LPI LINUX
CERTIFICATION
IN A NUTSHELL

A Desktop Quick Reference

LPI LINUX
CERTIFICATION
IN A NUTSHELL

A Desktop Quick Reference

Jeffrey Dean

O'REILLY®

Beijing • Cambridge • Farnham • Köln • Paris • Sebastopol • Taipei • Tokyo

LPI Linux Certification in a Nutshell

by Jeffrey Dean

Copyright © 2001 O'Reilly Media, Inc. All rights reserved.
Printed in the United States of America.

Published by O'Reilly Media, Inc., 1005 Gravenstein Highway North, Sebastopol, CA 95472.

Editor: Chuck Toporek

Production Editor: Mary Brady

Cover Designer: Ellie Volckhausen

Printing History:

June 2001:	First Edition.

 This book uses RepKover™, a durable and flexible lay-flat binding.

ISBN: 1-56592-748-6

Table of Contents

Part 2: General Linux Exam 102

Preface

Objective certification of professionals is a time-honored tradition in many fields, including medicine and law. As small computer systems and networks proliferated over the last decade, Novell and Microsoft produced extremely popular certification products for their respective operating system and network technologies. These two programs are often cited as having popularized a certification market where products that had previously been highly specialized and relatively rare. These programs have become so popular that a huge training and preparation industry has formed to service a constant stream of new certification candidates.

Certification programs, offered by vendors such as Sun and Hewlett-Packard, have existed in the Unix world for some time. However, since Solaris and HP-UX aren't commodity products, those programs don't draw the crowds that the PC platform does. Linux, however, is different. Linux is both a commodity operating system and is PC-based, and its popularity continues to grow at a rapid pace. As Linux deployment increases, so too does the demand for qualified and certified Linux system administrators.

A number of programs—the Linux Professional Institute, Sair Linux and GNU Certification, the Red Hat Certified Engineer (RHCE) program, and CompTIA's Linux+—have formed over the last few years to service this new market. Each of these programs seeks to provide objective measurements of a Linux administrator's skills, but they approach the problem in different ways.

The RHCE program requires that candidates pass a hands-on practical skills test, solving problems and performing configuration tasks. Though more involved from an exam delivery point of view, this type of test is very thorough and difficult to beat using purely good study habits. The Sair program is provided by Sair, Inc., a for-profit company that is also a vendor for courseware and texts. The Linux+ exam, scheduled for deployment in 2001, is an entry-level certification, which brings us to the LPI.

The Linux Professional Institute

The Linux Professional Institute, or LPI (*http://www.lpi.org*), is a nonprofit organization formed around the notion of certifying Linux administrators through a sort of open source process. The LPI seeks input from the public for its exam Objectives and questions, and anyone is welcome to participate. It has both paid and volunteer staff and receives funding from some major names in the computer industry. The result is a vendor-neutral, publicly developed program that is offered at a reasonable price.

The LPI organizes its Linux Professional Institute Certification (LPIC) series into three levels: LPIC Levels 1, 2, and 3. Each level consists of two exams that are priced at $100 each. This book covers the LPIC Level 1 exams, numbers 101 and 102.

LPI Level 1 Exams

The LPI offers its exams through Virtual University Enterprises (*http://www.vue.com*). You may establish an online account with VUE and resister for the exams using the company's web site. VUE has more than two thousand testing centers worldwide, making the exams accessible in most areas. The exams are presented in English using a PC-based automated examination program. Exam questions are presented in multiple-choice single-answer, multiple-choice multiple-answer, and fill-in-the-blank styles. However, a majority of the questions on the exams are multiple-choice single-answer.

Level 1 is aimed at junior to midlevel Linux administrators, who should be comfortable with Linux at the command line as well as capable of performing simple tasks, including system installation and troubleshooting. While Exams 101 and 102 are not constructed to be difficult or misleading, together they encompass a wide body of material, making preparation important for success even for experienced administrators.

Each of the exams covers a series of Topics, which are numbered using a *level.topic* notation (i.e., 1.2, 2.5, etc.). In the LPI's early stages of development, Topics were assigned to exams based on a different scheme than we see today. When the scheme changed, the Topics were redistributed to Exams 101 and 102, but the pairing of Topic numbers to exams was dropped. As a result, we have 1.x and 2.x Topics in both Level 1 Exams.

Each Topic contains a series of Objectives covering specific areas of expertise. The Level 1 Topics are distributed between the two exams to create tests of similar length and difficulty without subject matter overlap. As a result, there's no requirement for or advantage to taking them in sequence. Exam 101 tests five Topics in approximately 60 questions, and Exam 102 tests nine Topics in approximately 72 questions. Each exam is limited to 90 minutes.

Audience for This Book

The primary audience for this book is, of course, candidates seeking the LPIC Level 1 certification. These may range from administrators of other operating systems looking for a Linux certification to complement an MCSE or other certification to Unix administrators wary of a growing pool of Linux-certified job applicants. In any case, this book will help you with the specific information you require to be successful with the Level 1 exams.

Due to the breadth of knowledge required by the LPI Objectives and the book's 1-to-1 coverage, it also makes an excellent reference for skills and methods required for the day-to-day use of Linux. If you have a basic working understanding of Linux administration, the material in this book will help you fill in gaps in your knowledge while at the same time preparing you for the LPI exams, should you choose to take them.

This book should also prove to be a valuable introduction for new Linux users and administrators looking for a broad, detailed introduction to Linux. Part of the LPI exam–creation process includes a survey of Linux professionals in the field. The survey results drive much of the content found on the exams. Therefore, unlike general-purpose introductory Linux books, all of the information in this book applies directly to running Linux in the real world.

Organization

This book is designed to exactly follow the Topics and Objectives established by the LPI for Exams 101 and 102. That means that the presentation doesn't look like any other Linux book you've read. Instead, you can directly track the LPI Objectives and easily measure your progress as you prepare.

The book is presented in two parts. Part 1 covers Exam 101 and Part 2 covers Exam 102. Each part contains sections dedicated to the LPI Topics, and each of those sections contains information on all of the Objectives set forth for the Topic. In addition, each part contains a practice exam (with answers), review questions and exercises, and a handy "highlighter's index" that can help you review important details.

There is also a glossary at the back of the book, which you can use to help familiarize yourself with different Linux-related terms.

Parts 1 and 2: LPI Level 1 Exams 101 and 102

Parts 1 and 2 each contain these sections:

Exam overview
> Here you find an introduction to the exam along with details about the format of the questions.

Study guide
> This section offers a few tips for preparing for the LPI Level 1 exams and introduces the Objectives contained in the Topic sections that follow.

Topic sections

A separate section covers each of the Topic areas on the exam (five for Exam 101, nine for Exam 102). These sections provide background information and in-depth coverage for each Objective, with On the Exam tips dispersed throughout.

Review questions and exercises

This section reinforces important study areas with review questions. The purpose of this section is to provide you with a series of exercises that can be used on a running Linux system to give you valuable hands-on experience before you take the Level 1 exams.

Practice test

The practice test is designed to be similar in format and content to the actual LPI exams. You should be able to attain at least an 80 percent score on the sample test before attempting the live exam.

Highlighter's index

This unique section contains highlights and important facts culled from the Topic sections. You can use this as review and reference material prior to taking the actual exams.

Each Objective set forth by the LPI is assigned a numeric weight, which acts as an indicator of the importance of the Objective. Weights run between 1 and 10, with higher numbers indicating more importance. An Objective carrying a weight of 1 can be considered relatively unimportant and isn't likely to be covered in much depth on the exam. Objectives with larger weights are sure to be covered on the exam, so you should study these Topics closely. The weights of the Objectives are provided at the beginning of each Topic section.

Conventions Used in This Book

This desktop quick reference follows certain typographical conventions:

Bold

Used for commands, programs, and options. All terms shown in bold are typed literally.

Italic

Used to show arguments and variables that should be replaced with user-supplied values. Italic is also used to indicate filenames and directories and to highlight comments in examples.

`Constant Width`

Used to show the contents of files or the output from commands.

`Constant Width Bold`

Used in examples and tables to show commands or other text that should be typed literally by the user.

Constant Width Italic

    Used in examples and tables to show text that should be replaced with user-supplied values.

#, $

    Used in some examples as the root shell prompt (#) and as the user prompt ($) under the Bourne or **bash** shell.

On the Exam

These provide information about areas you should focus on when studying for the exam.

NOTE

These signify a tip, suggestion, or general note.

WARNING

These indicate a warning or caution.

A final word about syntax: in many cases, the space between an option and its argument can be omitted. In other cases, the spacing (or lack of spacing) must be followed strictly. For example, **-w***n* (no intervening space) might be interpreted differently from -w *n*. It's important to notice the spacing used in option syntax.

How to Contact Us

We have tested and verified the information in this book to the best of our ability, but you may find that features have changed (or even that we have made mistakes!). As a reader of this book and as an LPI examinee, you can help us to improve future editions. Please let us know about any errors you find, as well as your suggestions for future editions, by writing to:

O'Reilly & Associates, Inc.
1005 Gravenstein Highway North
Sebastopol, CA 95472
(800) 998-9938 (in the U.S. or Canada)
(707) 829-0515 (international/local)
(707) 829-0104 (fax)

You can also send us messages electronically. To be put on the mailing list or to request a catalog, send email to:

info@oreilly.com

To ask technical questions or comment on the book, send email to:

> bookquestions@ora.com

We have a web site for the book, where we'll list examples, errata, and any plans for future editions. The site also includes a link to a forum where you can discuss the book with the author and other readers. You can access this site at:

> http://www.oreilly.com/catalog/lpicertnut

For more information about this book and others, see the O'Reilly web site:

> http://www.oreilly.com

If you have taken one or both of the LPIC Level 1 exams after preparing with this book and find that parts of this book could better address your exam experience, we'd like to hear about it. Of course, you are under obligation to the LPI not to disclose specific exam details, but comments regarding the coverage of the LPI Objectives, level of detail, and relevance to the exam will be most helpful. We take your comments seriously and will do whatever we can to make this book as useful as it can be.

Acknowledgments

I'd like to thank the LPI, its staff, its contributors, and its sponsors for creating a unique and valuable community-based certification program. The LPI mission and organization are in line with the open source community it serves, and the LPIC series of certificates are respected and credible achievements.

For their general good advice as well as some specific information on PC hardware, my thanks go to Matt Welsh, Matthias Kalle Dalheimer, and Lar Kaufman, authors of *Running Linux, Third Edition*. Likewise, *Linux in a Nutshell, Third Edition*, by Ellen Siever, Stephen Spainhour, Jessica P. Hekman, and Stephen Figgins, is invaluable for reference information like **bash** programming details. I'm also indebted to the many volunteer authors and editors contributing to the Linux Documentation Project.

A lot of important feedback came from technical reviewers Kara Prichard and Richard Fifarek, and my hat's off to them for their detailed suggestions and corrections.

Of course, this book wouldn't be nearly as readable or as useful without the dedicated support of my editor, Chuck Toporek. His guidance and encouragement kept me consistent, accurate, and motivated, and the book wouldn't have been the same without him. Thanks, Chuck!

Thanks also to the others who helped with the completion of this book: Mary Brady, the production editor; Claire Cloutier, the production manager; and Ellie Volckhausen, the cover designer.

Finally, I'd like to thank my lovely wife Monica, whose love, vision, and support made this project possible in the first place, and my boys Austin and Alexander, my constant source of inspiration.

PART 1

General Linux Exam 101

Part 1 covers the Topics and Objectives for the LPI's General Linux Certification for Exam 101 and includes the following sections:

- Exam 101 Overview
- Exam 101 Study Guide
  - GNU and Unix Commands
  - Devices, Linux Filesystems, and the Filesystem Hierarchy Standard
  - Boot, Initialization, Shutdown, and Runlevels
  - Documentation
  - Administrative Tasks
- Exam 101 Review Questions and Exercises
- Exam 101 Practice Test
- Exam 101 Highlighter's Index

Exam 101
Overview

LPI Exam 101 is one of two exams required for the LPIC Level 1 certification. In total, 14 major Topic areas are specified for Level 1; this exam tests your knowledge on 5 of them.

Exam Topics are numbered using a *level.topic* notation (e.g., 1.2, 2.5). In the LPI's early stages of development, Topics were assigned to exams based on a different scheme than we see today. When the scheme changed, the Topics were redistributed to Exams 101 and 102, but the pairing of Topic numbers to exams was dropped. As a result, we have 1.*x* and 2.*x* Topics in both Level 1 exams.

The Level 1 Topics are distributed between the two exams to create tests of similar length and difficulty without subject matter overlap. As a result, there's no requirement for or advantage to taking them in sequence.

Each Topic contains a series of Objectives covering specific areas of expertise. Each of these Objectives is assigned a numeric weight, which acts as an indicator of the importance of the Objective. Weights run between 1 and 10, with higher numbers indicating more importance. An Objective carrying a weight of 1 can be considered relatively unimportant and isn't likely to be covered in much depth on the exam. Objectives with larger weights are sure to be covered on the exam, so you should study these Topics closely. The weights of the Objectives are provided at the beginning of each Topic section.

The Topics for Exam 101 are listed in Table 1-1.

Table 1-1: LPI Topics for Exam 101

Name	Number of Objectives	Description
GNU and Unix Commands (Topic 1.3)	7	This Topic covers many GNU and Unix commands used during day-to-day system administration activity. Objectives include command syntax, text filters, file management, pipes, redirects, process management, process execution priorities, and basic regular expressions.
Devices, Linux Filesystems, and the Filesystem Hierarchy Standard (Topic 2.4)	8	Objectives for this Topic include the creation of partitions and filesystems, filesystem integrity, mounting, quotas, permissions, ownership, links, and file location tasks.
Boot, Initialization, Shutdown, and Runlevels (Topic 2.6)	2	This short Topic covers system **boot, lilo, syslog, runlevels, shutdown,** and **reboot**.
Documentation (Topic 1.8)	4	This is an overview of Linux documentation sources, such as manpages, info pages, */usr/doc,* Linux-related web sites, and the generation of local documentation. It also includes some discussion of user support.
Administrative Tasks (Topic 2.11)	5	This core system administration Topic includes user and group accounts, user environment issues, **syslog, cron, at,** and **backup**.

As you can see from Table 1-1, the Topic numbers assigned by the LPI are not sequential. This is due to various modifications made by the LPI to its exam program as it developed. The Topic numbers serve only as reference and are not used on the exam.

Exam 101 lasts a maximum of 90 minutes and contains approximately 60 questions. The exam is administered using a custom application on a PC in a private room with no notes or other reference material. About 75 percent of the exam is made up of multiple-choice single-answer questions. These questions have only one correct answer and are answered using radio buttons. Some of them present a scenario needing administrative action. Others seek appropriate commands for a particular task or for proof of understanding of a particular concept.

About 10 percent of the exam questions are multiple-choice multiple-answer questions, which are answered using checkboxes. These questions can have multiple correct responses, each of which must be checked. This is probably the most difficult question style because the multiple answers increase the likelihood of mistakes. But they also are a good test of your knowledge of Unix commands, since an incorrect response on any one of the possible answers causes you to miss the entire question. The exam also has some fill-in-the-blank questions. These questions provide a one-line text area input box for you to fill in your answer. These questions check your knowledge of concepts such as important files and commands, plus common facts that you are expected to be aware of.

Exam 101
Study Guide

Part 1 of this book contains a section for each of the five Topics found on LPI Exam 101. Each section details certain Objectives, which are described here and on the LPI web site, *http://www.lpi.org/p-obj-101.html*.

Exam Preparation

LPI Exam 101 is thorough, but you should find it fairly straightforward if you have a solid foundation in Linux concepts. You won't come across questions that intend to trick you, and you're unlikely to find ambiguous questions.

Exam 101 mainly tests your knowledge of facts, including commands and their common options, important file locations, configuration syntax, and common procedures. Your recollection of these details, regardless of your level of Linux administration experience, will directly influence your results.

For clarity, the material in the following sections is presented in the same order as the LPI Topics and Objectives. However, you may choose to study the Topics in any order you wish. To assist you with your preparation, Table 1-2 through Table 1-6 list the Topics and Objectives found on Exam 101. Objectives within each Topic occupy rows of the corresponding table, including the Objective's number, description, and *weight*. The LPI assigns a weight for each Objective to indicate the relative importance of that Objective on the exam on a scale of 1 to 10. We recommend that you use the weights to prioritize what you decide to study in preparation for the exams. After you complete your study of each Objective, simply check it off here to measure and organize your progress.

Table 1-2: GNU and Unix Commands (Topic 1.3)

Objective	Weight	Description
1	4	Work Effectively on the Unix Command Line (see page 10).
2	7	Process Text Streams Using Text-Processing Filters (see page 19)

Table 1-2: GNU and Unix Commands (Topic 1.3) (continued)

Objective	Weight	Description
3	2	Perform Basic File Management (see page 33)
4	3	Use Unix Streams, Pipes, and Redirects (see page 41)
5	5	Create, Monitor, and Kill Processes (see page 45)
6	2	Modify Process Execution Priorities (see page 56)
7	3	Making Use of Regular Expressions (see page 59)

Table 1-3: Devices, Linux Filesystems, and the Filesystem Hierarchy Standard (Topic 2.4)

Objective	Weight	Description
1	3	Create Partitions and Filesystems (see page 71)
2	5	Maintain the Integrity of Filesystems (see page 82)
3	3	Control Filesystem Mounting and Unmounting (see page 89)
4	1	Set and View Disk Quotas (see page 95)
5	3	Use File Permissions to Control Access to Files (see page 104)
6	2	Manage File Ownership (see page 114)
7	2	Create and Change Hard and Symbolic Links (see page 116)
8	2	Find System Files and Place Files in the Correct Location (see page 122)

Table 1-4: Boot, Initialization, Shutdown, and Runlevels (Topic 2.6)

Objective	Weight	Description
1	3	Boot the System (see page 135)
2	3	Change Runlevels and Shutdown or Reboot the System (see page 137)

Table 1-5: Documentation (Topic 1.8)

Objective	Weight	Description
1	5	Use and Manage Local System Documentation (see page 147)
2	2	Find Linux Documentation on the Internet (see page 155)
3	1	Write System Documentation (see page 160)
4	1	Provide User Support (see page 163)

Table 1-6: Administrative Tasks (Topic 2.11)

Objective	Weight	Description
1	7	Manage Users and Group Accounts and Related System Files (see page 165)
2	4	Tune the User Environment and System Environment Variables (see page 174)
3	3	Configure and Use System Log Files to Meet Administrative and Security Needs (see page 176)
4	4	Automate System Administration Tasks by Scheduling Jobs to Run in the Future (see page 180)
5	3	Maintain an Effective Data Backup Strategy (see page 184)

GNU and Unix Commands
(Topic 1.3)

This Topic covers the ever-important aspect of working interactively with Linux command-line utilities. While it's true that GUI tools are already available to manage just about everything on a Linux system, a firm understanding of basic use of command-line utilities is essential.

The family of commands that are part of Linux and Unix systems has a long history. Individuals or groups that needed specific tools contributed many of the commands in the early days of Unix development. Those that were popular became part of the system and were accepted as default tools under the Unix umbrella. Today, Linux systems carry new, often more powerful *GNU* versions of these historical commands.

This section covers LPI Topic 1.3, *GNU and Unix Commands*. Even the Topic name implies the confusion that may exist regarding the origin of the commands we're using on GNU/Linux systems. Remember that for software to be freely distributed as part of your Linux distribution, it cannot be proprietary and must come with some form of redistribution ability in its licensing terms.

This LPI Topic has seven Objectives:

Objective 1: Work Effectively on the Unix Command Line
> This Objective covers the essentials of working at the command line in a shell, including environment variables, using the command history and editing facilities, invoking commands, command substitution, and recursively executing commands. Weight: 4.

Objective 2: Process Text Streams Using Text-Processing Filters
> There exists a diverse "toolbox" of interesting and powerful utilities from the GNU **textutils** package, which can be used to manipulate text in various ways. This Objective covers those utilities and how to use them. Weight: 7.

Objective 3: Perform Basic File Management
> If you're used to an entirely GUI computing environment, performing basic file management manually from the command line may be awkward at first. You'll find, however, that after mastering a few simple commands you will

achieve much finer control over file management chores. This Objective covers simple and recursive file management, including the use of wildcards (regular expressions). Weight: 2.

Objective 4: Use Unix Streams, Pipes, and Redirects

Among the most powerful concepts in the Linux and Unix worlds is the idea of creating text streams. This powerful tool offers you the ability to succinctly string various commands (such as those described in Objective 2) together into customized editing chains, which modify text in a serial fashion. Objective 4 includes redirection and the use of the **tee** command. Weight: 3.

Objective 5: Create, Monitor, and Kill Processes

Every running program on a Linux system is a *process*. Some processes are short-lived, like utility programs such as **ls**. Other processes, usually called *daemons*, are intended to run for extended periods or even constantly; these include processes such as web or database server software. Managing these processes is an important activity for a system administrator. This Objective covers foreground and background processing, process monitoring, signaling, and how to "kill" a process. Also covered are some of the commands used to manipulate running processes. Weight: 5.

Objective 6: Modify Process Execution Priorities

When you launch a process, you may wish to instruct the system to lower or raise its *scheduling priority* relative to the default. This action has the effect of giving more or less CPU time to your process. This is accomplished with the **nice** command, which modifies the default scheduling priority prior to running your command. This Objective covers these modifications. Weight: 2.

Objective 7: Perform Searches of Text Files Making Use of Regular Expressions

Many tools on your Linux system are capable of using *regular expressions*. At the most basic level, regular expressions are simply wildcard-matching mechanisms, such as you've probably used at the command line many times. While detailed use is beyond the scope of this book and the LPI exams, regular expressions are a powerful solution to a range of problems. This Objective covers basic regular expression usage with command-line tools such as **sed** and **grep**. Weight: 3.

The tools and concepts discussed here represent important and fundamental aspects of working with Linux, and are essential for your success on Exam 101.

Objective 1: Work Effectively on the Unix Command Line

Every computer system requires a human interface component. For Linux system administration, a text interface is typically used. The system presents the administrator with a *prompt*, which at its simplest is a single character such as $ or #. The prompt signifies that the system is ready to accept typed commands, which usually occupy one or more lines of text. This interface is generically called the *command line*.

It is the job of a program called a *shell* to provide the command prompt and to interpret commands. The shell provides an interface layer between the Linux kernel and the human user, which is how it gets its name. The original shell for Unix systems was written by Steve Bourne and was called simply **sh**. The default Linux shell is **bash**, the *Bourne-Again Shell*, which is a GNU variant of **sh**. The popular **tcsh** shell, a variant of the original **csh** (or C shell), is also provided. The **bash** shell is the subject of an entire LPI Topic, covered in Part 2, *Shells, Scripting, Programming, and Compiling (Topic 1.9)*. At this point, we are primarily concerned with our interaction with **bash** and the effective use of commands.

The Interactive Shell

The shell is a powerful programming environment, capable of automating nearly anything you can imagine on your Linux system. The shell is also your interactive interface to your system. When you first start a shell, it does some automated housekeeping to get ready for your use, and then presents a command prompt. The command prompt tells you that the shell is ready to accept commands from its *standard input* device, which is usually the keyboard. Shells can run standalone, as on a physical terminal, or within a window in a GUI environment. Whichever the case, their use is the same.

Shell variable basics

During execution, **bash** maintains a set of *shell variables* that contain information important to the execution of **bash**. Most of these variables are set when **bash** starts, but they can be set manually at any time.

The first shell variable of interest in this Topic is called PS1 (which simply stands for *Prompt String 1*). This special variable holds the contents of the command prompt that are displayed when **bash** is ready to accept commands (there is also a PS2 variable, used when **bash** needs multiple-line input to complete a command). You can easily display the contents of PS1, or any other shell variable, by using the **echo** command with the variable name preceded by the $ symbol:

```
$ echo $PS1
\$
```

The \$ output tells us that PS1 contains the two characters \ and $. The backslash character tells the shell not to interpret the dollar symbol in any special way (that is, as a *metacharacter*, described later in this section). A simple dollar sign such as this was the default prompt for **sh**, but **bash** offers options to make the prompt much more informative. On your system, the default prompt stored in PS1 is probably something like:

```
[\u@\h \W]\$
```

Each of the characters preceded by backslashes have a special meaning to **bash**, while those without backslashes are interpreted literally. In this example, \u is replaced by the username, \h is replaced by the system's hostname, \W is replaced by the "bottom" portion of the current working directory, and \\$ is replaced by a $ character.* This yields a prompt of the form:

```
[jdean@linuxpc jdean]$
```

How your prompt is formulated is really just a convenience and does not affect how the shell interprets your commands. However, adding information to the prompt, particularly regarding system, user, and directory location, can make life easier when hopping from system to system and logging in as multiple users (as yourself and **root**, for example). See the documentation on **bash** for more information on customizing prompts.

Another shell variable that is extremely important during interactive use is PATH, which contains a list of all the directories that hold commands or other programs you are likely to execute. A default path is set up for you when **bash** starts. You may wish to modify the default to add other directories that hold programs you need to run.

NOTE

Every file in the Linux filesystem can be specified in terms of its location. The **less** program, for example, is located in the directory */usr/bin*. Placing */usr/bin* in your PATH enables you to execute **less** by simply typing **less** rather than the explicit */usr/bin/less*.

In order for **bash** to find and execute the command you enter at the prompt, the command must be either:

- A *bash built-in* command that is part of **bash** itself
- An executable program located in a directory listed in the PATH variable
- Explicitly defined

The shell holds PATH and other variables for its own use. However, many of the shell's variables are needed during the execution of programs launched from the shell (including other shells). For these variables to be available, they must be *exported*, at which time they become *environment variables*. Environment variables are passed on to programs and other shells, and together they are said to form the *environment* in which the programs execute. PATH is always made into an environment variable.† Exporting a shell variable to turn it into an environment variable is done using the **export** command:

```
$ export MYVAR
```

When a variable is exported to the environment, it is passed into the environment of all child processes. That is, it will be available to all programs run by your shell.

---

* Unless you are **root**, in which case \\$ is replaced by #.

† In the case of **csh** and **tcsh**, there are *both* shell and environment variables for PATH; the shell takes care of keeping them synchronized.

Entering commands at the command prompt

Commands issued to the shell on a Linux system generally consist of four components:

- A valid command (a shell built-in, a program or script found among directories listed in the PATH, or an explicitly defined program)
- Command options, usually preceded by a dash
- Arguments
- Line acceptance (i.e., pressing the Enter key), which we assume in the examples

Each command has its own unique syntax, though most follow a fairly standard form. At minimum, a *command* is necessary:

```
$ ls
```

This simple command lists files in the current working directory. It requires neither options nor arguments. Generally, *options* are letters or words preceded by a single or double dash and are added after the command and separated from it by a space:

```
$ ls -l
```

The -l option modifies the behavior of the ls program by listing files in a longer, more detailed format. In most cases, single-dash options can be either combined or specified separately. To illustrate this, consider these two equivalent commands:

```
$ ls -l -a
$ ls -la
```

By adding the -a option, ls does not hide files beginning with a dot (which it does by default). Adding that option by specifying -la yields the same result. Some commands offer alternative forms for the same option. In the preceding example, the -a option can be replaced with --all:

```
$ ls -l --all
```

These double-dash full-word options are frequently found in programs from the GNU project. They cannot be combined as the single-dash options can. Both types of options can be freely intermixed. Although the longer GNU-style options require more typing, they are easier to remember and easier to read in scripts than the single-letter options.

Adding an *argument* further refines the command's behavior:

```
$ ls -l *.c
```

Now the command will give a detailed listing only of C program source files (those with the .c extension), if they exist, in the current working directory. In this example, if no .c files exist, no output will be given.* Sometimes, options and arguments can be mixed in order:

```
$ ls --all *.c -l
```

---

* If a Unix or GNU command has nothing of significance to tell you, it most likely will remain silent. This brevity may take some users by surprise, particularly if they are used to systems that yield messages indicating something like "successful completion, but sorry, no results."

In this case, ls was able to determine that –1 is an option and not another file descriptor.

Some commands, such as **tar** and **ps**, don't require the dash preceding an option because at least one option is expected or required. Also, an option often instructs the command that the subsequent item on the command line is a specific argument. For example:

```
$ tar cf mytarfile file1 file2 file3
$ tar -cf mytarfile file1 file2 file3
```

These equivalent commands use *tar* to create an archive file named *mytarfile* and put three files (*file1*, *file2*, and *file3*) into it. In this case, the f option tells **tar** that archive filename *mytarfile* follows immediately after the option.

Just as any natural language contains exceptions and variations, so does the syntax used for GNU and Unix commands. You should have no trouble learning the essential syntax for the commands you need to use often. The capabilities of the command set offered on Linux are extensive, making it highly unlikely that you'll memorize all of the command syntax you need. Most systems administrators are constantly learning about features they've never used in commands they use regularly. It is standard practice to regularly refer to man or info pages and other documentation on commands you're using, so feel free to explore and learn as you go.

Entering commands not in the PATH

Occasionally, you will need to execute a command that is not in your path and not built into your shell. If this need arises often, it may be best to simply add the directory that contains the command to your path. However, there's nothing wrong with explicitly specifying a command's location and name completely. For example, the **ls** command is located in */bin*. This directory is most certainly in your PATH variable (if not, it should be!), which allows you to enter the **ls** command by itself on the command line:

```
$ ls
```

The shell will look for an executable file named **ls** in each successive directory listed in your PATH variable and will execute the first one it finds. Specifying the *fully qualified filename* for the command eliminates the directory search and yields identical results:

```
$ /bin/ls
```

Any executable file on your system may be started in this way. However, it is important to remember that some programs may have requirements during execution about what is listed in your PATH. A program can be launched normally but may fail if it is unable to find a required resource if the PATH is incomplete.

Entering multiple-line commands interactively

In addition to its interactive capabilities, the shell also has a complete programming language of its own. Many programming features can be very handy at the interactive command line as well. Looping constructs, including **for**, **until**, and **while** are often used this way. When you begin a command such as these, which normally spans multiple lines, **bash** prompts you for the subsequent lines until a valid command has been completed. The prompt you receive in this case is stored in shell variable PS2, which by default is >. For example, if you wanted to repetitively execute a series of commands each time with a different argument from a known series, you could enter the following:

```
$ ...series of commands on arg1...
command output
$ ...series of commands on arg2...
command output
$ ...series of commands on arg2...
command output
```

Rather than entering each command manually, you can interactively use **bash**'s **for** loop construct to do the work for you. Note that indented style, such as what you might use in traditional programming, isn't necessary when working interactively with the shell:

```
$ for var in arg1 arg2 arg3
> do
> echo $var
> ...series of commands...
> done
arg1
command output
arg2
command output
arg3
command output
```

Mixing the command-line world with the shell-scripting world in this way can make certain tasks surprisingly efficient.

Entering command sequences

There may be times when it is convenient to place multiple commands on a single line. Normally, **bash** assumes you have reached the end of a command (or the end of the first line of a multiple-line command) when you press Return. To add more than one command to a single line, the commands can be separated and entered sequentially with the *command separator*, a semicolon. Using this syntax, the following commands:

```
$ ls
$ ps
```

are, in essence, identical to and will yield the same result as the following single-line command that employs the command separator:

```
$ ls; ps
```

On the Exam

Command syntax and the use of the command line is very important. Pay special attention to the use of options and arguments and how they are differentiated. Also be aware that some commands expect options to be preceded by a dash while other commands do not.

Command History and Editing

If you consider interaction with the shell as a kind of conversation, it's a natural extension to refer back to things "mentioned" previously. You may type a long and complex command that you want to repeat, or perhaps you need to execute a command multiple times with slight variation.

If you work interactively with the original Bourne shell, maintaining such a "conversation" can be a bit difficult. Each repetitive command must be entered explicitly, each mistake must be retyped, and if your commands scroll off the top of your screen, you have to recall them from memory. Modern shells such as **bash** and **tcsh** include a significant feature set called *command history, expansion,* and *editing.* Using these capabilities, referring back to previous commands is painless, and your interactive shell session becomes much simpler and more effective.

The first part of this feature set is command history. When **bash** is run interactively, it provides access to a list of commands previously typed. The commands are stored in the history list *prior* to any interpretation by the shell. That is, they are stored before wildcards are expanded or command substitutions are made. The history list is controlled by the HISTSIZE shell variable. By default, HISTSIZE is set to 500 lines, but you can control that number by simply adjusting HISTSIZE's value. In addition to commands entered in your current **bash** session, commands from previous **bash** sessions are stored by default in a file called *~/.bash_history* (or the file named in shell variable HISTFILE).* To view your command history, use the **bash** built-in **history** command. A line number will precede each command. This line number may be used in subsequent *history expansion.* History expansion uses either a line number from the history or a portion of a previous command to reexecute that command.† Table 1-7 lists the basic history expansion designators. In each case, using the designator as a command causes a command from the history to be executed again.

Table 1-7: Command History Expansion Designators

Designator	Description
! !	Often called *bang-bang,*[1] this command refers to the most recent command.
!*n*	Refer to command *n* from the history. You'll use the **history** command to display these numbers.
!-*n*	Refer to the current command minus *n* from the history.
! *string*	Refer to the most recent command starting with *string*.

---

* If you use multiple shells in a windowed environment (as just about everyone does), the last shell to exit will write its history to *~/.bash_history.* For this reason you may wish to use one shell invocation for most of your work.

† History expansion also allows a fair degree of command editing using syntax you'll find in the **bash** documentation.

Table 1-7: Command History Expansion Designators (continued)

Designator	Description
!? *string*	Refer to the most recent command containing *string*.
^ *string1*^ *string2*	Quick substitution. Repeat the last command, replacing the first occurrence of *string1* with *string2*.

1. The exclamation point is often called *bang* on Linux and Unix systems.

While using history substitution can be useful for executing repetitive commands, command history editing is much more interactive. To envision the concept of command history editing, think of your entire **bash** history (including that obtained from your `~/.bash_history` file) as the contents of an editor's buffer. In this scenario, the current command prompt is the last line in an editing buffer, and all of the previous commands in your history lie above it. All of the typical editing features are available with command history editing, including movement within the "buffer," searching, cutting, pasting, and so on. Once you're used to using the command history in an editing style, everything you've done on the command line becomes available as retrievable, reusable text for subsequent commands. The more familiar you become with this concept, the more useful it can be.

By default, **bash** uses *key bindings* like those found in the Emacs editor for command history editing.* If you're familiar with Emacs, moving around in the command history will be familiar and very similar to working in an Emacs buffer. For example, the key command **Ctrl-p** (depicted as **C-p**) will move up one line in your command history, displaying your previous command and placing the cursor at the end of it. This same function is also bound to the up arrow key. The opposite function is bound to **C-n** (and the down arrow). Together, these two key bindings allow you to examine your history line by line. You may reexecute any of the commands shown simply by pressing Return when it is displayed. For the purposes of Exam 101, you'll need to be familiar with this editing capability, but detailed knowledge is not required. Table 1-8 lists some of the common Emacs key bindings you may find useful in *bash*. Note that C- indicates the **Ctrl** key, while M- indicates the Meta key, which is usually **Alt** on PC keyboards.†

Table 1-8: Basic Command History Editing Emacs Key Bindings

Key	Description
C-p	Previous line (also up arrow)
C-n	Next line (also down arrow)
C-b	Back one character (also left arrow)
C-f	Forward one character (also right arrow)
C-a	Beginning of line
C-e	End of line

---

* An editing style similar to the **vi** editor is also available.

† In unusual circumstances, such as on a terminal, using the *meta* key means pressing the Escape (**Esc**) key, releasing it, and *then* pressing the defined key. The **Esc** key is not a modifier, but serves to modify meta keys when an **Alt**-style key is unavailable.

Table 1-8: Basic Command History Editing Emacs Key Bindings (continued)

Key	Description
C-l	Clear the screen, leaving the current line at the top of the screen
M-<	Top of history
M->	Bottom of history
C-d	Delete character from right
C-k	Delete (kill) text from cursor to end of line
C-y	Paste (yank) text previously cut (killed)
M-d	Delete (kill) word
C-r*text*	Reverse search for *text*
C-s*text*	Forward search for *text*

Command substitution

bash offers a handy ability to do *command substitution*. This feature allows you to replace the result of a command with a script. For example, wherever $(*command*) is found, its output will be substituted. This output could be assigned to a variable, as in the number of lines in the *.bashrc* file:

```
$ RCSIZE=$(wc -l ~/.bashrc)
```

Another form of command substitution is `` `command` ``. The result is the same, except that the *backquote* syntax has some special rules regarding metacharacters that the $(*command*) syntax avoids.

Applying commands recursively through a directory tree

There are many times when it is necessary to execute commands *recursively*. That is, you may need to repeat a command throughout all the branches of a directory tree. Recursive execution is very useful but also can be dangerous. It gives a single interactive command the power to operate over a much broader range of your system than your current directory, and the appropriate caution is necessary. Think twice before using these capabilities, particularly when operating as the superuser.

Some of the GNU commands on Linux systems have built-in recursive capabilities as an option. For example, **chmod** modifies permissions on files in the current directory:

```
$ chmod g+w *.c
```

In this example, all files with the *.c* extension in the current directory are modified with the group-write permission. However, there may be a number of directories and files in hierarchies that require this change. **chmod** contains the **-R** option (note the uppercase option letter; you may also use **--recursive**), which instructs the command to operate not only on files and directories specified on the command line, but also on all files and directories contained *under* the specified directories. For example, this command gives the group-write permission to all files in a source-code tree named **src**:

```
$ chmod -R g+w src
```

Provided you have the correct privileges, this command will descend into each subdirectory in the **src** directory and add the requested permission to each file and directory it finds. Other example commands with this ability include **cp** (copy), **ls** (list files), and **rm** (remove files).

A more general approach to recursive execution through a directory is available by using the **find** command. This is an extremely powerful command because it can tell you a lot about your system's file structure. **find** is inherently recursive and is intended to descend through directories looking for files with certain attributes or executing commands. At its simplest, **find** displays an entire directory hierarchy when you simply enter the command with a target directory:

```
$ find src
...files and directories are listed recursively...
```

To get more specific, add the **-name** option to search the same directories for C files:

```
$ find src -name "*.c"
....c files are listed recursively*...
```

find can also execute commands against its results with the **–exec** option, which can execute any command against each successive element listed by **find**. During execution, a special variable {} is replaced by these **find** results. The command entered after the **–exec** option must be terminated by a semicolon; any metacharacters used—including the semicolon—must be either quoted or escaped. To take the previous example a little further, rather than execute the **chmod** recursively against all files in the **src** directory, **find** can execute it against the C files only, like this:

```
$ find src -name "*.c" -exec chmod g+w {} \;
```

The **find** command is capable of much more than this simple example and can locate files with particular attributes such as dates, protections, file types, access times, and others. While the syntax can be confusing, the results are worth some study of **find**.

Objective 2: Process Text Streams Using Text-Processing Filters

Many of the commands on Linux systems are intended to be used as *filters*, which modify text in helpful ways. Text fed into the command's standard input or read from files is modified in some useful way and sent to standard output or to a new file. Multiple commands can be combined to produce *text streams,* which are modified at each step in a pipeline formation. This section describes basic use and syntax for the filtering commands important for Exam 101. Refer to a Linux command reference for full details on each command and the many other available commands.

---

* This can be done recursively with the **ls** command as well.

cut

Syntax

    cut options [*files*]

Description

Cut out (that is, print) selected columns or fields from one or more *files*. The source file is not changed. This is useful if you need quick access to a vertical slice of a file. By default, the slices are delimited by a **tab**.

Frequently used options

-b *list*

> Print bytes in *list* positions.

-c *list*

> Print characters in *list* columns.

-d *delim*

> Set field delimiter for **-f**.

-f *list*

> Print *list* fields.

Examples

Show usernames (in the first colon-delimited field) from */etc/passwd*:

    $ cut -d: -f1 /etc/passwd

Show first column of */etc/passwd*:

    $ cut -c 1 /etc/passwd

expand

Syntax

    expand [*options*] files

Description

Convert tabs to spaces. Sometimes the use of tab characters can make output that is attractive on one output device look bad on another. This command eliminates tabs and replaces them with the equivalent number of spaces. By default, tabs are assumed to be eight spaces apart.

Frequently used options

-t *tabs*

> Specify tab stops, in place of default 8.

-i

> Initial; convert only at start of lines.

fmt

Syntax

fmt [*options*] [*files*]

Description

Format text to a specified width by filling lines and removing newline characters. Multiple *files* from the command line are concatenated.

Frequently used options

-u
Use uniform spacing: one space between words and two spaces between sentences.

-w *width*
Set line width to *width*. The default is 75 characters.

head

Syntax

head [*options*] [*files*]

Description

Print the first few lines of one or more files (the "head" of the file or files). When more than one file is specified, a header is printed at the beginning of each file, and each is listed in succession.

Frequently used options

-c *n*
Print the first *n* bytes, or if *n* is followed by *k* or *m*, print the first *n* kilobytes or megabytes, respectively.

-l *n*
Print the first *n* lines. The default is 10.

join

Syntax

join [*options*] *file1 file2*

Description

Print a line for each pair of input lines, one each from *file1* and *file2*, that have identical *join fields*. This function could be thought of as a very simple database table join, where the two files share a common index just as two tables in a database would.

Frequently used options

-j1 *field*
> Join on *field* of file1.

-j2 *field*
> Join on *field* of file2.

-j *field*
> Join on *field* of both *file1* and *file2*.

Example

Suppose *file1* contains the following:

```
1 one
2 two
3 three
```

and *file2* contains:

```
1 11
2 22
3 33
```

Issuing the command:

```
$ join -j 1 file1 file2
```

yields the following output:

```
1 one 11
2 two 22
3 three 33
```

---

nl

Syntax

```
nl [options] [files]
```

Description

Number the lines of *files*, which are concatenated in the output. This command is used for numbering lines in the body of text, including special header and footer options normally excluded from the line numbering. The numbering is done for each *logical page*, which is defined as having a header, a body, and a footer. These are delimited by the special strings \:\:\:, \:\:, and \:, respectively.

Frequently used options

-b *style*
> Set body numbering style to *style*, **t** by default.

-f *style*
> Set footer number style to *style*, **n** by default.

-h *style*
> Set header numbering style to *style*, **n** by default.

Styles can be in these forms:

A

Number all lines.

t

Only number non-empty lines.

n

Do not number lines.

p*REGEXP*

Only number lines that contain a match for regular expression *REGEXP*.

Example

Suppose file *file1* contains the following text:

```
\:\:\:
header
\:\:
line1
line2
line3
\:
footer
\:\:\:
header
\:\:
line1
line2
line3
\:
footer
```

If the following command is given:

```
$ nl -h a file1
```

the output would yield numbered headers and body lines but no numbering on footer lines. Each new header represents the beginning of a new logical page and thus a restart of the numbering sequence:

```
1 header

2 line1
3 line2
4 line3

footer

1 header

2 line1
3 line2
4 line3

footer
```

od

Syntax

    od [options] [files]

Description

Dump files in octal and other formats. This program prints a listing of a file's contents in a variety of formats. It is often used to examine the byte codes of binary files but can be used on any file or input stream. Each line of output consists of an octal byte offset from the start of the file followed by a series of tokens indicating the contents of the file. Depending on the options specified, these tokens can be ASCII, decimal, hexadecimal, or octal representations of the contents.

Frequently used options

-t *type*

> Specify the *type* of output. Typical types include:
>
> A
>> Named character
>
> c
>> ASCII character or backslash escape
>
> o
>> Octal (the default)
>
> x
>> Hexadecimal

Example

If *file1* contains:

    a1\n
    A1\n

where **\n** stands for the newline character. The **od** command specifying named characters yields the following output:

    $ od -t a file1
    00000000   a   1   nl   A   1   nl
    00000006

A slight nuance is the ASCII character mode. This **od** command specifying named characters yields the following output with backslash-escaped characters rather than named characters:

    $ od -t c file1
    00000000   a   1   \n   A   1   \n
    00000006

With numeric output formats, you can instruct **od** on how many bytes to use in interpreting each number in the data. To do this, follow the type specification by a decimal integer. This **od** command specifying single-byte hex results yields the following output:

```
$ od -t x1 file1
00000000   61 31 0a 41 31 0a
00000006
```

Doing the same thing in octal notation yields:

```
$ od -t o1 file1
00000000   141 061 012 101 061 012
00000006
```

If you examine an ASCII chart with hex and octal representations, you'll see that these results match those tables.

paste

Syntax

paste [*options*] *files*

Description

Paste together corresponding lines of one or more *files* into vertical columns.

Frequently used options

-d'*n*'

Separate columns with character *n* in place of the default **tab**.

-s

Merge lines from one file into a single line. When multiple files are specified, their contents are placed on individual lines of output, one per file.

For the following three examples, *file1* contains:

```
1
2
3
```

and *file2* contains:

```
A
B
C
```

Example 1

A simple paste creates columns from each file in standard output:

```
$ paste file1 file2
1    A
2    B
3    C
```

Example 2

The column separator option yields columns separated by the specified character:

```
$ paste -d'@' file1 file2
1@A
2@B
3@C
```

Example 3

The single-line option (-s) yields a line for each file:

```
$ paste -s file1 file2
1    2    3
A    B    C
```

pr

Syntax

pr [*options*] [*file*]

Description

Convert a text *file* into a paginated, columnar version, with headers and page fills. This command is convenient for yielding nice output, such as for a line printer from raw uninteresting text files. The header will consist of the date and time, the filename, and a page number.

Frequently used options

-d
　　Double space.

-h *header*
　　Use *header* in place of the filename in the header.

-l *lines*
　　Set page length to *lines*. The default is 66.

-o *width*
　　Set the left margin to *width*.

split

Syntax

split [*option*] [*infile*] [*outfile*]

Description

Split *infile* into a specified number of line groups, with output going into a succession of files, *outfileaa*, *outfileab*, and so on (the default is *xaa*, *xab*, etc.). The *infile* remains unchanged. This command is handy if you have a very long text file that needs to be reduced to a succession of smaller files. This was often done to email large files in smaller chunks, because it was at one time considered bad practice to send single large email messages.

Frequently used option

-n
　　Split the *infile* into *n*-line segments. The default is 1000.

Example

Suppose *file1* contains:

```
1  one
2  two
3  three
4  four
5  five
6  six
```

Then the command:

```
$ split -2 file1 splitout_
```

yields as output three new files, *splitout_aa, splitout_ab,* and *splitout_ac.* The file *splitout_aa* contains:

```
1  one
2  two
```

splitout_ab contains:

```
3  three
4  four
```

and *splitout_ac* contains:

```
5  five
6  six
```

---

tac

Syntax

```
tac [file]
```

Description

This command is named as an opposite for the **cat** command, which simply prints text files to standard output. In this case, **tac** prints the text files to standard output with lines in reverse order.

Example

Suppose *file1* contains:

```
1  one
2  two
3  three
```

Then the command:

```
$ tac file1
```

yields as output:

```
3  three
2  two
1  one
```

tail

Syntax

```
tail [options] [files]
```

Description

Print the last few lines of one or more *files* (the "tail" of the file or files). When more than one file is specified, a header is printed at the beginning of each file, and each is listed in succession.

Frequently used options

-c *n*

> This option prints the last *n* bytes, or if *n* is followed by *k* or *m*, the last *n* kilobytes or megabytes, respectively.

-f

> Follow the output dynamically as new lines are added to the bottom of a file.

-n *m*

> Prints the last *m* lines. The default is 10.

-f

> Continuously display a file as it is actively written by another process. This is useful for watching log files as the system runs.

---

tr

Syntax

```
tr [options] [[string1 [string2]]
```

Description

Translate characters from *string1* to the corresponding characters in *string2*. **tr** does *not* have file arguments and therefore must use standard input and output. If *string1* and *string2* specify ranges (a-z or A-Z), they should represent the same number of characters.

Frequently used options

-d

> Delete characters in *string1* from the output.

-s

> Squeeze out repeated output characters in *string1*.

Example 1

To change all lowercase characters in *file1* to uppercase, use either of these commands:

```
$ cat file1 | tr a-z A-Z
```

or:

```
$ tr a-z A-Z < file1
```

Example 2

To suppress repeated "a" characters from *file1*:

```
$ cat file1 | tr -s a
```

Example 3

To remove all "a," "b," and "c" characters from *file1*:

```
$ cat file1 | tr -d abc
```

wc

Syntax

wc [*options*] [*files*]

Description

Print counts of characters, words, and lines for *files*. When multiple files are listed, statistics for each file output on a separate line with a cumulative total output last.

Frequently used options

-c
 Print the character count only.

-l
 Print the line count only.

-w
 Print the word count only.

Example 1

Show all counts and totals for *file1*, *file2*, and *file3*:

```
$ wc file[123]
```

Example 2

Count the number of lines in *file1*:

```
$ wc -l file1
```

xargs

Syntax

xargs [*options*] [*command*] [*initial-arguments*]

Description

Execute *command* followed by its optional *initial-arguments* and append additional arguments found on standard input. Typically, the additional arguments are filenames in quantities too large for a single command line. **xargs** runs *command* multiple times to exhaust all arguments on standard input.

Frequently used options

-n *maxargs*

> Limit the number of additional arguments to *maxargs* for each invocation of *command*.

-p

> Interactive mode. Prompt the user for each execution of *command*.

Example

Use **grep** to search a long list of files, one by one, for the word "linux":

```
$ find / -type f | xargs -n 1 grep linux
```

find searches for normal files (**-type f**) starting at the root directory. **xargs** executes **grep** once for each of them due to the **-n 1** option.

The Stream Editor, sed

Another filtering program found on nearly every Unix system is **sed**, the *stream editor*. It is called a stream editor because it is intended as a filter, with text usually flowing from standard input, through the utility, to standard output. Unlike the previously listed commands, **sed** is a programmable utility with a range of capabilities. During processing, **sed** interprets instructions from a *sed script*, processing the text according to those instructions. The script may be a single command or a longer list of commands. It is important to understand **sed** and its use for Exam 101, although detailed knowledge is not required or offered in this brief introduction.

The **sed** utility is usually used either to automate repetitive editing tasks or to process text in pipes of Unix commands (see Objective 4). The scripts that **sed** executes can be single commands or more complex lists of editing instructions. It is invoked using one of the following methods.

---

sed

Syntax

```
sed [options] 'command1' [files]
sed [options] -e 'command1' [-e 'command2'...] [files]
sed [options] -f script [files]
```

Description

The first form invokes **sed** with a one-line *command1*. The second form invokes **sed** with two (or more) commands. Note that in this case the **-e** parameter is required for all commands specified. The commands are specified in quotes to prevent the shell from interpreting and expanding them. The last form instructs **sed** to take editing commands from file *script* (which does not need to be executable). In all cases, if *files* are not specified, input is taken from standard input. If multiple *files* are specified, the edited output of each successive file is concatenated.

Frequently used options

-e *cmd*
>The next argument is a command. This is not needed for single commands but is required for all commands when multiple commands are specified.

-f *file*
>The next argument is a script.

-g
>Treat all substitutions as global.

The **sed** utility operates on text through the use of *addresses* and *editing commands*. The address is used to locate lines of text to be operated upon, and editing commands modify text. During operation, each line (that is, text separated by newline characters) of input to **sed** is processed individually and without regard to adjacent lines. If multiple editing commands are to be used (through the use of a script file or multiple **-e** options), they are all applied in order to each line before moving on to the next line.

Input to **sed** can come from standard input or from *files*. When input is received from standard input, the original versions of the input text are lost. However, when input comes from files, the files themselves are *not changed* by **sed**. The output of **sed** represents a modified version of the contents of the files but does not affect them.

Addressing

Addresses in **sed** locate lines of text to which commands will be applied. The addresses can be:

* A line number (note that **sed** counts lines continuously across multiple input files).

* A line number with an interval. The form is *n~s*, where *n* is the starting line number and *s* is the step, or interval, to apply. For example, to match every odd line in the input, the address specification would be *1~2* (start at line 1 and match every two lines thereafter). This feature is a GNU extension to **sed**.

* The symbol $, indicating the last line of the last input file.

* A regular expression delimited by forward slashes (*/regex/*). See Objective 7 for more information on using regular expressions.

Zero, one, or two such addresses can be used with a **sed** command. If no addresses are given, commands are applied to all input lines by default. If a single address is given, commands are applied only to a line or lines matching the address. If two comma-separated addresses are given, an inclusive range is implied. Finally, any address may be followed by the ! character, and commands are applied to lines that *do not match* the address.

Commands

The **sed** command immediately follows the address specification if present. Commands generally consist of a single letter or symbol, unless they have arguments. Following are some basic **sed** editing commands to get you started.

d

Delete lines.

s

Make substitutions. This is a very popular **sed** command. The syntax is:

s/*pattern*/*replacement*/ [*flags*]

The following *flags* can be specified for the **s** command:

g

Replace all instances of *pattern*, not just the first.

n

Replace *n*th instance of *pattern*; the default is 1.

p

Print the line if a successful substitution is done. Generally used with the **-n** command-line option.

w *file*

Print the line to *file* if a successful substitution is done.

y

Translate characters. This command works in a fashion similar to the **tr** command, described earlier.

Example 1

Delete lines 3 through 5 of *file1*:

```
$ sed '3,5d' file1
```

Example 2

Delete lines of *file1* that contain a # at the beginning of the line:

```
$ sed '/^#/d' file1
```

Example 3

Translate characters:

y/abc/xyz/

Every instance of *a* is translated to *x*, *b* to *y*, and *c* to *z*.

Example 4

Write the @ symbol for all empty lines in *file1* (that is, lines with only a newline character but nothing more):

```
$ sed 's/^$/@/' file1
```

Example 5

Remove all double quotation marks from all lines in *file1*:

```
$ sed 's/"//g' file1
```

Example 6

Using **sed** commands from external file *sedcmds*, replace the third and fourth double quotation marks with (and) on lines 1 through 10 in *file1*. Make no changes from line 11 to the end of the file. Script file *sedcmds* contains:

```
1,10{
s/"/(/3
s/"/)/4
}
```

The command is executed using the –f option:

```
$ sed -f sedcmds file1
```

This example employs the positional flag for the **s** (substitute) command. The first of the two commands substitutes (for the third double-quote character. The next command substitutes) for the fourth double-quote character. Note, however, that the position count is interpreted *independently* for each subsequent command in the script. This is important because each command operates on the results of the commands preceding it. In this example, since the third double quote has been replaced with (, it is no longer counted as a double quote by the second command. Thus, the second command will operate on the *fifth* double quote character in the original *file1*. If the input line starts out with:

```
""""""
```

after the first command, which operates on the third double quote, the result is:

```
""("""
```

At this point, the numbering of the double-quote characters has changed, and the fourth double quote in the line is now the fifth character. Thus, after the second command executes, the output is:

```
""(")"
```

As you can see, creating scripts with **sed** requires that the sequential nature of the command execution be kept in mind.

If you find yourself making repetitive changes to many files on a regular basis, a **sed** script is probably warranted. Many more commands are available in **sed** than are listed here.

Objective 3: Perform Basic File Management

This section covers basic file and directory management, including filesystems, files and directories, standard file management commands, their recursive capabilities where applicable, and wildcard patterns.

Filesystem Objects

Nearly every operating system that has ever been devised structures its collection of stored objects in a *hierarchy,*[*] which is a tree of objects containing other

---

[*] However, it wasn't so long ago that MS-DOS was "flat" and had no hierarchy.

objects. This hierarchy allows a sane organization of objects and allows identically named objects to appear in multiple locations—this is essential for multiuser systems like Linux. Information about each object in the filesystem is stored in a table (which itself is part of the filesystem), and each object is numbered uniquely within that table. Although there are a few special object types on Linux systems, the two most common are *directories* and *files*.

Directories and files

A directory is an object intended to contain other objects, while a file is an object intended to contain information. At the top of all Linux filesystem hierarchies is a directory depicted simply by /; this is known as the *root* directory.* Beneath / are named directories and files in an organized and well-defined tree. To describe these objects, you simply refer to them by name separated by the / character. For example, the object **ls** is an executable program stored in a directory called */bin* under the *root* directory; it is depicted simply as */bin/ls*.

Inodes

The identification information for a filesystem object is known as its *inode*. Inodes carry information about objects, such as where they are located on disk, their modification time, security settings, and so forth. Each Linux *ext2* filesystem is created with a finite number of inodes, which is a number calculated based on the number of objects contained by the filesystem. Multiple objects in the filesystem can share the same inode; this concept is called *linking*.

File and directory management commands

Once a hierarchy is defined, there is a constant need to manage the objects in the filesystem. Objects are constantly created, read, modified, copied, moved, and deleted, and wisely managing the filesystem is one of the most important tasks of a system administrator. In this section, we discuss the basic command-line utilities used for file and directory management. While the GUI has tools for this task, the spirit of the Linux system and the requirements of Exam 101 require your understanding of these commands.

---

cp

Syntax

```
cp [options] file1 file2
cp [options] files directory
```

Description

In the first command form, copy *file1* to *file2*. If *file2* exists and you have appropriate privileges, it will be overwritten without warning (unless you use the -i

---

* Not to be confused with the username **root**, which is separate and distinct. There's also often a directory named */root* for the root user. Keeping /, */root* and the *root user* straight in a conversation can be a challenge.

---

option). Both *file1* and *file2* can be any valid filename, either fully qualified or in the local directory. In the second command form, copy one or more *files* to *directory*. Note that the presence of multiple files *implies* that you wish to copy files to a directory. If *directory* doesn't exist, an error message will be printed. This command form can get you in trouble if you attempt to copy a single file into a directory that doesn't exist, as the command will be interpreted as the first form and you'll end up with *file2* instead of *directory*.

Frequently used options

-f

> Force an overwrite of existing files in the destination.

-i

> Prompt *interactively* before overwriting destination files. It is common practice (and advised) to alias the **cp** command to **cp -i** to prevent accidental overwrites. You may find that this is already done for you for user root on your Linux system.

-p

> Preserve all information, including owner, group, permissions, and timestamps. Without this option, the copied file or files will have the present date and time, default permissions, owner, and group.

-r, -R

> Recursively copy directories. You may use either upper- or lowercase for this option. If *file1* is actually a directory instead of a file and the recursive option is specified, *file2* will be a copy of the entire hierarchy under directory *file1*.

-v

> Display the name of each file verbosely before copying.

Example 1

Copy the messages file to the local directory (specified by .):

```
$ cp /var/log/messages .
```

Example 2

Make an identical copy, including preservation of file attributes, of directory *src* in new directory *src2*:

```
$ cp -Rp src src2
```

Copy *file1*, *file2*, *file5*, *file6*, and *file7* from the local directory into your home directory (under *bash*):

```
$ cp file1 file2 file[567] ~
```

On the Exam

Be sure to know the difference between a file destination and a directory destination and how to force an overwrite of existing objects.

---

mkdir

Syntax

mkdir [*options*] *directories*

Description

Create one or more *directories*. You must have write permission in the directory where *directories* are to be created.

Frequently used options

-m *mode*

Set the access *mode* for *directories*.

-p

Create intervening parent directories if they don't exist.

Examples

Create a read-only directory named *personal*:

```
$ mkdir -m 444 personal
```

Create a directory tree in your home directory, as indicated with a leading tilde (~), using a single command:

```
$ mkdir -p ~/dir1/dir2/dir3
```

In this case, all three directories are created. This is faster than creating each directory individually.

On the Exam

Verify your understanding of the tilde (~) shortcut for the home directory.

---

mv

Syntax

mv [*options*] *source target*

Description

Move or rename files and directories. For *targets* on the same filesystem (partition), moving a file doesn't relocate the contents of the file itself. Rather, the directory entry for the target is updated with the new location. For *targets* on different filesystems, such a change can't be made, so files are copied to the target location and the original sources are deleted.

NOTE

Note that **mv** is used to rename files and directories, because a rename operation requires the same directory entry update as a move.

If a *target* file or directory does not exist, *source* is renamed to *target*. If a *target* file already exists, it is overwritten with *source*. If *target* is an existing directory, *source* is moved into that directory. If *source* is one or more files and *target* is a directory, the files are moved into the directory.

Frequently used options

-f

Force the move even if *target* exists, suppressing warning messages.

-i

Query interactively before moving files.

On the Exam

Remember that, from the filesystem's point of view on a single partition, re-naming a file and moving it to a different location are nearly identical operations. This eliminates the need for a *rename* command.

---

rm

Syntax

rm [*options*] *files*

Description

Delete one or more *files* from the filesystem. To remove a file, you must have write permission in the directory that contains the file, but you do not need write permission on the file itself. The rm command also removes directories when the -d, -r, or -R option is used.

Frequently used options

-d

Remove directories even if they are not empty. This option is reserved for privileged users.

-f

Force removal of write-protected files without prompting.

-i

Query interactively before removing files.

-r, -R

If the *file* is a directory, recursively remove the entire directory and all of its contents, including subdirectories.

rmdir

Syntax

rmdir [*option*] *directories*

Description

Delete *directories*, which must be empty.

Frequently used option

-p

Remove *directories* and any intervening parent directories that become empty as a result. This is useful for removing subdirectory trees.

On the Exam

Remember that recursive remove using **rm -R** removes directories too, even if they're not empty.

---

touch

Syntax

touch [*options*] *files*

Description

Change the access and/or modification times of *files*. This command is used to refresh timestamps on files. Doing so may be necessary, for example, to cause a program to be recompiled using the date-dependant **make** utility.

Frequently used options

-a

Change only the access time.

-m

Change only the modification time.

-t *timestamp*

Instead of the current time, use *timestamp* in the form of [[CC]YY]MMDDhhmm[.ss]. For example, the *timestamp* for January 12, 2001, at 6:45 p.m. is 200101121845.

File-Naming Wildcards

When working with files on the command line, you'll often run into situations in which you need to perform operations on many files at once. For example, if you are developing a C program, you may want to **touch** all of your .c files in order to be sure to recompile them the next time you issue the **make** utility to build your program. There will also be times when you need to move or delete all the files in a directory or at least a selected group of files. At other times, filenames may be long or difficult to type, and you'll want to find an abbreviated alternative to typing the filenames for each command you issue.

In order to make these operations simpler, all shells* on Linux offer *file-naming wildcards* (Table 1-9). Rather than explicitly specifying every file or typing long filenames, specifying *wildcard characters* in place of portions of the filenames can usually do the work for you. For example, the shell expands things like *.txt* to a list of all the files that end in *.txt*. File wildcard constructs like this are called *file globs*, and their use is awkwardly called *globbing*. Using file globs to specify multiple files is certainly a convenience, and in many cases is required to get anything useful accomplished.

Table 1-9: Common File-Naming Wildcards

Wildcard	Description
*	Commonly thought to "match anything." It actually will match zero or more characters (which includes "nothing"!). For example, x* matches files or directories *x, xy, xyz, x.txt, xy.txt, xyz.c,* and so on.
?	Match exactly one character. For example, x? matches files or directories *xx, xy, xz,* but not *x* and not *xyz.* The specification x?? matches *xyz,* but not *x* and *xy.*
[characters]	Match any single character from among *characters* listed between the brackets. For example, x[yz] matches *xy* and *xz.*
[!characters]	Match any single character other than *characters* listed between the brackets. For example, x[!yz] matches *xa* and *x1* but does not match *xy* and does not match *xz.*
[a-z]	Match any single character from among the range of characters listed between the brackets and indicated by the dash (the dash character is not matched). For example, x[0-9] matches *x0* and *x1,* but does not match *xx.* Note that to match both upper- and lowercase letters,[1] you specify [a-zA-Z]. Using x[a-zA-Z] matches *xa* and *xA.*
[!a-z]	Match any single character from among the characters not in the range listed between the brackets.

---

* Wildcards are expanded by the shell, not by commands. When a command is entered with wildcards included, the shell first expands all the wildcards (and other types of expansion) and passes the full result on to the command. This process is invisible to you.

Table 1-9: Common File-Naming Wildcards (continued)

Wildcard	Description

{*frag1,frag2,frag3...*}	Create strings *frag1*, *frag2*, *frag3*, etc. For example, `file_{one,two,three}` yields the strings `file_one`, `file_two`, and `file_three`. This is a special operator named *brace expansion* that can be used to match filenames but isn't specifically a file wildcard operator and does not examine directories for existing files to match. Instead, it will expand *any string*. For example, it can be used with **echo** to yield strings totally unrelated to existing filenames:
	`$ echo string_{a,b,c}`
	`string_a string_b string_c`

1. Linux filenames are case-sensitive.

Here are a few common applications for wildcards:

- If you remember part of a filename but not the whole thing, use wildcards with the portion you remember to help find the file. For example, if you're working in a directory with a large number of files and you know you're looking for a file named for Linux, you may enter a command like this:

```
$ ls -l *inux*
```

- When working with groups of related files, wildcards can be used to help separate the groups. For example, suppose you have a directory full of scripts you've written. Some are Perl scripts, for which you've used an extension of *.pl*, and some are Python, with a *.py* extension. You may wish to separate them into new separate directories for the two languages like this:

```
$ mkdir perl python
$ mv *.pl perl
$ mv *.py python
```

- Wildcards match directory names as well. Suppose you have a tree of directories starting with *contracting*, where you've created a directory for each month (that is, *contracting/january*, *contracting/february*, through *contracting/december*). In each of these directories are stored invoices, named simply *invoice_custa_01.txt*, *invoice_custa_02.txt*, *invoice_custb_01.txt*, and so on, where *custa* and *custb* are customer names of some form. To display all of the invoices, wildcards can be used:

```
$ ls con*/*/inv*.txt
```

The first * matches *tracting*. The second matches all directories under the *contracting* directory (*january* through *december*). The last matches all the customers and each invoice number for each customer.

See the **bash** man or info pages for additional information on how **bash** handles expansions and on other expansion forms.

Objective 4: Use Unix Streams, Pipes, and Redirects

Among the many beauties of the Linux and Unix systems is the notion that *everything is a file*. Things such as disk drives and their partitions, tape drives, terminals, serial ports, the mouse, and even audio are mapped into the filesystem. This mapping allows programs to interact with many different devices and files in the same way, simplifying their interfaces. Each device that uses the file metaphor is given a *device file*, which is a special object in the filesystem that provides an interface to the device. The kernel associates device drivers with various device files, which is how the system manages the illusion that devices can be accessed as if they were files. Using a terminal as an example, a program reading from the terminal's device file will receive characters typed at the keyboard. Writing to the terminal causes characters to appear on the screen. While it may seem odd to think of your terminal as a file, the concept provides a unifying simplicity to Linux and Linux programming.

Standard I/O and Default File Descriptors

Standard I/O is a capability of the shell, used with all text-based Linux utilities to control and direct program input, output, and error information. When a program is launched, it is automatically provided with three *file descriptors*. File descriptors are regularly used in programming and serve as a "handle" of sorts to another file. Standard I/O creates the following file descriptors:

Standard input (abbreviated stdin)
> This file descriptor is a text input stream. By default it is attached to your keyboard. When you type characters into an interactive text program, you are feeding them to standard input. As you've seen, some programs take one or more filenames as command-line arguments and ignore standard input. Standard input is also known as *file descriptor 0*.

Standard output (abbreviated stdout)
> This file descriptor is a text output stream for normal program output. By default it is attached to your terminal (or terminal window). Output generated by commands is written to standard output for display. Standard output is also known as *file descriptor 1*.

Standard error (abbreviated stderr)
> This file descriptor is also a text output stream, but it is used exclusively for errors or other information unrelated to the successful results of your command. By default standard error is attached to your terminal just like standard output. This means that standard output and standard error are commingled in your display, which can be confusing. You'll see ways to handle this later. Standard error is also known as *file descriptor 2*.

Standard output and standard error are separated because it is often useful to process normal program output differently than errors.

The standard I/O file descriptors are used in the same way as those created during program execution to read and write disk files. They enable you to tie commands together with files and devices, managing command input and output in exactly the way you desire. The difference is they are provided to the program by the shell by default and do not need to be explicitly created.

Pipes

From a program's point of view there is no difference between reading text data from a file and reading it from your keyboard. Similarly, writing text to a file and writing text to a display are equivalent operations. As an extension of this idea, it is also possible to tie the output of one program to the input of another. This is accomplished using a *pipe* (|) to join two or more commands together. For example:

```
$ grep "01523" order* | less
```

This command searches through all files whose names begin with **order** to find lines containing the word *01523*. By creating this pipe, the standard output of **grep** is sent to the standard input of **less**. The mechanics of this operation are handled by the shell and are invisible to the user. Pipes can be used in a series of many commands. When more than two commands are put together, the resulting operation is known as a *pipeline* or *text stream*, implying the flow of text from one command to the next.

As you get used to the idea, you'll find yourself building pipelines naturally to extract specific information from text data sources. For example, suppose you wish to view a sorted list of inode numbers from among the files in your current directory. There are many ways you could achieve this. One way would be to use **awk** in a pipeline to extract the inode number from the output of **ls**, then send it on to the **sort** command and finally to a pager for viewing:[*]

```
$ ls -i * | awk '{print $1}' | sort -nu | less
```

The pipeline concept in particular is a feature of Linux and Unix that draws on the fact that your system contains a diverse set of tools for operating on text. Combining their capabilities can yield quick and easy ways to extract otherwise hard to handle information.

Redirection

Each pipe symbol in the previous pipelines example instructs the shell to feed output from one command into the input of another. This action is a special form of *redirection*, which allows you to manage the origin of input streams and the destination of output streams. In the previous example, individual programs are unaware that their output is being handed off to or from another program because the shell takes care of the redirection on their behalf.

Redirection can also occur to and from files. For example, rather than sending the output of an inode list to the pager **less**, it could easily be sent directly to a file with the > redirection operator:

```
$ ls -i * | awk '{print $1}' | sort -nu > in.txt
```

---

[*] Don't worry about the syntax or function of these commands at this point.

By changing the last redirection operator, the shell creates an empty file (*in.txt*), opens it for writing, and the standard output of **sort** places the results in the file instead of on the screen. Note that, in this example, anything sent to standard error is still displayed on the screen.

Since the > redirection operator *creates* files, the >> redirection operator can be used to append to existing files. For example, you could use the following command to append a one-line footnote to *in.txt*:

```
$ echo "end of list" >> in.txt
```

Since *in.txt* already exists, the quote will be appended to the bottom of the existing file. If the file didn't exist, the >> operator would create the file and insert the text "end of list" as its contents.

It is important to note that when creating files, the output redirection operators are interpreted by the shell *before* the commands are executed. This means that any output files created through redirection are opened first. For this reason, you cannot modify a file in place, like this:

```
$ grep "stuff" file1 > file1   # don't do it!
```

If *file1* contains something of importance, this command would be a disaster because an empty *file1* would overwrite the original. The **grep** command would be last to execute, resulting in a complete data loss from the original *file1* file because the file that replaced it was empty. To avoid this problem, simply use an intermediate file and *then* rename it:

```
$ grep "stuff" file1 > file2
$ mv file2 file1
```

Standard input can also be redirected. The input redirection operator is <. Using a source other than the keyboard for a program's input may seem odd at first, but since text programs don't care about where their standard input streams originate, you can easily redirect input. For example, the following command will send a mail message with the contents of the file *in.txt* to user *jdean*:

```
$ Mail -s "inode list" jdean < in.txt
```

Normally, the **Mail** program prompts the user for input at the terminal. However with standard input redirected *from* the file *in.txt,* no user input is needed and the command executes silently. Table 1-10 lists the common standard I/O redirections for the **bash** shell, specified in the LPI Objectives.

NOTE

The redirection syntax may be significantly different if you use another shell.

Table 1-10: Standard I/O Redirections for the bash shell

Redirection Function	Syntax for bash
Send *stdout* to *file*.	`$ cmd > file` `$ cmd 1> file`
Send *stderr* to *file*.	`$ cmd 2> file`
Send both *stdout* and *stderr* to *file*.	`$ cmd > file 2>&1`

Table 1-10: Standard I/O Redirections for the bash shell (continued)

Redirection Function	Syntax *for* bash
Send *stdout* to *file1* and *stderr* to *file2*.	`$ cmd > file1 2> file2`
Receive *stdin* from *file*.	`$ cmd < file`
Append *stdout* to *file*.	`$ cmd >> file` `$ cmd 1>> file`
Append *stderr* to *file*.	`$ cmd 2>> file`
Append both *stdout* and *stderr* to *file*.	`$ cmd >> file 2>&1`
Pipe *stdout* from *cmd1* to *cmd2*.	`$ cmd1	cmd2`
Pipe *stdout* and *stderr* from *cmd1* to *cmd2*.	`$ cmd1 2>&1	cmd2`

On the Exam

Be prepared to demonstrate the difference between filenames and command names in commands using redirection operators. Also, check the syntax on commands in redirection questions to be sure about which command or file is a data source and which is a destination.

Using the tee Command

Sometimes, you'll want to run a program and send its output to a file while at the same time viewing the output on the screen. The **tee** utility is helpful in this situation.

---

tee

Syntax

    tee [*options*] *files*

Description

Read from standard input and write both to one or more *files* and to standard output (analogous to a tee junction in a pipe).

Option

−a

    Append to *files* rather than overwriting them.

Example

Suppose you're running a pipeline of commands **cmd1**, **cmd2**, and **cmd3**:

    $ cmd1 | cmd2 | cmd3 > file1

This sequence puts the ultimate output of the pipeline into *file1*. However, you may also be interested in the intermediate result of **cmd1**. To create a new *file_ cmd1* containing those results, use **tee**:

    $ cmd1 | tee file_cmd1 | cmd2 | cmd3 > file1

The results in *file1* will be the same as in the original example, and the intermediate results of **cmd1** will be placed in *file_cmd1*.

Objective 5: Create, Monitor, and Kill Processes

This Objective looks at the management of *processes*. Just as file management is a
fundamental system administrator's function, the management and control of
processes is also essential for smooth system operation. In most cases, processes
will live, execute, and die without intervention from the user because they are
automatically managed by the kernel. However, there are times that a process will
die for some unknown reason and need to be restarted. Or, some process may
"run wild" and consume system resources, requiring that it be terminated. You will
also need to instruct running processes to perform operations, such as rereading a
configuration file.

Processes

Each program running on your system is considered to be a process by the kernel.
Your shell is a process, and each command you type into the shell starts one or
more processes during its execution. Attributes and concepts associated with
processes include:

Lifetime
> Each process "lives" as it executes. Short commands such as **ls** will execute for
> a very short time, generate results, and terminate on their own. User programs
> such as web browsers run for extended periods until terminated by the user.
> Daemons such as web servers run continuously from boot to shutdown or
> restart. When a process terminates, it is said to *die* (which is why the program
> used to manually signal a process to stop execution is called **kill**; succinct,
> though admittedly morbid).

Process ID (PID)
> Every process has a number assigned to it when it starts. PIDs are integer
> numbers unique among all running processes.

User ID (UID) and Group ID (GID)
> Processes must have associated privileges, and a process' UID and GID are
> associated with the user who started the process. This limits the process'
> access to objects in the filesystem.

Parent process
> The first process started by the kernel at system start time is a program called
> **init**. This process has PID 1 and is the ultimate parent of all other processes
> on the system. Your shell is a descendant of **init** and the parent process to
> commands started by the shell, which are its *child* processes, or *subprocesses*.*

Parent process ID (parent PID)
> *This is the PID of the process that created the process in question.* If that parent
> process has vanished, the parent PID will be 1, which is the PID of **init**.

---

* Note that shell's built-in commands, such as **alias**, **bg**, **cd**, **echo**, **jobs**, and **test**, do not start a
child process but are executed in the shell process itself. See the **bash** manpage for a full list
of built-in commands.

Environment

Each process holds a list of variables and their associated values. Collectively, this list is known as the process' *environment* and the variables are *environment variables*. The environment is inherited from the parent process unless it is replaced through the execution of startup scripts.

Current working directory

A default directory is associated with each process, which is where the process will seek and write files unless they are explicitly specified to be elsewhere in the filesystem.

NOTE

Processes are often referred to as *tasks*. Linux is a multitasking operating system, in that it runs many processes simultaneously. However, even though the terms *process* and *task* may be synonymous in this context, don't confuse multiprocessing with multitasking. Multiprocessing generally refers to systems with multiple central processing units, a definition that has little to do with system processes. Given the correct hardware and a multiprocessing kernel, Linux has multiprocessing capability.

Process Monitoring

At any time, there could be tens or even hundreds of processes running together on your Linux system. Monitoring these processes is done using three convenient utilities: **ps**, **pstree**, and **top**.

---

ps

Syntax

ps [*options*]

Description

This command generates a one-time snapshot of the current processes on standard output.

Frequently used options

–a

Show processes that are owned by other users and attached to a terminal. Normally, only the current user's processes are shown.

–f

"Forest" mode, which is used to display process family trees. For example, using this option will display all running child web servers (**httpd**) in a hierarchical diagram under the parent web server.*

–l

Long format, which includes priority, parent PID, and other information.

---

* There is also a separate command called **pstree** that does this nicely.

-u

    User format, which includes usernames and the start time of processes.

-w

    Wide output format, used to eliminate the default output line truncation. Useful for the **-f** option.

-x

    Include processes without controlling terminals. Often needed to see daemon processes and others not started from a terminal session.

-C *cmd*

    Display instances of command name *cmd.*

-U *usr*

    Display processes owned by username *usr.*

Examples

Simply entering the **ps** command with no options will yield a brief list of processes owned by you and attached to your terminal:

```
$ ps
```

Use the **-a**, **-u**, and **-x** options to include processes owned by others and not attached to terminals as well as to display them in the "user" mode. The command is valid with or without the dash:

```
$ ps -aux
$ ps aux
```

In this case, the dash is optional. However, certain **ps** options require the dash. (See the manpage for details.)

If you are interested in finding process information on a particular command, use the **-C** option. This command displays all web server processes:

```
$ ps u -C httpd
```

You'll note that the **-C** option *requires* the dash, but the **u** option won't work with it if a dash is included. This confusion exists because the **ps** command as implemented on Linux understands options in three differing forms:

Unix98 options

    These may be grouped and must be preceded by a dash.

BSD options

    These may be grouped and must *not* be used with a dash.

GNU long options

    These options are preceded by two dashes.

All of these option types may be freely intermixed. Instead of the **-C** option, you may wish to use **ps** with other options that you usually use and pipe the output to **grep**, searching for process names, PIDs, or anything else you know about the process:

```
$ ps -aux | grep httpd
```

In this case, the result would be the same list of **httpd** servers, as well as the **grep** command itself.

pstree

Syntax

    pstree [*options*] [*pid*|*user*]

Description

The **pstree** command is similar to the "forest" mode of **ps -f**. This command displays a hierarchical list of processes in a tree format. **pstree** is very handy for understanding how parent/child process relationships are set up.

If *pid* is specified, the displayed tree is rooted at that process. Otherwise, it is rooted at the *init* process, which has PID 1. If *user* (a valid username) is specified, trees for all processes owned by *user* are shown. The tree is represented using characters that appear as lines, such as | for vertical lines and + for intersections (VT100 line-drawing characters, displayed as solid lines by most terminals, are optional). The output looks similar to this:

    httpd-+-httpd
          |-httpd
          |-httpd
          |-httpd
          `-httpd

By default, visually identical branches of the tree are merged to reduce output. Merged lines are preceded by a count indicating the actual number of similar processes. The preceding example is normally displayed on a single line:

    httpd---5*[httpd]

This behavior can be turned off with the **-c** option.

Frequently used options

-a

Display command-line arguments used to launch processes.

-c

Disable the compaction of identical subtrees.

-G

Use the VT100 line-drawing characters instead of plain characters to display the tree. This yields a much more pleasing display but may not be appropriate for printing or paging programs.

-h

Highlight the ancestry of the current process (usually the shell). The terminal must support highlighting for this option to be meaningful.

-n

The default sort order for processes with the same parent is alphanumerically by name. This option changes this behavior to a numeric sort by PID.

-p

Include PIDs in the output.

Example

Display a process tree including PIDs:

```
# pstree -p
init(1)-+-atd(356)
        |-crond(370)
        |-gpm(526)
        |-httpd(540)-+-httpd(544)
        |            |-httpd(545)
        |            |-httpd(546)
        |            |-httpd(547)
        |            |-httpd(548)
        |-inetd(384)
        |-login(691)-bash(699)-startx(711)-xinit(718)
        | -+-X(719)
        |-lpd(412)
        |-mdrecoveryd(5)
        |-mingetty(692)
        |-mingetty(693)
        |-named(398)
        |-nfsd(467)---lockd(475)---rpciod(476)
        |-nfsd(468)
        |-portmap(284)
```

top

Syntax

top [*command-line options*]

Description

The **top** command also offers output similar to **ps**, but in a continuously updated display. This is useful in situations in which you need to watch the status of one or more processes or to see how they are using your system.

In addition, a header of useful uptime, load, CPU status, and memory information is displayed. By default, the process status output is generated with the most CPU-intensive processes at the top of the listing (and is named for the "top" processes). In order to format the screen, **top** must understand how to control the terminal display. The type of terminal (or terminal window) in use is stored in the environment variable TERM. If this variable is not set or contains an unknown terminal type, **top** may not execute.

Popular command-line options

Dashes are not required for **top** options:

-b

> Run in batch mode. This is useful for sending output from **top** to other programs or to a file. It executes the number of iterations specified with the -n option and terminate. This option is also useful if **top** cannot display on the terminal type you are using.

-d *delay*

> Specify the *delay* in seconds between screen updates. The default is five seconds.

-i

> Ignore idle processes, listing only the "interesting" ones taking system resources.

-n *num*

> Display *num* iterations and then exit, instead of running indefinitely.

-q

> Run with no delay. If the user is the superuser, run with highest possible priority. This option causes **top** to update continuously and will probably consume any idle time your CPU had. Running **top -q** as superuser will seriously affect system performance and is not recommended.

-s

> Run in secure mode. Some of **top**'s interactive commands can be dangerous if running as the superuser. This option disables them.

Frequently used interactive options

Once **top** is running interactively, it can be given a number of commands via the keyboard to change its behavior. These commands are single-key commands, some of which cause **top** to prompt for input:

Ctrl-L

> Repaint the screen.

h

> Generate a help screen.

k

> Kill a process. You will be prompted for the PID of the process and the signal to send it (the default signal is 15, *SIGTERM*). See the later section, "Terminating Processes."

n

> Change the number of processes to show. You will be prompted to enter an integer number. The default is 0, which indicates that the screen should be filled.

q

> Quit the program.

r

> **Renice** a process (change its priority). You will be prompted for the PID of the process and the value to nice it to (see **nice** and **renice** in Objective 6). Entering a positive value causes a process to lose priority. If the superuser is running top, a negative value may be entered, causing a process to get a higher than normal priority. This command is not available in secure mode.

s

> Change the delay in seconds between updates. You will be prompted for the delay value, which may include fractions of seconds (i.e., 0.5).

Example 1

Simply executing **top** without options gives a full status display updated every five seconds:

```
$ top
```

Use the **q** command to quit.

Example 2

To run **top** with a faster refresh rate, use the interval option, specified here with a one-second refresh:

```
$ top -d 1
```

Example 3

To have **top** update constantly, you could specify **-d 0**, or use the **-q** option. Here, this feature is used to watch only nonidle processes, which will include **top** itself:

```
$ top -qi
```

Example 4

You may wish to use **top** to log its output to a file. Use the **-b** (batch) option for this purpose. In this batch example, the **-i** option eliminates idle processes, the **-n** option, with its argument, indicates five iterations, and the **-d** option indicates a one-second interval. Results will be redirected to *file1*. This command will take five seconds to execute and does not use the optional dashes:

```
$ top bin 5 d 1 > file1
```

The single-key interactive commands can be used when **top** is running interactively. For example, if you type the **h** command, **top** yields a help screen. By entering the **n** command, **top** prompts you for the number of lines you wish to display.

On the Exam

The parent/child relationship of the processes on a Linux system is important. Be sure to understand how these relationships work and how to view them. Note that the *init* process always has PID 1 and is the ultimate ancestor of all system processes.

Using **top** to change the "nice" (priority modifier) value for a process is discussed in Objective 6.

Signaling Active Processes

Each process running on your system listens for *signals*, simple messages sent to the process either by the kernel or by a user. The messages are sent through interprocess communication. They are single-valued, in that they don't contain strings or command-like constructs. Instead, signals are numeric integer messages, predefined and known by processes. Most have an implied action for the process to take. When a process receives a signal, it can (or may be forced) to take action. For example, if you are executing a program from the command line that appears to hang, you may elect to type **Ctrl-C** to abort the program. This action actually sends an INTERRUPT signal to the process, telling it to stop running.

There are about 30 signals defined in Linux. Each signal has a name and a number (the number is sent to the process, the name is only for our convenience). Many signals are used by the kernel, and some are useful for users. Table 1-11 lists popular signals for interactive use.

Table 1-11: Frequently Used Interactive Signals

Signal Name[1]	Number	Meaning and Use
HUP	1	Hang up. This signal is sent automatically when you log out or disconnect a modem. It is also used by many daemons to cause the configuration file to be reread.
INT	2	Interrupt; stop running. This signal is sent when you type **Ctrl-C**.
KILL	9	Kill; stop unconditionally and immediately. Sending this signal is a drastic measure, as it cannot be ignored by the process. This is the "emergency kill" signal.
TERM	15	Terminate, nicely if possible. This signal is used to ask a process to exit gracefully.
TSTP	18	Stop executing, ready to continue. This signal is sent when you type **Ctrl-Z**. (See "*Shell Job Control*" later in this section for more information.)

1. Signal names will often be specified with a "SIG" prefix. That is, signal **HUP** is the same as signal **SIGHUP**.

As you can see from Table 1-11, some signals are invoked by pressing well-known key combinations such as **Ctrl-C** and **Ctrl-Z**. You can also use the **kill** command to send any message. The **kill** command is implemented both as a shell built-in command and as a standalone binary command.

---

kill

Syntax

```
kill [-s sigspec | -sigspec] [pids]
kill -l [signum]
```

Description

In the first form, **kill** is used with an optional *sigspec*. This is a signal value, specified as either an integer or the signal name (such as **SIGHUP**, or simply **HUP**). The *sigspec* is case-insensitive but usually specified with uppercase letters. You may use -s *sigspec* or simply -*sigspec* to make up the signal value or name. If a *sigspec*

---

is not given, then SIGTERM (signal 15, "exit gracefully") is assumed. The *sigspec* is followed by one or more *pids* to which the signal is to be sent. In the second form with the –l option, **kill** lists the valid signal names. If *signum* (an integer) is present, only the signal name for that number will be displayed.

Examples

This command displays the signal name **SIGTERM**, the name of signal 15, and the default when **kill** is used to signal processes:

```
$ kill -l 15
```

All of these commands will send a **SIGTERM** signal to the processes with PIDs 1000 and 1001:

```
$ kill 1000 1001
$ kill -15 1000 1001
$ kill -SIGTERM 1000 1001
$ kill -sigterm 1000 1001
$ kill -TERM 1000 1001
$ kill -s 15 1000 1001
$ kill -s SIGTERM 1000 1001
```

If those two processes are playing nicely on your system, they'll comply with the **SIGTERM** signal and terminate when they're ready (after they clean up whatever they're doing). Not all processes will comply, however. A process may be hung in such a way that it cannot respond, or it may have *signal handling* code written to trap the signal you're trying to send. To force a process to die, use the strongest **kill**:

```
$ kill -9 1000 1001
$ kill -KILL 1000 1001
```

These equivalent commands send the **KILL** signal to the process, which the process cannot ignore. The process will terminate immediately without regard to closing files or other cleanup procedures. Because of this, using the **KILL** signal is a last resort.* See the next section, "*Terminating Processes*."

The **inetd** superdaemon will respond to the **HUP** signal by rereading its configuration file. If you've made changes to that file and want **inetd** to reconfigure itself, send it the **HUP** signal:

```
$ kill -HUP `cat /var/run/inetd.pid`
```

On the Exam

Note that **kill** is used for sending all kinds of signals, not just termination signals. Also, be aware of the difference between the PID you intend to kill and the signal you wish to send it. Since they're both integers, they can sometimes be confused.

---

* There are situations in which the **KILL** signal won't stop a process. Most of them are hardware-related, such as a process trying to write to an unavailable NFS server or waiting for a tape device to complete rewinding.

The backward quotes are replaced by the shell with the contents of the file *inetd.pid*, which **inetd** creates when it starts.

Terminating Processes

Based on the type of service that has failed, you can use **ps** or **top** to identify one or more processes that may have a problem. Once you know the PID for the process that's causing the problem, you can use the **kill** command to stop the process nicely with SIGTERM (**kill -15** [*PID*]), escalating the signal to higher strengths if necessary until the process terminates.

NOTE

Occasionally you may see a process displayed by **ps** or **top** that is listed as a *zombie*. These are processes that are stuck while trying to terminate and are appropriately said to be in the *zombie state*. Just as in the cult classic film Night of the Living Dead, you can't kill zombies, because they're already dead!

If you have a recurring problem with zombies, there may be a bug in your system software or in an application

---

Killing a process may also kill all of its child processes. For example, killing a shell may kill all the processes initiated from that shell, including other shells.

Shell Job Control

Linux and most modern Unix systems offer *job control*, which is the ability of your shell (with support of the kernel) to place executing commands in the *background* where they can be executed. A program is said to be in the *foreground* when it is attached to your terminal. When executing in the background, you have no input to the process other than sending it signals. When a process is started in the background, you create a *job*. Each job is assigned a job number, starting at 1 and numbering sequentially.

The basic reason to create a background process is to keep your terminal or terminal window session free. There are many instances when a long-running program will never produce a result from standard output or standard error, and your shell will simply sit idle waiting for the program to finish. Noninteractive programs can be placed in the background by adding the **&** character to the command. For example, if you start **netscape** from the command line, you don't want the shell to sit and wait for it to terminate. The shell will respond by starting the browser in the background and will give you a new command prompt. It will also issue the job number, denoted in square brackets, along with the PID. For example:

```
$ netscape &
[1]  1748
```

Here, Netscape is started as a background process. Netscape is assigned to job 1 (as denoted by [1]), and is assigned PID *1748*. If you start a program and forget

---

the & character, you can still put it in the background by first stopping it by typing
Ctrl–Z:

```
^Z
[1]+  Stopped        netscape
```

Then issue the **bg** command to restart the job in the background:

```
$ bg
[1]+ netscape &
```

Putting interactive programs in the background can be quite useful. Suppose
you're logged into a remote Linux system, running Emacs in text mode. Realizing
that you need to drop back to the command line, you elect not to terminate the
editor but instead simply press **Ctrl–Z**. This stops Emacs and puts it in the background and returns you a command prompt.* When you're finished, you can go
back into Emacs by issuing the **fg** command, which puts your stopped job back
into the foreground.

Background jobs and their status can be listed by issuing the **jobs** command.
Stopped jobs can be brought to the foreground with the **fg** command and optionally placed into the background with the **Ctrl–Z** and **bg** sequence.

bg

Syntax

bg [*jobspec*]

Description

Place *jobspec* in the background, as if it had been started with **&**. If *jobspec* is not
present, then the shell's notion of the *current job* is used, as indicated by the plus
sign (**+**) in output from the *jobs* command. Using this command on a job that is
stopped will allow it to run in the background.

fg

Syntax

fg [*jobspec*]

Description

This command places the specified job in the foreground, making it the current
job. If *jobspec* is not present, then the shell's notion of the current job is used.

jobs

Syntax

jobs [*options*] [*jobspecs*]

---

* This example ignores the fact that Emacs is capable of hosting a shell itself, which would
probably eliminate your need to use job control to get to the command line.

Description

List the active jobs. If *jobspecs* are included, output is restricted to information about those jobs.

Frequently used option

-l

    Also list PIDs.

On the Exam

Be sure to know how to display background jobs and how to switch among them.

Objective 6: Modify Process Execution Priorities

Certain tasks on the system require more execution time than others, and thus deserve to be allocated more frequent execution and longer time slices by the kernel. For this reason, each process is given an *execution priority*. Usually, you don't need to worry about execution priority because the kernel handles it automatically. Each process' priority level is constantly and dynamically raised and lowered by the kernel according to a number of parameters, such as how much system time it has already consumed and its status (perhaps waiting for I/O—such processes are favored by the kernel). Linux gives you the ability to bias the kernel's priority algorithm, favoring certain processes over others.

The priority of a process can be determined by examining the PRI column in the results produced from issuing either the **top** or **ps -l** commands. The values displayed are relative; the higher the priority number, the more CPU time the kernel offers to the process. The kernel does this by managing a queue of processes. Those with high priority are given more time, and those with low priority are given less time. On a heavily loaded system, a process with a very low priority may appear stalled.

nice

One of the parameters used by the kernel to assign process priority is supplied by the user and is called a *nice number*. The **nice** command* is used to assign a priority number to the process. It is so named because it normally causes programs to execute with lower priority levels than with their default. Thus, the process is being "nice" to other processes on the system by yielding CPU time. With this scheme, more "niceness" implies a lower priority, and less niceness implies a higher priority.

---

* Some shells, not including **bash**, have a built-in **nice** command.

By default, user processes are created with a *nice number* of zero. With this setting, **nice** doesn't sway the kernel's prioritization scheme one way or another. Positive numbers lower the priority, and negative numbers raise the priority. Nice numbers range from -20 to +19. Any user can start a process with a positive nice number, but only the superuser (*root*) can lower a process' nice number to raise its priority. For example, if you have a long-running utility program but don't want to impact interactive performance, a positive nice number will lower the job's priority and improve interactive performance.

nice

Syntax

```
nice [-n adjustment] [command]
nice [-adjustment] [command]
```

Description

The **nice** command is used to alter another command's nice number at start time. For normal users, *adjustment* is an integer from 1 to 19. If you're the superuser, the *adjustment* range is from -20 to 19. If an *adjustment* number is not specified, the process' **nice** number defaults to 10. The *command* consists of any command that you might enter on the command line, including all options, arguments, redirections, and the background character **&**.

If both *adjustment* and *command* are omitted, nice displays the current scheduling priority, which is inherited.

Example 1

The following command starts a program in the background with reduced priority, using the default nice number of 10:

```
$ nice somecmd -opt1 -opt2 arg1 arg2 &
```

Example 2

As superuser, you can start programs with elevated priority. These equivalent commands start the **vi** editor with a higher priority, which may be necessary for administrative purposes if the system is exceptionally slow:

```
# nice --10 vi /etc/hosts.deny
# nice -n -10 vi /etc/hosts.deny
```

Note the double dash (**--10**) in the first form. The first dash indicates that an option follows, while the second dash indicates a negative number.

Be careful when using **nice** on interactive programs such as editors, word processors, or browsers. Assigning a program a positive nice number will most likely result in sluggish performance. Remember, the higher the positive number, the lower the resulting priority level.* For that reason, you should try not to assign positive nice numbers to foreground jobs on your terminal. If the system gets busy, your terminal could hang awaiting CPU time, which has been sacrificed by **nice**.

---

* The actual scheduling priority used by the kernel is dynamic and takes into account many more factors than the nice value.

Changing nice numbers on running processes

The **nice** command only works to change the nice number for new processes at the time that they're started. To modify a running program, use the **renice** command.

---

renice

Syntax

```
renice [+|-]nicenumber [option] targets
```

Description

Alter the *nicenumber* to set the scheduling priority of one or more running *target* processes. By default, **renice** assumes that the *targets* are numeric PIDs. One or more *options* may also be used to interpret *targets* as processes owned by specific users.

Frequently used options

-u
> Interpret *targets* as usernames, affecting all processes owned by those users.

-p
> Interpret *targets* as PIDs (the default).

Examples

This command will lower the priority of the process with PID 501 by increasing its **nice** number to the maximum:

```
$ renice 20 501
```

The following command can be used to increase the priority of all of user *jdean*'s processes as well as the process with PID 501:

```
# renice -10 -u jdean -p 501
```

In this command, -10 indicates a **nice** value of negative 10, thus giving PID 501 a higher priority on the system. A dash isn't used for the **nice** value because the dash could be confused for an option, such as -u.

On the Exam

Be sure to know the range and meaning of **nice** numbers and how to change them for new and existing processes. Also note that **nice** and **renice** specify their numbers differently. With **nice**, a leading dash can indicate a nice number (e.g., -10), including a negative one with a second dash (e.g., --10). On the other hand, **renice** does not need the hyphen.

The **renice** command is handy for managing groups of processes, particularly to affect user processes by username. In addition, if you're observing processes in

---

top, you may change nice numbers for them interactively from within the **top** program (discussed in Objective 5) by using the single-keystroke **r** command. You will be prompted for the PID of the process whose nice number you wish to change and for the new nice number (if you are the superuser, you may enter negative values). The new nice number will be displayed by **top** in the column labeled *NI* for the process you specify.

Objective 7: Making Use of Regular Expressions

In *Objective 3*, filename globbing with wildcards is described, which enables us to list or find files with common elements (i.e., filenames or file extensions) at once. File globs make use of special characters such as *, which have special meanings in the context of the command line. There are a handful of shell wildcard characters understood by **bash**, enough to handle the relatively simple problem of *globbing* filenames. Other problems aren't so simple, and extending the glob concept into any generic text form (files, text streams, program string variables, etc.) can open up a wide new range of capability. This is done using *regular expressions*.

Two tools that are important for the LPIC Level 1 exams and that make use of regular expressions are **grep** and **sed**. These tools are useful for text searches. There are many other tools that make use of regular expressions, including the *awk*, Perl, and Python languages and other utilities, but you don't need to be concerned with them for the purpose of the LPIC Level 1 exams.

Using grep

A long time ago, as the idea of regular expressions was catching on, the line editor **ed** contained a command to display lines of a file being edited that matched a given regular expression. The command is:

    g/regular expression/p

That is, "on a global basis, print the current line when a match for *regular expression* is found," or more simply, "global regular expression print." This function was so useful that it was made into a standalone utility named, appropriately, **grep**. Later, the regular expression grammar of **grep** was expanded in a new command called **egrep** (for "extended *grep*"). You'll find both commands on your Linux system today, and they differ slightly in the way they handle regular expressions. For the purposes of Exam 101, we'll stick with **grep**, which can also make use of the "extended" regular expressions when used with the –**E** option. You will find some form of **grep** on just about every Unix or Unix-like system available.

grep

Syntax

    grep [options] regex [files]

Description

Search *files* or standard input for lines containing a match to regular expression *regex*. By default, matching lines will be displayed and nonmatching lines will not be displayed. When multiple files are specified, **grep** displays the filename as a prefix to the output lines (use the -h option to suppress filename prefixes).

Frequently used options

-c
  Display only a count of matched lines, but not the lines themselves.

-h
  Display matched lines, but do not include filenames for multiple file input.

-i
  Ignore uppercase and lowercase distinctions, allowing *abc* to match both *abc* and *ABC.*

-n
  Display matched lines prefixed with their line numbers. When used with multiple files, *both* the filename and line number are prefixed.

-v
  Print all lines that *do not* match *regex*. This is an important and useful option. You'll want to use regular expressions, not only to *select* information but also to *eliminate* information. Using -v inverts the output this way.

Examples

Since regular expressions can contain both metacharacters and literals, **grep** can be used with an entirely literal *regex*. For example, to find all lines in *file1* that contain either *Linux* or *linux*, you could use **grep** like this:

```
$ grep -i linux file1
```

In this example, the *regex* is simply "linux." The uppercase *L* in "Linux" is matched by the command-line option -i. This is fine for literal expressions that are common. However, in situations in which *regex* includes regular expression metacharacters that are also shell special characters (such as $ or *), the *regex* must be quoted to prevent shell expansion and pass the metacharacters on to **grep**.

As a simplistic example of this, suppose you have files in your local directory named *abc*, *abc1*, and *abc2*. When combined with **bash**'s **echo** expression, the *abc** wildcard expression lists all files that begin with *abc*, as follows:

```
$ echo abc*
abc abc1 abc2
```

Now suppose that these files contain lines with the strings *abc*, *abcc*, *abccc*, and so on, and you wish to use **grep** to find them. You can use the shell wildcard expression *abc** to expand to all the *abc* files as displayed with **echo** above, and you'd use an identical regular expression **abc*** to find all occurrences of lines containing *abc*, *abcc*, *abccc*, etc. Without using quotes to prevent shell expansion, the command would be:

```
$ grep abc* abc*
```

After shell expansion, this yields:

```
$ grep abc abc1 abc2 abc abc1 abc2   # no!
```

This is *not* what you intended! **grep** would search for the literal expression *abc*, because it appears as the first command argument. Instead, quote the regular expression with single or double quotes to protect it:*

```
$ grep 'abc*' abc*
```

or:

```
$ grep "abc*" abc*
```

After expansion, both examples yield the same results:

```
$ grep abc* abc abc1 abc2
```

Now this is what you're after. The three files *abc*, *abc1*, and *abc2* will be searched for the regular expression *abc**. It is good to stay in the habit of quoting regular expressions on the command line to avoid these problems—they won't be at all obvious because the shell expansion is invisible to you unless you use the **echo** command.

On the Exam

The use of **grep** and its options is common. You should be familiar with what each option does, as well as the concept of piping the results of other commands into **grep** for matching.

Using sed

In Objective 2, we introduce **sed**, the *stream editor*. In that section, we talk about how **sed** uses *addresses* to locate text upon which it will operate. Among the addressing mechanisms mentioned is the use of regular expressions delimited between slash characters. Let's recap how **sed** can be invoked.

---

sed

Syntax

```
sed [options] 'command1' [files]
sed [options] -e 'command1' [-e 'command2'] [files]
sed [options] -f script [files]
```

Description

Note that *command1* is contained within single quotes. This is necessary for the same reasons as with **grep**. The text in *command1* must be protected from evaluation and expansion by the shell.

The address part of a **sed** command may contain regular expressions, which are enclosed in slashes. For example, to show the contents of *file1* except for blank lines, the **sed** delete (**d**) command could be invoked like this:

```
$ sed '/^$/ d' file1
```

---

* The difference between single quotes and double quotes on the command line is subtle and is explained later in this section.

In this case, the regular expression ^$ matches blank lines and the **d** command removes those matching lines from **sed**'s output.

Quoting

As shown in the examples for **grep** and **sed**, it is necessary to *quote* regular expression metacharacters if you wish to preserve their special meaning. Failing to do this can lead to unexpected results when the shell interprets the metacharacters as file globbing characters. There are three forms of quoting you may use to preserve special characters:

\ *(an unquoted backslash character)*
> By applying a backslash before a special character, it will not be interpreted by the shell but will be passed through unaltered to the command you're entering. For example, the * metacharacter may be used in a regular expression like this:

> `$ grep abc\* abc abc1 abc2`

> Here, files *abc*, *abc1*, and *abc2* are searched for the regular expression *abc*.*

Single quotes
> Surrounding metacharacters with the single-quote character also protects them from interpretation by the shell. All characters inside a pair of single quotes are assumed to have their literal value.

Double quotes
> Surrounding metacharacters with the double-quote character has the same effect as single quotes, with the exception of the $, ' (single quote), and \ (backslash) characters. Both $ and ' retain their special meaning within double quotes. The backslash retains its special meaning when followed by $, ', another backslash, or a newline.

In general, single quotes are safest for preserving regular expressions.

On the Exam

Pay special attention to quoting methods used to preserve special characters, because the various forms don't necessarily yield the same result.

Regular Expressions

Linux offers many tools for system administrators to use for processing text. Many, such as **sed** and the *awk* and Perl languages, are capable of automatically editing multiple files, providing you with a wide range of text-processing capability. To harness that capability, you need to be able to define and delineate specific text segments from within files, text streams, and string variables. Once the text you're after is identified, you can use one of these tools or languages to do useful things to it.

These tools and others understand a loosely defined pattern language. The language and the patterns themselves are collectively called regular expressions (often abbreviated just *regexp* or *regex*). While regular expressions are similar in

---

concept to file globs, many more special characters exist for regular expressions, extending the utility and capability of tools that understand them.

Regular expressions are the topic of entire books (such as Jeffrey E. F. Friedl's excellent and very readable *Mastering Regular Expressions*, published by O'Reilly & Associates). Exam 101 requires the use of simple regular expressions and related tools, specifically to perform searches from text sources. This section covers only the basics of regular expressions, but it goes without saying that their power warrants a full understanding. Digging deeper into the regular expression world is highly recommended when you have the chance.

Regular expression syntax

It would not be unreasonable to assume that some specification defines how regular expressions are constructed. Unfortunately, there isn't one. Regular expressions have been incorporated as a feature in a number of tools over the years, with varying degrees of consistency and completeness. The result is a cart-before-the-horse scenario, in which utilities and languages have defined their own flavor of regular expression syntax, each with its own extensions and idiosyncrasies. Formally defining the regular expression syntax came later, as did efforts to make it more consistent. Regular expressions are defined by arranging strings of text, or *patterns*. Those patterns are composed of two types of characters:

Metacharacters

Like the special file *globbing* characters, regular expression *metacharacters* take on a special meaning in the context of the tool in which they're used. There are a few metacharacters that are generally thought of to be among the "extended set" of metacharacters, specifically those introduced into **egrep** after **grep** was created. Now, most of those can also be handled by **grep** using the −E option. Examples of metacharacters include the ^ symbol, which means "the beginning of a line," and the $ symbol, which means "the end of a line." A complete listing of metacharacters follows in Table 1-12, Table 1-13, and Table 1-14.

Literals

Everything that is not a metacharacter is just plain text, or literal text.

It is often helpful to consider regular expressions as their own language, where literal text acts as words and phrases. The "grammar" of the language is defined by the use of metacharacters. The two are combined according to specific rules (which, as mentioned earlier, may differ slightly among various tools) to communicate ideas and get real work done. When you construct regular expressions, you use metacharacters and literals to specify three basic ideas about your input text:

Position anchors

A position anchor is used to specify the position of one or more character sets in relation to the entire line of text (such as the beginning of a line).

Character sets

A character set matches text. It could be a series of literals, metacharacters that match individual or multiple characters, or combinations of these.

Quantity modifiers

Quantity modifiers follow a character set and indicate the number of times the set should be repeated. These characters "give elasticity" to a regular expression by allowing the matches to have variable length.

The next section lists commonly used metacharacters. The examples given with the metacharacters are very basic, intended just to demonstrate the use of the metacharacter in question. More involved regular expressions are covered later.

Regular Expression Examples

Now that the gory details are out of the way, here are some examples of simple regular expression usage that you may find useful.

Anchors

Anchors are used to describe position information. Table 1-12 lists anchor characters.

Table 1-12: Regular Expression Position Anchors

Regular Expression	Description
^	Match at the beginning of a line. This interpretation makes sense only when the ^ character is at the lefthand side of the *regex*.
$	Match at the end of a line. This interpretation makes sense only when the $ character is at the righthand side of the *regex*.

Example 1

Display all lines from *file1* where the string "Linux" appears at the start of the line:

```
$ grep '^Linux' file1
```

Example 2

Display lines in *file1* where the last character is an "x":

```
$ grep 'x$' file1
```

Display the number of empty lines in *file1* by finding lines with nothing between the beginning and the end:

```
$ grep -c '^$' file1
```

Display all lines from *file1* containing only the word "null" by itself:

```
$ grep '^null$' file1
```

Groups and ranges

Characters can be placed into groups and ranges to make regular expressions more efficient, as shown in Table 1-13.

Table 1-13: Regular Expression Character Sets

Regular Expression	Description
[abc] [a-z]	Single-character groups and ranges. In the first form, match any single character from among the enclosed characters a, b, or c. In the second form, match any single character from among the range of characters bounded by a and z. The brackets are for grouping only and are not matched themselves.
[^abc] [^a-z]	Inverse match. Match any single character not among the enclosed characters a, b, and c or in the range a-z. Be careful not to confuse this inversion with the anchor character ^, described earlier.
\<word\>	Match words. Words are essentially defined as being character sets surrounded by whitespace and adjacent to the start of line, the end of line, or punctuation marks. The backslashes are required and enable this interpretation of < and >.
. (the single dot)	Match any single character except a *newline*.
\	As mentioned in the section on quoting earlier, turn off (escape) the special meaning of the character that follows, turning metacharacters in to literals.

Study Guide
101

Example 1

Display all lines from *file1* containing either "Linux," "linux," "TurboLinux," and so on:

```
$ grep '[Ll]inux' file1
```

Example 2

Display all lines from *file1* which contain three adjacent digits:

```
$ grep '[0-9][0-9][0-9]' file1
```

Example 3

Display all lines from *file1* beginning with any single character other than a digit:

```
$ grep '^[^0-9]' file1
```

Example 4

Display all lines from *file1* that contain the whole word "Linux" or "linux," but not "LinuxOS" or "TurboLinux":

```
$ grep '\<[Ll]inux\>' file1
```

Example 5

Display all lines from *file1* with five or more characters on a line (excluding the newline character):

```
$ grep '.....' file1
```

Example 6

Display all nonblank lines from *file1* (i.e., that have at least one character):

```
$ grep '.' file1
```

Example 7

Display all lines from *file1* that contain a period (normally a metacharacter) using escape:

```
$ grep '\.' file1
```

Modifiers

Modifiers change the meaning of other characters in a regular expression. Table 1-14 lists these modifiers.

Table 1-14: Regular Expression Modifiers

Regular Expression	Description
*	Match an unknown number (zero or more) of the single character (or single-character *regex*) that precedes it.
?	Match zero or one instance of the preceding regex. This modifier is an "extended" feature and available in **grep** only when the –E command-line option is used.
+	Match one or more instances of the preceding *regex*. This modifier is an "extended" feature and available in **grep** only when the –E command-line option is used.
\{n,m\}	Match a range of occurrences of the single character or regex that precedes this construct. \{n\} matches n occurrences, \{n,\} matches at least n occurrences, and \{n,m\} matches any number of occurrences between n and m, inclusively. The backslashes are required and enable this interpretation of{ and }.
|	Alternation. Match either the *regex* specified before *or* after the vertical bar. This modifier is an "extended" feature and available in **grep** only when the –E command-line option is used.

Example 1

Display all lines from *file1* that contain "ab," "abc," "abcc," "abccc," and so on:

```
$ grep 'abc*' file1
```

Example 2

Display all lines from *file1* that contain "abc," "abcc," "abccc," and so on, but not "ab":

```
$ grep 'abcc*' file1
```

Example 3

Display all lines from *file1* that contain two or more adjacent digits:

```
$ grep '[0-9][0-9][0-9]*' file1
```

Example 4

Display lines from *file1* that contain "file" (because ? can match zero occurrences), *file1*, or *file2*:

```
$ grep -E 'file[12]?' file1
```

Example 5

Display all lines from *file1* containing at least one digit:

```
$ grep -E '[0-9]+' file1
```

Example 6

Display all lines from *file1* that contain "111," "1111," or "11111" on a line by itself:

```
$ grep '^1\{3,5\}$' file1
```

Example 7

Display all lines from *file1* that contain any three-, four-, or five-digit number:

```
$ grep '\<[0-9]\{3,5\}\>' file1
```

Example 8

Display all lines from *file1* that contain "Happy," "happy," "Sad," "sad," "Angry," or "angry":

```
$ grep -E '[Hh]appy|[Ss]ad|[Aa]ngry' file1
```

Basic regular expression patterns

Example 1

Match any letter:

```
[A-Za-z]
```

Example 2

Match any symbol (not a letter or digit):

```
[^0-9A-Za-z]
```

Example 3

Match an uppercase letter, followed by zero or more lowercase letters:

```
[A-Z][a-z]*
```

Example 4

Match a U.S. Social Security Number (123-45-6789) by specifying groups of three, two, and four digits separated by dashes:

```
[0-9]\{3\}-[0-9]\{2\}-[0-9]\{4\}
```

Example 5

Match a dollar amount, using an escaped dollar sign, zero or more spaces or digits, an escaped period, and two more digits:

```
\$[ 0-9]*\.[0-9]\{2\}
```

Example 6

Match the month of June and its abbreviation, "Jun." The question mark matches zero or one instance of the *e*:

```
June?
```

Using regular expressions as addresses in sed

These examples are commands you would issue to **sed**. For example, the commands could take the place of *command1* in this usage:

```
$ sed [options] 'command1' [files]
```

These commands could also appear in a standalone **sed** script.

Example 1

Delete blank lines:

```
/^$/d
```

Example 2

Delete any line that doesn't contain #keepme::

```
/#keepme/!d
```

Example 3

Delete lines containing only whitespace (spaces or tabs). In this example, *tab* means the single tab character and is preceded by a single space:

```
/^[ tab]*$/d
```

Example 4

Delete lines beginning with periods or pound signs:

```
/^[.#]/d
```

Example 5

Substitute a single space for any number of spaces wherever they occur on the line:

```
s/  */ /g
```

Example 6

Substitute *def* for *abc* from line 11 to 20, wherever it occurs on the line:

```
11,20s/abc/@@@/g
```

Example 7

Translate the characters *a*, *b*, and *c* to the @ character from line 11 to 20, wherever they occur on the line:

```
11,20y/abc/@@@/
```

On the Exam

Make certain you are clear about the difference between *file globbing* and the use of regular expressions.

Devices, Linux Filesystems, and the Filesystem Hierarchy Standard (Topic 2.4)

Filesystem management is among the most critical activities that you must perform to maintain a stable Linux system. In simple situations, after a successful installation, you may never have a problem or need to manage filesystem specifics. However, understanding how to configure and maintain Linux filesystems is essential to safely manage your system and to pass Exam 101. This section contains these Objectives:

Objective 1: Create Partitions and Filesystems
Most Linux distributions will automate initial filesystem creation on your system for you. However, subsequent management of partitions, particularly on large systems and multiboot configurations, requires specific knowledge. This Objective involves the creation of disk partitions using **fdisk**, and filesystem creation using **mkfs**. Weight: 3.

Objective 2: Maintain the Integrity of Filesystems
At one time or another, you will probably find yourself stuck with an ailing filesystem. It could be a small problem resulting from a system crash, or it could be a total disk failure. Whatever the cause, you must be prepared to work with **fsck** to repair problems. This Objective also covers the handy **du** and **df** commands, which will help you with monitoring filesystem properties. Weight: 5.

Objective 3: Control Filesystem Mounting and Unmounting
Under Linux, a filesystem is not available for use unless it is *mounted*. When the system boots, it mounts its filesystems according to instructions in the important */etc/fstab* file. This Objective covers the management of this file, manual mounting of filesystems, and configuration of user-mountable removable filesystems. Weight: 3.

Objective 4: Set and View Disk Quotas
When running a system with multiple users, you may find some of them competing for disk space. Managing that problem gets much easier when you enforce *disk quotas*, which allocate finite amounts of space to individual user accounts. Setup and management of quotas is covered by this Objective. Weight: 1.

Objective 5: Use File Permissions to Control Access to Files
Linux file permissions are a critical part of any system's security policy. This Objective covers permissions on files and directories, including special modes. Weight: 3.

Objective 6: Manage File Ownership
File ownership is a fundamental part of the access control described in Objective 5. This Objective covers the management of user and group ownership. Weight: 2.

Objective 7: Create and Change Hard and Symbolic Links
The Linux filesystem allows the creation of filesystem links. Links allow multiple filenames to point to the same file, a handy way of having the same file appear in more than one place or under different names. This Objective covers both hard and soft (symbolic) links. Weight: 2.

Objective 8: Find System Files and Place Files in the Correct Location
Linux distributions share a common *Filesystem Hierarchy Standard* (FHS), which describes where files are located in the filesystem and how they are named. This Objective covers that standard, as well as methods of locating files. Weight: 2.

Objective 1: Create Partitions and Filesystems

In many PCs, disk organization schemes use a single disk containing a single filesystem. This filesystem contains all data on the computer, mixing system files and user files together. On MS-DOS and Windows systems, that volume is usually labeled *C:* and thought of as the *C drive.* If additional space is made available, it is seen as one or more additional volumes, each with a separate drive letter. If these separate drives are intended for user data, it is the user's responsibility to remember which drive letter to use when storing files. While this simplicity has some value for most users, others prefer the ability to create filesystems across multiple partitions, devices, and even multiple computers. Linux offers this ability.

Disk Drives Under Linux

Linux supports many types of disk devices and formats. Any SCSI or IDE hard disk will work with Linux, as will floppy disks, CD-ROMs, CD-Rs, Zip® and Jaz® disks, and other types of removable media. These media can contain the standard Linux *ext2* filesystem, FAT, FAT32, NTFS, as well as other filesystem types. This flexibility makes Linux coexist nicely with other operating systems on multiboot systems.

The most commonly found hard disks on PCs are IDE (Integrated Device Electronics) drives. These disks feature a relatively simple system interface, and most of the "smarts" of the disk are onboard the disk itself. The IDE standard allows disk manufacturers to sell their product at a very attractive price point. Also used on PCs are Small Computer System Interface (SCSI, pronounced "scuzzy") drives. SCSI is an older standard for connecting peripherals; however, modern SCSI versions are quite fast and flexible.

In general, IDE disks offer reasonable performance at a low price point, which is highly desirable for consumer products. A single IDE interface is capable of attaching two disk drives to a system. One device is named *master* and the other is the *slave* (an unfortunate naming convention). Most PCs have a *primary* and *secondary* IDE interface. Together, these interfaces allow up to four devices (primary master, primary slave, secondary master, and secondary slave). At a minimum, these devices will include a hard disk and a CD-ROM, leaving two available positions for CD-R, Zip, tape, or other IDE devices. Adding additional IDE controllers or specialized IDE subsystems can further expand a PC's capabilities.

Compared to IDE, SCSI offers excellent performance, lower CPU utilization, and a much more flexible connection scheme capable of handling up to 15 devices on a single bus. These conveniences allow SCSI systems to grow as space requirements increase without major hardware reconfiguration. Unfortunately, SCSI usually implies higher cost, which reduces demand for SCSI in the cost-sensitive PC market.

Typically, IDE is considered appropriate for desktop use. SCSI is usually specified for servers, for high-performance workstations, and in situations in which expansion capability is a concern.

Hard disk devices

By default, Linux defines IDE device files as follows:

/dev/hda
  Primary master IDE (often the hard disk)

/dev/hdb
  Primary slave IDE

/dev/hdc
  Secondary master IDE (often a CD-ROM)

/dev/hdd
  Secondary slave IDE

SCSI device files are similar, except that there is no four-device limitation:

/dev/sda
  First SCSI drive

/dev/sdb
  Second SCSI drive

/dev/sdc
  Third SCSI drive (and so on)

Under Linux, a typical PC with a single hard disk on the primary IDE interface and a single CD-ROM on the secondary IDE interface would have disk drive */dev/hda* and CD-ROM */dev/hdc*.

On the Exam

You should be prepared to identify IDE and SCSI devices based on their device filenames.

Disk partitions

On each disk in a PC, there may be between 1 and 16 *partitions*. A partition can be thought of as a container on the disk, into which a filesystem (or in one circumstance, more partitions) can be placed. Unlike MS-DOS, which assigns letter names to partitions, each partition under Linux is assigned an integer number on the disk, which is appended to the disk's device name. For example, the first partition on IDE disk */dev/hda* is */dev/hda1*. There are three types of partitions found on PCs:

Primary partitions

> This type of partition contains a filesystem. At least one primary partition must exist, and up to four can exist on a single physical disk. If all four primary partitions exist, they are numbered as follows:
>
> – */dev/hda1*
> – */dev/hda2*
> – */dev/hda3*
> – */dev/hda4*
>
> One of these primary partitions may be marked *active*, in which case the PC BIOS will be able to select it for boot.

Extended partitions

> An extended partition is a variant of the primary partition but cannot contain a filesystem. Instead, it contains *logical partitions*. Only one extended partition may exist on a single physical disk. If an extended partition exists, it takes one of the four possible spots for primary partitions, leaving room for only three primary partitions. The partitions on a disk with one primary partition and the sole extended partition are numbered as follows:
>
> – */dev/hda1* (primary)
> – */dev/hda2* (extended)

Logical partitions

> Logical partitions exist *within* the extended partition. 1 to 12 logical partitions may be created. Logical partitions are numbered from 5 to 16. The partitions on a disk with one primary partition, the sole extended partition, and four logical partitions are numbered as follows:
>
> – */dev/hda1* (primary)
> – */dev/hda2* (extended)
> – */dev/hda5* (logical)
> – */dev/hda6* (logical)
> – */dev/hda7* (logical)
> – */dev/hda8* (logical)

Under this PC partitioning scheme, a maximum of 15 partitions with filesystems may exist on a single physical disk (3 primary plus 12 logical), more than enough for any Linux installation. In practice, the last example is typical for a Linux installation. It is unlikely that all of the 15 possible partitions on a disk would be necessary just to support Linux.

The root filesystem and mount points

As a Linux system boots, the first filesystem that becomes available is the top level, or *root* filesystem, denoted with a single forward slash.[*] In a simple installation, the root filesystem could contain nearly everything on the system. However, such an arrangement could lead to system failure if the root filesystem fills to capacity. Instead, multiple partitions are typically defined, each containing one of the directories under /. As the Linux kernel boots, the partitions are *mounted* to the root filesystem, and together create a single unified filesystem. (Mounting is the subject of Objective 3.) Everything on the system that is not stored in a mounted partition is stored locally in /. The mounted filesystems are placed on separate partitions and possibly multiple disk drives.

The choice of which directories are placed into separate partitions is both a personal and technical decision. Here are some guidelines for individual partitions:

/ (the root directory)
> Since the only filesystem mounted at the start of the boot process is /, certain directories must be part of it in order to be available for the boot process. These include:

/bin and /sbin
> Contain required system binary programs

/dev
> Contains device files

/etc
> Contains boot configuration information

/lib
> Contains program libraries

> These directories are always part of the single / partition. See the description of the FHS in Objective 8 for more on the requirements for the root filesystem.

---

[*] The *root* filesystem /, often called the *root directory*, shouldn't be confused with the *root* superuser account or the superuser's home directory, */root*. The distinct directories / and */root* are unrelated and are not required to share the same disk partition.

/boot

> This directory holds static files used by the boot loader, including kernel images. On systems where kernel development activity occurs regularly, making */boot* a separate partition eliminates the possibility that / will fill with kernel images and associated files during development.

/home

> User files are usually placed in a separate partition. This is often the largest partition on the system and may be located on a separate physical disk or disk array.

/tmp

> This directory is often a separate partition used to prevent temporary files from filling.

/var

> Log files are stored here. Just like */tmp*, log files could grow unchecked unless they are rotated regularly, filling.

/usr

> This directory holds a hierarchy of directories containing user commands, source code, and documentation. It is often quite large, making it a good candidate for its own partition. Because much of the information stored under */usr* is static, some users prefer that it be mounted as read-only, making it impossible to corrupt.

In addition to the preceding six partitions listed, a */swap* partition is also necessary for a Linux system to enable virtual memory. For information on determining the size of a swap partition, see "Part 2: *Linux Installation and Package Management (Topic 2.2)*, Objective 1: Design a Hard Disk Layout" later in this book.

Using these guidelines at installation time, the disk partitions for an IDE-based system with two physical disks on the primary IDE controller might look as described in Table 1-15.

Table 1-15: An Example Partitioning Scheme

Partition	Type	Mounted Filesystem	Size
/dev/hda1	Primary	/	300 MB
/dev/hda2	Extended	-	-
/dev/hda5	Logical	/boot	300 MB
/dev/hda6	Logical	/opt	300 MB
/dev/hda7	Logical	/tmp	300 MB
/dev/hda8	Logical	/usr	600 MB
/dev/hda9	Logical	/var	300 MB
/dev/hda10	Logical	(/swap partition)	128 MB
/dev/hdb1	Primary	/home	6 GB

See Figure 1-1 later in this chapter for a graphical depiction of this partitioning scheme.

Once a disk is partitioned, it can be difficult or risky to change the partition sizes. Commercial and open source tools are available for this task, but a full backup is recommended prior to their use.

Managing partitions

Linux has two basic options for partitioning disk drives. The **fdisk** command is a text-based program that is easy to use and exists on every Linux distribution. It is also required for Exam 101. Another option you may wish to explore after mastering **fdisk** is **cfdisk**, which is still a text-mode program but which uses the *curses* system to produce a GUI-style display.

fdisk

Syntax

```
fdisk [device]
```

Description

Manipulate or display the partition table for *device* using a command-driven interactive text interface. *device* is a physical disk such as */dev/hda*, not a partition such as */dev/hda1*. If omitted, *device* defaults to */dev/hda*. Interactive commands to **fdisk** are a single letter followed by a carriage return. The commands do not take arguments, but start an interactive dialog. Commands that operate on a partition will request the *partition number*, which is an integer. For primary and extended partitions, the partition number is from 1 to 4. For logical partitions, which are available only if the extended partition already exists to contain them, the partition number is from 5 to 16.

When making changes to the partition table, **fdisk** accumulates changes without writing them to the disk, until it receives the **write** command.

Frequently used commands

a

Toggle the *bootable* flag on/off for a primary partition.

d

Delete a partition. You are prompted for the partition number to delete. If you delete a logical partition when higher numbered logical partitions exist, the partition numbers are decremented to keep logical partition numbers contiguous.

l

List the known partition types. A table of partition types is printed.

m

Display the brief help menu for these commands.

n

Add a new partition. You are prompted for the partition type (primary, extended, or logical).* For primary and extended partitions, you are asked for

---

* Note that **fdisk** displays options for extended and primary partition types if an extended partition does not yet exist. If the extended partition already exists, **fdisk** displays options for logical and primary partition types.

the partition number (1–4). For logical partitions, the next logical partition number is selected automatically. You are then prompted for the starting disk cylinder for the partition and are offered the next free cylinder as a default. Finally, you are prompted for the last cylinder or a size, such as "+300M." By default, new partitions are assigned as Linux *ext2*, type 83. To create another partition type, such as a swap partition, first create the partition with the **n** command, then change the type with the **t** command.

p

Display the partition table as it exists in memory. This depiction will differ from the actual partition table on disk if changes have not been saved.

q

Quit without saving changes.

t

Change a partition's system ID. This is an octal number that indicates the type of filesystem the partition is to contain. Linux *ext2* partitions are type 83, and Linux swap partitions are type 82.

w

Write (save) the partition table to disk and exit. No changes are saved until the **w** command is issued.

Example 1

Display the existing partition table on */dev/hda* without making any changes:

```
# fdisk /dev/hda
Command (m for help): p

Disk /dev/hda: 255 heads, 63 sectors, 1027 cylinders
Units = cylinders of 16065 * 512 bytes

    Device Boot    Start      End    Blocks   Id  System
/dev/hda1    *        1      250   2008093+   83  Linux
/dev/hda2           251      280    240975    82  Linux swap
/dev/hda3           281     1027   6000277+    5  Extended
/dev/hda5           281      293    104391    83  Linux
/dev/hda6           294      306    104391    83  Linux
/dev/hda7           307      319    104391    83  Linux

Command (m for help): q

#
```

In this configuration, */dev/hda* has two primary partitions, */dev/hda1*, which is bootable, and */dev/hda2*, which is the swap partition. The disk also has an extended partition */dev/hda3*, which contains three logical partitions, */dev/hda5*, */dev/hda6*, and */dev/hda7*. All other primary and logical partitions are Linux *ext2* partitions.

Example 2

Starting with a blank partition table, create a bootable primary partition of 300 MB on */dev/hda1*, the extended partition on */dev/hda2* containing the remainder of the disk, a logical partition of 200 MB on */dev/hda5*, a logical swap partition of 128 MB on */dev/hda6*, and a logical partition on */dev/hda7* occupying the remainder of the extended partition:

```
# fdisk /dev/hda

Command (m for help): n
Command action
   e   extended
   p   primary partition (1-4)
p
Partition number (1-4): 1
First cylinder (1-1027, default 1):
Using default value 1
Last cylinder or +size or +sizeM or +sizeK (1-1027,
   default 1027): +300M

Command (m for help): a
Partition number (1-4): 1

Command (m for help): n
Command action
   e   extended
   p   primary partition (1-4)
e
Partition number (1-4): 2
First cylinder (40-1027, default 40):
Using default value 40
Last cylinder or +size or +sizeM or +sizeK (40-1027,
   default 1027):<return>
Using default value 1027

Command (m for help): n
Command action
   l   logical (5 or over)
   p   primary partition (1-4)
l
First cylinder (40-1027, default 40):
Using default value 40
Last cylinder or +size or +sizeM or +sizeK (40-1027,
   default 1027): +200M

Command (m for help): n
Command action
   l   logical (5 or over)
   p   primary partition (1-4)
l
First cylinder (79-1027, default 79):
Using default value 79
```

```
Last cylinder or +size or +sizeM or +sizeK (79-1027,
    default 1027): +128M

Command (m for help): t
Partition number (1-6): 6
Hex code (type L to list codes): 82
Changed system type of partition 6 to 82 (Linux swap)

Command (m for help): n
Command action
    l   logical (5 or over)
    p   primary partition (1-4)
l
First cylinder (118-1027, default 118):
Using default value 118
Last cylinder or +size or +sizeM or +sizeK (118-1027,
    default 1027):<return>
Using default value 1027

Command (m for help): p

Disk /dev/hda: 255 heads, 63 sectors, 1027 cylinders
Units = cylinders of 16065 * 512 bytes

    Device Boot    Start      End    Blocks   Id  System
/dev/hda1    *        1       39    313236   83  Linux
/dev/hda2            40     1027   7936110    5  Extended
/dev/hda5            40       65    208813+  82  Linux swap
/dev/hda6            66       82    136521   83  Linux
/dev/hda7            83     1027   7590681   83  Linux

Command (m for help): w

The partition table has been altered!

Calling ioctl() to re-read partition table.
Syncing disks.


#
```

Note the use of defaults for the partition start cylinders and for end cylinder selections, indicated by **<return>** in this example. Other partition sizes are specified in megabytes using responses such as **+128M**.

At boot time, the BIOS of many PCs can access only the first 1024 cylinders of the disk. The Linux kernel, however, has no such limitation, but the BIOS must be able to load the boot loader LILO and the entire kernel image into memory. Thus, the entire contents of */boot*, either as part of */* or as a separate partition, must be located within the 1024-cylinder boundary. In April 2000, Version 0.21.4.2 of LILO was released; which is within the 1024-cylinder limit. If you have a Linux distribution that includes a newer version of LILO, you may not need to worry about this issue. Check your LILO documentation to be sure.

WARNING

If you are attempting to create partitions for other operating systems with the Linux **fdisk** utility, you could run into a few problems. As a rule, it is safest to prepare the partitions for an operating system using the native tools of that operating system.

As you might expect, using **fdisk** on a working system can be dangerous, because one errant **w** command can render your disk useless. Use extreme caution when working with the partition table of a working system, and be sure you know exactly what you intend to do and how to do it.

On the Exam

You should understand disk partitions and the process of creating them using **fdisk**.

Creating filesystems

Once a disk is partitioned, filesystems may be created in those partitions using the **mkfs** utility. Usually, partitions intended for use with Linux will use the native *second extended* filesystem, or *ext2*. MS-DOS filesystems can also be created.* In reality, **mkfs** is a front-end program for filesystem-specific creation tools named *mkfs.ext2* and *mkfs.msdos*, which are in turn linked to *mke2fs* and *mkdosfs*, respectively. **mkfs** offers a unified front-end, while the links provide convenient names. The choice of which executable to call is up to you.

---

mkfs

Syntax

```
mkfs [-t fs_type] [fs_options] device
```

Description

Make a filesystem of type *fs_type* on *device*. The *fs_type* is either *ext2* or *msdos*. If *fs_type* is omitted, *ext2* is used by default. When called by **mkfs**, these programs are passed any *fs_options* included on the command line. See the manpages for **mke2fs** and **mkdosfs** for full details on their individual options.

---

* You can also use **mkfs** to create filesystems of type *minix*, in the rare event that you encounter such a requirement.

Frequently used fs_options

-c

Check *device* for bad blocks (**mke2fs** and **mkdosfs**).

-L *label*

Set the volume *label* for the filesystem (**mke2fs** only).

-n *label*

Set the 11-character volume label for the filesystem (**mkdosfs** only).

-q

Uses **mkfs** in quiet mode, resulting in very little output (**mke2fs** only).

-v

Used to enter verbose mode (**mke2fs** and **mkdosfs**).

Example 1

Using defaults, quietly create an *ext2* partition on */dev/hda3*:

```
# mkfs -q /dev/hda3
mke2fs 1.14, 9-Jan-1999 for EXT2 FS 0.5b, 95/08/09
#
```

Example 2

Create an *ext2* filesystem labeled *rootfs* on existing partition */dev/hda3*, checking for bad blocks and with full verbose output:

```
# mkfs -t ext2 -L rootfs -cv /dev/hda3
mke2fs 1.14, 9-Jan-1999 for EXT2 FS 0.5b, 95/08/09
Linux ext2 filesystem format
Filesystem label=rootfs
26208 inodes, 104422 blocks
5221 blocks (5.00%) reserved for the super user
First data block=1
Block size=1024 (log=0)
Fragment size=1024 (log=0)
13 block groups
8192 blocks per group, 8192 fragments per group
2016 inodes per group
Superblock backups stored on blocks:
        8193, 16385, 24577, 32769, 40961, 49153,
        57345, 65537, 73729, 81921, 90113, 98305

Checking for bad blocks (read-only test): done
Writing inode tables: done
Writing superblocks and filesystem accounting
   information: done

#
```

Additional options are available in the **mke2fs** and **mkdosfs** programs, which may be needed to fine-tune specific filesystem parameters for special situations. In most cases, the default parameters are appropriate and adequate.

An additional command not specifically cited in the LPI Objectives for this Topic is **mkswap**. This command prepares a partition for use as Linux swap space and is needed if you plan to fully configure a disk from scratch. It is also needed if you need to add an additional swap partition.

---

mkswap

Syntax

    mkswap *device*

Description

Prepare a partition for use as swap space. This command can also set up swap space in a file on another filesystem.

Example

On an existing partition, which should be set to type 82 (Linux swap), ready swap space:

```
# mkswap /dev/hda5
Setting up swapspace version 1, size = 139792384 bytes
#
```

Running any of the filesystem creation programs is, like **fdisk**, potentially dangerous. All data in any previously existing filesystems in the specified partition will be deleted. Since **mkfs** does not warn you prior to creating the filesystem, be certain that you are operating on the correct partition.

On the Exam

The exam is likely to contain general questions about using *mkfs*, though details such as inode allocation are beyond the scope of the LPIC Level 1 exams.

Objective 2: Maintain the Integrity of Filesystems

Over the course of time, active filesystems can develop problems, such as:

- A filesystem fills to capacity, causing programs or perhaps the entire system to fail.

- A filesystem is corrupted, perhaps due to a power failure or system crash.

- A filesystem runs out of inodes, meaning that new filesystem objects cannot be created.

Carefully monitoring and checking Linux filesystems on a regular basis can help prevent and correct these types of problems.

Monitoring Free Disk Space and Inodes

A read/write filesystem isn't much good if it grows to the point that it won't accept any more files. This could happen if the filesystem fills to capacity or runs out of *inodes.*

Inodes are the data structures within filesystems that describe files on disk. Every filesystem contains a finite number of inodes, set when the filesystem is created. This number is also the maximum number of files that the filesystem can accommodate. Because filesystems are created with a huge number of inodes, you'll probably never create as many files as it would take to run out of inodes. However, it is possible to run out of inodes if a partition contains many small files.

It is important to prevent space and inode shortages from occurring on system partitions. The df command gives you the information you need on the status of both disk space utilization and inode utilization.

---

df

Syntax

df [*options*] [*directories*]

Description

Display overall disk utilization information for mounted filesystems on *directories.* Usually, *directories* are device files for partitions, such as */dev/hda1*, but using another file or directory name yields information on the partition that holds the file or directory. If *directories* are omitted, information for mounted filesystems on all devices in */etc/fstab* are displayed.

Frequently used options

-h

Displays results in a human-readable format, including suffixes such as M (megabytes) and G (gigabytes).

-i

Displays information on remaining inodes rather than the default disk space information.

Example 1

Check disk space utilization on all filesystems:

```
# df -h
  Filesystem        Size  Used Avail Use% Mounted on
  /dev/sda1         387M   56M  311M  15% /
  /dev/sda5         296M  5.2M  276M   2% /boot
  /dev/sda9         1.9G  406M  1.4G  22% /home
  /dev/sda6          53M   12M   39M  23% /root
  /dev/sda10         99M  104k   93M   0% /tmp
  /dev/sda8         972M  507M  414M  55% /usr
  /dev/sda7         296M  9.3M  272M   3% /var
```

This example shows that of the seven filesystems mounted by default, none exceeds 55 percent capacity.

Example 2

Check the same filesystems for inode utilization:

```
# df -i
Filesystem          Inodes   IUsed   IFree IUse% Mounted on
/dev/sda1           102800    7062   95738    7% /
/dev/sda5            78312      29   78283    0% /boot
/dev/sda9           514000     934  513066    0% /home
/dev/sda6            14056     641   13415    5% /root
/dev/sda10           26104      60   26044    0% /tmp
/dev/sda8           257040   36700  220340   14% /usr
/dev/sda7            78312     269   78043    0% /var
```

Among these partitions, the largest consumption of inodes is a mere 14 percent. It is clear that none of the filesystems is anywhere near consuming the maximum number of inodes available. Note that the /usr partition (with 14 percent of inodes used) has used 55 percent of the disk space. With utilization like this, the /usr volume will most likely fill to capacity long before the inodes are exhausted.

Example 3

Quickly determine which partition the current working directory (represented simply by a single dot) is located:

```
# df .
/dev/sda1           102800    7062   95738    7% /
```

When a filesystem is nearing capacity, files may simply be deleted to make additional space available. However, in the rare case in which an inode shortage occurs, the filesystem must be recreated with a larger number of inodes unless a significant number of files can be deleted.

Monitoring Disk Usage

Have you ever found yourself wondering, "Where did all the disk space go?" Some operating systems make answering this question surprisingly difficult using only native tools. On Linux, the **du** command can help display disk utilization information on a per-directory basis and perhaps answer that question. **du** recursively examines directories and reports detailed or summarized information on the amount of space consumed.

---

du

Syntax

du [options] [directories]

Description

Display disk utilization information for directories. If directories are omitted, the current working directory is searched.

Frequently used options

-a

Shows all files, not just directories.

-c

Produces a grand total for all listed items.

-h

Displays results in a human-readable format, including suffixes such as M (megabytes) and G (gigabytes).

-s

Prints a summary for each of the *directories* specified, instead of totals for each subdirectory found recursively.

-S

Excludes subdirectories from counts and totals, limiting totals to *directories*.

Example 1

Examine disk utilization in */etc/rc.d*:

```
# du /etc/rc.d
882     /etc/rc.d/init.d
1       /etc/rc.d/rc0.d
1       /etc/rc.d/rc1.d
1       /etc/rc.d/rc2.d
1       /etc/rc.d/rc3.d
1       /etc/rc.d/rc4.d
1       /etc/rc.d/rc5.d
1       /etc/rc.d/rc6.d
904     /etc/rc.d
```

Example 2

Display utilization by files in */etc*, including subdirectories beneath it:

```
# du -s /etc
13002   /etc
```

Example 3

Display utilization by files in */etc*, but not in subdirectories beneath it:

```
# du -Ss /etc
1732    /etc
```

Example 4

Show a summary of all subdirectories under */home*, with human-readable output:

```
# du -csh /home/*
42k     /home/bsmith
1.5M    /home/httpd
9.5M    /home/jdean
42k     /home/jdoe
12k     /home/lost+found
1.0k    /home/samba
11M     total
```

This result shows that 11 MB of total disk space is used.

Example 5

Show the same summary, but sort the results to display in order of largest to smallest disk utilization:

```
# du -cs /home/* | sort -nr
11386   total
9772    jdean
1517    httpd
42      jdoe
42      bsmith
12      lost+found
1       samba
```

This result shows that user *jdean* is consuming the largest amount of space. Note that the human-readable format does not sort in this way, since **sort** is unaware of the human-readable size specifications.

Checking Filesystem Integrity

No matter how stable, computers do fail, even due to something as simple as a power cable being accidentally unplugged. Unfortunately, such an interruption can make a mess of a filesystem. If a disk write operation is aborted before it completes, the data in transit could be lost, and the portions of the disk that were allocated for it are left marked as used. In addition, filesystem writes are cached in memory, and a power loss or other crash prevents the kernel from synchronizing the cache with the disk. Both of these scenarios lead to inconsistencies in the filesystem and must be corrected to ensure reliable operation.

Filesystems are checked with **fsck**. Like **mkfs**, **fsck** is a front-end to filesystem-specific utilities—including *fsck.ext2*, which is a link to the **e2fsck** program (see its manpage for detailed information).

Part of the information written on disk to describe a filesystem is known as the *superblock*, written in block 1 of the partition. If this area of the disk is corrupted, the filesystem is inaccessible. Because the superblock is so important, copies of it are made in the filesystem at regular intervals, by default every 8192 blocks. The first superblock copy is located at block 8193, the second copy is at block 16385, and so on. As you'll see, **fsck** can use the information in the superblock copies to restore the main superblock.

---

fsck

Syntax

fsck [*options*] [-t *type*] [*fs-options*] *filesystems*

Description

Check *filesystems* for errors and optionally correct them. By default, **fsck** assumes the *ext2* filesystem type and runs interactively, pausing to ask for permission before applying fixes.

Frequently used options for fsck

-A

Run checks on all filesystems specified in */etc/fstab*. This option is intended for use at boot time, before filesystems are mounted.

-N

Don't execute, but show what would be done.

-t *type*

Specify the type of filesystem to check; the default is *ext2*. The value of *type* determines which filesystem-specific checker is called.

Frequently used options for e2fsck

-b *superblock*

Use an alternative copy of the *superblock*. In interactive mode, e2fsck automatically uses alternative *superblocks*. Typically, you'll try -b 8193 in non-interactive mode to restore a bad *superblock*.

-c

Check for bad blocks.

-f

Force a check, even if the filesystem looks clean.

-p

Automatically repair the filesystem without prompting.

-y

Answers "yes" to all interactive prompts, allowing e2fsck to be used noninteractively.

Example 1

Check the *ext2* filesystem on */dev/hda5*, which is not mounted:

```
# fsck /dev/hda5
[/sbin/fsck.ext2 -- ] fsck.ext2 /dev/hda5
Parallelizing fsck version 1.14 (9-Jan-1999)
e2fsck 1.14, 9-Jan-1999 for EXT2 FS 0.5b, 95/08/09
/dev/hda5: clean, 1011/34136 files, 4360/136521 blocks
```

The partition was clean, so **fsck** didn't really check it.

Example 2

Force a check:

```
# fsck -f /dev/hda5
Parallelizing fsck version 1.14 (9-Jan-1999)
e2fsck 1.14, 9-Jan-1999 for EXT2 FS 0.5b, 95/08/09
Pass 1: Checking inodes, blocks, and sizes
Pass 2: Checking directory structure
Pass 3: Checking directory connectivity
Pass 4: Checking reference counts
Pass 5: Checking group summary information
/dev/hda5: 1011/34136 files (0.1% non-contiguous),
    4360/136521 blocks
```

Example 3

Force another check, this time with verbose output:

```
# fsck -fv /dev/hda5
Parallelizing fsck version 1.14 (9-Jan-1999)
e2fsck 1.14, 9-Jan-1999 for EXT2 FS 0.5b, 95/08/09
Pass 1: Checking inodes, blocks, and sizes
Pass 2: Checking directory structure
Pass 3: Checking directory connectivity
Pass 4: Checking reference counts
Pass 5: Checking group summary information

    1011 inodes used (2%)
       1 non-contiguous inodes (0.1%)
         # of inodes with ind/dind/tind blocks: 0/0/0
    4360 blocks used (3%)
       0 bad blocks

    1000 regular files
       2 directories
       0 character device files
       0 block device files
       0 fifos
       0 links
       0 symbolic links (0 fast symbolic links)
       0 sockets
--------
    1002 files
```

Example 4

Allow **fsck** to automatically perform all repairs on a damaged filesystem by speci-fying the **-y** option to run the command automatically:

```
[root@smp /mnt]# fsck -y /dev/hda5
Parallelizing fsck version 1.14 (9-Jan-1999)
e2fsck 1.14, 9-Jan-1999 for EXT2 FS 0.5b, 95/08/09
Couldn't find ext2 superblock, trying backup blocks...
/dev/hda5 was not cleanly unmounted, check forced.
Pass 1: Checking inodes, blocks, and sizes
Pass 2: Checking directory structure
Pass 3: Checking directory connectivity
Pass 4: Checking reference counts
Pass 5: Checking group summary information
Block bitmap differences:  +1 +2 +3 +4
Fix? yes

Inode bitmap differences:  +1 +2 +3 +4 +5 +6
Fix? yes

/dev/hda5: ***** FILE SYSTEM WAS MODIFIED *****
/dev/hda5: 1011/34136 files (0.1% non-contiguous),
    4360/136521 blocks
```

When Linux boots, the kernel performs a check of all filesystems in */etc/fstab* using the –A option to **fsck.**[*] Any filesystems that were not cleanly unmounted are checked. If that check finds any significant errors, the system drops into single-user mode so you can run **fsck** manually. Unfortunately, unless you have detailed knowledge of the inner workings of the filesystem, there's little you can do other than to have **fsck** do all of the repairs. As a result, it is common to use the –y option and hope for the best.

On the Exam

Familiarity with **du**, **df**, and **fsck** is important. Be sure you understand the differences between the commands and when each is used.

Objective 3: Control Filesystem Mounting and Unmounting

As discussed in Objective 1, the Linux directory hierarchy is usually made up of multiple partitions, each joined to the root filesystem. Filesystems on removable media, such as CD-ROMs, Zip disks, and floppy disks, are joined in the same way, but usually on a temporary basis. Each of these separate filesystems is *mounted* to the parent filesystem as a directory (or *mount point*) in the unified hierarchy.

Directories intended as mount points usually don't contain files or other directories. Instead, they're just empty directories created solely to mount a filesystem. If a directory that already contains files is used as a mount point, its files are obscured and unavailable until the filesystem is unmounted. Typical mount points include the directories */usr*, */home*, */var*, and others.

Managing the Filesystem Table

Since the Linux filesystem hierarchy is spread across separate partitions and/or multiple drives, it is necessary to automatically mount those filesystems at boot time. In addition, removable media and filesystems on remote NFS servers may be used regularly with recurring mount properties. All of this information is recorded in the */etc/fstab* file. Filesystems defined in this file are checked and mounted when the system boots. Entries in this file are consulted for default information when users wish to mount removable media.

The */etc/fstab* file (see Example 1-1) is plain text and consists of lines with six fields:

Device

This field specifies the device file of the partition holding the filesystem—for example, */dev/hda1*. This field cannot contain a whole device, such as */dev/hda*.

---

[*] Unless the */etc/fstab* entry contains the **noauto** option.

Mount point

    This field specifies the directory upon which the filesystem is to be mounted. For example, if */dev/hda1* contains the root filesystem, it is mounted at */.* The root filesystem will contain additional directories intended as mount points for other filesystems. For example, */boot* may be an empty directory intended to mount the filesystem that contains kernel images and other information required at boot time.

Filesystem type

    Next, the type of filesystem is specified. These include some *ext2* filesystems, as well as *swap, iso9660* (CD-ROM), and others.

Mount options

    This field contains a comma-separated list of options. Some options are specific to particular filesystem types. Options are described later in this Objective.

Dump frequency

    The **dump** program, a standard Unix backup utility, may consult */etc/fstab* for information on how often to dump each filesystem. This field holds an integer, usually set to 1 for *ext2* filesystems and to 0 for others.

Pass number for **fsck**

    This field is used by the **fsck** utility when the **-A** option is specified, usually at boot time. It is a flag that may contain only the values *0, 1,* or *2.*

    –   A *0* instructs **fsck** not to check the filesystem.

    –   A *1* should be entered for the root filesystem and instructs **fsck** to check that filesystem first.

    –   A *2* instructs **fsck** to check corresponding filesystems after those with a *1.*

Example 1-1: Sample /etc/fstab File

```
/dev/sda1     /               ext2      defaults          1 1
/dev/sda5     /boot           ext2      defaults          1 2
/dev/sda9     /home           ext2      defaults          1 2
/dev/sda6     /root           ext2      defaults          1 2
/dev/sda10    /tmp            ext2      defaults          1 2
/dev/sda8     /usr            ext2      defaults          1 2
/dev/sda7     /var            ext2      defaults          1 2
/dev/sda11    swap            swap      defaults          0 0
/dev/fd0      /mnt/floppy     ext2      noauto,users      0 0
/dev/hdc      /mnt/cdrom      iso9660   noauto,ro,users   0 0
/dev/hdd      /mnt/zip        vfat      noauto,users      0 0
fs1:/share    /fs1            nfs       defaults          0 0
```

The **fstab** in Example 1-1 depicts a system with a single SCSI disk, */dev/sda.* The first partition, */dev/sda1*, contains an *ext2* root filesystem. Partition */dev/sda11* is swap. Partitions */dev/sda5* through */dev/sda10* contain *ext2* partitions for */boot, /home, /root, /tmp, /usr,* and */var,* respectively. All of the local *ext2* partitions are to be checked by **fsck** and dumped. Entries for the floppy disk (*/dev/fd0*), CD-ROM (*/dev/hdc*), and IDE Zip drive (*/dev/hdd*) hold appropriate mount properties, making manual mounting of these devices simple. Finally, this example

---

shows a remote NFS mount of directory */share* of system *fs1*. It is mounted locally at */fs1*.

The */etc/fstab* file is automatically created when Linux is installed and is based on the partitioning and mount point configuration specified. This file can be changed at any time to add devices and options, tailoring the filesystem to meet your specific needs.

Mounting Filesystems

Filesystems are mounted using the **mount** command. At boot time, those filesystems with a nonzero pass number in */etc/fstab* are checked and automatically mounted. Later, you can run **mount** manually to add other filesystems to the filesystem hierarchy.

---

mount

Syntax

```
mount [command_line_options]  device
mount [command_line_options]  directory
mount [command_line_options]  device directory
```

Description

Used to mount filesystems onto the filesystem hierarchy. The first and second forms consult */etc/fstab* and mount the filesystem located on *device* or intended to be attached to *directory*, respectively. In both cases, information necessary to complete the mount operation is taken from */etc/fstab*. The third form is independent of */etc/fstab* and mounts the filesystem on *device* at mount point *directory*.

The **mount** command accepts two kinds of options: *command-line* and *mount*. The command-line options provide general direction for the **mount** command. The mount options, which are generally alphanumeric words, word fragments, or abbreviations, are used to specify additional information about the device being mounted.

Command-line options

−a

    Mounts all of the partitions specified in */etc/fstab*, except those with the **noauto** option.

−h

    Displays help on the **mount** command.

-o *mount_options*

Specifies mount options on the command line.

-r

Mounts the filesystem as read-only.

-t *fstype*

Specifies that the filesystem to be mounted is of type *fstype*. This option is typically used interactively, when no entry for the mount exists in */etc/fstab*.

-v

Sets verbose mode.

-w

Mounts the filesystem read/write mode.

Mount options

A number of parameters are available as options for mounting filesystems. These options may be specified in */etc/fstab* or as arguments of the **-o** command-line **mount** argument. These options modify the way **mount** configures the mounted filesystem. Some of the options can provide added security by controlling some operations on the filesystem. Others protect the filesystem from damage. Here is a partial list:

async

Establishes asynchronous I/O to the mounted filesystem. The opposite is *sync*.

auto

Enables a mount specification in */etc/fstab* to be processed with the **-a** command-line option, as needed at boot time. The opposite is *noauto*.

defaults

Implies *rw, suid, dev, exec, auto, nouser*, and *async*. It is commonly found on */etc/fstab* entries for *ext2* mount points.

dev

Interprets character or block special devices on the filesystem.

exec

Enables the execution of programs contained on the mounted partition. The opposite is **noexec**.

noauto

Prohibits automatic mounting with the **-a** option. This is usually specified for removable media.

noexec

Prohibits the execution of executable programs, a potential security measure.

nosuid

Prohibits the effect of **suid** or **sgid** bits on executable files.

nouser

Forbids non-root users from mounting and unmounting the filesystem. See **user** and **users** for the opposite effect.

ro

Equivalent to specifying the command-line option **-r**.

rw

Equivalent to specifying the command-line option **-w**.

suid

Enables the effect of **suid** and **sgid** bits on executable files.

sync

Establishes synchronous I/O to the mounted filesystem. The opposite is **async**.

user

Allows an ordinary user to mount the filesystem but prohibits other ordinary users from unmounting it. This is useful for removable media that an individual requires control over. See also **users**.

users

Allows any user to mount and unmount the filesystem.

Note that the **user** and **users** options make the **mount** and **umount** commands available to non-root users. This may be important for some systems where end users must have the ability to mount removable media.

Filesystem types

Mount must be aware of the type of filesystem it is mounting, which is specified with a single *filesystem type*. This parameter may be included on the command line using the **-t** option, or in the third field in */etc/fstab*. Linux can mount a variety of filesystems. Here are some of the more popular ones:

ext2

The standard Linux filesystem.

msdos

The MS-DOS FAT filesystem, limited to "8.3" filenames (eight characters, a dot, and a three-character extension).

vfat

Virtual FAT, used instead of *msdos* when long filenames must be preserved. For example, you may wish to have access to Windows partitions on systems configured to boot both Linux and Windows.

iso9660

The CD-ROM format, also the default type.

nfs

Remote servers.

swap

Swap partitions.

proc

This type represents the *proc* filesystem, which is not really a filesystem at all. The virtual files found in this virtual filesystem provide a window into the kernel. It is usually mounted on */proc*.

Example 1

Display filesystems currently mounted on the system:

```
# mount
/dev/sda1 on / type ext2 (rw)
none on /proc type proc (rw)
/dev/sda5 on /boot type ext2 (rw)
/dev/sda9 on /home type ext2 (rw)
/dev/sda6 on /root type ext2 (rw)
/dev/sda10 on /tmp type ext2 (rw)
/dev/sda8 on /usr type ext2 (rw)
/dev/sda7 on /var type ext2 (rw)
none on /dev/pts type devpts (rw,mode=0622)
/dev/hdd on /mnt/zip type vfat (rw,noexec,nosuid,nodev)
```

In this example, you can see that most of the filesystems specified in the */etc/fstab* from Example 1-1 are already mounted.

Example 2

Mount the IDE CD-ROM device found on */dev/hdc* to the existing directory */cdrom*, read-only of course:

```
# mount -rt iso9660 /dev/hdc /cdrom
```

Note that without the **-r** option, you will receive a warning but still get appropriate results:

```
# mount -t iso9660 /dev/hdc /mnt/cdrom
mount: block device /dev/hdc is write-protected,
    mounting read-only
```

Example 3

Mount an MS-DOS floppy in the first floppy disk drive */dev/fd0* (*A:* in MS-DOS) to the existing directory */floppy*:

```
# mount -t msdos /dev/fd0 /floppy
```

Example 4

The filesystems mounted at */home* and */opt* have been unmounted for some kind of maintenance and are now remounted using the **-a** option:

```
# mount -av
mount: /dev/hda5 already mounted on /root
mount: /dev/hda9 already mounted on /usr
mount: /dev/hda7 already mounted on /var
mount: none already mounted on /proc
mount: none already mounted on /dev/pts
mount: 192.168.0.2:/ already mounted on /smp
/dev/hda10 on /home type ext2 (rw)
/dev/hda8 on /opt type ext2 (rw)
```

Note that **mount** should work silently without the **-v** option. It also safely skips filesystems that have been previously mounted.

Unmounting Filesystems

Filesystems can be unmounted using the **umount** command. When a filesystem is unmounted, the buffers of the filesystem are synchronized with the actual contents on disk and the filesystem is made unavailable, freeing the mount point. If the filesystem is busy, **umount** yields an error. This will happen, for example, when the filesystem contains open files or when a process has a working directory within the filesystem. Other less obvious errors can occur when removable media are exchanged without being unmounted first.

umount

Syntax

umount [*options*] *device*
umount [*options*] *directory*

Description

Unmount the filesystem on *device* or mounted on *directory*.

-a

Unmounts all of the filesystems described in */etc/mtab*. This file is maintained by the **mount** and **umount** commands and contains an up-to-date list of mounted filesystems. This option is typically used at shutdown time.

-t *fstype*

Unmounts only filesystems of type *fstype*.

Example 1

Unmount the CD-ROM mounted on */dev/hdc* at */cdrom*:

umount /cdrom

or:

umount /dev/hdc

Example 2

Unmount all NFS filesystems:

umount -at nfs

On the Exam

Be sure that you understand how to use **mount** and mount points and how */etc/fstab* is used when mounting files.

Objective 4: Set and View Disk Quotas

Managing disk space can be a difficult problem. The available space is a finite resource and is often consumed at an alarming rate, turning today's carefully sized filesystem into tomorrow's expansion requirement. On multiuser systems—no matter how big the filesystem—users will find a way to fill it. The last thing you want is for a filesystem to fill to capacity too early. One way to prevent that from happening is to enforce *disk quotas*, which allow you assign a limit to the amount of space individual users or groups have on a filesystem.

A typical quota size is usually much smaller than the filesystem it is configured on, thus preventing the user or group from consuming too much space. Quotas can be configured for each filesystem mentioned in */etc/fstab*, though they are usually applied only where multiple end users store files (i.e., */home/username*). There is no need for a quota on */usr*, for example, since end users cannot store files there. Quotas may be configured for individual users listed in */etc/passwd* and for groups listed in */etc/group*.

Quota Limits

Each filesystem has up to five types of quota limits that can be enforced on it. These limits are specified in disk *blocks*, usually 1024 bytes each:

Per-user hard limit
> The *hard limit* is the maximum amount of space an individual user can have on the system. Once the user reaches his quota limit, he won't be allowed to write files to the disk.

Per-user soft limit
> Each user is free to store data on the filesystem until reaching her *soft limit*. The soft limit implements a sort of warning zone, instructing the user to clean up while still allowing her to work. When the amount of data exceeds this limit but does not exceed the hard limit, a message is printed on the user's terminal, indicating that her quota has been exceeded; however, the write operation will succeed.

Per-group hard limit
> This is the final limit set for a group by the quota system. Once this limit has been reached, none of the users within that group will be allowed to write files to the disk—even if the user's individual limits are not exceeded.

Per-group soft limit
> This limit behaves in the same way as a user's soft limit but is enforced based on group ownership instead of individual ownership.

Grace period
> Once a soft limit is reached, the user or group enters the *grace period*. After the grace period expires, the soft limit becomes a hard limit until enough files are deleted to eliminate the over-quota situation. The grace period may be specified for any number of months, weeks, days, hours, minutes, or seconds. A typical value is seven days.

These limits are set using the **edquota** command, detailed in the next section.

NOTE

When a disk write exceeds a hard limit or an expired soft limit, only part of the write operation will complete, leaving a truncated and probably useless file. The messages reported to the user when a quota is exceeded may be lost if the shell he is using is hidden. This could confuse the user, because the error message generated by the application indicates that the disk is full or write-protected.

Quota Commands

Linux offers a host of commands to manage, display, and report on filesystem quotas. Some of the setup required to initially enable quotas is done manually and without specific quota commands, a process that is covered in the next section.

quota

Syntax

```
quota [-u] [options] user
quota -g [options] group
```

Description

Displays quota limits on *user* or *group*. The -u option is the default. Only the superuser may use the -u flag and *user* to view the limits of other users. Other users can use the -g flag and *group* to view only the limits of groups of which they are members, provided that the *quota.group* files are readable by them.

Frequently used options

-q

  Sets quiet mode, which shows only over-quota situations.

-v

  Enables verbose mode to display quotas even if no storage space is allocated.

Example 1

As *root*, examine all quotas for user *jdoe*:

```
# quota -uv jdoe
Disk quotas for user jdoe (uid 500):
Filesystem  blks  quota limit grace  files quota limit grace
/dev/sda9   9456  10000 10200          32     0     0
/dev/hda1     23      0     0           17     0     0
```

This example shows that *jdoe* is barely within her soft limit of 10,000 blocks, with a corresponding hard limit of 10,200 blocks on */dev/sda9*, and has no quota on */dev/hda1*. The entry for */dev/hda1* is displayed in response to the -v option. No values are shown for the grace periods, because the soft limit has not been exceeded.

Example 2

As user *jdoe*, examine quotas for the *finance* group, of which he is a member:

```
$ quota -gv finance
Disk quotas for group finance (gid 501):
Filesystem  blks   quota  limit grace  files quota limit grace
/dev/sda9   1000*  990    1000  6days     34  3980  4000
/dev/hda1      0     0       0              0     0     0
```

Here, the *finance* group has exceeded its meager soft limit of 990 blocks and has come up against its hard limit of 1000 blocks. (The write operation that wrote the 1000th block was probably incomplete.) The original grace period in this example was set to seven days and has six days remaining, meaning that one day has elapsed since the soft limit was exceeded.

quotaon

Syntax

```
quotaon [options] [filesystems]
quotaon [options] -a
```

Description

Enable previously configured disk quotas on one or more *filesystems*.

Frequently used options

-a

Turns quotas on for all filesystems in */etc/fstab* that are marked read-write with quotas. This is normally used automatically at boot time to enable quotas.

-g

Turns on group quotas. This option is not necessary when using the **-a** option, which includes both user and group quotas.

-u

Turns on user quotas; this is the default.

-v

Enables verbose mode to display a message for each filesystem where quotas are turned on.

Example 1

Turn on all quotas as defined in */etc/fstab*:

```
# quotaon -av
/dev/sda9: group quotas turned on
/dev/sda9: user quotas turned on
/dev/hda1: group quotas turned on
/dev/hda1: user quotas turned on
```

Example 2

Turn on user quotas only on the */home* filesystem:

```
# quotaon -gv /home
/dev/sda9: group quotas turned on
```

quotaoff

Syntax

```
quotaoff [options] [filesystems]
quotaoff [options] -a
```

Description

Disables disk quotas on one or more *filesystems.*

Frequently used options

-a

    Turns quotas off for all filesystems in */etc/fstab.*

-g

    Turns off group quotas. This option is not necessary when using the -a option, which includes both user and group quotas.

-u

    Turns off user quotas; this is the default.

-v

    Enables verbose mode to display a message for each filesystem where quotas are turned off.

Example

Turn off all quotas:

```
# quotaoff -av
/dev/sda9: group quotas turned off
/dev/sda9: user quotas turned off
/dev/hda1: group quotas turned off
/dev/hda1: user quotas turned off
```

quotacheck

Syntax

```
quotacheck [options] filesystems
quotacheck [options] -a
```

Description

Examine filesystems and compile quota databases. This command is not specifically called out in the LPI Objectives for Exam 101, but is an important component of the Linux quota system. You should run the **quotacheck -a** command on a regular basis (perhaps weekly) via **cron**.

Frequently used options

-a

    Checks all of the quotas for the filesystems mentioned in */etc/fstab.* Both user and group quotas are checked as indicated by the **usrquota** and **grpquota** options.

-g *group*

    Compiles information only on *group.*

-u *user*

    Compiles information only on *user*; this is the default action. However, if the
    -g option is specified, then this option should also be specified when both
    group and user quotas are to be processed.

-v

    Enables verbose mode to display information about what the program is
    doing. This option shows activity by displaying a spinning character in the
    terminal. This is nice but could be a problem if you are logged in over a slow
    modem link.

Example 1

Initialize all quota files:

```
# quotaoff -a
# quotacheck -aguv
Scanning /dev/sda9 [/home] done
Checked 237 directories and 714 files
Using quotafile /home/quota.user
Using quotafile /home/quota.group
Scanning /dev/hda1 [/mnt/hd] done
Checked 3534 directories and 72673 files
Using quotafile /mnt/hd/quota.user
Using quotafile /mnt/hd/quota.group
# quotaon -a
```

By turning off quotas during the update, the quota database files are updated.

Example 2

With quotas active, update the user quotas in memory for */home*:

```
# quotacheck -v /home
Scanning /dev/sda9 [/home] done
Checked 237 directories and 714 files
Using quotafile /home/quota.user
Updating in-core user quotas
```

---

edquota

Syntax

```
edquota [-p proto-user] [options] names
edquota [options] -t
```

Description

Modify user or group quotas. This interactive command uses a text editor to
configure quota parameters for users or groups. The **vi** editor is used by default
unless either the EDITOR or VISUAL environment variables are set to another
editor, such as Emacs. When the command is issued, the **vi** editor is launched with
a temporary file containing quota settings. When the temporary file is saved and
the editor is terminated, the changes are saved in the quota databases.

In the first form, a space-separated list of users or groups specified in *names* is modified. If *proto-user* is specified with the -p option, quotas of that user or group are copied and used for *names* and no editor is launched. In the second form with the -t option, the soft limit settings are edited interactively for each filesystem.

Frequently used options

-g

> Modify group quotas. If **-g** is specified, all *names* are assumed to be groups and not users, even if **-u** is also specified.

-p *proto-user*

> Duplicate the quotas of the prototypical user or group *proto-user* for each user or group specified. This is the normal mechanism used to initialize quotas for multiple users or groups at the same time.

-t

> Modify soft limits. Time units of *sec*(onds), *min*(utes), *hour*(s), *day*(s), *week*(s), and *month*(s) are understood.

-u

> Modify user quotas. This is the default action. This option is ignored if **-g** is also specified.

NOTE

The following examples use the **vi** editor. The contents of the edit buffer —not program output—are shown after each example.

Example 1

Modify the user quotas for *jdoe*:

```
# edquota -u jdoe
Quotas for user jdoe:
/dev/sda9: blocks in use: 87, limits (soft = 99900,
        hard = 100000)
        inodes in use: 84, limits (soft = 0, hard = 0)
/dev/hda1: blocks in use: 0, limits (soft = 0, hard = 0)
        inodes in use: 0, limits (soft = 0, hard = 0)
~
~
"/tmp/EdP.auHTZJ0" 5 lines, 241 characters
```

Here, *jdoe* has been allocated a soft limit of 99,900 blocks, a hard limit of 100,000 blocks, and no file limits on */dev/sda9*. She has no limits on */dev/hda1*.

Example 2

Modify soft limits for users on all filesystems:

```
# edquota -tu
Time units may be: days, hours, minutes, or seconds
Grace period before enforcing soft limits for users:
/dev/sda9: block grace period: 7 days,
   file grace period: 3 days
```

```
/dev/hda1: block grace period: 7 days,
   file grace period: 3 days
~
~
"/tmp/EdP.aiTShJB" 5 lines, 249 characters
```

Here, the user grace periods have been set to seven days for blocks (disk space) and three days for files (inodes).

repquota

Syntax

```
repquota [options] filesystems
repquota -a [options]
```

Description

Used to report on the status of quotas. In the first form, **repquota** displays a summary report on the quotas for the given *filesystems* on a per-user or per-group basis. In the second form, the **-a** option causes a summary for all filesystems with quotas to be displayed. This command fails for non-root users unless the quota database files are world-readable. The current number of files and the amount of space utilized are printed for each user, along with any quotas created with **edquota**.

Frequently used options

-a

Report on all of the quotas for the read-write filesystems mentioned in */etc/fstab*. Both user and group quotas are reported as indicated by the **usrquota** and **grpquota** options.

-g

Report quotas for groups.

-u

Report quotas for users; this is the default action.

-v

Enable verbose mode, which adds a descriptive header to the output.

Example

Report user quotas for */home:*

```
# repquota -v /home
*** Report for user quotas on /dev/sda9 (/home)
                        Block limits      File limits
User          used  soft   hard grace used soft hard grace
root    --  418941     0      0          269    0    0
328     --    1411     0      0           20    0    0
jdean   --    9818 99900 100000          334    0    0
```

u1	--	44	0	0	43	0	0
u2	--	44	0	0	43	0	0
u3	--	127	155	300	124	0	0
jdoe	--	87	99900	100000	84	0	0
bsmith	--	42	1990	2000	41	0	0

Enabling Quotas

In order to use quotas, they must first be enabled.[*] This is not a difficult process, but unfortunately it is not completely straightforward either. To clarify the procedure, this section provides a brief tutorial on how to enable user and group quotas for a filesystem on */dev/sda9* mounted under */home*. Note that you may enable user quotas only, group quotas only, or both, as your needs dictate.

1. Set options in */etc/fstab*. On the line containing the */home* filesystem, add the **userquota** and **grpquota** options to the existing *default* option, like this:

   ```
   /dev/sda9   /home   ext2   defaults,usrquota,grpquota 1  2
   ```

   These options tell quota configuration utilities which partitions should be managed when the utilities reference */etc/fstab*.

2. Create the *quota.user* and *quota.group* files at the top of the */home* filesystem and set their protection bits for root access only:

   ```
   # touch /home/quota.user /home/quota.group
   # chmod 600 /home/quota.user /home/quota.group
   ```

   These two files are the databases for user and group quotas. Each filesystem with quotas uses its own quota databases. When quotas are enabled, these files will contain binary data (that is, they're not text files). Note that if you want end users to be able to examine quotas on groups to which they belong, *quota.group* will need a protection mode of 644 instead of 600.

3. Run **quotacheck** to initialize the databases:

   ```
   # quotacheck -avug
   Scanning /dev/sda9 [/home] done
   Checked 236 directories and 695 files
   Using quotafile /home/quota.user
   Using quotafile /home/quota.group
   ```

4. Then verify that your quota database files have been initialized by noting that they are no longer of size zero (here they're 16,192 bytes each):

   ```
   # ls -al /home/quota.*
   -rw-------  1 root  root 16192 Dec 27 19:53 /home/quota.group
   -rw-------  1 root  root 16192 Dec 27 19:53 /home/quota.user
   ```

5. Run **quotaon** to enable the quota system:

   ```
   # quotaon -a
   ```

---

[*] Quota support must also be compiled into the kernel. In the unlikely event that your kernel does not contain quota support, you will need to recompile the kernel (see Part 2, *Kernel (Topic 1.5)*, for more details on how to compile a kernel).

6. Verify that your system's initialization script (*/etc/rc.d/rc.sysinit* or similar) will turn on quotas when your system boots. Something along these lines is appropriate, although your system may be very different:

```
if [ -x /sbin/quotacheck ]
then
    echo "Checking quotas."
    /sbin/quotacheck -avug
    echo " Done."
fi
if [ -x /sbin/quotaon ]
then
    echo "Turning on quotas."
    /sbin/quotaon -avug
fi
```

7. Add a command script to a system *crontab* directory (such as the directory */etc/crontab.weekly*) to execute **quotacheck** on a routine basis. An executable script file like the following will work:

```
#!/bin/bash
/sbin/quotacheck -avug
```

If you prefer, you could instead put */sbin/quotacheck* in root's *crontab* file (using the **crontab -e** command) for weekly execution, like this:

```
# run quotacheck weekly
0 3 * * 0    /sbin/quotacheck -avug
```

At this point the */home* filesystem is ready to accept quotas on a per-user and per-group basis, enforce them, and report on them.

On the Exam

A general understanding of quotas is necessary for the exam. In particular, you should know the function of each command. Also remember that quotas are set on a per-filesystem basis.

Objective 5: Use File Permissions to Control Access to Files

Filesystem security is a fundamental requirement for any multiuser operating system. The system's files, such as the kernel, configuration files, and programs, must be protected from accidents and tampering by unauthorized people. Users' files must be protected from modification by other users and sometimes must be kept completely private. In general, a form of *access control* must be implemented to allow secure operations.

Linux Access Control

Native Linux filesystem access control is implemented using a set of properties, maintained separately for each file. These properties are collectively called the *access mode*, or simply the *mode*, of the file. The mode is a part of the file's inode, the information retained in the filesystem that describes the file. A file's mode controls access by these three classes of users:

User
> The user that owns the file.

Group
> The group that owns the file.

Other
> All other users on the system.

Like the *mode*, user and group ownership properties are a part of the inode, and both are assigned when a file is created. Usually, the owner is the user who created the file. The file's group is usually set to its creator's default group.* Group ownership adds flexibility in situations in which a team shares files. The "other" users are those who aren't members of the file's group and are not the file's owner. For each of these three user classes, the access mode defines three types of permissions, which apply differently for files and directories. The permissions are listed in Table 1-16.

Table 1-16: File Permissions

Permission	Mnemonic	File Permission	Directory Permission
Read	r	Examine the contents of the file.	List directory contents.
Write	w	Write to, or change, the file.	Create and remove files in the directory.
Execute	x	Run the file as a program.	Read and write files contained in the directory.

These three permissions apply to the three different classes of users: *user, group,* and *other.* Each has *read, write,* and *execute* capabilities, as shown in Figure 1-1.

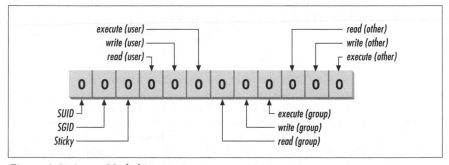

Figure 1-1: Access Mode bits

---

* On some Linux distributions, the default group for all new accounts is set to a general *users* group. However, if everyone is in the same group by default, group permissions don't offer added security. For this reason, other distributions define a unique default group for every user.

All of the permissions are binary (either granted or not granted) and are thought of as single binary bits in the access mode. When written, the permissions use the mnemonic in Table 1-16 for the true state and a hyphen for the false state. To represent only the read permission, for example, r-- would be used. Read and execute together, typical for directories, would be denoted r-x. These notations are usually offered in sets of three, such as:

rw-rw-r--

A file with this setting would give read/write permission to the user and group, and read-only permission to everyone else.

In addition to the nine bits for user, group, and other, the access mode contains three more bits, which control special attributes for executable files and directories:

SUID (Set User ID)

The SUID property is for executable files only and has no effect on directories. Normally the user who launches a program owns the resulting process. However, if an executable file has its SUID bit set, the *file's owner* owns the resulting process, no matter who launched it. When SUID is used, the file's owner is usually root. This offers anyone temporary root access for the duration of the command. An example of an SUID program is **lpr**, the *line print* command. This command needs special access to manipulate the print spools, and runs as user root.

Using the SUID bit in cases like **lpr** enhances security by allowing access to secure functions without giving away the root password. On the other hand, SUID can be a security risk if access is granted unwisely.

SGID (Set Group ID)

The SGID property works the same way as SUID for executable files, setting the process group owner to the file's group. In addition, the SGID property has a special effect on directories. When SGID is set on a directory, new files created within that directory are assigned the same group ownership as the directory itself. For example, if directory */home/fin* has the group *finance* and has SGID enabled, then all files under */home/fin* are created with group ownership of *finance*, regardless of the creator's group. This is an important attribute for teams, ensuring that shared files all have the same group ownership.

Sticky

At one time, the sticky property (more commonly known as the *sticky bit*), applied to executable programs, flagging the system to keep an image of the program in memory after the program finished running. This capability increased performance for subsequent uses by eliminating the programs' load phase, and was applied to programs that were large or were run frequently. Modern virtual memory techniques have made this use unnecessary, and under Linux there is no need to use the sticky bit on executable programs.

When applied to a directory, the sticky bit offers additional security for files within the directory. Regardless of file permissions, the only users who can rename or delete the files from a directory with the sticky bit set are the file owner, the directory owner, and root. When used in a team environment, the sticky bit allows groups to create and modify files but allows only file owners the privilege of deleting or renaming them.

Like the other access controls, these special properties are binary and are considered bits in the access mode.

The mode bits

The *special, user, group,* and *other* permissions can be represented in a string of 12 binary bits, as shown in Figure 1-2.

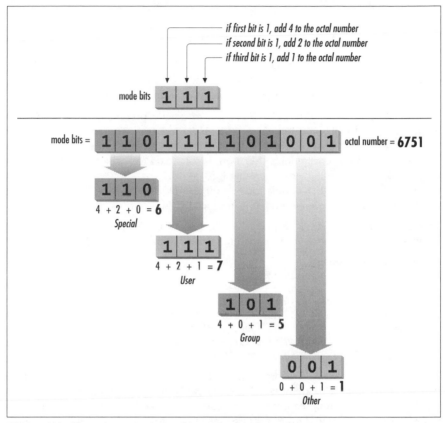

Figure 1-2: Changing permission bits to an octal number.

It is common to refer to these bits in four sets of three, translated into four octal (base-8) digits. The first octal digit represents the special permissions SUID, SGID, and sticky. The other three represent the read, write, and execute permissions, respectively, in each of the user, group, and other user classes. Octal notation is used as shorthand for binary strings like the access mode, and each group of three bits has 2^3 = 8 possible values, listed in Table 1-17.

Table 1-17: Octal Numbers

Octal Value	Binary Equivalent
0	000
1	001

Table 1-17: Octal Numbers (continued)

Octal Value	Binary Equivalent
2	010
3	011
4	100
5	101
6	110
7	111

The read permission by itself is r--, which can be thought of as binary 100, or octal 4. Adding the write permission yields rw-, or binary 110, which is octal 6. Figure 1-3 shows how to total bit values into the octal equivalents.*

To turn the mode bits 110111101001 into an octal representation, first separate them into chunks of three bits: 110, 111, 101, and 001. The first group, representing the special permissions, is 110. This can be thought of as $4 + 2 + 0 = 6$. The second group, representing user permissions, is 111, or $4 + 2 + 1 = 7$. The third group, representing group permissions, is 101, or $4 + 0 + 1 = 5$. The last group, representing other permissions, is 001, or $0 + 0 + 1 = 1$. The mode string for this example can then be written as the octal 6751.

This is the form used to display the file mode in the output from the **stat** command. Here, the octal access mode for the **lpr** command is 4755:

```
# stat /usr/bin/lpr
  File: "/mnt/hd/usr/bin/lpr"
  Size: 235672       Filetype: Regular File
  Mode: (4755/-rwsr-xr-x)  Uid: ( 0/ root)  Gid: ( 0/  root)
Device:  3,1   Inode: 176133    Links: 1
Access: Tue Aug 10 23:57:11 1999(00144.11:34:49)
Modify: Tue Aug 10 23:57:11 1999(00144.11:34:49)
Change: Wed Dec  8 20:59:02 1999(00024.13:32:58)
```

The special permissions are represented in this example by octal 4, or binary 100, indicating that the SUID permission is set (-rws). The user permission is octal 7, or binary 111, indicating read, write, and execute for the file's owner (in this case, root). Both the group and other permissions are set to octal 5, or binary 101, indicating read and execute, but not write.

The mode string

As mentioned earlier, the user, group, and other permissions are often spelled out in symbolic mode descriptions such as rwxr-xr-x. This notation is found in the output of the **ls -l** and **stat** commands. As you can see in the access mode for **lpr**, this scheme is modified slightly in the presence of special permissions. Instead of adding three more bits to the left of rwxr-xr-x, the SUID permission is indicated in the string by changing the user execute position from x to s. SGID permission is handled the same way. The sticky permission is indicated by replacing x in the

---

* Memorizing, or even writing, the binary-to-octal equivalents may be easier on the exam than adding bit values. Use the technique that works best for you.

other execute position with T. For example, an executable program with mode 6755 would have the following equivalent symbolic mode:

```
rwsr-sr-x
```

A directory with mode 1774 would have this equivalent string:

```
rwxr-xr-T
```

While this layering of special permissions may appear to obscure the underlying execute permissions, it makes sense. The special permissions are relatively rare in the filesystem, so depicting the three extra bits would waste space on your terminal or terminal window. In addition, the special permissions are used only for executable programs and directories, where the underlying executable permission is understood to be set.*

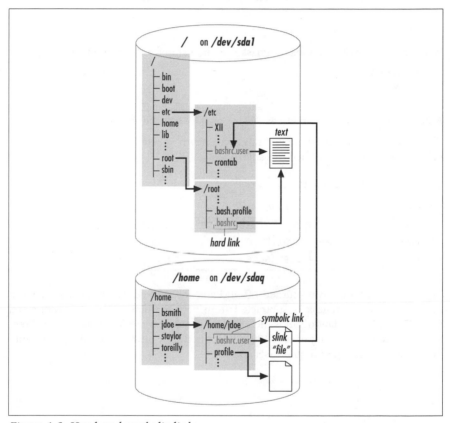

Figure 1-3: Hard and symbolic links

---

* For the purists among us, note that the special bits may be set without setting the execute permission, although to do so is meaningless. In this case, the string's s and t values are replaced with S and T, respectively.

Setting Access Modes

New files are created with a default access mode to automatically set the permission levels. But just because a permission level is set automatically doesn't mean that you have to live with what you're given. Access modes on existing files can be changed or modified.

New files

When new files are created, the protection bits are set according to the user's default setting. That default is established using the **umask** command, probably in a startup script. This command accepts only one argument, which is a three-digit octal string that masks the user, group, and other permission bits for newly created files and directories. Without a value, **umask** reports the current value:

```
$ umask
22
```

When provided with an integer, **umask** sets the value for the current shell:

```
$ umask 2
$ umask
2
```

A **umask** of 22 can be rewritten as 022, or as 000010010 in binary.

The process of creating the initial mode for newly created files begins with a raw initial mode string, as defined in Table 1-18.

Table 1-18: Initial Access Modes

Form	For Files	For Directories
Symbolic	rw-rw-rw-	rwxrwxrwx
Binary	110110110	111111111
Octal	6 6 6	7 7 7

The special bits are always turned off and are not masked by the **umask**. When a file is created, the **umask** is subtracted from 666; for directories, it is subtracted from 777. This calculation yields the effective protection mode for the file or directory. For example, a **umask** of 2 (002) is applied to a new file, masking the write permission for group and other user classes:

```
  110 110 110
- 000 010 010
  110 100 100
```

This is the same as mode 644, or rw-r--r--.

Using the same mask on a directory yields a similar result:

```
  111 111 111
- 000 010 010
  111 101 101
```

This is the same as mode 755 or rwxr-xr-x, which is appropriate for directories. A **umask** of 002 or 022 is typical, though if you wish to ensure maximum privacy, a **umask** of 077 blocks all access except for the superuser. To set a custom **umask**, enter the **umask** command in a startup script, such as *.bash_profile*. Here's an example of the **umask** in action:

```
$ umask 27
$ touch afile
$ mkdir adir
$ ls -ld adir afile
drwxr-x---  2 jdean    jdean          1024 Jan  2 20:31 adir
-rw-r-----  1 jdean    jdean             0 Jan  2 20:31 afile
```

In this case, the **umask** of 27 makes the file *afile* read-only to members of the group and disallows access to the file to all others.

In the previous example, the command **ls -ld** adds an extra letter at the beginning of the mode string for the *adir* directory. This symbol indicates the type of file being listed and is not part of the access mode. The letter **d** indicates a directory, a – indicates a file, the letter **l** indicates a symbolic link, a **b** indicates a block device (such as a disk), and a **c** indicates a character device (such as a terminal).

Changing access modes

Access modes can be changed with the **chmod** command, which accepts either *octal* or *symbolic* access mode specifications. Octal bits, as shown in the previous section, are specified explicitly. However, some people prefer to use symbolic forms because they usually modify an existing mode instead of completely replacing it. Symbolic mode specifications have three parts, made up of individual characters, as shown in Table 1-19.

Table 1-19. Symbolic Modes for the chmod Command

Category	Mode	Description
User class	u	User.
	g	Group.
	o	Other.
	a	All classes.
Operation	–	Take away permission.
	+	Add permission.
	=	Set permission exactly.
Permissions	r	Read permission.
	w	Write permission.
	x	Execute permission.
	X	Execute permission for directories and files with another execute permission, but not plain files.
	s	SUID or SGID permissions.
	t	Sticky bit.

The individual user class characters and permissions characters may be grouped to form compound expressions, such as **ug** for *user* and *group* combined or **rw** for *read* and *write*. Here are some examples of symbolic mode specifications:

u+x

Add execute permission for the *user*.

go-w

Remove write permission from *group* and *other* classes.

o+t

Set the sticky bit.

a=rw

Set read and write, but not execute, permissions for everyone.

a+X

Give everyone execute permission for directories and for those files with any existing execute permission.

The **chmod** command is used to modify the mode.

---

chmod

Syntax

```
chmod [options] symbolic_mode[,symbolic_mode]... files
chmod [options] octal_mode files
chmod [options] --reference=rfile files
```

Description

Modify the access mode on *files*. In the first form, use one or more comma-separated *symbolic_mode* specifications to modify *files*. In the second form, use an *octal_mode* to modify *files*. In the third form, use the mode of *rfile* as a template to be applied to *files*.

Frequently used options

-c

Like verbose mode, but report only changes.

-R

Use recursive mode, descending through directory hierarchies under *files* and making modifications throughout.

-v

Use verbose behavior, reporting actions for all *files*.

Example 1

Set the mode for a file to rw-r--r--, using an octal specification:

```
$ chmod 644 afile
$ ls -l afile
-rw-r--r--   1 jdean     jdean          0 Jan  2 20:31 afile
```

Example 2

Set the same permission using a symbolic specification, using the verbose option:

```
$ chmod -v u=rw,go=r afile
mode of afile retained as 0644 (rw-r--r--)
```

Example 3

Recursively remove all permissions for *other* on a directory:

```
$ chmod -v o-rwx adir
mode of adir retained as 0770 (rwxrwx---)
mode of adir/file1 changed to 0660 (rw-rw----)
mode of adir/file2 changed to 0660 (rw-rw----)
mode of adir/file3 changed to 0660 (rw-rw----)
mode of adir/file4 changed to 0660 (rw-rw----)
mode of adir/dir1 changed to 0770 (rwxrwx---)
mode of adir/dir1/file6 changed to 0660 (rw-rw----)
mode of adir/dir1/file5 changed to 0660 (rw-rw----)
mode of adir/dir2 changed to 0770 (rwxrwx---)
```

Example 4

Set the sticky bit on a directory:

```
$ chmod -v +t adir
mode of adir changed to 1770 (rwxrwx--T)
```

Setting Up a Workgroup Directory

The steps you may use to create a useful workgroup directory for a small team of people are briefly described here. The goals of the directory are as follows:

- The workgroup is to be called *sales* and has members *jdoe*, *bsmith*, and *jbrown*.

- The directory is */home/sls.*

- Only the creators of files in */home/sls* should be able to delete them.

- Members shouldn't need to worry about file ownership, and all group members require full access to files.

- Nonmembers should have no access to any of the files.

The following steps will satisfy the goals:

1. Create the new group:

   ```
   # groupadd sales
   ```

2. Add the existing users to the group:

   ```
   # usermod -G sales jdoe
   # usermod -G sales bsmith
   # usermod -G sales jbrown
   ```

3. Create a directory for the group:

   ```
   # mkdir /home/sls
   ```

4. Set the ownership of the new directory:

```
# chgrp sales /home/sls
```

5. Protect the directory from others:

```
# chmod 770 /home/sls
```

6. Set the SGID bit to ensure that the *sales* group will own all new files. Also set the sticky bit to protect files from deletion by non-owners:

```
# chmod g+s,o+t /home/sls
```

7. Test it:

```
# su - jdoe
$ cd /home/sls
$ touch afile
$ ls -l afile
-rw-rw-r--   1 jdoe      sales      0 Jan  3 02:44 afile
$ exit
# su - bsmith
# cd /home/sls
# rm afile
rm: cannot unlink `afile': Operation not permitted
```

After the **ls** command, we see that the group ownership is correctly set to *sales*. After the **rm** command, we see that *bsmith* cannot delete *afile*, which was created by *jdoe*. We also note that although *afile* has mode 664, the directory containing it has mode 770, preventing *other* users from reading the file.

On the Exam

For the exam, you should be prepared to answer questions on file and directory permissions in both symbolic and numeric (octal) forms. You should also be able to translate between the two forms given an example.

Objective 6: Manage File Ownership

Modification of ownership parameters may become necessary when moving files, setting up workgroups, or working in a user's directory as root. This is accomplished using the **chown** command, which can change user and group ownership, and the **chgrp** command for modifying group ownership.

The **chown** command supersedes **chgrp** because all of the **chgrp** command's functions are available in **chown**. However, many system administrators still habitually use **chgrp**, and it is often found in scripts and makefiles.

chown

Syntax

```
chown [options] user-owner files
chown [options] user-owner. files
chown [options] user-owner.group-owner files
chown [options] .group-owner files
chown [options] --reference=rfile files
```

Description

Used to change the owner and/or group of *files* to *user-owner* and/or *group-owner*. In the first form, *user-owner* is made the owner of *files* and the group is not affected. In the second form (note the trailing dot on *user-owner*), the *user-owner* is made the owner of *files* and the group of the files is changed to *user-owner*'s default group. In the third form, both *user-owner* and *group-owner* are assigned to *files*. In the fourth form, only the *group-owner* is assigned to *files,* and the user is not affected. In the fifth form, the owner and group of *rfile* is used as a template and applied to *files*. Since this program can handle all types of changes to groups, it replaces the **chgrp** command. Only the superuser may change file ownership, but group ownership may be set by anyone belonging to the target *group-owner*.

Frequently used options

-c
> Like verbose mode, but report only changes.

-R
> Use recursive mode, descending through directory hierarchies under *files* and making modifications throughout.

-v
> Use verbose behavior, reporting actions for all *files*.

Example 1

As root, set the user of a file:

```
# chown -v jdoe afile
owner of afile changed to jdoe
```

Example 2

As root, set the user and group of a file:

```
# chown -v jdoe.sales afile
owner of afile changed to jdoe.sales
```

Example 3

Recursively change the group of the entire *sls* directory:

```
# chown -Rv .sales sls
owner of sls changed to .sales
owner of sls/file1 changed to .sales
owner of sls/file2 changed to .sales
...
```

chgrp

Syntax

```
chgrp [options] group-owner files
chgrp [options] --reference=rfile files
```

Description

Change the group parameter of *files* to *group-owner*. In the first form, set the *group-owner* of *files*. In the second form, the group of *rfile* is used as a template and applied to *files*. Options and usage are the same as that of **chown**.

On the Exam

Remember that only root can change file ownership. Also remember that **chown** can change not only the user but also the group ownership.

Objective 7: Create and Change Hard and Symbolic Links

A *link* is a pseudofile that creates a shortcut to the original file located elsewhere on the filesystem. Links don't take up very much space, as they don't contain any real data. While the concept of links may seem a little odd, they are very useful and can be used for anything from creating a shortcut, to launching an application, to mirroring the kernel's source.

There are two types of links used on Linux:

Symbolic links
> A symbolic link is really a tiny file that contains a pointer to another file. When Linux opens a symbolic link, it reads the pointer and then finds the intended file that contains the actual data. Symbolic links can point to other filesystems, both local and on networked computers, and they can point to directories. They are clearly listed as being a link with the **ls -l** command by displaying a special "l" (a lowercase *l*) in column one, and they have no file protections of their own (the actual file's permissions are used instead). Note that if a file with a symbolic link is deleted, then the symbolic link points to nothing and is said to be stale.

Hard links
> A hard link is not really a "link" at all, but a copy of another directory entry. The two directory entries have different names but point to the same inode and thus to the same actual data, ownership, permissions, and so on. In fact, if a file with a hard link is deleted, the link remains, still pointing to the valid inode. Except for its name, including its location in the directory hierarchy, the link is indistinguishable from the original file.

Hard links have two important limitations. First, because they share inodes, files and any hard links to them must reside on the same filesystem (inode numbers aren't expected to be unique across filesystems). Second, hard links cannot point to directories. However, hard links take no disk space beyond an additional directory entry.

Symbolic links are used more often than hard links because they are more versatile and easier to manage, yet still consume a trivial amount of disk space.

Why Links?

To see an example of the use of links in practice, consider the directories in */etc/rc.d*:

```
drwxr-xr-x   2 root      root       1024 Dec 15 23:05 init.d
-rwxr-xr-x   1 root      root       2722 Apr 15  1999 rc
-rwxr-xr-x   1 root      root        693 Aug 17  1998 rc.local
-rwxr-xr-x   1 root      root       9822 Apr 13  1999 rc.sysinit
drwxr-xr-x   2 root      root       1024 Dec  2 09:41 rc0.d
drwxr-xr-x   2 root      root       1024 Dec  2 09:41 rc1.d
drwxr-xr-x   2 root      root       1024 Dec 24 15:15 rc2.d
drwxr-xr-x   2 root      root       1024 Dec 24 15:15 rc3.d
drwxr-xr-x   2 root      root       1024 Dec 24 15:16 rc4.d
drwxr-xr-x   2 root      root       1024 Dec 24 15:16 rc5.d
drwxr-xr-x   2 root      root       1024 Dec 14 23:37 rc6.d
```

Inside *init.d* are scripts to start and stop many of the services on your system, such as **httpd**, **cron**, and **syslog**. Some of these files are to be executed with a **start** argument, while others are run with a **stop** argument, depending upon the *runlevel* of your system. To determine just which files are run and what argument they receive, a scheme of additional directories has been devised. These directories are named *rc0.d* through *rc6.d*, one for each runlevel (see the next section, *Part 1, Boot, Initialization, Shutdown, and Runlevels (Topic 2.6),* for a complete description of this scheme). Each of the runlevel-specific directories contains several links, each with a name that helps determine the configuration of services on your system. For example, *rc3.d* contains the following links, among many others:

```
S30syslog -> ../init.d/syslog
S40crond -> ../init.d/crond
S85httpd -> ../init.d/httpd
```

All of these links point back to the scripts in *init.d* as indicated by the arrows (->) after the script name. If these links were copies of the scripts, editing would be required for all of the runlevel-specific versions of the same script just to make a single change. Instead, links allow us to:

- Make changes to the original file once. References to the links will yield the updated contents as long as the filename doesn't change.

- Avoid wasting disk space by having multiple copies of the same file in different places for "convenience."

As another example, consider the directory for the kernel source, */usr/src/linux*:

```
linux -> linux-2.2.10
linux-2.2.10
```

Makefiles and other automated tools can refer to *usr/src/linux*, but in reality, they reference *usr/src/linux-2.2.10*. If a new kernel is added, say Version 2.2.14, its source would be placed into an appropriately named directory and the *linux* link would be reset, as follows:

```
linux -> linux-2.2.14
linux-2.2.10
linux-2.2.14
```

Now the appropriate directory can be selected simply by changing the link. No files need to be moved or deleted. Once created, links are normal directory entries, which may be copied, renamed, deleted, and backed up.

Symbolic and hard links are created with the **ln** command.

---

ln

Syntax

```
ln [options] file link
ln [options] files directory
```

Description

Create links between files. In the first form, a new *link* is created to point to *file*, which must already exist. In the second form, links are created in *directory* for all *files* specified.

Frequently used options

−f

Overwrite (force) existing links, or existing files in the destination *directory*.

−i

Prompt interactively before overwriting destination files.

−s

Create a symbolic link rather than a hard link.

Example 1

Note that the Bourne shell **sh** on a Linux system is a symbolic link to **bash**:

```
$ ls -l /bin/bash /bin/sh
/bin/bash
/bin/sh -> bash
```

Example 2

Create a file named *myfile*, a symbolic link to that file named *myslink*, and a hard link to that file named *myhlink*, then examine them:

```
$ touch myfile
$ ln -s myfile myslink
$ ln myfile myhlink
$ ls -l my*
-rw-r--r--   2 jdoe   jdoe   0 Jan  3 13:21 myfile
-rw-r--r--   2 jdoe   jdoe   0 Jan  3 13:21 myhlink
lrwxrwxrwx   1 jdoe   jdoe   6 Jan  3 13:21 myslink -> myfile
```

Using the **stat** command on **my*** demonstrates that they all ultimately reference the same inode (the inode numbers are the same) and indicates the number of links to the file (two links, one symbolic and one hard):

```
# stat my*
File: "myfile"
  Size: 0              Filetype: Regular File
  Mode: (0644/-rw-r--r--) Uid: (0/ root)  Gid: (0/ root)
Device: 8,6    Inode: 30        Links: 2
Access: Mon Jan  3 14:33:04 2000(00000.00:06:05)
Modify: Mon Jan  3 14:33:04 2000(00000.00:06:05)
Change: Mon Jan  3 14:33:25 2000(00000.00:05:44)

  File: "myhlink"
  Size: 0              Filetype: Regular File
  Mode: (0644/-rw-r--r--) Uid: (0/ root)  Gid: (0/ root)
Device: 8,6    Inode: 30        Links: 2
Access: Mon Jan  3 14:33:04 2000(00000.00:06:05)
Modify: Mon Jan  3 14:33:04 2000(00000.00:06:05)
Change: Mon Jan  3 14:33:25 2000(00000.00:05:44)

  File: "myslink"
  Size: 0              Filetype: Regular File
  Mode: (0644/-rw-r--r--) Uid: (0/ root)  Gid: (0/ root)
Device: 8,6    Inode: 30        Links: 2
Access: Mon Jan  3 14:33:04 2000(00000.00:06:05)
Modify: Mon Jan  3 14:33:04 2000(00000.00:06:05)
Change: Mon Jan  3 14:33:25 2000(00000.00:05:44)
```

However, the symbolic link has an inode of its own, which is displayed using the -i option to **ls**:

```
# ls -li my*
30 -rw-r--r--   2 root root  0 Jan  3 14:33 myfile
30 -rw-r--r--   2 root root  0 Jan  3 14:33 myhlink
41 lrwxrwxrwx   1 root root  6 Jan  3 14:33 myslink -> myfile
```

Here you can see that the directory entries for *myfile* and *myhlink* both point to inode 30, while the directory entry for *myslink* points to inode 41. That inode contains the symbolic link to *myfile*.

As another example, consider the two filesystems in Figure 1-4. The root partition on */dev/sda1* holds a file intended as an example **bash** startup file, located in */etc/bashrc_user*. On the same filesystem, the *root* user has elected to use */etc/bashrc_user*. Not wanting to maintain both files individually, *root* has created a hard link, */root/.bashrc*, to the example file. Both of the directory entries, */etc/bashrc_user* and */root/.bashrc*, point to the same text data in the same file, described by the same inode, on */dev/sda1*. User *jdoe* has also elected to link to the example file. However, since his home directory is located in */home* on */dev/sda9*, *jdoe* cannot use a hard link to the file on */dev/sda1*. Instead, he created a symbolic link,   */home/jdoe/.bashrc*, which points to a small file on */dev/sda9*. This contains the pointer to directory entry */etc/bashrc_user*, which finally points at the *text*. The result for *root* and *jdoe* is identical, though the two styles of links implement the reference in completely different ways.

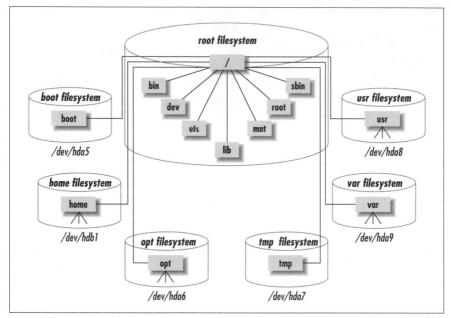

Figure 1-4: Hard and symbolic links

Preserving links

Programs such as **tar** and **cp** contain options that control whether symbolic links are followed during operation. In the case of a **tar** backup, this may be important if you have multiple links to large files, because you would get many redundant backups of the same data.

When a symbolic link is encountered with **cp**, the contents of the file to which the link points are copied unless the **–d** option is specified. This "no dereference" operator causes **cp** to copy the links themselves instead. For example, consider a directory *dir1* containing a symbolic link, which is recursively copied to other directories with and without the **–d** option:

```
# ls -l dir1
total 13
lrwxrwxrwx 1 root root         19 Jan  4 02:43 file1 -> /file1
-rw-r--r-- 1 root root      10240 Dec 12 17:12 file2
# cp -r dir1 dir2
# ls -l dir2
total 3117
-rw-r--r-- 1 root root 3164160 Jan  4 02:43 file1
-rw-r--r-- 1 root root   10240 Jan  4 02:43 file2
# cp -rd dir1 dir3
# ls -l dir3
total 13
lrwxrwxrwx 1 root root         19 Jan  4 02:43 file1 -> /file1
-rw-r--r-- 1 root root      10240 Jan  4 02:43 file2
```

Directory *dir2* has a copy of the entire *file1*, which is large, probably wasting disk space. Directory *dir3*, created with **cp -rd**, is the same as *dir1* (including the symbolic link) and takes very little space.

Finding links to a file

Finding the file pointed to by a symbolic link is simple. The **ls -l** command displays a convenient pointer notation, indicating just where links are pointing:

```
lrwxrwxrwx 1 root root      19 Jan  4 02:43 file1 -> /file1
```

Study Guide 101

Going the other way and finding symbolic links to a file is less obvious but is still relatively easy. The **-lname** option to the **find** utility locates them for you by searching for symbolic links containing the original filename. Here, the entire local filesystem is searched for *myfile*, turning up three symbolic links:

```
# find / -lname myfile
/home/world/rootsfile
/home/finance/hisfile
/root/myslink
```

Remember that symbolic links could be anywhere, including being located on a remote system (if you're sharing files), so you may not be able to locate them all. (See "Part 1: *GNU and Unix Commands (Topic 1.3)*, Objective 1: Work Effectively on the Unix Command Line" for additional information on the **find** command).

Since hard links aren't really links, but duplicate directory entries, you can locate them by searching directory entries for the inode, which is identical in all the links. Unlike symbolic links, you are guaranteed to find all of the links since hard links cannot cross filesystem boundaries. First, identify the inode you're interested in, as well as the filesystem that contains the links:

```
# df file1
Filesystem     1k-blocks      Used Available Use% Mounted on
/dev/sda9        1981000    451115   1427473  24% /home
# ls -i file
90469 file1
```

Here, *file1* is on the */home* filesystem, and its inode number is 90469. Next, **find** is used with the **–inum** option to locate all instances of inode 90469:

```
# find /home -inum 90469
/home/world/file1
/home/finance/file1
/home/jdoe/private/.myfile1
```

This example turns up three links to *file1*, including one that user *jdoe* appears to be hiding!

On the Exam

You should be prepared to identify the differences between hard and symbolic links, when each is used, and their limitations.

Objective 8: Find System Files and Place Files in the Correct Location

In 1993, the Linux community formed a project to provide a standardized file-system layout for all general-purpose distributions of Linux. The intent of this standardization was to provide advice on how to create a low-maintenance file-system, and to reduce the proliferation of proprietary Linux filesystem layouts and their possible contribution to market fragmentation.

The project released a document describing the Linux Filesystem Standard, usually abbreviated FSSTND, in 1994. The following year, the group began to reduce Linux-specific content and to refine the standard to include other Unix or Unix-like operating systems. As the FSSTND attracted broader appeal, it was renamed the *Filesystem Hierarchy Standard*, or FHS. Although the FHS is not a requirement of Linux developers and distributors, the Linux community understands the impor-tance of standards, and all major distributions support the standard.

Data Types

In order to frame its recommendations, the FHS defines two categories of data use, each with two opposing subtypes:

Data sharing
> This category defines the scope of data use in a networked environment:
>
> *Sharable*
>> Sharable data can be used by multiple host systems on a network. Shar-able files contain general-purpose information, without ties to any specific host. Examples include user datafiles, many executable program files, and common configuration files such as *hosts*.
>
> *Non-sharable*
>> Data is not sharable when linked to a specific host, such as a unique configuration file. Examples include the *passwd* file, network configura-tion files, and system logs.

Data modification
> This category specifies how data changes:
>
> *Variable*
>> Data is considered variable when changed by natural, frequent processes. Examples include user files and system log files, such as */var/log/ messages*.
>
> *Static*
>> Static data is left alone for the most part, remaining the same from day to day or even year to year. Examples include binary programs such as **ls** and **bash**, which change only when the system administrator performs an upgrade.

Some directories in the Linux filesystem are intended to hold specific types of data. For example, the executable files in */usr* are rarely changed, and thus could be defined as *static* because they are needed by all users on a network. Before disks were as large as they are today, the files commonly found in */usr* were often mounted from remote servers to preserve local disk space. Thus, in addition to being static, */usr* is said to be *sharable*. Keeping files organized with respect to these attributes can simplify file sharing, system administration, and backup complexity, as well as reduce storage requirements. The FHS arranges the preceding data categories into a 2 × 2 matrix, as shown with a few example directories in Table 1-20.

Table 1-20: FHS Data Types

	Sharable	Non-sharable
Static	*/usr*	*/etc*
	/usr/local	*/boot*
Variable	*/var/mail*	*/var/log*
	/home	*/proc*

On many networks, */usr* and */usr/local* are mounted by individual workstations from an NFS server. This can save a considerable amount of local storage on the workstations. More important, placing these directories on another system can make upgrades and additions much simpler. These directories are usually shared as read-only filesystems because they are never modified by most end users. The */var/mail* and */home* directories, on the other hand, are shared but must be changed regularly by users. The */etc* and */boot* directories contain files that are static in the sense that only the administrator changes them, but sharing them is not necessary or advised, since they are local configuration files. The */var/log* and */proc* directories are very dynamic but also of local interest only.

The root Filesystem

The FHS offers a significant level of detail describing the exact locations of files, using rationale derived from the static/variable and sharable/nonsharable definitions. However, knowledge of the location of every file is not necessary or required for Exam 101. This section discusses the major portions of the FHS directory hierarchy overall, with specific example files offered as illustrations.

NOTE

While the FHS is a defining document for the Linux filesystem, it does not follow that all directories described in the FHS will be present in all Linux installations. Some directory locations cited in the FHS are package-dependent or open to customization by the vendor.

The root filesystem is located at the top of the entire directory hierarchy. The FHS defines these goals for the root filesystem:

- It must contain utilities and files sufficient to boot the operating system, including the ability to mount other filesystems. This includes utilities, device files, configuration, boot loader information, and other essential start-up data.

- It should contain the utilities needed by the system administrator to repair or restore a damaged system.

- It should be relatively small. Small partitions are less likely to be corrupted due to a system crash or power failure than large ones are. In addition, the root partition should contain non-sharable data to maximize the remaining disk space for sharable data.

- Software should not create files or directories in the root filesystem.

While a Linux system with everything in a single root partition may be created, doing so would not meet these goals. Instead, the root filesystem should contain only essential system directories, along with mount points for other filesystems. Essential root filesystem directories include:

/bin

> The */bin* directory contains executable system commands such as **cp**, **date**, **ln**, **ls**, **mkdir**, and **more**. These commands are deemed essential to system administration in case of a problem.

/dev

> Device files, necessary for accessing disks and other devices, are stored in */dev*. Examples include disk partitions, such as *hda1*, and terminals, such as *tty1*. Devices must be present at boot time for proper mounting and configuration.

/etc

> The */etc* directory contains configuration information unique to the system and is required for boot time. No binary executable programs are stored here.* Example files include *passwd*, *hosts*, and *login.defs*.

/lib

> The */lib* directory contains shared libraries and kernel modules, both essential for system initialization.

/mnt

> This directory is empty except for some mount points for temporary partitions, including *cdrom* and *floppy*.

/root

> The typical home directory for the superuser is */root*. While it is not absolutely essential for */root* to be on the root filesystem, it is customary and convenient, because doing so keeps root's configuration files available for system maintenance or recovery.

/sbin

> Essential utilities used for system administration are stored in */sbin*. Examples include **fdisk**, **fsck**, and **mkfs**.

The remaining top-level directories in the root filesystem are considered non-essential for emergency procedures:

/boot

> The */boot* directory contains files for LILO. Because it is typically small, it can be left in the root filesystem. However, it is often separated to keep the boot loader files within the first 1024 cylinders of a physical disk.

---

* Prior practice in various versions of Unix had administrative executable programs stored in */etc*. These have been moved to */sbin* under the FHS.

/home

> The */home* directory contains home directories for system users. This is usually a separate filesystem and is often the largest variable filesystem in the hierarchy.

/opt

> The */opt* directory is intended for the installation of software other than that packaged with the operating system. This is often the location selected by third-party software vendors for their products.

/tmp

> The */tmp* directory is for the storage of temporary files. The contents are deleted upon every system boot.

/usr

> The */usr* directory contains a significant hierarchy of executable programs deemed nonessential for emergency procedures. It is usually contained in a separate partition. It contains sharable, read-only data, and is often mounted locally read-only and shared via NFS read-only. */usr* is described in detail in the next section.

/var

> Like */usr*, the */var* directory contains a large hierarchy and is usually contained in a separate partition. It holds data that varies over time, such as logs, mail, and spools.

The /usr filesystem

The */usr* filesystem hierarchy contains system utilities and programs that do not appear in the root partition. For example, user programs such as **awk**, **less**, and **tail** are found in */usr/bin*. */usr/sbin* contains system administration commands such as **adduser** and **traceroute**, and a number of daemons needed only on a normally operating system. No host-specific or variable data is stored in */usr*. Also disallowed is the placement of directories directly under */usr* for large software packages. An exception to this rule is made for X11, which has a strong precedent for this location. The following subdirectories can be found under */usr*:

/usr/X11R6

> This directory contains files for XFree86. Because X is deployed directly under */usr* on many Unix systems, X breaks the rule that usually prohibits a custom */usr* directory for a software package.

/usr/bin

> The */usr/bin* directory is the primary location for user commands that are not considered essential for emergency system maintenance (and thus are stored here rather than in */bin*).

/usr/games

> It's unlikely that you'll find anything of significant interest here. This location was used for older console (text) games and utilities.

/usr/include

> */usr/include* is the standard location for *include* or *header* files, used for C and C++ programming.

/usr/lib

> This directory contains shared libraries that support various programs. FHS also allows the creation of software-specific directories here. For example, */usr/lib/perl5* contains the standard library of Perl modules that implement programming functions in that language.

/usr/local

> */usr/local* is the top level of another hierarchy of binary files, intended for use by the system administrator. It contains subdirectories much like */usr* itself, such as */bin*, */include*, */lib*, and */sbin*. After a fresh Linux installation, this directory contains no files but may contain an empty directory hierarchy. Example items that may be found here are locally created documents in */usr/local/doc* or */usr/local/man*, and executable scripts and binary utilities provided by the system administrator in */usr/local/bin*.

/usr/sbin

> The */usr/sbin* directory is the primary location for system administration commands that are not considered essential for emergency system maintenance (and thus are stored here rather than in */sbin*).

/usr/share

> */usr/share* contains a hierarchy of datafiles that are independent of, and thus can be shared among, various hardware architectures and operating system versions. This is in sharp contrast to architecture-dependant files such as those in */usr/bin*. For example, in an enterprise that uses both i386- and Alpha-based Linux systems, */usr/share* could be offered to all systems via NFS. However, since the two processors are not binary-compatible, */usr/bin* would have two NFS shares, one for each architecture.

> The information stored in */usr/share* is static data, such as the GNU **info** system files, dictionary files, and support files for software packages.

/usr/src

> */usr/src* contains Linux source code, if installed. For example, if kernel development files are installed, */usr/src/linux* contains the complete tree of source and configuration files necessary to build a custom kernel.

The */var* filesystem

The */var* filesystem contains data such as printer spools and log files that vary over time. Since variable data is always changing and growing, */var* is usually contained in a separate partition to prevent the root partition from filling. The following subdirectories can be found under */var*:

/var/account

> Some systems maintain process accounting data in this directory.

/var/cache

> */var/cache* is intended for use by programs for the temporary storage of intermediate data, such as the results of lengthy computations. Programs using this directory must be capable of regenerating the cached information at any time, which allows the system administrator to delete files as needed. Because it holds transient data, */var/cache* never has to be backed up.

/var/crash

> This directory holds crash dumps for systems that support that feature.

/var/games

> Older games may use this directory to store state information, user score data, and other transient items.

/var/lock

> Lock files, used by applications to signal their existence to other processes, are stored here. Lock files usually contain no data.

/var/log

> The */var/log* directory is the main repository for system log files, such as those created by the *syslog* system. For example, the default system log file is */var/log/messages*.

/var/mail

> This is the system mailbox, with mail files for each user. */var/mail* is a replacement for */var/spool/mail* and aligns FHS with many other Unix implementations. You may find that your Linux distribution still uses */var/spool/mail*.

/var/opt

> This directory is defined as a location for temporary files of programs stored in */opt*.

/var/run

> */var/run* contains various files describing the present state of the system. All such files may be deleted at system boot time. This is the default location for PID files, which contain the PIDs of the processes for which they are named. For example, if the Apache web server, **httpd**, is running as process number 534, */var/run/httpd.pid* will contain that number:

```
# cat /var/run/httpd.pid
534
```

> Such files are needed by utilities that must be able to find a PID for a running process. Also located here is the *utmp* file, used by commands such as **last** and **who**, to display logged-in users.

/var/spool

> The */var/spool* directory contains information that is queued for processing. Examples include print queues, outgoing mail, and crontab files.

/var/state

> The */var/state* directory is intended to contain information that helps applications preserve state across multiple invocations or multiple instances.

/var/tmp

> As with */tmp* in the root filesystem, */var/tmp* is used for storage of temporary files. Unlike */tmp*, the files in */var/tmp* are expected to survive across multiple system boots. The information found in */var/tmp* could be considered more persistent than information in */tmp*.

/var/yp

> This directory contains the database files of the Network Information Service (NIS), if implemented. NIS was formerly known as the *yellow pages* (not to be confused with the big yellow book).

Figure 1-5 depicts an example filesystem hierarchy. This figure is a graphical depiction of the partitioning scheme listed in Table 1-15 earlier in this chapter. The root partition contains full directories for */bin*, */dev*, */etc*, */lib*, */mnt*, */root*, and */sbin*.

Top-level directories */boot*, */home*, */opt*, */tmp*, */usr*, and */var* exist on the root file-system, but they are empty and act as mount points for other filesystems.

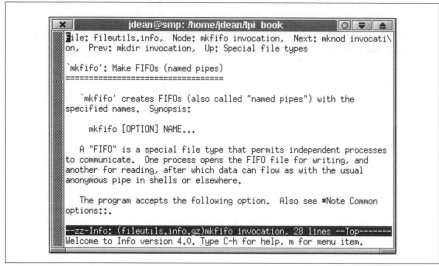

Figure 1-5: Example filesystem hierarchy

Linux annex

Since FHS migrated away from being a Linux-only document and expanded to cover other operating systems, information specific to any one operating system was moved to an *annex*. The only annex listed in v2.0 of FHS is the Linux annex, which mentions a few guidelines and makes allowances for the placement of additional program files in */sbin*. The Linux annex also mentions and supports the use of the */proc* filesystem for the processing of kernel, memory, and process information.

Where's that binary?

Compiled executable files, called *binary files,* or just *binaries,* can be located in a number of places in an FHS-compliant filesystem. However, it's easy to become a little confused over why a particular executable file is placed where it is in the FHS. This is particularly true for *bin* and *sbin* directories, which appear in multiple locations. Table 1-21 lists these directories and shows how each is used.

Table 1-21: Binary File Locations

	User Commands	*System Admininistration Commands*
Vendor-supplied, essential (*root* filesystem)	*/bin*	*/sbin*
Vendor-supplied, nonessential (*/usr* filesystem)	*/usr/bin*	*/usr/sbin*
Locally supplied, nonessential (*/usr* filesystem)	*/usr/local/bin*	*/usr/local/sbin*

Locating Files

FHS offers the Linux community an excellent resource that assures consistency across distributions and other operating systems. In practice, however, file location problems can be frustrating, and the need arises to find files in the system quickly. These file location tools are required for Exam 101: **which**, **find**, **locate**, **updatedb**, **whatis**, and **apropos**.

which uses the PATH variable to locate executable files. **find** searches specified areas in the filesystem. **updatedb**, **whatis**, and **apropos** utilize databases to do quick searches to identify and locate files. **locate** offers a quick alternative to **find** for filename searches and is suited for locating files that are not moved around in the filesystem. Without a fresh database to search, **locate** is not suitable for files recently created or renamed.

whatis and **apropos** work similarly to **locate** but use a different database. The **whatis** database is a set of files containing short descriptions of system commands, created by **makewhatis**. Note that these commands are not specifically mentioned in this Objective but may appear on Exam 101.

---

which

Syntax

which *command*

Description

Determine the location of *command* and display the full pathname of the executable program that the shell would launch to execute it. **which** has no options.

Example

Determine the shell that would be started by entering the *tcsh* command:

```
# which tcsh
/bin/tcsh
```

which is small and does only one thing: determines what executable program will be found and called by the shell. Such a search is particularly useful if you're having trouble with the setup of your PATH environment variable or if you are creating a new version of an existing utility and want to be certain you're executing the experimental version.

---

find

Syntax

find *paths expression*

Description

Locate files that match an *expression* starting at *paths* and continuing recursively. The **find** command has a rich set of *expression* directives for locating just about anything in the filesystem.

Example

To find files by name located in the *usr* directory hierarchy that might have something to do with the **csh** shell or its variants, you might use the **–name** *filename*
directive:

```
# find /usr -name "*csh*"
/usr/bin/sun-message.csh
/usr/doc/tcsh-6.08.00
/usr/doc/tcsh-6.08.00/complete.tcsh
/usr/doc/vim-common-5.3/syntax/csh.vim
/usr/man/man1/tcsh.1
/usr/share/apps/ktop/pics/csh.xpm
/usr/share/apps/ktop/pics/tcsh.xpm
/usr/share/emacs/20.3/etc/emacs.csh
/usr/share/vim/syntax/csh.vim
/usr/src/linux-2.2.5/fs/lockd/svcshare.c
```

Some of these results are clearly related to **csh** or to **tcsh**, while others are questionable. In addition, this command may take a while because **find** must traverse
the entire */usr* hierarchy, examining each filename for a match. This example
demonstrates that if filename wildcards are used, the entire string must be quoted
to prevent expansion by the shell prior to launching **find**.

find is among the most useful commands in the Linux administrator's toolkit and
has a variety of useful options. **find** is handy in certain cases. For example:

- You need to limit a search to a particular location in the filesystem.

- You must search for an attribute other than the filename.

- Files you are searching for were recently created or renamed, in which case
  locate may not be appropriate.

Unfortunately, **find** can take a long time to run. Refer to "Part 1: *GNU and Unix
Commands (Topic 1.3),* Objective 1: Work Effectively on the Unix Command
Line"for additional information on the **find** command.

On the Exam

You should have a general understanding of **find**. Remember that by default, **find** prints matching directory entries to the screen. However, detailed
knowledge of **find** options and usage are beyond the scope of LPIC Level 1
exams.

---

locate

Syntax

locate *patterns*

Description

Locate files whose names match one or more *patterns* by searching an index of
files previously created.

Example

Locate files by name in the entire directory hierarchy that might have something to do with the **csh** shell or its variants:

```
# locate "*csh*"
/home/jdean/.tcshrc
/root/.cshrc
/root/.tcshrc
/usr/bin/sun-message.csh
/usr/doc/tcsh-6.08.00
/usr/doc/tcsh-6.08.00/FAQ
/usr/doc/tcsh-6.08.00/NewThings
/usr/doc/tcsh-6.08.00/complete.tcsh
/usr/doc/tcsh-6.08.00/eight-bit.txt
/usr/doc/vim-common-5.3/syntax/csh.vim
/usr/man/man1/tcsh.1
/usr/share/apps/ktop/pics/csh.xpm
/usr/share/apps/ktop/pics/tcsh.xpm
/usr/share/emacs/20.3/etc/emacs.csh
/usr/share/vim/syntax/csh.vim
/usr/src/linux-2.2.5/fs/lockd/svcshare.c
/etc/csh.cshrc
/etc/profile.d/kde.csh
/etc/profile.d/mc.csh
/bin/csh
/bin/tcsh
```

The **locate** command must have a recent database to search, and that database must be updated periodically to incorporate changes in the filesystem. If the database is stale, using **locate** yields a warning:

```
# locate tcsh
locate: warning: database /var/lib/slocate/slocate.db' is
    more than 8 days old
```

---

updatedb

Syntax

updatedb [*options*]

Description

Refresh (or create) the *slocate* database in */var/lib/slocate/slocate.db*.

Option

-e *directories*
Exclude a comma-separated list of *directories* from the database.

Example

Refresh the *slocate* database, excluding files in temporary locations:

```
# updatedb -e "/tmp,/var/tmp,/usr/tmp,/afs,/net,/proc"
```

updatedb is typically executed periodically via **cron**.

Some Linux distributions (Debian, for example) come with a version of **updatedb** that accepts additional options that can be specified on the command line:

Additional options

–netpaths='*path1 path2 . . .***'**
 Add network *paths* to the search list.

–prunepaths='path1 path2 ...'
 Eliminate *paths* from the search list.

–prunefs='filesystems ...'
 Eliminate entire types of *filesystems*, such as NFS.

These options modify the behavior of **updatedb** on some Linux systems by prohibiting the parsing of certain filesystem locations and by adding others. There are a few more of these options than those listed here, but these three are special in that they can also be specified through the use of environment variables set prior to **updatedb** execution. The variables are NETPATHS, PRUNEPATHS, and PRUNEFS. These variables and the options to **updatedb** are discussed here because this Objective makes specific mention of *updatedb.conf*, a sort of control file for **updatedb**. Despite its name, *updatedb.conf* isn't really a configuration file, but rather a fragment of a Bourne shell script that sets these environment variables. Example 1-2 shows a sample *updatedb.conf* file.

Example 1-2: Sample updatedb.conf File

```
# This file sets environment variables used by updatedb
# filesystems which are pruned from updatedb database:
PRUNEFS="NFS nfs afs proc smbfs autofs auto iso9660"
export PRUNEFS

# paths which are pruned from updatedb database:
PRUNEPATHS="/tmp /usr/tmp /var/tmp /afs /amd /alex"
export PRUNEPATHS

# netpaths which are added:
NETPATHS="/mnt/fs3"
export NETPATHS
```

In this example, the PRUNEFS and PRUNEPATHS variables cause **updatedb** to ignore types of filesystems and particular paths, respectively. NETPATHS is used to add network paths from remote directory */mnt/fs3*.

updatedb.conf doesn't directly control **updatedb**, but eliminates the need for lengthy options on the **updatedb** command line, which can make **crontab** files a bit cleaner.

On the Exam

Remember that **updatedb** does not require configuration to execute. On systems that provide for configuration, *updatedb.conf* can specify a few extra options to **updatedb** by way of environment variables.

---

whatis

Syntax

whatis *keywords*

Description

Search the **whatis** database for exact matches to *keywords* and display results.

Example

```
# whatis mksw
mksw: nothing appropriate
```

apropos

Syntax

apropos *keywords*

Description

Search the **whatis** database for partial word matches to *keywords* and display results.

Example

```
# apropos mksw
mkswap (8)            - set up a Linux swap area
```

On the Exam

You must be familiar with the FHS concept and the contents of its major directories. Be careful about the differences between (and reasons for) */bin* and */sbin*, root partition and */usr* partition, and locally supplied commands. Also practice with various file location techniques and be able to differentiate among them.

Boot, Initialization, Shutdown, and Runlevels (Topic 2.6)

Even the most inexpensive PC has a fairly complex series of steps to execute on its way from idle hardware to productive system. When a system is powered on, a computer's electronics are in a random state and must be reset to a known condition. After this occurs, the CPU in the system begins processing instructions at a specific, hardcoded memory location in Read-Only Memory (ROM). For PCs, the ROM is usually called the Basic Input/Output System (BIOS). The startup instructions stored in the BIOS perform basic initialization chores to discover and configure peripheral hardware. When the system is initialized and ready, it begins looking in known locations for an operating system (or operating system loader software). This could be stored on fixed or removable disk media, or even placed in memory during initialization. Once an operating system is launched, it begins an initialization sequence of its own.

This section covers the latter portions of the boot process, from the point where the BIOS looks for an operating system, as required for Exam 101.* This Topic has two Objectives:

Objective 1: Boot the System
This Objective covers the Linux boot process, including boot-time kernel options, examining log file events, and the **dmesg** and **lilo** commands. We also examine some boot-related configuration files. Weight: 3.

Objective 2: Change Runlevels and Shutdown or Reboot System
Linux and many Unix systems share the concept of *runlevels*. A Linux runlevel describes a mode of operation, such as single-user mode or multiuser mode. Runlevels and the associated shutdown and system reboot topics are covered in this Objective. Weight: 3.

---

* The BIOS is covered in "Part 2: *Hardware and Architecture (Topic 1.1)*, Objective 1: Configure Fundamental System Hardware."

Objective 1: Boot the System

It is the Linux Loader's (LILO) job to launch a Linux kernel or other operating system at boot time (LILO configuration is described in "Part 2: *Linux Installation and Package Management (Topic 2.2)*, Objective 2: Install a Boot Manager." In some cases, that task requires the ability to deliver to the Linux kernel certain information, which may be required to configure peripherals. This information is sent using kernel parameters on the LILO command line.

Boot-Time Kernel Parameters

The Linux kernel has the capability to accept information at boot time in the form of a sort of command line. The idea is similar to an argument list in *name* or *name=value* forms that might be specified for a program. These values are used to supply the kernel with information that it may not be able to determine on its own. Kernel parameters can also be used to override known values. In either case, they convey vital information to hardware drivers compiled into the kernel.*

Kernel parameters are entered either in the *lilo* configuration file or at the LILO prompt. For example, to boot with a root partition other than the one specified in Example 1-1 (see "Part 1: *Devices, Linux Filesystems, and the Filesystem Hierarchy Standard (Topic 2.4)*, Objective 3: Control Filesystem Mounting and Unmounting"), the user could enter the following at the LILO prompt:

```
LILO: linux root=/dev/hda9
```

This command boots the kernel whose label is linux and overrides the default value of */dev/hda1* to */dev/hda9* for the root filesystem.

On the Exam

There are far too many kernel parameters to list in this book. Consequently, you must familiarize yourself with them in general terms so that you can answer questions on their form. Remember that they are specified to LILO *after* a kernel image name, and that they consist of either a single item, such as *ro*, or *name=value* pairs such as *root=/dev/hda2*. Multiple parameters are space-separated.

There are many boot-time kernel parameters. While unlikely, depending upon your hardware configuration and use of modules, you may need to use these parameters to specify resource settings (such as I/O ports and interrupts) for hardware such as Ethernet or SCSI adapters. For detailed information on these parameters, see the Linux */usr/doc/HOWTO/BootPrompt-HOWTO*.

Introduction to Kernel Module Configuration

Modern Linux kernels are *modular*, in that modules of code traditionally compiled into the kernel (say, a sound driver) are loaded as needed. The modules are

---

* Boot prompt arguments do not affect kernel modules.

separate from the kernel and can be inserted and removed by the superuser if necessary. While parameters in the *lilo* configuration file and the **lilo** command line affect the kernel, they do not control kernel modules.

To send parameters to a kernel module, they are inserted into the file */etc/conf.modules* (*/etc/modules.conf* on some Linux distributions) as text. Common module options you may find in your module configuration file are I/O address, interrupt, and DMA channel settings for your sound device. This file will also probably carry PCMCIA driver information when installed on laptops. Module configuration will probably be handled by your distribution's installation procedure but may require modifications if hardware is added or changed later. Example 1-3 shows a typical */etc/conf.modules* file.

Example 1-3: A Typical /etc/conf.modules File

```
alias scsi_hostadapter aic7xxx
alias eth0 3c59x
alias parport_lowlevel parport_pc
pre-install pcmcia_core /etc/rc.d/init.d/pcmcia start
alias sound opl3sa2
pre-install sound insmod sound dmabuf=1
alias midi opl3
options opl3 io=0x388
options opl3sa2 mss_io=0x530 irq=5 dma=0 dma2=1 mpu_io=0x388
    io=0x370
```

On the Exam

Read questions that ask about kernel or module parameters carefully. Kernel options can be passed on the LILO command line; module options are specified in *conf.modules*.

In this example, note first that an alias named *sound* is created for the audio driver *opl3sa2*. Further, you can see that various I/O port, interrupt request (IRQ), and DMA channel settings are specified for that driver. The installer determines the settings. Unless you're aware of a specific parameter or option that needs to be sent to a specific kernel module, you probably won't need to change *conf.modules*.

Kernel boot-time messages

As the Linux kernel boots, it gives detailed status of its progress in the form of console messages.* Modules that are loaded also yield status messages. These

---

* These messages may take users used to other, less verbose, operating systems by surprise due to their detailed nature. You'll learn a lot about your hardware by booting a Linux kernel.

messages contain important information regarding the health and configuration of your hardware. Generally, the kinds of messages you will see are:

- Kernel identification

- Memory and CPU information

- Information on detected hardware, such as pointers (mice), serial ports, and disks

- Partition information and checks

- Network initialization

- Kernel module output for modules that load at boot time

These messages are displayed on the system console at boot time but often scroll off the screen too fast to be read. The messages are also logged to disk. They can easily be viewed using the **dmesg** command, which displays messages logged at the last system boot. For example, to view messages from the last boot sequence, simply pipe the output of **dmesg** to **less**:

```
# dmesg | less
```

It is also common to use **dmesg** to dump boot messages to a file for later inspection or archive, by simply redirecting the output:

```
# dmesg > bootmsg.txt
```

NOTE

For more information on the Linux kernel, including the compilation and installation of a new kernel and modules, see Part 2, *Kernel (Topic 1.5)*.

Reviewing system logs

In addition to kernel messages, many other boot-time messages will be logged using the *syslog* system. Such messages will be found in the system log files such as */var/log/messages*. For example, **dmesg** displays information on your network adapter when it was initialized. However, the configuration and status of that adapter is logged in */var/log/messages* as a result of the network startup. When examining and debugging boot activity on your system, you need to review both kinds of information. *syslog*, its configuration, and log file examination are covered in "Part 1: *Administrative Tasks (Topic 2.11)*, Objective 3: Configure and Use System Log Files."

Objective 2: Change Runlevels and Shutdown or Reboot the System

As mentioned in the introduction, Linux and many Unix systems share the concept of runlevels. This concept specifies how a system is used by controlling which services are running. For example, a system that operates a web server program is configured to boot and initiate processing in a runlevel designated for sharing data, at which point the web server is started. However, the same system would

---

not run the web server in a runlevel used for emergency administration, when all but the most basic services are shut down.

Runlevels are specified by the integers 0 through 6 as well as a few single characters. Runlevels 0 and 6 are unusual in that they specify the transitional states of shutdown and reboot, respectively. By instructing Linux to enter runlevel 0, it begins a clean shutdown procedure. Similarly, the use of runlevel 6 begins a reboot. The remaining runlevels differ in meaning slightly among Linux distributions and other Unix systems.

When a Linux system boots, the **init** process is responsible for taking the system to the default runlevel, which is usually either 3 or 5. Typical runlevel meanings are listed in Table 1-22.

Table 1-22: Typical Runlevels

Runlevel	Description
0	Halt the system; runlevel 0 is a special transitional device used by administrators to shut down the system quickly. This, of course, shouldn't be a default runlevel, because the system would never come up—it would shutdown immediately when the kernel launches the **init** process. Also see runlevel 6.
1, s, S	Single-user mode, sometimes called "maintenance mode." In this mode, system services such as network interfaces, web servers, and file sharing are not started. This mode is usually used for interactive filesystem maintenance.
2	Multiuser with no NFS file sharing.
3	Full multiuser mode. This is often used as the default runlevel by the **init** process.
4	Typically unused.
5	Full multiuser mode with GUI login. In runlevel 3, **init** does not attempt to launch the X11 system. In runlevel 5, X11 is started and the text-mode login is replaced with a GUI login. This is often used as the default runlevel but can cause problems if X11 cannot start for some reason.
6	Reboot the system; used by system administrators. Just like runlevel 0, this is a transitional device for administrators. It shouldn't be a default runlevel because the system would eternally reboot.

Single-User Mode

Runlevel 1, the *single-user* runlevel,* is a bare-bones operating environment intended for system maintenance. In single-user mode, remote logins are disabled, networking is disabled, and most daemons are shut down. One common reason

---

* Runlevel 1 can also be specified using *S* or *s*. The three designations are equivalent.

you might be forced to use single-user mode is to correct problems with a corrupt filesystem that the system cannot handle automatically. Single-user mode is also used for the installation of software and other system configuration tasks that must be performed with no user activity.

If you wish to boot directly into single-user mode, you may specify it at boot time at the LILO prompt. After entering your kernel image name, give the argument **single** or simply the numeral **1**. These arguments are not interpreted as kernel arguments but are instead passed along to the **init** process. For example, if your kernel image is named "*linux,*" these commands would take the system to single-user mode, bypassing the default:

LILO: **linux single**

or:

LILO: **linux 1**

To switch into single-user mode from another runlevel, you can simply issue a runlevel change command with **init**:

init 1

If others are using resources on the system, they will be unpleasantly surprised, so be sure to give users plenty of warning before doing this. To change from the text-mode login to the X login screen, simply initiate the X-enabled runlevel, usually 5:

init 5

On the Exam

Make certain that you understand the use of the transitional runlevels 0 and 6, the single-user runlevel, and the difference between GUI and text login configurations. You should also be prepared to demonstrate how to change the runlevel of a running system.

If X is configured improperly, starting the X login screen will lead to problems because X may die. It will be automatically restarted, and this will go on in an infinite loop until you reconfigure X. It is important to be sure X is working correctly before attempting the GUI logon.*

Overview of the /etc/rc.d directory tree and the init process

By themselves, the runlevels listed in Table 1-22 don't mean much. It's what the **init** process does as a result of a runlevel specification or change that affects the system. The actions of **init** for each runlevel are derived from Unix System V–style initialization and are specified in a series of directories and script files under */etc/rc.d*.

---

* The X Window System is described in Part 2, *X (Topic 2.10).*

When a Linux system starts, a number of scripts in */etc/rc.d* are used to initially configure the system and switch among runlevels:[*]

rc.sysinit

This file is a script launched by **init** at boot time. It handles some essential chores to ready the system for use, such as mounting filesystems.

rc.local

This file is a script that is called by *rc.sysinit*. It contains local customizations affecting system startup and provides an alternative to modifying *rc.sysinit*. Many administrators prefer to avoid changing *rc.sysint* because those changes could be lost during a system upgrade. The contents of *rc.local* are not lost in an upgrade.

rc

This file is a script that is used to change between runlevels.

The job of starting and stopping system services such as web servers is handled by the files and symbolic links in */etc/rc.d/init.d* and by a series of runlevel-specific directories, *rc0.d* through *rc6.d*:

init.d

This directory contains individual startup/shutdown scripts for each service on the system. For example, the script */etc/rc.d/init.d/httpd* is a Bourne shell script that safely starts or stops the Apache web server. These scripts have a standard basic form and take a single argument. Valid arguments are at least the words **start** and **stop**. Additional arguments are sometimes required by the script; examples are **restart**, **status**, and sometimes **reload** (to ask the service to reconfigure itself without exiting). Administrators can use these scripts directly to start and stop services. For example, to restart Apache, an administrator could issue commands like these:

```
# /etc/rc.d/init.d/httpd stop
# /etc/rc.d/init.d/httpd start
```

or simply:

```
# /etc/rc.d/init.d/httpd restart
```

Either form would completely shut down and start up the web server. To ask Apache to remain running but reread its configuration file, you might enter:

```
# /etc/rc.d/init.d/httpd reload
```

This has the effect of sending the SIGHUP signal to the running **httpd** process, instructing it to initialize.[†]

If you add a new service (a daemon, intended to always run in the background), one of these initialization files may be installed automatically for you. In other cases, you may need to create one yourself, or as a last resort, place startup commands in the *rc.local* file.

---

[*] System initialization techniques differ among Linux distributions. The examples here are typical of a Red Hat Linux system.

[†] Signals such as SIGHUP are covered in "Part 1: *GNU and Unix Commands (Topic 1.3)*, Objective 5: Create, Monitor, and Kill Processes."

Directories rc0.d through rc6.d

The initialization scripts in */etc/rc.d/init.d* are not directly executed by the **init** process. Instead, each of the directories */etc/rc.d/rc0.d* through *rc6.d* contain symbolic (soft) links* to the scripts in directory *init.d.* When the **init** process enters runlevel *n*, it examines all of the links in the associated *rcn.d* directory. These links are given special names in the form of [*K| S*][*nn*][*init.d_name*], described as follows:

K and S prefixes

The *K* and *S* prefixes mean **kill** and **start**, respectively. A runlevel implies a state in which certain services are running and all others are not. The *S* prefix is used for all services that are to be running (**start**ed) for the runlevel. The *K* prefix is used for all other services, which should not be running.

nn

Sequence number. This part of the link name is a two-digit integer (with a leading zero, if necessary). It specifies the relative order for services to be started or stopped. The lowest number is the first link executed by **init**, and the largest number is the last. There are no hard-and-fast rules for choosing these numbers, but it is important when adding a new service to be sure that it starts *after* any other required services are already running. If two services have an identical start order number, the order is indeterminate but probably alphabetical.

init.d_name

By convention, the name of the script being linked is used as the last part of the link name. **init** does not use this name, but excluding it makes things difficult for human readers.

As an example, when **init** enters runlevel 3 at boot time, all of the links with the *S* prefix in */etc/init.d/rc3.d* will be executed in the order given by their sequence number. They will be run with the single argument **start** to launch their respective services. After the last of the scripts is executed, the requirements for runlevel 3 are satisfied.

Setting the default runlevel

To determine the default runlevel at boot time, **init** reads the configuration file */etc/inittab* looking for a line containing the word *initdefault*, which will look like this:

```
id:n:initdefault:
```

In the preceding, n is a valid runlevel number, such as 3. This number is used as the default runlevel by **init**. The *S* scripts in the corresponding */etc/rc.d/rcn.d* directory are executed to start their respective services. If you change the default runlevel for your system, it will most likely be to switch between the standard text login runlevel and the GUI login runlevel. In any case, never change the default runlevel to 0 or 6, or your system will not boot to a usable state.

---

* These symbolic links could also be files, but using script files in each of the directories would be an administrative headache, as changes to any of the startup scripts would mean identical edits to multiple files.

Determining your system's runlevel

From time to time, you may be unsure just what runlevel your system is in. For example, you may have logged into a Linux system from a remote location and not know how it was booted or maintained. You may also need to know what runlevel your system was in prior to its current runlevel—perhaps wondering if the system was last in single-user mode for maintenance.

To determine this runlevel information, use the **runlevel** command. When executed, **runlevel** displays the previous and current runlevel as integers, separated by a space, on standard output. If no runlevel change has occurred since the system was booted, the previous runlevel is displayed as the letter *N*. For a system that was in runlevel 3 and is now in runlevel 5, the output is:

```
# runlevel
3 5
```

For a system with a default runlevel of 5 that has just completed booting, the output would be:

```
# runlevel
N 5
```

On the Exam

Determining the present and previous runlevel—including the correct interpretation of the *N* response in the output from **runlevel**—is important.

---

runlevel does not alter the system runlevel. To do this, use either the **init** or the **telinit** commands.

Changing runlevels with init and telinit

The **init** process is the "grandfather" of all processes. If used as a command on a running system, **init** sends signals to the executing **init** process, instructing it to change to a specified runlevel. You must be logged in as the superuser to use the **init** command.

---

init

Syntax

```
init n
```

Description

The number of the runlevel, *n*, can be changed to an integer from 0 through 6 or with the letter arguments S, s, or q. The numeric arguments instruct **init** to switch to the specified runlevel. The S and s runlevels are equivalent to runlevel 1. The q argument is used to tell **init** to reread its configuration file, */etc/inittab*.

Examples

Shut down immediately:

```
# init 0
```

Reboot immediately:

```
# init 6
```

Go to single-user mode immediately:

```
# init 1
```

or:

```
# init s
```

The **telinit** command may be used in place of **init**. **telinit** is simply a hard link to **init**, and the two may be used interchangeably.

Generally, you will use a runlevel change for the following reasons:

* To shut down the system using runlevel 0.

* To go to single-user mode using runlevel 1.

* To reboot the system using runlevel 6.

* To switch between text-based and X11 GUI login modes, usually runlevels 3 and 5, respectively.

On the Exam

Remember that **init** and **telinit** can be used interchangeably, since they both point to the same file.

If you are working on a personal Linux workstation with no logged-in users, shared files, or other shared resources, changing the state of your system is pretty much at your discretion. You're aware of the important processes that are active and will surely save your work before any runlevel change. You can then simply direct **init** to change the runlevel as desired. However, if you are working on a system acting as a file or web server, or some other public resource, changing a runlevel without notification could be a disaster for other users. It is imperative to notify users before any major system changes are made. Using **init** to shutdown the system doesn't automatically provide this courtesy, and in these situations the **shutdown** command is preferred.

System shutdown with shutdown

When **shutdown** is initiated, all users who are logged into terminal sessions are notified that the system is going down. In addition, further logins are blocked to prevent new users from entering the system as it is being shut down.

shutdown

Syntax

shutdown [*options*] *time* [*warning message*]

Description

The **shutdown** command brings the system down in a secure, organized fashion. By default, **shutdown** takes the system to single-user mode. Options can be used to either halt or reboot instead. The command uses **init** with an appropriate runlevel argument to affect the system change.

The mandatory *time* argument tells the shutdown command when to initiate the shutdown procedure. It can be a time of day in the form *hh:mm*, or it can be in the form +*n*, where *n* is a number of minutes to wait. The *time* can also be the word *now*, in which case the shutdown proceeds immediately. If the *time* specified is more than 15 minutes away, **shutdown** waits until 15 minutes remain before shutdown before making its first announcement.

If *warning message* (a text string) is provided, it is used in the system's announcements to end users. No quoting is necessary for *warning message* unless the message includes special characters such as * or &.

Frequently used options

−f

Fast boot; this skips filesystem checks on the next boot.

−F

Force filesystem checks on the next boot.

−h

Halt after shutdown.

−k

Don't really shutdown, but send the warning messages anyway.

−r

Reboot after shutdown.

Examples

To reboot immediately:

```
# shutdown -r now
```

To reboot in five minutes with a maintenance message:

```
# shutdown -r +5 System maintenance is required
```

To halt the system just before midnight tonight:

```
# shutdown -h 23:59
```

The two most common uses of shutdown by individuals are:

```
# shutdown -h now
```

and

```
# shutdown -r now
```

These initiate for immediate halts and reboots, respectively. Although it's not really a bug, the **shutdown** manpage notes that omission of the required *time* argument yields unusual results. If you do forget the *time* argument, **shutdown** will probably exit without an error message. This might lead you to believe that a shutdown is starting, so it's important to be sure of your syntax when using **shutdown**.

On the Exam

Make certain that you are aware of the differences between system shutdown using **init** (and its link **telinit**) and **shutdown**.

Documentation
(Topic 1.8)

As system administrators, our ability to navigate through daily computing tasks, both common and esoteric, depends to a large degree on our access to documentation. Even experts must have detailed system information available and refer to it on a routine basis. It is appropriate then that the LPI has made Linux documentation a minor but important part of Exam 101. There are four Objectives for documentation:

Objective 1: Use and Manage Local System Documentation
This Objective covers two primary areas of documentation on Linux systems: the **man** (manual) facility and files stored in */usr/doc*. Weight: 5.

Objective 2: Find Linux Documentation on the Internet
Just as Linux itself is available via the Internet, a variety of documentation is also available. Weight: 2.

Objective 3: Write System Documentation
As a system administrator, you'll no doubt be creating programs and utilities of your own, often for consumption by other users. At those times, you'll also need to provide documentation for your work and make it available using man and info pages. Weight: 1.

Objective 4: Provide User Support
One of the biggest challenges in the IT world is providing excellent end user support. A methodical approach, which draws on your experience and available system documentation, is needed to respond to the variety of problems that are presented to a help desk. Weight: 1.

Objective 1: Use and Manage Local System Documentation

Each Linux system is configured out of the box with extensive documentation from programmers, authors, and other contributors. Some of this documentation is formal while some is quite informal. Combined, this documentation offers a comprehensive body of knowledge for Linux users.

Text and Paging

At a fundamental level, documents stored electronically may be encoded in a bewildering variety of formats. For example, most word processors use proprietary file formats to store characters, text formatting, and printing control languages such as Adobe PostScript to manage printer hardware. While these relatively modern features can be found on Linux systems, most of the documents and configuration files are in plain text.

In the context of Linux systems, "plain text" means files or streams of both printable characters and control characters. Each is represented using a standard encoding scheme, such as the American Standard Code for Information Interchange (ASCII) and its relatives. Text files are most conveniently viewed using a *paging* program.

Paging programs

The most popular pager for Unix systems was once the **more** command, so named because it gave you "one more screen." **more** exists on Linux systems and probably every recent Unix variant; however, **more** is somewhat limited in its capability. The **less** command (so named because, of course, "less is more!") is more commonly used. The **less** command is a full-featured text pager that emulates **more** but offers an extended set of capabilities.

One particularly important feature of **less** is that it does not read all of its input before starting, which makes it faster for large input than an editor. **less** also offers many useful features and is available for almost every operating environment.

less begins execution by first examining the environment in which it is running. It needs to know some things about the terminal (or window) in which its output will be displayed. Once that's known, **less** formats the text and displays the first screen's output. The last line of the screen is reserved for user interaction with the program. **less** will display a colon on the first column of the last line and leave the cursor there. This colon is a command prompt, awaiting command input from the user. Most commands to **less** are single-character entries, and **less** will act upon them immediately and without a subsequent carriage return (this is known as *cbreak* mode). The most basic command to **less** (and **more**) is a single space, which instructs the pager to move ahead in the text by one screen. Table 1-23 lists commonly used **less** commands.

Table 1-23: Commonly Used less Commands

Command	Description
Space	Scroll forward one screen.
D	Scroll forward one-half screen.
Return	Scroll forward one line.
B	Scroll backward one screen.
U	Scroll backward one-half screen.
Y	Scroll backward one line.
g	Go to the beginning of the text (could be slow with large amounts of text).
G	Go to the end of the text (could be slow with large amounts of text).
/pattern	Search forward for *pattern*, which can be a regular expression.
?pattern	Search backward for *pattern*, which can be a regular expression.
H	Display a help screen.
:n	Display next file from command line (two-character command).
:p	Display previous file from command line (two-character command).

less has a rich command set, and its behavior can be modified as needed for your use. See the **less** manpage for further details.

Pagers are important to the topic of manpages because they provide the user with an interface to the **man** program. For each **man** command you enter, the **man** program works quietly to locate a manual page (or pages) to match your query, then displays the result using a pager.

The man Facility

Traditional computer manuals covered everything from physical maintenance to programming libraries. While the books were convenient, many users didn't always want to dig through printed documentation. So, as space became available, the **man** (for *manual*) facility was created to put the books on the system, allowing users immediate access to the information they needed.

There is a manpage for most commands on your system. There are also manpages for important files, library functions, shells, languages, devices, and other features. The **man** facility is to your system what a dictionary is to your written language. That is, nearly everything is defined in exacting detail, but you probably need to know in advance just what you're looking for. Manpages are generally written for those who already have an idea of what the item in question does, but regardless of your level of experience, manpages are invaluable.

man

Syntax

man [*options*] [*section*] *command*

Description

Format and display manpages from manual *section* on the topic of *command* using a pager. If *section* is omitted, the first manpage found is displayed.

Frequently used options

-a

> Normally, **man** exits after displaying a single manpage. The **-a** option instructs **man** to display all manpages that match *name*, in a sequential fashion.

-d

> Display debugging information.

-w

> Print the locations of manpages instead of displaying them.

Example 1

View a manpage for **mkfifo**:

```
$ man mkfifo
...
```

Results for the first manpage found are scrolled on the screen using a pager.

Example 2

Determine what manpages are available for **mkfifo**:

```
$ man -wa mkfifo
/usr/man/man1/mkfifo.1
/usr/man/man3/mkfifo.3
```

This shows that two manpages are available, one in section 1 (*mkfifo.1*) of the manual and another in section 3 (*mkfifo.3*). See the next section for a description of manpage sections.

Example 3

Display the **mkfifo** manpage from manual section 3:

```
$ man 3 mkfifo
```

Manual sections

Manpages are grouped into *sections*, and there are times when you should know the appropriate section in which to search for an item. For example, if you were interested in the **mkfifo** C-language function rather than the command, you must tell the **man** program to search the section on library functions (in this case, section 3, *Linux Programmer's Manual*):

```
$ man 3 mkfifo
```

An alternative would be to have the **man** program search all manual sections:

```
$ man -a mkfifo
```

The first example returns the *mkfifo(3)* manpage regarding the library function. The second returns pages for both the command and the function. In this case, the pages are delivered separately; terminating the pager on the first manpage with **Ctrl-C** causes the second to be displayed.

Manual sections are numbered 1 through 9 and N. They are searched in the order shown in Table 1-24 by default.

Table 1-24: Man Sections and Search Order

Section	Description
1	Executable programs or shell commands
8	System administration commands
2	System calls
3	Library calls
4	Special files (usually found in */dev*)
5	File formats and conventions
6	Games (sorry, no Quake here!)
7	Macro packages and conventions
9	Kernel routines
N	Tcl/Tk commands

Manpage format

Most manpages are presented in a concise format with information grouped under well-known standard headings such as those shown in Table 1-25. Other manpage headings depend on the context of the individual manpage.

Table 1-25: Standard Manpage Headings

Heading	Description
Name	The name of the item, along with a description
Synopsis	A complete description of syntax or usage
Description	A brief description of the item
Options	Detailed information on each command-line option (for commands)
Return values	Information on function return values (for programming references)
See also	A list of related items that may be helpful
Bugs	Descriptions of unusual program behavior or known defects
Files	A list of important files related to the item, such as configuration files

Table 1-25: Standard Manpage Headings (continued)

Heading	Description
Copying or Copyright	A description of how the item is to be distributed or protected
Authors	A list of those who are responsible for the item

man mechanics

System manpages are stored in */usr/man* and elsewhere. At any time, the manual pages available to the **man** command are contained within directories configured in your **man** configuration file, */etc/man.config*. This file contains directives to the **man**, telling it where to search for pages (the MANPATH directive), the paging program to use (PAGER), and many others. This file essentially controls how **man** works on your system. To observe this, use the debug (**-d**) option to **man** to watch as it constructs a *manpath* (a directory search list) and prepares to display your selection:

```
$ man -d mkfifo
```

Information in /usr/doc

Manpages are particularly useful when you know what you're looking for, or at least have some good leads on how to find it. However, they are not tutorial in nature, nor do they often describe overall concepts. Fortunately, individuals in the Linux world not only contribute their programming skills, but many also generate excellent tutorial documents to assist others with features, procedures, or common problems. Many of these documents end up as HOWTO guides, FAQs (lists of Frequently Asked Questions), README files, or even exhaustive user manuals. These documents are often part of the source distribution of a particular program, and while valuable, don't fit elsewhere on the Linux system and are deposited in */usr/doc*. Most of these files are ASCII text, which can be viewed with a pager, such as **less**, or with your favorite text editor. Some documents may be written in HTML for use with your web browser. Some text files may also be compressed with the **gzip** program, and thus have the *.gz* extension. The handy **zless** utility allows you to page these files without first decompressing them.

The contents of */usr/doc* can be classified broadly into these categories:

Package-related
> These documents are typically useful snippets of information included with program source distributions. Packages offering this type of documentation will install a subdirectory in */usr/doc* that contains the documentation files and may be specific to a version of the package.

> For example, */usr/doc/tcsh-6.08.00* contains the following files related to the **tcsh** shell, Version 6.08.00:

FAQ
> A list of frequently asked questions about **tcsh**

NewThings
> Aptly named, contains descriptions of new features in this release (and previous releases) of **tcsh**

Complete.tcsh

An interesting portion of source code from **tcsh**

eight-bit.txt

A description of ways to use 8-bit (international) characters with **tcsh**

In this example, no general documentation is included in */usr/doc*, though this particular command has a thorough manpage. Of the files available, the FAQ and perhaps the version information file (see the next section, "Info Pages") will be of interest to most users.

Frequently Asked Questions

A Frequently Asked Questions (FAQ) page contains detailed information in a Q&A format. FAQ topics can range from simple questions such as "What is Linux," to more specific questions about how to configure or troubleshoot a particular program. While FAQs may be found for specific packages in a */usr/ doc* package directory (as with **tcsh**), a number of important FAQs reside in */usr/doc/FAQ*. FAQ lists are generated in many different formats. Inside */usr/ doc/FAQ* are subdirectories for these formats, including:

html

HTML files suitable for viewing with a web browser

ps

PostScript files, suitable for viewing with a reader such as Ghostscript or in a printer-friendly format

txt

Plain text files

HOWTO documents

A HOWTO document details information on completing a particular task. They can be as simple as a narrative describing one individual's success in configuring some software under Linux, or they can be a complete author's description. For example, */usr/doc/HOWTO/Printing-HOWTO* (a text file) tells you how to configure a printer under Linux. HOWTOs often serve as reference material for new administrators working with printers. Like FAQs, many HOWTO documents are stored in their own directory under */usr/doc/HOWTO*. Some smaller HOWTO documents are titled *mini-HOWTOs*, which are generally of limited scope and can be found in */usr/doc/HOWTO/mini*.

Info Pages

Among the many contributions from the Free Software Foundation (*http:// www.fsf.org*) is the GNU documentation format called *info*. Info pages are part of a system called *Texinfo*, which uses a single source file to display information on screen and on paper. Texinfo is hypertext and creates a browser-like interface on a terminal or terminal window (Emacs users will recognize the menu system as the editor's online help). For GNU software, Texinfo is the definitive documentation mechanism. Texinfo can be viewed by running the **info** command. For example, the Texinfo document on **mkfifo** can be displayed using the following command:

```
$ info mkfifo
```

The result will be a display similar to the example in Figure 1-6.

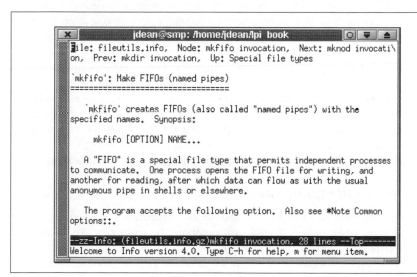

Figure 1-6: Info display in a terminal window

Basic navigation commands for the info system are listed in Table 1-26.

Table 1-26: Info Commands

Command	Description
Tab	Move among hypertext links.
Enter	Follow hypertext links.
d	Return to the top (directory node) of the menu.
?	List all info commands.
p and n	Move to previous and next pages, respectively.
u	Move up one level in the Texinfo hierarchy.
q	Terminate the system.
h	Show a primer for first-time users.
/*string*	Enter a string.
/*pattern*	Search forward for *pattern*, which can be a regular expression.

Manpages and other types of system documentation are packaged and installed by default with most Linux distributions. For example, this means that both the manpage and executable program for **wc** are contained in the **textutils** package.

Other documentation, such as LDP guides and HOWTOs, may be contained in standalone packages, depending on the distribution.

Oddities

Occasionally you'll come across an application or program that provides excellent documentation but places it in nonstandard locations. Perl is one such program. Perl's online documentation is very thorough and detailed. However, Perl uses the man facility to document not just the syntax and options for the perl program, but just about anything you'd want to know about the Perl interpreter and language. By adding a large number of man targets, the Perl distribution documents its function library, its FAQ, data structures, syntax, and many others. This extensive use of man ensures that the Perl documentation will be available to anyone who needs it. However, despite Perl's ubiquitous presence on the Linux system, it is not mentioned in */usr/doc*. It's worth remembering that documentation for the concept you're after is probably available, but you may need to check multiple sources.

Using the locate Command

While the availability of these various sources of information is reassuring, finding what you want when time is limited can sometimes be frustrating. To assist, most Linux systems will periodically create a database of files on the system that you can query using the locate command. If the database is configured correctly, such a query returns all instances of the command or command fragment you enter. For example, entering a locate request for the gzip utility, using only a fragment of "gzip," yields something similar to this:

```
$ locate gzi
/usr/bin/gzip
/usr/doc/gzip-1.2.4
/usr/doc/gzip-1.2.4/NEWS
/usr/doc/gzip-1.2.4/README
/usr/info/gzip.info.gz
/usr/man/man1/gzip.1
/bin/gzip
```

These results can be extremely helpful, as they tell you:

*   The only item matching "*gzi*" is gzip, because nothing other than *gzip* was found.

*   Exactly where gzip is located in the filesystem (*/bin/gzip*, and its symbolic link */usr/bin/gzip*).

*   That there is a package directory under */usr/doc* (*/usr/doc/gzip-1.2.4*).

*   That there are both man and info pages for gzip.

*   gzip is a user command, because its manpage is found in section 1 (*/usr/man/man1*).

Typically, to proceed from this point with researching **gzip**, you would use **info gzip** or perhaps **man gzip**.

NOTE

locate is dependent on a database created by the **updatedb** command. This utility searches the filesystem and constructs the index used by **locate**. Depending on your system's configuration, this update could be set to occur periodically at night when your system might be off. The cron facility is used to schedule these updates. Many routine tasks such as the use of updatedb will be placed in special files under the /etc directory, grouped for their frequency. The /etc/crontab file contains instructions for cron to execute the commands in these special files on a routine basis. In this case, your locate database may be stale. To refresh the database, you can run **updatedb** manually or leave your system running overnight to execute periodic updates. See "Part 1: *Devices, Linux Filesystems, and the Filesystem Hierarchy Standard (Topic 2.4)*, Objective 8: Find System Files and Place Files in the Correct Location" for more on **locate** and **updatedb**.

Objective 2: Find Linux Documentation on the Internet

No doubt you've heard media reports regarding the genesis of Linux from a bunch of hackers, the profits of the major distributions, high-profile corporate relationships with Linux, and Linux as a Wall Street darling. It is well known that coders around the world are contributing to the Linux code base. Rarely mentioned, however, are the many dedicated writers working in the public domain to make sure that Linux is as well understood as it is stable. Most of the people who contribute to the LDP do so on their own time, providing information learned from their own experiences. In most cases, the people who write for the LDP provide their names and email addresses so you can contact them with questions that remain unanswered. These writers are partially responsible for the widespread growth of Linux, because they make it understandable to individuals through documentation efforts not usually seen with commercial software.

The Linux Documentation Project

Most of the documentation in */usr/doc* and elsewhere on a Linux system is part of an organized approach to system documentation. The Linux Documentation Project, or *LDP*, is a loosely knit team of writers, proofreaders, and editors who work together to create the definitive set of documentation for Linux. The main web site can be found at *http://www.linuxdoc.org* and at many mirror sites throughout the world.

The LDP contains a collection of freely contributed documents. Like Linux, all of the LDP's content may be freely distributed, copied, and even published for a fee

---

without royalties to authors or to the LDP. Documents that are contributed to the LDP can be licensed a variety of ways. The LDP offers its own licensing terms, but authors aren't tied to using it. Some have opted to write their own license, while others have published their work under the GNU Public License (GPL). The Free Software Foundation has recently produced the GNU Free Documentation License (GFDL), which may become a standard for many of the LDP content.

The scope of the LDP is broad, ranging from online documents such as manpages to complete books in the form of reference guides. Some of the documents have software-style version numbers to assist with keeping up-to-date. Some of the more commonly used LDP reference guides include:

- Installation and Getting Started Guide

- The Linux Users' Guide

- The Linux System Administrators' Guide

- The Linux Network Administrators' Guide

- The Linux Programmer's Guide

- The Linux Kernel

- The Linux Kernel Hackers' Guide

- The Linux Kernel Module Programming Guide

Some of these LDP guides have been published in traditional book form, with mixed success. Any publisher can produce its own edition of the text, but since content must be identical, competing publishers can find themselves in a discounting exercise. This, coupled with frequent and unadvertised modifications, makes printed versions of LDP documents a speculative business venture at best.

Usenet Newsgroups

Usenet newsgroups can be thought of as a worldwide bulletin board service, with topics beyond your imagination (some of which probably belong beyond your imagination!). Unlike the older traditional proprietary bulletin board services you may remember from the early online days, Usenet is a distributed system, where messages are posted to a user's local *news server* in a *newsgroup*. The message is then copied among thousands of news servers worldwide that also serve that same newsgroup. Some newsgroups are moderated by a responsible party to keep the content from getting out of hand. Many are not monitored at all and are a free-for-all of opinions, ideas, and occasional off-topic color.

You can access Usenet content through your Internet Service Provider's news server, if one is offered, or you may use a web-based news reading service, such as Google Groups (*http://groups.google.com*). Regardless of the method you choose, the content is the same. Messages posted to newsgroups are stored on your news server and not on a remote origin server. This fact sometimes leads ISPs and corporations to abandon news services altogether, due to the sheer volume of information that gets relayed on a daily basis.

If you use a Usenet news server, you will read messages with a *news reader* application. Many mail programs and web browsers contain news readers that communicate with Usenet news servers. Standalone GUI- and text-based news readers are also available. Since Usenet messages are plain text, they can be viewed by any paging or editing program. However, many news readers optionally group messages by thread, which makes following a particular discussion easy. Another benefit of using a news reader is that they manage *read* and *unread* message status, marking messages for later review, and so on.

A search for Linux in the growing list of newsgroups yields hundreds of individual groups, far too many for any single individual to keep up with. There are groups specific to development, to distributions, and to hardware platforms. There are Linux advocacy groups (both pro and con) and security groups. Perhaps the most popular are those under the *comp.os* hierarchy, which are moderated by a person who filters incoming messages before sending them out to subscribers. Some Linux-related newsgroups you should follow include:

comp.os.linux
> A general discussion on Linux

comp.os.linux.advocacy
> A less technical discussion of Linux, mainly by enthusiastic supporters

comp.os.linux.development
> A Linux-related software development discussion

comp.os.linux.announce
> Announcements from vendors, programmers, and so on

comp.os.linux.hardware
> A discussion on hardware issues specific to Linux

comp.os.linux.answers
> A Q&A forum

comp.os.linux.networking
> Internetworking discussion, with such topics as TCP/IP, the Internet, etc.

comp.os.linux.x
> A discussion on the X Window System

Subscribing to one or more of these groups for at least a few weeks will give you a good feel for the type of communication that goes on and how useful they may be to you.

Newsgroup archives

Given the explosive growth of the Usenet service, many people turn to newsgroup archives on the Internet rather than watch specific groups on a daily basis. Many groups serve hundreds of messages a day, so unless the topic is very close to your daily activity (or heart), monitoring a busy group can become a full-time job. For example, unless you are a kernel developer or are debugging specific kernel problems, watching *redhat.kernel.general* won't be of much interest to you. Archives offer information as you need it. A few popular newsgroup archives are:

Google groups (http://groups.google.com)
> Google.com has acquired the Usenet group archive of Deja.com. They provide a searchable archive of Usenet postings that can be helpful when you need to find recent or historical comments on a particular topic.

Remarq (http://www.remarq.com)
> This site purports to join people together in communities. Like *deja.com*, *remarq.com* contains a searchable database of Usenet articles.

Newsgroup archives provide you with an alternate view of Usenet threaded topics. Rather than posting a request for information and waiting for a response, searching an archive may yield immediate answers found in communications that have already occurred. An archive can free you from reading the headers to messages that are ultimately of no interest to you.

Contributing to Usenet

Depending on your level of expertise on the topic you're reading, you will inevitably come across a user question that you can answer with authority. Such a question is an opportunity for you to help someone. Think of the time needed to construct a helpful response as the payment for all the tips and assistance you yourself have received from other Usenet users over time.

Mailing Lists

Usenet provides an organized set of communications channels on specific topics. Often, however, a system administrator or an organization will want to set up a limited group of users with basic messaging capabilities. Without universal demand, or failing to make the case for a legitimate new Usenet group, a *mailing list* is often constructed using list-processing software.

A mailing list is an email autoresponder with a known list of mail recipients. Any inbound mail to the list server from among the known list members will be mirrored to each of the other recipients on the list. This service keeps list subscribers tuned into their topic but increases email volume, and subscriptions to a few active mailing lists can fill your inbox daily.

On the other hand, a mailing list is proactive, and email received may be more likely to be read than Usenet newsgroup information. Usenet messages are easily missed simply because recipients are not paying attention. Mailing lists can be found on many web sites, where instructions for joining the lists are available. For example, the LDP maintains a general-discussion mailing list that you can join by sending email to *ldp-discuss-request@linuxdoc.org*. This list is for the discussion of LDP issues, document proposals, and other commentary. Your local Linux User's Group (LUG) probably also has a mailing list to keep members up-to-date on events, meetings, and opinions.

Vendor Web Sites and Other Resources

It is impossible to list the ever-increasing number of Linux-related sites on the Internet. Each distribution and many major projects have their own sites, as do groups such as the Free Software Foundation. Table 1-27 lists some of the most popular, grouped into categories, in case you've missed them.

Table 1-27: Some Linux-Related Web Sites

Category	Web Sites
Certification	*http://www.brainbench.com* *http://www.linuxcertification.com* *http://www.lpi.org* *http://www.redhat.com/rhce*
Commerce	*http://www.elinux.com* *http://www.linuxcentral.com* *http://www.linuxmall.com*
Distributions	*http://www.calderasystems.com* *http://www.debian.org* *http://www.linux-mandrake.com* *http://www.redhat.com* *http://www.slackware.com* *http://www.suse.com* *http://www.turbolinux.com*
Documentation	*http://www.linuxdoc.org* *http://linux.oreilly.com* *http://www.searchlinux.com*
General	*http://www.linux.com* *http://www.linux.org* *http://www.linuxberg.com*
GUIs	*http://www.afterstep.org* *http://www.eazel.com* *http://www.gnome.org* *http://www.kde.org*
News	*http://slashdot.org* *http://www.linuxplanet.com* *http://www.lwn.com* *http://www.linuxjournal.com* *http://www.linuxtoday.com* *http://www.linuxpr.com* *http://www.oreillynet.com*
Open source	*http://www.fsf.org* *http://www.gnu.org* *http://www.kernelnotes.org* *http://freshmeat.org* *http://www.sourceforge.net*
Projects	*http://www.apache.org* *http://www.squidcache.org* *http://www.linuxrouter.org* *http://www.linuxppc.org*
Search engines	*http://www.google.com* *http://www.altavista.com* *http://www.northernlight.com* *http://www.yahoo.com*
Support	*http://www.linuxcare.org*

Table 1-27: Some Linux-Related Web Sites (continued)

Category	Web Sites
Training	http://www.lintraining.com
X Window System	http://www.x.org
	http://www.xfree86.com

Of course, it's impossible to create a static list of resources that will fulfill your ever-changing needs. If standard and familiar sources don't offer what you're looking for, don't hesitate to use a search engine. A targeted search on a quality search site can be surprisingly fruitful.

Objective 3: Write System Documentation

Through daily activity as a system administrator, you have a unique opportunity to observe the needs of multiple users on your systems. Based on that vantage point, you will probably be writing scripts and other utilities specific to your location and business. Such things can be as simple as login or shell scripts, or as complex as full-featured applications. As these tools make their way into the lives of other people, the need to document your work becomes a necessary part of being a system administrator. To be useful, such documentation should appear in locations where end users will expect to find it. In effect, creating a tool that is intended for an audience beyond yourself implies the responsibility to document that tool.

Creating Manpages

System manpages are an excellent place to create local documentation. Manpages are simple to create; the mechanism is well known, and your users will be comfortable using it. You can produce formatted documentation, including bold and underlined text from **nroff** source files. These text files contain extra markup information that controls the display formatting on screen. However, you can also use plain text files by employing a special performance feature of the man system.

Typically, the raw files used by **man** are processed from their raw **nroff** form to create the displayable form. At one time, this processing took a long time, particularly for large manpages. To make manpage access faster for subsequent requests for the same manpage, the system often would save a version of the formatted page on disk. The raw, unformatted system pages are stored in */usr/man/man.1*, */usr/man/man.2*, and so on for each section in the manual. In addition, the directories */usr/cat/cat.1*, */usr/cat/cat.2*, and so on, can hold the previously formatted files. The **cat** *directory* setup on your system may be different and is defined by */etc/man.config*. Wherever they are, these directories can contain text files for use with **man** rather than raw **nroff** files.

You can take advantage of this feature to create simple manpages for your own system. Simply generate a text file that looks like a typical manpage (sans fancy formatting) and place it in the appropriate **cat** directory. The file must be named with a trailing dot and the section name, just as the formatted files are. This method couldn't get any easier and yields a result expected by the end user. The missing formatting probably won't be noticed.

For those of you needing to get a little more serious and generate formatted manpages, you may want to start with an existing manpage to use as a template. To do this, simply find a manpage that makes a suitable starting point and copy it to the appropriate name in the appropriate man directory. Again, the name must have the trailing dot and man section. For example, we could copy the existing file */usr/man/man1/ln.1* to */usr/local/man/man1/mycmd.1*:

```
cp /usr/man/man1/ln.1 /usr/local/man/man1/mycmd.1
```

Edit the file with a text editor, changing sections and text as needed but leaving the formatting macros intact. When editing your new file, you'll find a number of *man macros* inside that handle complex text formatting. The macros consist of a dot (.) and one or two characters representing the formatting feature. Some of the more important macros are listed in Table 1-28.

Table 1-28: Commonly Used man Macros

Macro	Function
.TH	A manpage header. Includes title, section, date, description, and author.
.SH	A section heading. You can add your own sections to the standard sections as required.
.PP	A paragraph separator. Without this macro, lines of text will flow together.
.TP	A hanging indent macro, used for command options.
.B	Everything on the line following this macro is bold.
.I	Everything on the line following this macro is italic (or sometimes underlined).
\fB	This inline macro makes text following on the line bold.
\fI	This inline macro makes text following on the line italic (or sometimes underlined).
\fR	This inline macro returns the text to the default style.

Using these macros, you can create and format your own manpages. Example 1-4 contains an example of a very simple manpage using these macros.

Example 1-4: Sample Source for a Manpage

```
.\" This is a comment line.
.\"
.\" .TH defines your man page header, including
.\" the title, manual section, date, description, and author.
.TH MYPAGE 1 "TheDate" "My Page Description" "Me"
.\"
.\" .SH defines a section.  This is the NAME section.
.SH NAME
mypage \- make your own manpage
.\"
```

Example 1-4: Sample Source for a Manpage (continued)

```
.\" This is the SYNOPSIS section.
.SH SYNOPSIS
.\"
.\" .B is a font change macro, yielding bold for
.\" everything on the line.
.B mypage
.\"
.\" \fI, \fB, and \fR are in-line font changes for italic,
.\" bold, and roman, respectively.
.\"
.\"
.\" This is the DESCRIPTION section.
.SH DESCRIPTION
.\"
This is paragraph 1 of your description.
.\"
.\" .PP is a paragraph separator.
.PP
This is paragraph 2 of your description.
To create a manpage, the most important man macros
are \fB.TH\fR
.\"
.\" .TP precedes command options.
.TP
\fB\-a\fR
option a
.TP
\fB\-b\fR
option b
.\"
.\" This is the multiword "reporting bugs" section,
.\" which is why it is quoted.
.SH "REPORTING BUGS"
Report bugs to <someone@somewhere.com>.
.\"
.\" This is the multiword "see also" section.
.SH "SEE ALSO"
.\"
.B yourpage(1)
```

Your manpages will most likely go in the directory reserved for local additions to the system, */usr/local/man*. While there's nothing preventing you from storing your manpages in the system */man* directories, you may forget about customizations you make there—therefore, you could lose customizations when you upgrade your system and that directory gets overwritten with newer manpages.

NOTE

At the time of this writing, there are no questions for "Objective 3: Write System Documentation," on the LPIC Level 1 Exam.

Objective 4: Provide User Support

If you have spent any time working support calls on a help desk, then you already know you're an unsung hero. Within every help desk phone call received or help ticket dispatched, a problem of unknown origin and complexity awaits. Problems large and small, self-inflicted and accidental, technical and personal, will all be presented. You'll be expected to handle each of these situations with finesse, and of course deliver a timely, friendly, and helpful response even if you're given misleading information.

User support in any computing environment requires patience, perseverance, reliability, a genuine desire to help, and above all, tact. Tact is of utmost importance because, though the topic is computers, we're dealing with people in need who just want to get their job done. Often they're frustrated or even embarrassed to make a help desk call—it's the last thing they really want to do. Once they do contact you, individuals have a unique set of expectations for your help desk performance. Corporate executives will expect kid-glove treatment even if their problems are trivial and of little importance. Uninformed users may expect immediate fixes to new and perplexing problems. Highly technical users may know a great deal about what they're asking and expect detailed responses to detailed questions. Many users will simply want to dump their problems on you so they can move on to other tasks. Despite the attendant frustrations involved with staffing a help desk, the work you encounter responding to this diversity, particularly in large enterprises, will yield an excellent education on the systems you support.

Administrative Tasks
(Topic 2.11)

As a system administrator in a multiuser environment, much of your activity is related to users and their system accounts, the automation of routine tasks, and system backup. This chapter covers these administrative aspects of Linux as required for Exam 101. This chapter has five Objectives:

Objective 1: Manage Users and Group Accounts and Related System Files
This Objective covers the management of user accounts and the commands used to create and modify them. We also examine the files that store user account information. Weight: 7.

Objective 2: Tune the User Environment and System Environment Variables
A user's environment, including shell selection, environment variables, aliases, and the like, is somewhat personal. Each user will want to customize her environment for individual tastes and needs. However, a default setup is needed for new user accounts, and certain system setup items must be provided to all users. This Objective covers the system */etc/profile* (a system-wide startup file for the **bash** shell) and the */etc/skel* directory, used as an image for new user accounts. Weight: 4.

Objective 3: Configure and Use System Log Files to Meet Administrative and Security Needs
This Objective covers the configuration and use of standard system logging with the **syslog** system. Weight: 3.

Objective 4: Automate System Administration Tasks by Scheduling Jobs to Run in the Future
This Objective covers the use of the **cron** facility for automating routine system maintenance. Weight: 4.

Objective 5: Maintain an Effective Data Backup Strategy
While many commercial tools exist in the market for system backup, you can form an effective basic strategy with tools already available on your Linux system. This Objective covers basic backup strategy using the **tar** program, including verification of backups and restoration of files. Weight: 3.

Objective 1: Manage Users and Group Accounts

Whether on a corporate server or personal desktop machine, managing user accounts is an important aspect of running a Linux system. The root, or super-user, account is established when you first install Linux. Unlike single-user systems (such as MS-DOS), multiuser systems (such as Linux) require the notion of an *owner* for files, processes, and other system objects. In many cases, an object's owner is a human system user who created the object. Many objects are also owned by system services, such as web servers. Each of these owners is differentiated from others by a unique *user account*, which is assigned to it by the system administrator.

If you're building your own desktop system, you may be tempted to use the root account for daily activity, thus avoiding user account issues. In most cases, however, the privileges that come with the superuser account aren't required for much of your daily activity and can be a double-edged sword. It is easy to make big mistakes when you have full privileges across the entire system. Instead, running your daily tasks with a standard user account and reserving the use of the root account for tasks that require those privileges is always safer, even for experts.

User Accounts and the Password File

When a new user account is added to a Linux system, an entry is added to a list of users in the *password file*, which is stored in */etc/passwd*. This file gets its name from its original use, which was to store user information including an encrypted form of the user's password. The password file is in plain text and is readable by everyone on the system. Each line in the password file contains information for a single user account, with item detail separated by colons as illustrated in Figure 1-7.

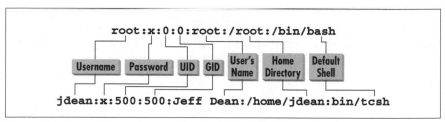

Figure 1-7: Sample lines from a password file

Each line in the file contains information for a single system account and contains the following pieces of information in colon-separated fields:

Username

> The first field on a line is a unique *username* for the person or service using the account. The username is usually a short form of the person's name, such as *jdean*.

Password

Each username has an associated *password*. The password stored in this field is in an encrypted (unreadable) form. Despite the encryption, for security reasons, most systems now store users passwords in a separate */etc/shadow* file. If the password is not included, its field is filled by the letter *x*, which indicates that the shadow password system is in use.

User ID

Each username requires a unique *user identifier*, or *UID*. The UID is simply a nonnegative integer. The root account is assigned the UID of 0, which affords it global privilege on the system. Other users have a positive UID, and it is not unusual to begin the sequence for new users at a large number like 100, or on some Linux distributions, 500. By convention, the UID values from 0 to 99 are reserved for administrative use; those over 99 are for regular system users.

Group ID

Each username has a default *group identifier*, or *GID*. The GID is also a nonnegative integer. Groups are a way of allowing users to share files through mutual group membership. Group numbers and their associated names are specified in the */etc/group* file. The GID stored for each user in */etc/passwd* is its default group ID, though a user may belong to many groups.

User's name (or other comment)

The user's name or other information is stored as plain text and usually contains the user's full name. This field may contain spaces.

Home directory

The *home directory* is the default directory in the filesystem for the account. If a new account is meant for a person, a home directory will probably be created in the filesystem with standard configuration files that the user may then personalize. The full path to that home directory is listed here.

Default shell

This field specifies the default shell for the user or service, which is the shell that runs when the user logs in or opens a shell window. In most cases, the shell will be */bin/bash* or */bin/tcsh*, but it can be any shell, or even another executable program.[*]

In looking back at Figure 1-7, the first line shows the definition of the root account with UID and GID of 0, a name of "root," a home directory of */root*, and a default shell of */bin/bash*. The second line shows a standard user account for Jeff Dean, with UID and GID of 500. The home directory is */home/jdean* and the default shell is */bin/tcsh*.

On the Exam

You must be prepared to name the fields in the *passwd* file.

---

[*] Non-shell entries may be seen in the case of some services that should own files but never log in interactively. You may see the shell field filled with */bin/false*, a small program that does nothing but yield an error and terminate. This ensures that a service account is secured from login.

In both cases, note that the password field contains a single letter *x*. This indicates that the password is stored in */etc/shadow* and not */etc/passwd*; */etc/shadow* is secured and readable only by the root user. This technique reduces the likelihood of an attack against passwords on your system. Shadow passwords and the attacks they defend against are discussed later in this Objective.

Groups and the Group File

In addition to ownership by individual system users, filesystem objects have separate ownership settings for groups of users. This *group ownership* allows an additional level of user-specific access control beyond that of a file's individual owner. Groups are similar to users in their administration and are defined in the file */etc/group*. Like the *passwd* file, the *group* file contains colon-separated fields:

Group name
> Each group must have a unique name.

Group password
> Just as user accounts have passwords, groups can have passwords for their membership. If the password field is empty, the group does not require a password.

Group ID
> Each group requires a unique GID. Like a UID, a GID is a nonnegative integer.

Group member list
> The last field is a list of group members by username, separated by commas.

Together, these pieces of information define a group; colons separate the fields. Here are a few sample lines from a group file:

```
root:x:0:root
pppusers:x:230:jdean,jdoe
finance:x:300:jdean,jdoe,bsmith
jdean:x:500:
jdoe:x:501:
bsmith:x:502:
```

On the Exam

Remember that some distributions assign all accounts to the *users* group while others assign a group for each account. Red Hat Linux, for example, creates single-user groups for all users. In contrast, SuSE Linux assigns the *users* group (GID 100) as the default for all users.

In this example, both jdean and jdoe are members of the pppusers group (GID 230), and jdean, jdoe, and bsmith are all members of the finance group (GID 300). The remaining groups, root, jdean, jdoe, and bsmith are single-user groups. These groups are not intended for multiple users and do not contain additional members. For security purposes, it is common to create new users with their own personal single-user group. Doing this enhances security because new files and directories will not have group privileges for other users.*

The Shadow Password and Shadow Group Systems

At one time, the encryption used on passwords in the world-readable /etc/passwd file was a roadblock to anyone trying to break into a Unix system account. The encrypted passwords were meaningless, and there was no way to reverse-engineer them. However, improved computer performance has led to tools that can process encrypted passwords through what is known as a *dictionary attack*. In this form of attack, a list of common words and typical passwords is encrypted. The encrypted words are then compared against the publicly available encrypted passwords. If a match is found, the account in question is compromised and can then be used by someone other than its owner.

Shadow passwords

Encrypted passwords must be secure from all users on the system, while leaving the remainder of the information in /etc/passwd world-readable. To do this, the encrypted password is moved to a new file that "shadows" the password file line for line. The file is aptly called /etc/shadow and is generally said to contain *shadow passwords*. Here are a few example lines from a shadow file:

```
root:$1$oxEaSzzdXZESTGTU:10927:0:99999:7:-1:-1:134538444
jdean:$1$IviLopPn461z47J:10927:0:99999:7::11688:134538412
```

The first two fields contain the username and the encrypted passwords. The remaining fields contain optional additional information on password aging information.

Group passwords and shadow groups

Just as user accounts listed in /etc/passwd are protected by encrypted passwords, groups listed in /etc/group can also be protected by passwords. A group password can be used to allow access to a group by a user account that is not actually a member of the group.† Account users can use the **newgrp** command to change their default group and enter the group password. If the password is correct, the account is granted the group privileges, just as a group member would be.

The group definition file, like the password file, is readable by everyone on the system. If group passwords are stored there, a dictionary attack could be made against them. To protect against such attacks, passwords in /etc/group can be shadowed. The protected passwords are stored in /etc/gshadow, which is readable only by *root*. Here are a few sample lines from a *gshadow* file:

---

* Although the GID of these single-user groups may match the UID of the user for which they're created, there is no direct relationship between the UID and GID.

† This begs the question "Why not simply make that user a member of the group instead of handing out group passwords?" Indeed, group passwords are rarely used, precisely because group membership is so simple to administer and is more secure than publicly known passwords. It is unlikely that you will need to use group passwords. Nevertheless, understanding group passwords is a requirement for Exam 101.

```
root:::root
pppusers:x::
finance:0cf7ipLtpSBGg::
jdean:x::
jdoe:x::
bsmith:x::
```

In this example, the groups pppusers, jdean, jdoe, and bsmith do not have group passwords as indicated by the x in the password field. The finance group is the only one with a password, which is encrypted.

On the Exam

A major contrast between *passwd/group* and *shadow/gshadow* is the permissions on the files. The standard files are readable by everyone on the system, but the shadow files are readable only by *root*, which protects encrypted passwords from theft and possible cracking.

User and Group Management Commands

Although possible, it is rarely necessary (or advised) to manipulate the account and group definition files manually with a text editor. Instead, a family of convenient administrative commands is available for managing accounts, groups, password shadowing, group shadowing, and password aging.*

---

useradd

Syntax

useradd [*options*] *user*

Description

Create the account *user* on the system. Both system defaults and specified *options* define how the account is configured. All system account files are updated as required. An initial password must subsequently be set for new users using the passwd command. It is the user's responsibility to go back and change that password when he first logs in to the system.

Frequently used options

-c *"comment"*
    Define the comment field, probably the user's name.

-d *homedir*
    Use *homedir* as the user's home directory.

-D
    List (and optionally change) system default values.

---

* Password aging (rules governing change intervals and automated expiration of passwords) is not an explicit Objective for the LPIC Level 1 exams.

-m
> Create and populate the home directory.

-s *shell*
> Use *shell* as the default for the account.

Examples

Add a new user, *bsmith*, with all default settings:

```
# useradd bsmith
```

Add a new user, *jdoe*, with a name, default home directory, and the **tcsh** shell:

```
# useradd -mc "Jane Doe" -s /bin/tcsh jdoe
```

---

usermod

Syntax

```
usermod [options] user
```

Description

Modify an existing user account. The **usermod** command accepts many of the same options as **useradd** does.

Frequently used options

-L
> Lock the password, disabling the account.

-U
> Unlock the user's password, enabling the user to once again log into the system.

Examples

Change *jdoe*'s name in the comment field:

```
# usermod -c "Jane Deer-Doe" jdoe
```

Lock the password for *bsmith*:

```
# usermod -L bsmith
```

---

userdel

Syntax

```
userdel [-r] user
```

Description

Delete an existing user account. When combined with the **-r** option, the user's home directory is deleted. Note that completely deleting accounts may lead to confusion when files owned by the deleted user remain in other system directories. For this reason, it is common to disable an account rather than delete it. Accounts can be disabled using the **chage**, **usermod**, and **passwd** commands.

Example

Delete the user *bsmith*, including the home directory:

```
# userdel -r bsmith
```

groupadd

Syntax

```
groupadd group
```

Description

Add *group* to the system. In the rare case that a group password is desired on *group*, it must be added using the **gpasswd** command after the group is created.

groupmod

Syntax

```
groupmod [option] group
```

Description

Modify the parameters of *group*.

Option

-n *name*
  Change the name of group to *name*.

groupdel

Syntax

```
groupdel group
```

Description

Delete *group* from the system. Deleted groups can lead to the same confusion in the filesystem as described previously for deleting a user (see **userdel**).

passwd

Syntax

```
passwd [options] username
```

Description

Interactively set the password for *username*. The password cannot be entered on the command line.

Option

−l

Available only to the superuser, this option locks the password for the account.

---

gpasswd

Syntax

gpasswd *groupname*

Description

Interactively set the group password for *groupname*. The password cannot be entered on the command line.

Additional user and group management commands

While they are not specifically required for this Objective, this discussion would not be complete without a few additional commands for managing users and groups.

---

pwconv

Syntax

pwconv

Description

Convert a standard password file to a password and shadow password combination, enabling shadow passwords on the system.

---

pwunconv

Syntax

pwunconv

Description

Revert from a shadow password configuration to a standard password file.

---

grpconv

Syntax

grpconv

Description

Convert a standard group file to a group and shadow group combination, enabling shadow groups on the system. Shadow passwords are rarely necessary.

---

grpunconv

Syntax

grpunconv

Description

Revert from a shadow group configuration to a standard group file.

chage

Syntax

chage [*options*] *user*

Description

Modify password aging and expiration settings for *user*. Nonprivileged users may use this command with the –l option for their username only.

Frequently used options

–E *expiredate*
    Set the account to expiration date *expiredate* in the form MM/DD/YY or MM/DD/YYYY.

–l
    List a user's password settings.

Example 1

Display password settings for user *jdoe* (including nonprivileged user *jdoe*):

    $ **chage -l jdoe**

Example 2

Set *jdoe's* account expiration date to January 1, 2002:

    # **chage -E 01/01/2002 jdoe**

On the Exam

You must be familiar with these account management commands as well as be ready to specify methods for adding, removing, and modifying user accounts.

Objective 2: Tune the User Environment

When you create a new user account on your Linux system, some basic setup information is necessary for the user to initially become productive. When the user logs into the system, she will need:

- A minimal set of environment variables, including a **PATH** that is meaningful for your system.

- Basic configuration files in her home directory.

The amount of default information you provide can range from minimal to extremely detailed. In general, you'll want to provide the setup information that will allow the user to begin working without extensive personal customization.

System-wide Startup Scripts

When the **bash** shell starts, it looks for a number of configuration script files, including */etc/profile*. Commands in this file are executed at login time and contain global startup information and settings for all **bash** users.* Example 1-5 contains an example profile.

Example 1-5: Sample /etc/profile File

```
# /etc/profile

# System wide environment and startup programs
# Functions and aliases go in /etc/bashrc

PATH="$PATH:/usr/X11R6/bin"
PS1="[\u@\h \W]\\$ "

ulimit -c 1000000
if [ `id -gn` = `id -un` -a `id -u` -gt 14 ]; then
umask 002
else
umask 022
fi

USER=`id -un`
LOGNAME=$USER
MAIL="/var/spool/mail/$USER"

HOSTNAME=`/bin/hostname`
HISTSIZE=1000
HISTFILESIZE=1000

INPUTRC=/etc/inputrc
PATH="$PATH:/usr/local/bin"
export PATH PS1 HOSTNAME HISTSIZE HISTFILESIZE
USER LOGNAME MAIL INPUTRC
```

---

* This does not apply to users of other shells, such as **tcsh**. Those shells require different global startup setup and are not among the Objectives for the LPIC Level 1 exams.

The syntax for **bash** programming is in Part 2, *Shells, Scripting, Programming, and Compiling (Topic 1.9)*. However, you can see that this file does basic shell setup for the user, including the assignment of a number of environment variables. As an example of a common local customization, note the line containing PATH= adds an additional directory to those already listed in the PATH environment variable. In this case, the system administrator expects that most users will need to run programs stored in */usr/local/bin*. Making this modification once in */etc/profile* eliminates the need for individuals to make it in their personal **bash** profiles.

On the Exam

Remember that */etc/profile* is executed only once, while */etc/bashrc* is called for each new shell invocation. Also note that these startup scripts are specific to **bash** and that users of other shells will have a different configuration.

As you may have noted in the comments at the top of Example 1-5, the definition of functions and aliases typically is not done in */etc/profile*, but instead in */etc/bashrc*. This is because functions and aliases are not *inherited* by new shells. Since commands in */etc/profile* are executed only at login time, functions and aliases defined there would only be available in the login shell. Commands in the *bashrc* file are executed each time a new shell starts; their effects will apply to all shells.

Setting the Home Directory for New Accounts

When creating a new account, usually you'll want to create a default home directory for the user of the account. On Linux systems, the home directory is most likely something like */home/username*, but you can define it in any way you like.

When you create a new home directory, it is a courtesy to the new user to initially populate the directory with useful files. These might include startup files for the user's shell, his desktop, or for X Window applications. To facilitate the automated population of new user directories, an example home directory is created in a "skeleton" directory */etc/skel*. This directory should contain all of the files and subdirectories that all new users will need. Example 1-6 shows the contents of an example */etc/skel* directory.

Example 1-6: Sample Skeleton (/etc/skel) Directory

```
-rw-r--r--  1 root    root    1422 Mar 29  1999 .Xdefaults
-rw-r--r--  1 root    root      24 Jul 13  1994 .bash_logout
-rw-r--r--  1 root    root     230 Aug 22  1998 .bash_profile
-rw-r--r--  1 root    root     124 Aug 23  1995 .bashrc
drwxr-xr-x  3 root    root    1024 Dec  2 09:37 .kde
-rw-r--r--  1 root    root     966 Apr 16  1999 .kderc
drwxr-xr-x  5 root    root    1024 Dec  2 09:37 Desktop
```

This example */etc/skel* directory contains:

* An X application startup file (*.Xdefaults*).
* Three configuration files for the shell (*.bash_logout*, *.bash_profile*, and *.bashrc*).

- A directory and a startup file for KDE (*.kde* and *.kderc*).

- A *Desktop* directory, which defines the appearance of the user's desktop.

The specifics of this example are not important, but illustrate that a number of default files can be included in a new user's account setup. Additions could include default files for other desktop environments such as GNOME as well as startup files for other shells.

When a new account is created with a home directory, the entire contents of */etc/skel* are copied recursively (that is, including subdirectories) to the new home directory location. The home directory and its entire contents are then set to the new account's UID and GID, making the new user owner of her initial files. She is then free to modify these files and directories as necessary.

As the system administrator, you may add, modify, and delete files in */etc/skel* as needed for your environment.

Objective 3: Configure and Use System Log Files

Many events occur on your Linux system that should be logged for administrative purposes. Linux uses the **syslog** system to display and record messages describing these events. This system allows finely controlled logging of messages from the kernel as well as processes running on your system and remote systems. Messages can be placed on the console display, in log files, and on the text screens of users logged in to the system.

Configuring syslog

The behavior of **syslog** is controlled by its configuration file, */etc/syslog.conf*. This text file contains lines indicating what is to be logged and where. Each line contains directives in this form:

> *facility.level action*

The directives are defined as follows:

facility
> This represents the creator of the message (that is, the kernel or a process) and is one of the following: *auth, authpriv, cron, daemon, kern, lpr, mail, mark, news, syslog, user,* or *local0* through *local7*. The use of these facility designators allows you to control the destination of messages based on their origin. Facilities *local0* through *local7* are for any use you may wish to assign to them in your own programs and scripts.*

level
> Specifies a severity threshold beyond which messages are logged, and is one of the following (from lowest to highest severity): *debug, info, notice, warning, err, crit, alert,* or *emerg*. There is also a special level called *none* that will disable a facility. The level defines the amount of detail recorded in

---

* It's possible that your distribution has assigned one or more of the local facilities already. Check your configuration before using a local facility.

the log file. A single period separates the facility from the level, and together they comprise the *message selector*. The asterisk (*) can be used to describe all facilities or all levels.

action

The *action* directive is arguably misnamed. It represents the destination for messages that correspond to a given selector (*facility.level*). The action can be a filename (including the full pathname), a hostname preceded by the @ sign, or a comma-separated list of users or asterisk (this means all logged-in users will be included). The action is to send the message to the specified destination.

For example, if you wanted to create a separate log file for activity reported by the scripts you write, you might include a line like this in */etc/syslog.conf*:

```
# Define a new log file for the local5 facility
local5.*                          /var/log/local5
```

You could then use the **logger** utility to write messages to the facility from your shell script:[*]

```
$ logger -p local5.info "Script terminated normally"
```

The message "Script terminated normally" would be placed into */var/log/local5*, along with a timestamp and the hostname that sent the message. Example 1-7 contains an example */etc/syslog.conf* file.

Example 1-7: Sample /etc/syslog.conf File

```
# Log everything except mail & authpriv of level info
# or higher to messages
*.info;mail.none;authpriv.none     /var/log/messages

# The authpriv file has restricted access.
authpriv.*                         /var/log/secure

# Log all the mail messages in one place.
mail.*                             /var/log/maillog

# Everybody gets emergency messages
*.emerg                                    *

# Save boot messages also to boot.log
local7.*                           /var/log/boot.log
```

On the Exam

If you're not yet familiar with **syslog**, spend some time with it, modifying */etc/syslog.conf* and directing messages to various files. An understanding of **syslog** is critical because so many programs depend on it.

---

[*] **syslog** must be restarted or signaled to reinitialize before the new log file is created.

If you examine this *syslog.conf* file, you'll see that nearly all system messages are sent to the */var/log/messages* file via the **.info* message selector. In this case, the asterisk directs **syslog** to send messages from all facilities except *mail* and *auth-priv*, which are excluded using the special none level. The */var/log/messages* file is the default system message destination, and you will consult it frequently for information on processes running (or failing to run) and other events on your system. In this example, the low severity level of info is used for the *messages* file, which logs all but debugging messages. On heavily loaded servers, this may result in an unwieldy file size due to message volume. Depending upon your available disk space, you may choose to save less information by raising the level for the *messages* file.

Log File Rotation

Most distributions will install a default **syslog** configuration for you, including logging to *messages* and other log files in */var/log*. To prevent any of these files from growing unattended to extreme sizes, a *log file rotation* scheme should be installed as well. The **cron** system issues commands on a regular basis (usually once per day) to establish new log files; the old files are renamed with numeric suffixes (see Objective 4 for more on **cron**). With this kind of rotation, yesterday's */var/log/messages* file becomes today's *messages.1*, and a new *messages* file is created. The rotation is configured with a maximum number of files to keep, and the oldest log files are deleted when the rotation is run.

The utility that establishes the rotation is **logrotate**. This privileged command is configured using one or more files, which are specified as arguments to the **logrotate** command. These configuration files can contain directives to include other files as well. The default configuration file is */etc/logrotate.conf*. Example 1-8 depicts an example *logrotate.conf* file.

Example 1-8: Sample /etc/logrotate.conf File

```
# global options
# rotate log files weekly
weekly

# keep 4 weeks worth of backlogs
rotate 4

# send errors to root
errors root

# create new (empty) log files after rotating old ones
create

# compress log files
compress

# specific files

/var/log/wtmp {
    monthly
```

Example 1-8: Sample /etc/logrotate.conf File (continued)

```
    create 0664 root utmp
    rotate 1
}

/var/log/messages {
    postrotate
        /usr/bin/killall -HUP syslogd
    endscript
}
```

This example specifies rotations for two files, */var/log/wtmp* and */var/log/messages*. Your configuration will be much more complete, automatically rotating all log files on your system. A complete understanding of *logrotate* configuration is not necessary for LPIC Level 1 exams, but you must be familiar with the concepts involved. See the *logrotate* manpages for more information.

Examining Log Files

You can learn a lot about the activity of your system by reviewing the log files it creates. At times, it will be necessary to debug problems using logged information. Since most of the log files are plain text, it is very easy to review their contents with tools such as **tail**, **less**, and **grep**.

syslog stores the messages it creates with the following information, separated by (but also including) spaces:

*   Date/time
*   Origin hostname
*   Message sender (such as *kernel*, *sendmail*, or a username)
*   Message text

Typical messages will look like this:

```
    Dec  8 10:41:23 smp kernel: Symbols match kernel
        version 2.2.5.
    Dec  8 10:41:23 smp kernel: Loaded 182 symbols
        from 12 modules.
    Dec  8 10:50:19 smp kernel: Kernel logging (proc) stopped.
    Dec  8 10:50:19 smp kernel: Kernel log daemon terminating.
```

In this case, **smp** is the hostname, and the messages are coming from the kernel. At any time you can review the entire contents of your log files using **less**:

```
    # less /var/log/messages
```

You can then page through the file. This is a good way to become familiar with the types of messages you'll see on your system. To actively monitor the output to your *messages* file, you could use **tail**:

```
    # tail -f /var/log/messages
```

This might be useful, for example, to watch system activity as an Internet connection is established via modem. To look specifically for messages regarding your mouse, you might use **grep**:

```
# grep '[Mm]ouse' /var/log/messages
Dec  8 00:15:28 smp kernel: Detected PS/2 Mouse Port.
Dec  8 10:55:02 smp gpm: Shutting down gpm mouse services:
```

Often, if you are using **grep** to look for a particular item you expect to find in */var/log/messages*, you will need to search all of the rotated files with a wildcard. For example, to look for all messages from *sendmail*, you may issue a command like this:

```
# grep 'sendmail:' /var/log/messages*
```

When you note problems in log files, look at the hostname and sender of the message first, then the message text. In many cases, you will be able to determine what is wrong from the message. Sometimes the messages are only clues, so a broader review of your logs may be necessary. In this case, it may be helpful to temporarily turn on more messaging by using the debug level in */etc/syslog.conf* to help yield additional information that can lead you to the problem.

Objective 4: Automate System Administration Tasks

There is a surprising amount of housekeeping that must be done to keep a complex operating system such as Linux running smoothly. Log file rotation, cleanup of temporary files and directories, system database rebuilds, backups, and other tasks should be done routinely. Clearly such mundane things should be automated by the system, freeing weary system administrators for more interesting work. Fortunately, any system task that can be accomplished without real-time human intervention can be automated on Linux using the **cron** and **at** facilities. Both have the ability to execute system commands, which may start any executable program or script, at selectable times. Further, **cron** and **at** can execute these commands on behalf of any authorized system user. **cron** is intended mainly for regularly scheduled recurring activities, and **at** is most useful for scheduling single commands for execution in the future. **cron** gets its name from the "*chron-*" prefix of "*chronology*" (time).

Using cron

The **cron** facility consists of two programs:[*]

crond

> This is the **cron** daemon. This is the process that executes your instructions. It starts at system initialization time and runs in the background thereafter.

crontab

> This is the *cron table* manipulation program. This program gives you access to your cron table or **crontab** file. Each authorized user may have his own **crontab** file to run commands and processes on a regular basis.

---

[*] There is no individual program called "cron," which is the overall name given to the facility. If you execute **man cron** however, you will, see the manpage for **crond**.

The **cron** daemon wakes up every minute and examines all **crontab** files, executing any commands scheduled for that time.

User crontab files

To use the **cron** facility, users do not need to interact directly with the **crond** daemon. Instead, each system user has access to the **cron** facility through her **crontab** file. These files are stored together in a single directory (usually */var/spool/ cron*) and are created and maintained using the **crontab** utility.

crontab

Syntax

    crontab [options]

Description

View or edit **crontab** files.

Frequently used options

-e

> Interactively edit the **crontab** file. Unless otherwise specified in either the EDITOR or VISUAL environment variables, the editor is **vi**.

-l

> Display the contents of the **crontab** file.

-r

> Remove the **crontab** file.

-u *user*

> Operate on *user*'s **crontab** file instead of your own. Only *root* can edit or delete the **crontab** files of other users.

Examples

Display the **crontab** file for user *jdoe*:

    # crontab -l -u jdoe

Edit your own **crontab** file:

    $ crontab -e

crontab files use a flexible format to specify times for command execution. Each line contains six fields:

    minute hour day month dayofweek   command

These fields are specified as follows:

- Minute (0 through 59)
- Hour (0 through 23)
- Day of the month (1 through 31)
- Month (1 through 12 or jan through dec)

- Day of the week (0 through 6 [where 0 is Sunday] or sun through sat)
- Command (any valid command, including spaces and standard bourne shell syntax)

For example, to execute *myprogram* once per day at 6:15 a.m., use this **crontab** entry:

```
# run myprogram at 6:15am
15 6 * * *   myprogram
```

Lines that begin with the pound sign (#) are *comment lines* and are ignored by **crond**. Comments must begin on a new line and may not appear within commands. The asterisks in this **crontab** are placeholders and match any date or time for the field where they're found. Here, they indicate that *myprogram* should execute at 6:15 a.m. on all days of the month, every month, all days of the week.

Each of the time specifications may be single, list (1,3,5), or range (1-5 or wed-fri) entries or combinations thereof. To modify the previous example to execute at 6:15 and 18:15 on the 1st and 15th of the month, use:

```
# run myprogram at 6:15am and 6:15pm on the 1st and 15th
15 6,18 1,15 * *   myprogram
```

As you can see, the time specifications are very flexible.

Because the **cron** daemon evaluates each **crontab** entry when it executes each minute, it is not necessary to restart or reinitialize **crond** when **crontab** entries are changed or new files are created.

System crontab files

In addition to **crontab** files owned by individual users, **crond** also looks for the system **crontab** files */etc/crontab* and files in the directory */etc/cron.d*. The format for these system **crontab**s differs slightly from user **crontab**s. System **crontab**s have an additional field for a username between the time specifications and the command. For example:

```
# /etc/crontab
# run myprogram at 6:15am as root
15 6 * * *   root   myprogram
```

In this example, myprogram will be executed by **cron** as the *root* user.

System **crontab** files located in */etc/cron.d* are of the same form as */etc/crontab*, including the extra user field. These files are usually associated with some package or service that includes a system **crontab**. Allowing a collection of files in */etc/cron.d* allows software installation and upgrade procedures to keep the **cron** configuration up-to-date on an individual package basis. In most cases, however, you won't need to change the **crontab** files in */etc/cron.d*.

On the Exam

Memorize the sequence of time/date fields used in **crontab** files.

On most Linux distributions, */etc/crontab* contains some standard content to enable the execution of programs and scripts on the minute, hour, week, and month. These arrangements allow you to simply drop executable files into the appropriate directory (such as */etc/cron.hourly*), where they are executed automatically. This eliminates **cron** configuration altogether for many tasks and avoids cluttering the root **crontab** file with common commands.

Using at

The **cron** facility is intended for the execution of commands on a regular, periodic schedule. When you need to simply delay execution of a command or a group of commands to some other time in the future, you should use **at**. The **at** facility accepts commands from standard input or from a file.

---

at

Syntax

> at [*-f file*] *time*
> at [*options*]

Description

In the first form, enter commands to the **at** queue for execution at *time*. at allows fairly complex time specifications. It accepts times of the form *HH:MM* to run a job at a specific time of day. (If that time is already past, the next day is assumed.) You may also specify *midnight, noon,* or *teatime* (4 p.m.), and you suffix a time of day with *AM* or *PM* for running in the morning or evening. You can also say what day the job will be run by giving a date in month-day form, with the year being optional, or by giving a date in *MMDDYY, MM/DD/YY* or *DD.MM.YY* form. The date specification must follow the time-of-day specification. You can also give times like *now + count time-units*, where time-units can be minutes, hours, days, or weeks, you can tell **at** to run the job today by suffixing the time with *today*, and you can tell it to run the job tomorrow by suffixing the time with *tomorrow*.

If *-f file* is given, commands are taken from the *file*, otherwise **at** will prompt the user for commands.

In the second form, list or delete jobs from the **at** queue.

Frequently used options

-d *job1* [, *job2*, ...]
> Delete jobs from the **at** queue by number (same as the **atrm** command).

-l
> List items in the **at** queue (same as the **atq** command).

Example 1

Run *myprogram* once at 6:15 p.m. tomorrow:

```
$ at 6:15pm tomorrow
at> myprogram
at> ^D
```

In the previous code listing, ^D indicates that the user typed **Ctrl-D** on the keyboard, sending the end-of-file character to terminate the **at** command.

Example 2

Run commands that are listed in the file *command_list* at 9 p.m. two days from now:

```
$ at -f command_list 9pm + 2 days
```

List items in the **at** queue (root sees all users' entries):

```
$ at -l
```

Remove job number 5 from the **at** queue:

```
$ at -d 5
```

Using **at** to schedule jobs for delayed execution, such as while you're asleep or on vacation, is simple and doesn't require creation of a recurring **cron** entry.

Controlling User Access to cron and at

In most cases, it is safe to allow users to use the **cron** and **at** facilities. However, if your circumstances dictate that one or more users should be prohibited from using these services, two simple authorization files exist for each:

- *cron.allow, cron.deny*
- *at.allow, at.deny*

These files are simply lists of account names. If the *allow* file exists, only those users listed in the *allow* file may use the service. If the *allow* file does not exist but the *deny* file does, only those users not listed in the *deny* file may use the service. For **cron**, if neither file exists, all users have access to **cron**. For **at**, if neither file exists, only root has access to **at**. An empty *at.deny* file allows access to all users and is the default.

Objective 5: Maintain an Effective Data Backup Strategy

Regardless of how careful we are or how robust our hardware might be, it is highly likely that sometimes data will be lost. Though fatal system problems are rare, accidentally deleted files or mistakes using **mv** or **cp** are common. Routine system backup is essential to avoid losing precious data.

There are many reasons to routinely back up your systems:

- Protection against disk failures
- Protection against accidental file deletion and corruption
- Protection against disasters, such as fire, water, or vandalism
- Retention of historical data
- Creation of multiple copies of data, with one or more copies stored at off-site locations for redundancy

---

All of these reasons for creating a backup strategy could be summarized as insurance. Far too much time and effort goes into a computer system to allow random incidents to force repeated work.

Backup Concepts and Strategies

Most backup strategies involve copying data between at least two locations. At a prescribed time, data is transferred from a source media (such as a hard disk) to some form of backup media. Backup media are usually removable, and include tapes, floppy disks, Zip disks, and so on. These media are relatively inexpensive, compact, and easy to store off-site. On the other hand, they are slow relative to hard disk drives.

Backup types

Backups are usually run in one of three general forms:

Full backup
> A full, or complete, backup saves all of the files on your system. Depending on circumstances, "all files" may mean all files on the system, all files on a physical disk, all files on a single partition, or all files that cannot be recovered from original installation media. Depending on the size of the drive being backed up, a full backup can take hours to complete.

Differential backup
> Save only files that have been modified or created since the last full backup. Compared to full backups, differentials are relatively fast because of the reduced number of files written to the backup media. A typical differential scheme would include full backup media plus the latest differential media. Intermediate differential media are superseded by the latest and can be recycled.

Incremental backup
> Save only files that have been modified or created since the last backup, including the last incremental backup. These backups are also relatively fast. A typical incremental backup would include full backup media plus the entire series of subsequent incremental media. All incremental media are required to reconstruct changes to the filesystem since the last full backup.

Typically, a full backup is coupled with a series of *either* differential backups *or* incremental backups, but not both. For example, a full backup could be run once per week with six daily differential backups on the remaining days. Using this scheme, a restoration is possible from the full backup media and the most recent differential backup media. Using incremental backups in the same scenario, the full backup media and *all* incremental backup media would be required to restore the system. The choice between the two is related mainly to the tradeoff between media consumption (incremental backup requires more media) versus backup time (differential backup takes longer, particularly on heavily used systems).

For large organizations that require retention of historical data, a backup scheme longer than a week is created. Incremental or differential backup media are retained for a few weeks, after which the tapes are reformatted and reused. Full backup media are retained for an extended period, perhaps permanently. At the very least, one full backup from each month should be retained for a year or more.

A backup scheme such as this is called a *media rotation scheme*, because media are continually written, retained for a defined period, and then reused. The media themselves are said to belong to a *media pool*, which defines the monthly full, the weekly full, and differential or incremental media assignments, as well as when media can be reused. When media with full backups are removed from the pool for long-term storage, new media join the pool, keeping the size of the pool constant. Media may also be removed from the pool if your organization chooses to limit the number of uses media are allowed, assuming that reliability goes down as the number of passes through a tape mechanism increases.

Your organization's data storage requirements dictate the complexity of your backup scheme. On systems in which many people frequently update mission-critical data, a conservative and detailed backup scheme is essential. For casual-use systems, such as desktop PCs, only a basic backup scheme is needed, if at all.

Backup verification

To be effective, backup media must be capable of yielding a successful restoration of files. To ensure this, a backup scheme must also include some kind of backup verification in which recently written backup media are tested for successful restore operations. This could take the form of a comparison of files after the backup, an automated restoration of a select group of files on a periodic basis, or even a random audit of media on a recurring basis. However the verification is performed, it must prove that the media, tape drives, and programming will deliver a restored system. Proof that your backups are solid and reliable ensures that they will be useful in case of data loss.

Device Files

Before discussing actual backup procedures, a word on so-called *device files* is necessary. When performing backup operations to tape and other removable media, you must specify the device using its device file. These files are stored in */dev* and are understood by the kernel to stimulate the use of device drivers that control the device. Archiving programs that use the device files need no knowledge of how to make the device work. Here are some typical device files you may find on Linux systems:

/dev/st0
> First SCSI tape drive

/dev/ft0
> First floppy-controller tape drive, such as Travan drives

/dev/fd0
> First floppy disk drive

/dev/hdd
> An ATAPI Zip or other removable disk

These names are just examples. The names on your system will be hardware- and distribution-specific.

Did I Rewind That Tape?

When using tape drives, the kernel driver for devices such as */dev/st0* and */dev/ft0* automatically sends a rewind command after any operation. However, there may be times when rewinding the tape is not desirable. Since the archive program has no knowledge of how to send special instructions to the device, a *nonrewinding device file* exists that instructs the driver to omit the rewind instruction. These files have a leading *n* added to the filename. For example, the nonrewinding device file for */dev/ st0* is */dev/nst0*. When using nonrewinding devices, the tape is left at the location just after the last operation by the archive program. This allows the addition of more archives to the same tape.

Using tar and mt

The **tar** (*t*ape *ar*chive) program is used to recursively read files and directories, and then write them onto a tape or into a file. Along with the data goes detailed information on the files and directories copied, including modification times, owners, modes, and so on. This makes **tar** much better for archiving than simply making a copy does, because the restored data has all of the properties of the original.

The **tar** utility stores and extracts files from an archive file known as a *tarfile*, which has the *.tar* file extension. Since tape drives and other storage devices in Linux are viewed by the system as files, one type of tarfile is a device file, such as */dev/st0* (SCSI tape drive 0). However, nothing prevents using regular files with **tar** —this is common practice and a convenient way to distribute complete directory hierarchies as a single file.

During restoration of files from a tape with multiple archives, the need arises to position the tape to the archive that holds the necessary files. To accomplish this control, use the **mt** command. (The name comes from "*m*agnetic *t*ape.") The **mt** command uses a set of simple instructions that directs the tape drive to perform a particular action.

---

tar

Syntax

    tar [*options*] *files*

Description

Archive or restore files. **tar** recursively creates archives of files and directories, including file properties. It *requires at least one basic mode option* to specify the operational mode.

Basic mode options

-c

> Create a new tarfile.

-t

> List the contents of a tarfile.

-x

> Extract files from a tarfile.

Frequently used options

-f *tarfile*

> Unless **tar** is using standard I/O, use the **-f** option with **tar** to specify the tarfile. This might be simply a regular file or it may be a device such as */dev/st0*.

-v

> Verbose mode. By default, **tar** runs silently. When **-v** is specified, **tar** reports each file as it is transferred.

-w

> Interactive mode. In this mode, **tar** asks for confirmation before archiving or restoring files. This option is useful only for small archives.

-z

> Enable compression. When using **-z**, data is filtered through the **gzip** compression program prior to being written to the tarfile, saving additional space. The savings can be substantial, at times better than an order of magnitude depending on the data being compressed. An archive created using the **-z** option *must* also be listed and extracted with **-z**; **tar** will not recognize a compressed file as a valid archive without the **-z** option. Tarfiles created with this option will have the *.tar.gz* file extension.

-N *date*

> Store only files newer than the *date* specified. This option can be used to construct an incremental or differential backup scheme.

-V *"label"*

> Adds a *label* to the *.tar* archive. Quotes are required to prevent the label from being interpreted as a filename. A label is handy if you find an unmarked tape or poorly named tarfile.

Example 1

Create an archive on SCSI tape 0 of the */etc* directory, reporting progress:

```
# tar cvf /dev/st0 /etc
tar: Removing leading `/' from absolute path names
in the archive
etc/
etc/hosts
etc/csh.cshrc
etc/exports
etc/group
etc/host.conf
etc/hosts.allow
```

```
etc/hosts.deny
etc/motd
...
```

Note the message indicating that **tar** will strip the leading slash from */etc* for the filenames in the archive. This is done to protect the filesystem from accidental restores to */etc* from this archive, which could be disastrous.

Example 2

List the contents of the **tar** archive on SCSI tape 0:

```
# tar tf /dev/st0
...
```

Example 3

Extract the entire contents of the **tar** archive on SCSI tape 0, reporting progress:

```
# tar xvf /dev/st0
...
```

Example 4

Extract only the */etc/hosts* file:

```
# tar xvf /dev/st0 etc/hosts
etc/hosts
```

Note that the leading slash is omitted in the file specification (*etc/hosts*), in order to match the archive with the stripped slash as noted earlier.

Example 5

Create a compressed archive of *root*'s home directory on a floppy:

```
# tar cvzf /dev/fd0 -V "root home dir" /root
tar: Removing leading `/' from absolute path names
in the archive
root/
root/lost+found/
root/.Xdefaults
root/.bash_logout
root/.bash_profile
root/.bashrc
root/.cshrc
root/.tcshrc
...
tar (grandchild): Cannot write to /dev/fd0: No space
left on device
tar (grandchild): Error is not recoverable: exiting now
```

As you can see from reading the error messages, there isn't enough room on the floppy, despite compression. In this case, try storing the archive to an ATAPI Zip drive:

```
# tar cvzf /dev/hdd -V "root home dir" /root
...
```

As mentioned earlier, tape drives have more than one device file. A tape drive's nonrewinding device file allows you to write to the tape without sending a rewind instruction. This allows you to use **tar** again on the same tape, writing another archive to the media. The number of archives written is limited only by the available space on the tape.

Often multiple archives are written on a single tape to accomplish a backup strategy for multiple computers, multiple disks, or some other situation in which segmenting the backup makes sense. One thing to keep in mind when constructing backups to large media such as tape is the reliability of the media itself. If an error occurs while **tar** is reading the tape during a restore operation, it may become confused and give up. This may prevent a restore of anything located beyond the bad section of tape. Segmenting the backup into pieces may enable you to position the tape beyond the bad section to the next archive, where **tar** would work again. In this way, a segmented backup could help shield you from possible media errors.

See the **tar** info page for full details; **info** is described in "Part 1: *Documentation (Topic 1.8)*, Objective 1: Use and Manage Local System Documentation."

---

mt

Syntax

> mt [-h] [-f *device_file*] *operation* [*count*]

Description

Control a tape drive. The tape drive is instructed to perform the specified *operation* once, unless *count* is specified.

Frequently used options

-h
> Print usage information, including operation names, and exit.

-f *device_file*
> Specify the device file; if omitted, the default is used, as defined in the header file */usr/include/sys/mtio.h*. The typical default is */dev/tape*.

Popular tape operations

fsf *[count]*
> Forward space files. Move forward the number of files specified by *count* (archives, in the case of **tar**), leaving the tape positioned at the first block of the next file.

rewind
> Rewind to the beginning of the tape.

offline
> Eject the tape. This is appropriate for 8 mm or similar drives, where the tape is handled automatically by the mechanism. Ejecting the tape at the end of a backup may prevent an accidental subsequent backup to the same media. This operation is meaningless on devices that cannot eject the tape.

---

status

>Displays status information about the tape drive being used.

tell

>For some SCSI tape drives, report the position of the tape in blocks.

Many more operations exist; consult the **mt** manpage for a complete list of options.

Example 1

Move the tape in */dev/st0* to the third archive on the tape by skipping forward over two archives:

```
# mt -f /dev/nst0 fsf 2
```

Note that the nonrewinding device file is specified (*/nst0*). If the standard device is specified, the tape drive dutifully skips forward to the appropriate location on the tape, then promptly rewinds.

Example 2

Rewind the tape in */dev/st0*:

```
# mt -f /dev/st0 rewind
```

Example 3

Eject the tape cartridge:

```
# mt -f /dev/st0 offline
```

Example 4

Determine what device is represented by the default */dev/tape*:

```
# ls -l /dev/tape
lrwxrwxrwx 1 root root 8 Dec 9 15:32 /dev/tape -> /dev/st0
```

If you wish to use the default tape device */dev/tape* and it is not set on your system, you may need to set it manually:

```
# ln -s /dev/tape /dev/st0
```

Backup Operations

Using **tar** or **mt** interactively for routine system backups can become tedious. It is common practice to create backup scripts called by **cron** to execute the backups for you. This leaves the administrator or operator with the duty of providing correct media and examining logs. This section describes a basic backup configuration using **tar**, **mt**, and **cron**.

What should I back up?

It's impossible to describe exactly what to back up on your system. If you have enough time and media, complete backups of everything are safest. However, much of the data on a Linux system, such as commands, libraries, and manpages, don't change routinely and probably won't need to be saved often. Making a full backup of the entire system makes sense after you have installed and configured your system. Once you've created a backup of your system, there are some directories that you should routinely back up:

/etc

> Most of the system configuration files for a Linux system are stored in /etc, which should be backed up regularly.

/home

> User files are stored in /home. Depending on your configuration, you may also store web server files in /home/httpd. On multiuser systems or large web servers, /home can be quite large.

/usr/src

> If you've done any kernel compilation, back up /usr/src to save your work.

/var/log

> If you have security or operational concerns, it may be wise to save log files stored in /var/log.

/var/spool/mail

> If you use email hosted locally, the mail files are stored in /var/spool/mail and should be retained.

/var/spool/at and /var/spool/cron

> Users' **at** and **crontab** files are stored in /var/spool/at and /var/spool/cron, respectively. These directories should be retained if these services are available to your users.

Of course, this list is just a start, as each system will have different backup requirements.

A scripted backup with tar, mt, and cron

This section presents a simple yet effective backup methodology. The backups are scheduled to run via **cron** using a shell script. This example is not intended as a production solution, but rather as an illustration of the general concepts involved in automating a backup scheme.

In Example 1-9, we back up /etc and /home using **tar**, executing both full and differential backups to two independent segments on a tape. We use a **bash** script scheduled in **cron** using root's **crontab** file. The script will perform full backups once per week early on Monday morning and differential backups on the remaining six mornings of the week. Differential backups will be done using **tar**'s -N option. The line numbers are for reference only and not part of the code.

Example 1-9: A Simple Backup Script

```
1  #!/bin/bash
2
3  # This script performs a weekly-full/daily-differential tar backup
4  # to tape. Each item in "targets" is placed in a separate tape
5  # tarfile. Gzip compression is enabled in tar.
6
7  # what to back up
```

Example 1-9: A Simple Backup Script (continued)

```
 8 targets="/etc /home"
 9
10 # the day we want a full backup (others are differential)
11 fullday=Mon
12
13 # the target tape drive and its non-rewinding twin
14 device="/dev/st0"
15 device_n="/dev/n`/bin/basename $device`"
16
17 # get the last full backup date and the present date
18 datefile="/var/tmp/backup_full_date"
19 prev_full=`/bin/cat $datefile`
20 now=`/bin/date`
21
22 # See if today is the full backup day
23 if (`echo $now | grep $fullday > /dev/null`)
24 then
25     # create and secure the new date file
26     /bin/echo $now > $datefile
27     /bin/chmod 600 $datefile
28
29     # full backup
30     for target in $targets
31     do
32     /bin/tar -cvzf $device_n \
33         -V "Full backup of $target on $now" \
34         $target
35         # let the tape drive flush its buffer
36         sleep 5
37     done
38 else
39     # If today isn't the day to perform the full backup
40     # then the differential backup is performed
41     for target in $targets
42     do
43     /bin/tar -cvzf $device_n \
44         -V "Differential backup of $target from $prev_full to $now" \
45         -N "$now" \
46         $target
47           # let the tape drive flush its buffer
48           sleep 5
49     done
50 fi
51
52 # rewind and eject the tape
53 /bin/mt -f $device rewind
54 sleep 1
55 /bin/mt -f $device offline
```

Now let's look at some of the key elements of this script:

Lines 7-8
> The `targets` variable contains a space-separated list of directories to back up.

Lines 10-11
> `fullday` contains the day that full backups should run.

Lines 13-15
> We define the `device` and its nonrewinding version.

Lines 17-20
> We specify a `datefile`, which will simply contain the output of the **date** command at the start time of each full backup. This date is used by **tar** to determine which files belong in subsequent differential backups.

Lines 22-46
> We then check to see if we're on the full backup day and then run **tar** on each `target` accordingly, with all output going to the same tape.

Lines 36, 48, and 54
> Sometimes a tape drive indicates that it has completed an operation before it is ready for another. By adding some delays to the script, we can be sure that the tape drive is ready.

Lines 53 and 55
> Finally, we rewind and unload the tape.

To execute this script daily, the following entry is made in *root*'s **crontab**:

```
# run the backup script at 00:05 every day
5 0 * * * /root/backup
```

On Sunday night, a blank tape is inserted in the drive for the full backup. During the week, other tapes are used to record each differential backup.

If necessary, a few weeks of full backups can be retained for historical purposes. Differential backups are sometimes retained for a short period, perhaps two weeks, to allow the restoration of a file on a particular day. This is a nice policy to implement, as it protects users by allowing them access to intermediate versions of their work.

As stated earlier, this is only a simple backup scheme, and many improvements could be made to it. For example, *root* will receive all of the output from the **tar** commands in the script via email, even for successful runs. Since the system administrator may not wish to view all of this good news, the script could be modified to alert the administrator only when an error occurs. The script also does not attempt to read the tape it just created, leaving the administrator to verify backups manually.

Locked files and single-user mode

Running the script in Example 1-9 late at night may be sufficient to create a reasonable general backup scheme in many situations. However, if users or over-night processes are actively working in a filesystem as it is backed up, the state of the files in the archive will be in question. To avoid this problem, it may be safest to eliminate the users and processes from the backup scheme completely by putting Linux into single-user mode (runlevel 1) before executing the backup. In this mode, users will not be logged on, and most services, such as web or database servers, will be shut down. With no active processes running, the filesystem can be safely backed up. See *Part 1, Boot, Initialization, Shutdown, and Runlevels (Topic 2.6),* for more information on changing runlevels.

Maintenance, Verification, and Restoration

Verifying the integrity of your backups and performing occasional file restorations and system maintenance are easy processes. As mentioned earlier, backup schemes are useless unless they successfully yield positive results during a restoration.

Caring for tape drive mechanisms

Modern tape drives store large volumes of data onto compact and relatively inexpensive media with a surprisingly high degree of reliability. Their reliability is so good that it is easy to forget that the tape drives require routine cleaning.

The surface of magnetic media is coated with one or more layers of microscopic metal oxide particles. As tapes pass over the tape drive mechanism, some of these particles begin to accumulate on the heads of the tape drive. A tape head is a very small and sensitive set of electromagnets that pass over the tape. When oxide particles accumulate on the heads, they become less effective and can fail completely in extreme cases. Some devices are capable of cleaning the heads themselves, but most require periodic insertion of special cleaning media. These media look like ordinary tapes, but they are formulated to extract loose particles from the tape heads. In a production environment with daily tape drive activity, it is common to use cleaning media once every week or two.

It is important to follow the recommendations of the tape drive manufacturer for cleaning media selection and cleaning frequency, and to keep the cleaning procedure a prominent part of a solid backup methodology.

Media expiration

Some media manufacturers make claims that their media are "guaranteed for life." But be careful here—the guarantee is probably good for only the cost of the media, not for the data you've stored on it. The manufacturer's guarantee won't get you very far if you're having difficulty restoring priceless data from an old, overused, worn-out tape. It's imperative that you implement a media rotation scheme to place a limit on the number of uses of any given medium. Adding a usage limit can help to avoid getting into trouble by over-using a tape. There is no hard rule on how many times a tape can be used, and any guidelines should be based on the drive technology, recommendations from drive and tape manufacturers, and direct personal experience. You may find that your situation shows that media can be reused quite often. Regardless, it is best to avoid thinking of media in perpetual rotation. At the very least, replace your backup media once or twice a year, just to be safe.

Verifying tar archives

Keeping tape drives clean and using fresh media lay a solid foundation for reliable backups. In addition to those preventive measures, you'll want to routinely verify your backups to ensure that everything ran smoothly. Verification is important on many levels. Clearly, it is important to ensure that the data is correctly recorded. Beyond that, you should also verify that the tape drives and the backup commands function correctly during restoration. Proper file restoration techniques should be established and tested during normal operations, before tragedy strikes and places your operation into an emergency situation.

You can verify the contents of a **tar** archive by simply listing its contents. For example, suppose a backup has been made of the */etc* directory using the following command:

```
# tar cvzf /dev/st0 /etc
```

After the backup is complete, the tape drive rewinds. The archive can then be verified immediately by reviewing the contents with the –t option:

```
# tar tf /dev/st0
```

This command lists the contents of the archive so that you can verify the contents of the tarfile. Additionally, any errors that may prevent **tar** from reading the tape is displayed at this time. If there are multiple archives on the tape, they can be verified in sequence using the nonrewinding device file:

```
# tar tf /dev/nst0
# mt -f /dev/nst0 fsf 1
# tar tf /dev/nst0
# mt -f /dev/st0 rewind
```

While this verification tells you that the tapes are readable, it does not tell you that the data being read is identical to that in the filesystem. If your backup device supports them, the **tar** utility contains two options—**verify** and **compare**—that may be useful to you. However, comparisons of files on the backup media against the live filesystem may yield confusing results if your files are changing constantly. In this situation, it may be necessary to select specific files for comparison that you are certain will not change after they are backed up. You would probably restore those files to a temporary directory and compare them manually, outside of **tar**. If it is necessary to compare an entire archive, be aware that doing so doubles the time required to complete the combined backup and verify operation.

File restoration

Restoring files from a **tar** archive is simple. However, you must exercise caution regarding exactly where you place the restored files in the filesystem. In some cases, you may be restoring only one or two files, which may be safely written to their original locations if you're sure the versions on tape are the ones you need. However, restoring entire directories to their original locations on a running system can be disastrous, resulting in changes being made to the system without warning as files are overwritten. For this reason, it is common practice to restore files to a different location and move those files you need into the directories where you want them.

Reusing a previous example, suppose a backup has been made of the */etc* directory:

```
# tar cvzf /dev/st0 /etc
```

To restore the */etc/hosts* file from this archive, the following commands can be used:

```
# cd /tmp
# tar xzf /dev/st0 etc/hosts
```

The first command puts our restore operation out of harm's way by switching to the */tmp* directory. (The directory selected could be anywhere, such as a home directory or scratch partition.) The second command extracts the specified file from the archive. Note that the file to extract is specified without the leading slash. This file specification will match the one originally written to the media by **tar**, which strips the slash to prevent overwriting the files upon restore. **tar** will search the archive for the specified file, create the *etc* directory under */tmp*, and then create the final file: */tmp/etc/hosts*. This file should then be examined by the system administrator and moved to the appropriate place in the filesystem only after its contents have been verified.

To restore the entire */etc* directory, simply specify that directory:

```
# tar xzf /dev/st0 etc
```

To restore the *.bash_profile* file for user *jdean* from a second archive on the same tape, use **mt** before using **tar**:

```
# cd /tmp
# mt -f /dev/nst0 fsf 1
# tar xzf /dev/st0 /home/jdean/.bash_profile
```

In this example, the nonrewinding tape device file is used with **mt** to skip forward over the first archive. This leaves the tape positioned before the second archive, where it is ready for tar to perform its extraction.

On the Exam

This Objective on system backup isn't specific about particular commands or techniques. However, **tar** is among the most common methods in use for simple backup schemes.

You should also know how to use the **mt** command to position a tape to extract the correct archive.

Exam 101
Review Questions and Exercises

This section presents review questions to highlight important concepts and hands-on exercises that you can use to gain experience with the Topics covered on the LPI Exam 101. The exercises can be particularly useful if you're not accustomed to routine Linux administration and should help you better prepare for the exam. To complete the exercises, you'll need a working Linux system that is not in production use. You might also find it useful to have a pen and paper handy to write down your responses as you work your way through the review questions and exercises.

GNU and Unix Commands (Topic 1.3)

Review questions

1. Describe the difference between shell variables and environment variables.

2. Compare and contrast built-in and explicitly defined commands and those found in PATH.

3. After a lengthy session of file manipulation on the command line, what will the !ls command produce?

4. What program was the source for the default history editing key bindings in **bash**?

5. Explain the notion of *pipes* as they refer to shell capabilities, and illustrate using an example of two or more filter programs.

6. Explain the -p option to **cp** and give an example of why it is necessary.

7. Give two examples of files matched by the wildcard ??[!1-5].

8. Name the three Standard I/O streams and their functions.

9. Give an example of the redirection operator, >, and describe how the outcome would be different using the >> operator.

10. What process is the ultimate ancestor of all system processes? Give both the PID and the program name.

11. Name three common utilities used for process monitoring.

12. What happens to a typical daemon when it receives SIGHUP? How would the behavior be different if it received SIGKILL?

13. Compare and contrast background and foreground jobs, and state the syntax to put a command in the background on the command line.

14. Explain the relationship between a process' *nice number* and its execution priority.

15. What two classifications of characters make up regular expressions?

16. How are the regular expressions [A-Z]* and ^[A-Z]*$ different?

Exercises

Exercise 1.3-1. Bash

1. Start a **bash** shell in a console or terminal window and enter the following commands:

```
$ MYVAR1="Happy"
$ MYVAR2="Birthday"
$ export MYVAR1
$ bash
$ echo $MYVAR1 $MYVAR2
$ exit
$ echo $MYVAR1 $MYVAR2
```

   a. Was the behavior of the two **echo** commands identical?

   b. If so, why? If not, why not?

   c. What happened immediately after the **bash** command?

   d. Which variable is an environment variable?

2. Continuing the previous exercise, enter Ctrl-P until you see the last **echo** command. Enter Ctrl-P again.

   a. What do you see?

   b. Why wasn't it the **exit** command?

   c. Enter Ctrl-P again so that the **export** command is displayed. Add a space and MYVAR2 so that the line now looks like this:

```
$ export MYVAR1 MYVAR2
```

   What happens when you enter this command?

3. Still continuing the previous exercise, enter the command **!echo**. Does anything change as a result of the revised **export** command?

4. The **file** command is used to examine a file's contents and displays the file type. Explain the result of using **file** as follows:

```
$ cd / ; file $(ls | head -10)
```

Exercise 1.3-2. GNU commands in pipes

1. Execute this command on your system:

   ```
   $ cut -d: -f1 /etc/passwd | fmt -w 20 | head -1
   ```

   a. What was displayed?

   b. How many lines of output did you see? Why?

   c. What was the width of the output? Why?

2. Execute the following **sed** substitution command and explain why it might be used on */etc/passwd*:

   ```
   $ sed 's/:[^:]*:/:---:/' /etc/passwd | less
   ```

Exercise 1.3-3. File management

1. Execute this command:

   ```
   $ cd /sbin ; ls -li e2fsck fsck.ext2
   ```

   a. What is the significance of the first field of the output?

   b. Why is it identical for both listings?

   c. Why are the file sizes identical?

2. Execute the following command sequence and explain the result at each step (this example assumes that **cp** is not aliased to **cp -i**, which is a common default alias):

   ```
   $ cd
   $ cp /etc/skel .
   $ cp -r /etc/skel .
   $ cp -rfv /etc/skel .
   $ cp -rfvp /etc/skel .
   ```

3. Remove the directory created in the previous exercise, using **rmdir** and/or **rm**. Which command can complete the task in a single step?

4. Explain when the wildcard {htm,html} might be useful.

5. Give an example of how the wildcard *.[Tt][Xx][Tt] could be used with directory listings.

6. What can be said about filenames matched by the *.? wildcard?

Exercise 1.3-4. Redirection

1. Experiment with redirecting the output of **ls** as follows:

   ```
   $ cp /etc/skel . 2> info.txt
   ```

   a. How is the terminal output different than that observed in Exercise 1.3-3?

   b. What is written to *info.txt*?

2. Experiment with the various forms of redirection in Table 1-10 on page 43, including the **tee** command.

Exercise 1.3-5. Processes

1. Experiment with **ps**, **pstree**, and **top** to monitor active processes on your system. Include **top**'s interactive commands.

2. If you have Apache running, use **ps** (and perhaps **grep**) to identify the **httpd** process and its *pid*, which is owned by root. Send that process the HUP signal as follows:

   ```
   $ kill -SIGHUP pid
   ```

   Using **tail**, examine the Apache error log (the location of your log file may differ):

   ```
   $ tail /var/log/httpd/error_log
   ```

   What was the effect of HUP on Apache?

3. While running X, start some interactive processes in the background and experiment with using **jobs**, **bg**, and **fg**. For example:

   ```
   $ netscape &
   $ xterm &
   $ emacs &
   $ jobs
   $ fg 1
   $ fg 2
   ...
   ```

   Were you able to bring each of the jobs to the foreground successfully?

Exercise 1.3-6. Process priority

1. This exercise starts a process, using various methods to view and modify the process execution priority:

   a. Start an editing session in the background using **nice**:

   ```
   $ nice vi &
   ```

   b. Observe that the process was **nice**'d using **ps**:

   ```
   $ ps -u
   ```

   c. Check it again using **top**:

   ```
   $ top -i
   ```

   d. Within **top**, renice the **vi** process using the **r** command and observe the effect on priority.

   e. Exit **top** and use **renice** to set the nice value back to zero.

Exercise 1.3-7. Regular expressions

1. Use a simple regular expression with **grep** to find **sh** and **bash** users in */etc/passwd*:

   ```
   $ grep "/bin/..sh" /etc/passwd
   ```

2. Determine the number of empty lines in */etc/inittab*:

   ```
   $ grep "^ *$" /etc/inittab | wc -1
   ```

   Explain the regular expression and the use of **wc**.

Devices, Linux Filesystems, and the Filesystem Hierarchy Standard (Topic 2.4)

Review questions

1. How many IDE devices can be installed in a Linux system? If all of them are installed and they're all disk drives, what are their device names?

2. What are the three types of disk partitions found on a Linux system? Which type can contain other partitions and which type does it contain?

3. Name the directories that must be within the *root* partition.

4. Describe the differences between physical disks, partitions, and filesystems.

5. What is a */swap* partition used for? Why not just use swap files?

6. What kind of output will **df –h** yield?

7. Describe a common situation that is likely to cause the automatic use of **fsck** on the next system boot.

8. Name the fields in */etc/fstab*.

9. Give the command to mount a CD-ROM drive on the secondary master IDE device, assuming that */etc/fstab* does not contain a line for the device.

10. If the **ro** option is used in */etc/fstab* for */usr*, what limitation is placed on that filesystem?

11. Compare and contrast hard and soft quota limits.

12. What three types of users can be granted or denied access to filesystem objects and how do they apply to files and directories?

13. Name the symbolic permission that is equivalent to 0754.

14. Describe a situation that requires the SUID permission. What ramifications does this permission imply?

15. Compare and contrast the differences between hard and symbolic links.

16. Name the document to which Linux directory assignments should conform.

17. Compare and contrast the differences between the **locate** and **find** commands.

Exercises

WARNING

Working with partitions and filesystems can damage your system. It is recommended that you use an expendable Linux system to perform the following exercises to be certain that mistakes won't harm a production system.

Exercise 2.4-1. Partitions and filesystems

1. As root, run **fdisk** and enter the **p** command to print the partition table. Examine your system's configuration and make sure you understand everything you see. Enter the l (a lowercase *L*) command and review the many partition types Linux can accommodate. Enter the **q** command to quit without saving changes.

2. If you have available disk space, use **fdisk** to create a new *ext2* partition, then format it with **mkfs**. Pay close attention to the output from **mkfs**.

Exercise 2.4-2, Filesystem integrity

1. Use a pager to examine */var/log/messages* and search for entries made by **fsck**. Did it find any problems?

2. If you created a new *partition* in Exercises 2.4-1 and 2.4-2, check it now with **fsck** and observe the output:

   $ **fsck -f /dev/***partition*

3. Check on the status of filesystems using **df**:

   $ **df -h**

   a. How does the **-h** flag assist you with interpreting the results?

   b. Are any of your filesystems nearly full?

   c. Which are underutilized?

4. As root, get a top-level view of disk usage by user using **du**:

   $ **du -s /home/***

   a. Are there any surprises?

   b. How could you use **sort** to make this output more useful?

Exercise 2.4-3. Mounting and unmounting

1. Review */etc/fstab*. Be sure you can name all six fields and their order as well as describe their function.

2. Examine the output of the **mount** command without options. Compare the output with the contents of */etc/fstab*.

3. If you created a new *partition* in Exercises 2.4-1 and 2.4-2, mount it on */mnt/new* or some other location of your choosing:

   $ **mkdir /mnt/new**
   $ **mount /dev/***partition* **/mnt/new**
   $ **df /mnt/new**

   a. Did the filesystem mount correctly? Can you store files on it?

   b. Next, unmount it:

      $ **umount /dev/***partition* **/mnt/new**

   c. Add a line to */etc/fstab* for the new partition:

      /dev/*partition*   /mnt/new   ext2   defaults   1 2

Exercise 2.4-4. Disk quotas

1. Using the instructions in "Part 1: *Devices, Linux Filesystems, and the Filesystem Hierarchy Standard (Topic 2.4)*, Objective 4: Set and View Disk Quotas," enable quotas on your */home* filesystem.

2. Test the quotas by setting them low for a particular user, then start adding files as that user until the quota is exceeded. What is the observable consequence of exceeding the quota?

Exercise 2.4-5. File permissions

1. Practice converting these file modes from octal to symbolic form:

   a. 0777

   b. 0754

   c. 0666

   d. 1700

   e. 7777

2. Practice converting these file modes from symbolic to octal form. You can assume that **x** bits are set under SUID, SGID, and sticky bits:

   a. -rwxr-xr-x

   b. -r--r--r--

   c. -rwsrwsrwx

   d. -rw-rw---t

   e. -rws-w--w-

3. Create temporary files and use **chmod** with both symbolic and numeric mode modifications. Include SUID, SGID, and sticky bits.

4. Using the instructions in "Part 1: *Devices, Linux Filesystems, and the Filesystem Hierarchy Standard (Topic 2.4)*, Objective 5: Use File Permissions to Control Access to Files," to set up a workgroup directory using group and sticky bits for access control. Verify that the directory meets the defined requirements.

Exercise 2.4-6. File ownership

1. As root, create temporary files and use **chown** to modify user ownership and group ownership.

2. Use **chgrp** to modify group ownership on the temporary files created in the previous exercise.

Exercise 2.4-7. Links

1. Create a temporary file and links as follows:

```
$ touch a_file
$ ln -s a_file an_slink
$ ln a_file an_hlink
```

Now verify that the file and the hard link indeed share an inode and that the symbolic link points to the original file:

```
$ ls -a_file an_slink an_hlink
```

Exercise 2.4-8. File location

1. Read the latest version of the FHS (it's not very long).

2. Examine your filesystem. Does it match the FHS? If you find discrepancies, is it clear why they don't?

3. Use **which** to check on the location of executable files.

4. Use **find** to search for **bash**:

```
$ find / -name bash
```

Now use **locate** for the same file:

```
$ locate bash
```

How are the results different? Describe a context in which each command would be useful.

5. Update your **locate** database using **updatedb**. Note the amount of time this command takes and the resources it consumes on your system.

Boot, Initialization, Shutdown, and Runlevels (Topic 2.6)

Review questions

1. Name and briefly describe the two parts of LILO. Which part has a configuration file and what is that file called?

2. What are the ramifications relating to new hardware when running a monolithic kernel?

3. Which three runlevels are well defined across Linux distributions, and what actions to they perform?

4. Describe a situation that would imply the need to switch to single-user mode.

5. What are the two alphabetic prefixes used in the **rd** directories, and what do they stand for?

6. How can you shutdown and halt a Linux system immediately using **shutdown**?

Exercises

Exercise 2.6-1. Boot

1. Examine the contents of */etc/lilo.conf.* How many kernel images or operating systems are configured for load by LILO? Explain the options you find in the file.

2. Install the boot loader by executing **lilo**. What happened?

3. Boot your system and manually specify the root filesystem using the **root=** keyword at the LILO prompt. What happens if you specify the wrong partition?

4. Use **dmesg** and **less** to examine boot-time messages. Compare what you find to the latest boot messages found in */var/log/messages.*

5. Boot your system and use the **single** or **1** option to boot directly into single-user mode.

Exercise 2.6-2. Runlevels

1. After booting to single-user mode, switch to your normal runlevel using **init n**.

   a. Does the system come up as expected?

   b. Enter **init 1** to go back to single-user mode. What daemons are still running?

2. Familiarize yourself with the contents of a few of the scripts in */etc/rc.d/init.d* (your system directories may vary).

3. Look in *rc0.d* through *rc6.d* for links to the scripts you examined. How are the scripts used? In which runlevels is the corresponding service active?

4. Shut down your system with **init 0**.

5. Shut down your system with **shutdown -h now**.

Documentation (Topic 1.8)

Review questions

1. Describe the PAGER environment variable.

   a. How does it affect the **man** facility?

   b. If PAGER is not set, how docs **man** display output?

   c. Does this environment variable affect the **info** facility?

2. In response to your query on a library function, **man** returns a page on an identically named user command. Why does this happen?

   a. How do you display the page for the function and not the command?

   b. How do you display both?

3. Where are the HOWTO documents located on a typical Linux system?

4. Name the program that displays GNU Texinfo pages.

5. What is probably the most important skill you can offer to end users while staffing a helpdesk service?

Exercises

Exercise 1.8-1. man and /usr/doc

1. Run a **man** inquiry as follows:

   ```
   $ man -a -Pless mkfifo
   ```

   There is both a **mkfifo** command and a **mkfifo** function. You'll be looking at the **mkfifo** command from section 1 of the manual. Note MKFIFO(1) at the top of the page.

   Press the letter **q** to terminate the pager program. The pager is then invoked again and displays the **mkfifo** function from section 3 of the manual. Note MKFIFO(3) at the top of the page.

   Run the **man** command again, using the **-Pmore** option as follows:

   ```
   $ man -a -Pmore mkfifo
   ```

   a. What differences do you see in the output?

   b. What does the **-P** option do?

2. Run another **man** inquiry as follows:

   ```
   $ man -d ln
   ```

   a. What output do you get from **man**?

   b. What is the **-d** option?

   c. Did you see information on the **ln** command?

   Now examine the **man** configuration file:

   ```
   $ less /etc/man.config
   ```

   Notice how the contents of this file coincide with the result you received from the **-d** option.

3. Enter the following command:

   ```
   $ locate whois
   ```

   Note that **locate** shows two commands that match **whois**, along with a directory and a *README* file.

   Now use the **stat** program to evaluate the two commands:

   ```
   $ stat /usr/bin/whois /usr/bin/fwhois
   ```

   Examine the inode number for both files. An inode is a unique identifier, or node, of your Linux filesystem. The fact that these two files show the same inode indicates that they are links to the same file. That is, one file has two directory entries with different names. This means that you'll be running the same program regardless of which command name you use.

Next, examine the *README* file that **locate** reported:

```
$ less /usr/doc/fwhois-1.00/README
```

Your version may be different. Now look for a manpage and an **info** page for this program:

```
$ man fwhois
$ info fwhois
```

As you can see, the program author chose not to offer a manpage or an **info** page for **fwhois**, leaving the *README* in */usr/doc* as the sole documentation for the program.

4. Suppose you are Spanish-speaking and would like to learn about how to use Linux in your native tongue. Try the following commands:

```
$ man spanish
$ info spanish
$ find /usr/doc -name "*anish*"
```

   a. Do the **man** and **info** utilities have anything to offer on Spanish?

   b. Did you find a document in */usr/doc* that concerns Spanish?

Exercise 1.8-2. Internet documentation resources

1. Using a Usenet news reader program, subscribe to *comp.os.linux* and *comp.os.linux.advocacy*.

   a. Of these, which has the highest volume, as indicated by the number of unread messages?

   b. Do you see messages of interest in these groups?

Exercise 1.8-3. Creating system documentation

1. Using a text editor, create a text file named *mycmd.1*. Complete the following steps:

   a. This page is intended as an example of local documentation, so store it in */usr/local/man/man1/mycmd.1*. Are there other files in this directory already? Why or why not?

   b. What happens when you execute the command:

```
$ man mycmd
```

   Did you get the result you expected? Experiment with the formatting macros by adding italic and bold both on a per-line basis (`.B`) and an in-line basis (`\fB`).

Exercise 1.8-4. Acting as a Linux helpdesk

Suppose you are a helpdesk technician in a mixed-systems office, and you are relatively new to Linux. A user calls your helpdesk with a general question about Linux system shutdown. He indicates that he's heard from Unix gurus that using the **halt** command could be unsafe. He also reports getting frustrated with

Windows NT users who use the **Ctrl-Alt-Del** key combination on his system console, which causes his Linux server to shut down. He asks for specific information on:

- How to safely shut down Linux.

- How to allow nonsuperusers the ability to shut down cleanly.

- How to disable the **Ctrl-Alt-Del** shutdown.

Let's further assume you don't know how to answer these questions and that you have access to system documentation. Complete the following steps:

1. Use the **man** facility to investigate the **halt** command. Based on what you find there, answer the following:

   a. In what section of the manual is **halt** located? Why?

   b. Determine if it is "safe" to use **halt** to shut down Linux. What caused the Unix gurus to instruct the caller that using **halt** was not safe?

   c. Determine if it would still be safe if the user uses the **-n** option to **halt**.

   d. Is it appropriate to use **halt** on a multiuser system to which others are logged in?

   e. Use **man** on the other commands referred to by the **halt** manpage in the *SEE ALSO* section.

2. Evaluate the other commands:

   a. Which commands can be used to shut down the system in place of **halt**?

   b. Which commands would be the most appropriate for shutting down a multiuser system?

3. From what you see in the manpages:

   a. Where is the **Ctrl-Alt-Del** system shutdown configured?

   b. Explain how to disable it.

   c. Do you need to reboot to enable the change? If so, why?

   d. How can you configure the system to allow specified nonsuperusers to shut down cleanly?

   e. If you use the **info** command, are you provided with additional information?

4. After successfully following your instructions, the user calls again. This time he is puzzled by error messages that are produced when his users attempt a clean shutdown from multiuser mode using the **shutdown** command without arguments.

   a. Re-evaluate the manpages in question. Are there any clues to common problems? (Hint: see *BUGS*.)

   b. State the typical **shutdown** command to issue from multiuser mode.

Administrative Tasks (Topic 2.11)

Review questions

1. Why is it considered insecure to store encrypted passwords in */etc/passwd*?

    a. What is the alternative?

    b. When the alternative is implemented, what happens to the password field in */etc/passwd*?

2. What would happen to a user account if the default shell were changed to */bin/false*?

3. When a new account is created with **useradd -m**, what files are used to populate the new home directory?

4. Compare and contrast the execution of */etc/profile* and */etc/bashrc*.

5. What is the complete filename for the file where most **syslog** messages are sent?

6. Describe the three **syslog** parameters: *facility*, *level*, and *action*.

7. Compare and contrast **cron** and **at**.

8. Is there a **cron** command?

9. State the format of a **crontab** file, describing each of the six fields.

10. What does an asterisk mean in **crontab** fields 1 through 5?

11. Compare and contrast the differential and incremental backup methods.

12. Why is **mt** usually used along with **tar** to implement simple backup schemes?

    a. What special measures must be taken with regard to device names when using **mt** for multiple-volume **tar** backups?

Exercises

Exercise 2.11-1. User accounts

1. Examine the */etc/passwd* file on your system.

    a. Is this the only means of user authentication on your system?

    b. Are shadow passwords in use?

    c. Are user accounts handled by NIS or are they all local?

2. Repeat the first exercise for groups.

3. If you have an expendable system available, experiment with implementing shadow passwords.

4. Add a user with **useradd**, including a new home directory populated with files from */etc/skel*.

5. Add a group with **groupadd**.

6. Use **usermod** to add your new user to the new group.

7. Set the new user's password using **passwd**.

8. Log into the new account, and use **newgrp** to change to the new group.

9. Delete the new group and user (including home directory) using **groupdel** and **userdel**.

Exercise 2.11-2. User environment and variables

1. Examine the contents of */etc/skel*. How similar are they to your own home directory?

2. Review the contents of */etc/profile* and */etc/bashrc*.

Exercise 2.11-3. Syslog and log files

1. Add the *local5* facility to your configuration as described in "Part 1: *Administrative Tasks (Topic 2.11)*, Objective 3: Configure and Use System Log Files." Use **logger** to write to your new log file, and verify its contents. Compare your log entries with those in */var/log/messages*.

2. Examine */etc/logrotate.conf*. What happens after */var/log/messages* is rotated?

Exercise 2.11-4. cron and at

1. Add an entry in your personal **crontab** file to perform a task, such as sending you an email message. Confirm that the action occurs as expected. Experiment with the five time specifiers.

2. Schedule a command in the future with **at**. How is **at** different from **cron**?

Exercise 2.11-5. Backup

1. Imagine that you have recently been made responsible for an important production system. No formalized backup procedures are in place. Backup operations that are run are not cataloged and media are scattered. Now imagine that after a holiday weekend the system has crashed due to a power failure. Upon restart, the system has severe disk errors requiring manual **fsck**. After repairs are complete, the system is again usable, but users complain about missing, truncated, or corrupt files. If a formalized backup procedure had been in place, would the outcome have been different?

2. If you have a tape drive available, experiment with **tar**, creating small tarfiles on a tape.

   a. Using the nonrewinding tape device, create multiple archives on the tape, and use **mt** to position among them.

   b. Verify that the various archives you create are accessible to **tar**.

Exam 101
Practice Test

Exam 101 consists approximately of 60 questions. Most are multiple-choice single-answer, a few are multiple-choice multiple-answer, and the remainder are fill-in questions. No notes or other materials are permitted, and you have 90 minutes to complete the exam. The answers are provided on page 224.

Questions

1. What section of the online user's manual and command reference holds administrative (not user) commands? Select one.

    a. Section 1

    b. Section 2

    c. Section 8

    d. Section n

    e. Section s

2. What two commands will display the status of processes on a Linux system? Select one.

    a. ls and df

    b. ps and top

    c. ps and df

    d. df and top

    e. du and df

3. What does the device file */dev/hdb6* represent? Select one.

    a. An extended partition on a SCSI disk drive

    b. A logical partition on a SCSI disk drive

    c. An extended partition on an IDE disk drive

d. A primary partition on an IDE disk drive

e. A logical partition on an IDE disk drive

4. Which command will display the last lines of text file *file1*? Select one.

    a. **head -b** *file1*

    b. **head --bottom** *file1*

    c. **head -v** *file1*

    d. **tail** *file1*

    e. **tail -n 1** *file1*

5. In the **bash** shell, entering the !! command has the same effect as which one of the following?

    a. **Ctrl-P** and **Enter**

    b. **Ctrl-N** and **Enter**

    c. **Ctrl-U** and **Enter**

    d. !-2

    e. !2

6. Which of the following commands can be used to check an *ext2* filesystem? Select all that apply.

    a. **fsck -ext2 /dev/hda5**

    b. **fsck /dev/hda5**

    c. **e2fsck /dev/hda5**

    d. **fsck.ext2 /dev/hda5**

    e. **fsck.linux /dev/hda5**

7. Name the command that displays pages from the online user's manual and command reference.

_____

8. In response to the **df** command, the system reports a **Use%** of **98%** for the file-system mounted on */home*. Which one of the following best describes the significance of this information?

    a. Files on */home* are consuming 98 percent of the physical disk.

    b. File read/write activity on */home* are consuming 98 percent of system I/O capacity.

    c. Files on */home* are consuming 98 percent of the */home* filesystem.

    d. Inodes on */home* are nearly exhausted.

    e. Inodes on */home* are 98 percent free.

9. Of the following directories, which one is the most important to back up on a routine basis?

    a. */var*

    b. */tmp*

c. */usr*

d. */root*

e. */etc*

10. Carolyn has a text file named *guest_list* containing 12 lines. She executes the following command. What is the result? Select one.

    # **split -4 guest_list gl**

    a. The first four columns in the text are written to new files *glaa*, *glab*, *glac*, and *glad*.

    b. The first four columns in the text are written to new files *aagl*, *abgl*, *acgl*, and *adgl*.

    c. The lines of *guest_list* are evenly divided among new files *glaa*, *glab*, *glac*, and *glad*.

    d. The lines of *guest_list* are evenly divided among new files *glaa*, *glab*, and *glac*.

    e. The lines of *guest_list* are evenly divided among new files *aagl*, *abgl*, and *acgl*.

11. Which one of the following commands would be best suited to mount a CD-ROM containing a Linux distribution, without depending on any configuration files?

    a. **mount /dev/cdrom /dev/hdc**

    b. **mount -f linux /dev/hdc /mnt/cdrom**

    c. **mount -t iso9660 /dev/cdrom /mnt/cdrom**

    d. **mount -t linux /dev/cdrom /mnt/cdrom**

    e. **mount -t iso9660 /mnt/cdrom /dev/cdrom**

12. An *ext2* filesystem is configured with user quotas enabled. The soft limit is set at 100 MB per user, the hard limit is set at 110 MB per user, and the grace period is seven days. User *bsmith* already owns 90 MB of the data stored on the filesystem. What happens when *bsmith* writes a new file of size 30 MB? Select one.

    a. The write will fail, but the superuser can recover the entire file within seven days.

    b. The write will fail, and the file will be truncated permanently.

    c. The write will succeed, but the file will be truncated permanently.

    d. The write will succeed, but the file will be available for only seven days.

    e. The write will succeed, but the file will be truncated in seven days.

13. User *jdoe*, a member of the *finance* group, owns a text file with group owner *finance* and mode *0077*. Which statements are true regarding access to view the contents of the file, assuming the directory that contains it has mode *0777*? Select all that apply.

a. *jdoe* can view the file's contents.

b. *jdoe* can first change the protection mode of the file and then view the file's contents.

c. *root* cannot view the file's contents.

d. Everyone in the *finance* group can view the file's contents except *jdoe*.

e. Everyone in the *finance* group can view the file's contents including *jdoe*.

14. Which of the following commands displays the comments from a **bash** script? Select all that apply.

   a. `find "^#" /etc/rc.d/rc.local`

   b. `sed '/^#/ !d' /etc/rc.d/init.d/httpd`

   c. `grep ^# /etc/rc.d/init.d/httpd`

   d. `grep ^# /etc/passwd`

   e. `locate "^#" /etc/skel/.bashrc`

15. State the syntax to direct the standard output of **cmd1** directly into the standard input of **cmd2**.

   _____

16. Which one of the following answers creates an environment variable VAR1, present in the environment of a **bash** child process?

   a. `VAR1="fail" ; export VAR1`

   b. `VAR1="fail" \ export VAR1`

   c. `VAR1="fail"`

   d. `set VAR1="fail" ; enable VAR1`

   e. `export VAR1 \ VAR1="fail"`

17. Name the full path and name of the file that holds most of the information on system user groups.

   _____

18. Which of the following directories *must* be part of the root filesystem? Select all that apply.

   a. */etc*

   b. */home*

   c. */lib*

   d. */usr*

   e. */root*

19. Name the facility that independently executes commands on a periodic basis for multiple users.

   _____

20. Alex is currently working in a directory containing only one file, *Afile1*. What is displayed after the following commands are entered in **bash**? Select one.

```
# MYVAR=ls
# echo $MYVAR "$MYVAR" '$MYVAR' `$MYVAR`
```

   a. *Afile1 Afile1 Afile1 Afile1*

   b. **ls** *Afile1 Afile1 Afile1*

   c. **ls ls** *Afile1 Afile1*

   d. **ls ls** *$MYVAR Afile1*

   e. **ls ls ls** *$MYVAR*

21. What does the **&** character do when placed at the end of a command? Select one.

   a. It allows another command to be entered on the same line.

   b. It causes the process to be stopped.

   c. It restarts a stopped process.

   d. It causes the process to be placed into the foreground.

   e. It causes the process to be placed into the background.

22. Which one of the following commands could be used to change all upper-case characters to lowercase in the middle of a pipe?

   a. **grep**

   b. **egrep**

   c. **wc**

   d. **tr**

   e. **pr**

23. What is the PID of **init**? Select one.

   a. 0

   b. 1

   c. 2

   d. undefined

   e. unknown

24. Which one of the following outcomes results from the following command?

```
# chmod g+s /home/software
```

   a. The SUID bit will be set for */home/software*.

   b. The SGID bit will be set for */home/software*, preventing access by those not a member of the *software* group.

   c. The SGID bit will be set for */home/software*, in order to keep group membership of the directory consistent for all files created.

   d. The sticky bit will be set for */home/software*.

   e. The sticky bit will be applied to all files in */home/software*.

25. Which one of the following commands is equivalent to the following command for user *jdoe* whose home directory is */home/jdoe*?

    # chmod 754 ~/file1

    a. # chmod u=rwx,g=rx,o=r /home/jdoe/file1

    b. # chmod ugo=rwx ~/file1

    c. # chmod u=7,g=5,o=4 ~/file1

    d. # chmod 754 \home\jdoe\file1

    e. # chmod 754 /usr/jdoe/file1

26. What command and single required option creates a symbolic link in a Linux *ext2* filesystem?

    _____

27. What command can display the contents of a binary file in a readable hexadecimal form? Select one.

    a. xd

    b. hd

    c. od

    d. Xd

    e. dump

28. Which one of the following commands copies files with the *.txt* extension from */dir1* into */dir2*, while preserving file attributes such as dates?

    a. mv --copy /dir1/*.txt /dir2

    b. mv /dir1/*.txt /dir2

    c. cp -k /dir1/*.txt /dir2

    d. cp -p /dir1/*.txt /dir2

    e. cp -p /dir2 < /dir1/*.txt

29. Which one of the following file globs matches "Linux" and "linux," but not "linux.com" and not "TurboLinux"?

    a. [L/linux]

    b. ?inux

    c. \L\linux

    d. [Ll]inux

    e. [Ll]inux?

30. A process with PID 4077 is misbehaving on your system. As superuser, you enter the following command:

    # kill 4077

    However, nothing changes as a result. What can you do to terminate the process? Select one.

a. # **kill -9 4077**

b. # **kill -1 4077**

c. # **kill +9 4077**

d. # **kill 4078**

e. # **kill --die 4077**

31. Which one of the following key sequences is used to put a noninteractive text-mode program that is attached to the terminal into the background to allow it to continue processing?

 a. **Ctrl-C**

 b. **Ctrl-B**

 c. **Ctrl-B** and then enter the **bg** command

 d. **Ctrl-Z**

 e. **Ctrl-Z** and then enter the **bg** command

32. What basic command is used to create hard disk partitions?

_____

33. With a **umask** of 027, how is the initial mode set for a newly created file? Select one.

 a. 0750

 b. 0640

 c. 0027

 d. 1027

 e. 1640

34. Consider the following script, stored in a file with proper modes for execution:

```
#!/bin/bash
for $v1 in a1 a2
do
echo $v1
done
```

Which one of the following best represents the output produced on a terminal by this script?

 a. in

 a1

 a2

 b. a1

 a2

 c. $v1

 $v1

 $v1

d. No output is produced, but the script executes correctly.

e. No output is produced, because the script has an error.

35. Which one of the following commands verbosely extracts files from a **tar** archive on a magnetic tape device?

    a. **tar cvf /dev/st0**

    b. **tar cvf /dev/ttyS0**

    c. **tar xvf /dev/st0**

    d. **tar xvf /dev/ttyS0**

    e. **tar rvf /dev/st0**

36. Alex wants to protect himself from inadvertently overwriting files when copying them, so he wants to alias **cp** to prevent overwrite. How should he go about this? Select one.

    a. Put alias cp='cp –i' in ~/.bashrc.

    b. Put alias cp='cp –i' in ~/.bash_profile.

    c. Put alias cp='cp –p' in ~/.bashrc.

    d. Put alias cp='cp –p' in ~/.bash_profile.

    e. Put alias cp = `cp –I` in ~/.bashrc.

37. Which one of the following utilities outputs a text file with line numbers along the left margin?

    a. **tar**

    b. **wc**

    c. **tr**

    d. **nl**

    e. **ln**

38. The following line comes from an /etc/fstab file. Which of the statements is accurate given the contents of this line? Choose all that apply.

    ```
    /dev/fd0    /mnt/fd0    vfat    noauto,users  0 0
    ```

    a. Users are prohibited from mounting and unmounting the filesystem.

    b. Users are permitted to mount and unmount the filesystem.

    c. The filesystem will be mounted on mount point /dev/fd0.

    d. The filesystem is expected to be a Linux native filesystem.

    e. The filesystem is on a floppy disk.

39. Which one of the following is an accurate statement regarding this regular expression?

    ```
    [^1-8A-Za-z]
    ```

    a. It matches all letters and numbers.

    b. It matches all letters and numbers except 9.

    c. It matches all letters and numbers except 9 and 0, but only at the beginning of a line.

d. It matches 9, 0, and other nonletter and nonnumber characters.

e. It matches characters other than letters or numbers.

40. Monica consults the */etc/passwd* file expecting to find encrypted passwords for all of the users on her system. She sees the following:

```
jdoe:x:500:500::/home/jdoe:/bin/bash
bsmith:x:501:501::/home/bsmith:/bin/tcsh
```

Which of the following is true? Select one.

   a. Accounts *jdoe* and *bsmith* have no passwords.

   b. Accounts *jdoe* and *bsmith* are disabled.

   c. The passwords are in */etc/passwd-*

   d. The passwords are in */etc/shadow*

   e. The passwords are in */etc/shadow-*

41. Name the briefest form of the command to initiate a change to runlevel 5.

_____

42. Where does *The Linux System Administrators' Guide* originate? Select one.

   a. Red Hat Software, Inc.

   b. O'Reilly and Associates, Inc.

   c. The Free Software Foundation.

   d. The Linux Documentation Project.

   e. Usenet newsgroup *comp.os.linux.*

43. What does the "sticky bit" do? Select one.

   a. It prevents files from being deleted by anyone.

   b. It marks files for deletion.

   c. It prevents files from being deleted by nonowners except *root.*

   d. It prevents files from being deleted by nonowners including *root.*

   e. It marks files for archive.

44. What variable holds the list of directories searched by the shell to find executable programs?

_____

45. Which one of the following commands displays the full path and name of the executable program **myprog** that the shell would execute if **myprog** were entered as a command?

   a. # **which myprog**

   b. # **find −name myprog**

   c. # **find myprog**

   d. # **locate myprog**

   e. # **apropos myprog**

46. Alex executes the **runlevel** command and gets 3 5 as the response. What does this tell Alex? Select one.

    a. The system is in runlevel 3 and the default is 5.

    b. The system is in runlevel 3 and will next go to runlevel 5.

    c. The system was in runlevel 3 and is now in runlevel 5.

    d. The system does not have a default runlevel.

    e. The system default runlevel is improperly configured.

47. Which one of these files determines how messages are stored using **syslogd**?

    a. */etc/sysconfig/logger.conf*

    b. */etc/syslog.conf*

    c. */etc/syslogd.conf*

    d. */etc/conf.syslog*

    e. */etc/conf.syslogd*

48. What does the **pr** command do? Select one.

    a. It prints files to the default printer.

    b. It displays a list of active processes.

    c. It modifies the execution priority of a process.

    d. It paginates text files.

    e. It modifies the command-line prompt.

49. Dave has a Linux system with an interrupt conflict caused by his 3C509 network card. Dave's kernel is fully modular. How could Dave instruct the system to use interrupt 11 for his network adapter? Select one.

    a. Enter `linux eth0=irq11` at the LILO boot loader prompt.

    b. Enter `linux 3c509=irq11` at the LILO boot loader prompt.

    c. Add `options 3c509 irq=11` to */etc/conf.modules*.

    d. Add `options irq=11 3c509` to */etc/conf.modules*.

    e. Add `ifup -irq 11 eth0` to */etc/rc.d/rc.sysinit*.

50. What is contained in directory */sbin*? Select the single best answer.

    a. Commands needed in the event of a system emergency of interest to all system users.

    b. Commands of interest to all system users.

    c. Commands needed in the event of a system emergency of interest mainly to the administrator.

    d. Commands of interest mainly to the administrator.

    e. Libraries needed in the event of an emergency.

51. What *ext2* filesystem attribute allows a process to take on the ownership of the executable file's owner?

52. What is appended to the beginning of a command line in order to modify the execution priority of the resulting process?

_____

53. How are the **cat** and **tac** commands related? Select one.

    a. **cat** displays files and **tac** does the same but in reverse order.

    b. **cat** concatenates files while **tac** splits a file into pieces.

    c. **cat** creates file catalogs while **tac** displays the catalogs.

    d. The two commands are links to the same executable.

    e. There is no relation or similarity between **cat** and **tac**.

54. With regard to the use of regular expressions to match text in a file, describe a metacharacter. Select one.

    a. They are standard text characters used in the regular expression.

    b. They are special control characters used in the regular expression.

    c. They are used to display results after using a regular expression.

    d. They are used by the shell to display graphics.

    e. Metacharacters aren't used in regular expressions.

55. How many IDE devices can be installed and simultaneously used in a typical Intel-based system? Select one.

    a. 1

    b. 2

    c. 3

    d. 4

    e. 5

56. Which one of the following would be a consequence of a filesystem running out of inodes?

    a. More inodes would be automatically created in the filesystem.

    b. Quotas would become disabled on the filesystem.

    c. The filesystem would be corrupted.

    d. The filesystem would be marked read-only.

    e. No writes would be possible on the filesystem until existing files were deleted.

57. Consider the following line of console output, excerpted from among other lines of output. Which one of the commands produced it?

    ```
    /dev/hda8      1.9G  559M  1.2G  30%  /home
    ```

    a. **du -s**

    b. **du -k**

    c. **df -h**

d. **df -k**

e. **df -m**

58. How can you configure your system at shutdown time to suppress **fsck** upon the next boot? Select one.

    a. **init 6**

    b. **init --suppress 6**

    c. **shutdown -h**

    d. **shutdown -f**

    e. **shutdown -F**

59. Which one of the following is true about the LILO boot loader?

    a. It can start the Windows NT Loader.

    b. It is started using the **lilo** command.

    c. It is the only boot loader available for Linux.

    d. It can start multiple Linux kernels, but no foreign operating systems.

    e. It resides entirely in the boot sector.

60. Which one of the following statements correctly describes the > and >> symbols in the context of the **bash** shell?

    a. > appends standard output to an existing file, and >> writes standard output to a new file.

    b. > writes standard output to a new file, and >> appends standard output to an existing file.

    c. > writes standard error to a new file, and >> appends standard error to an existing file.

    d. > pipes standard output to a new file, and >> pipes standard output to an existing file.

    e. > pipes standard output to an existing file and >> pipes standard error to a new file.

Answers

1. c. Section 8 holds administrative commands such as **fsck** and **mkfs**.

2. b. Both **ps** and **top** yield process status. None of the other listed commands are related to processes.

3. e. IDE disk drives are referred to as */dev/hdx*, where x is a, b, c, or d. Partitions are numbered from 1 through 4 for primary and extended partitions and 5 through 16 for logical partitions.

4. d. The **tail** command is used for checking the last lines of a text file. By default, it displays 10 lines.

5. a. The **!!** command history expansion executes the previous command. Entering the **Ctrl-P** keystroke uses the Emacs key-binding **bash** to move up one line in the history; pressing **Enter** executes that command.

6. b, c, and d. **fsck** is a frontend for the programs that actually do the checking. *e2fsck* and *fsck.ext2* are links to the program that checks native Linux *ext2* filesystems.

7. The **man** command displays manpages.

8. c. **df** reports disk information, including a percentage of the filesystems used. Answer a is incorrect because */home* may not be the only partition on the physical disk.

9. e. */var* and */tmp* are mainly transient, */usr* is typically static, */root* is simply a home directory for *root*, but */etc* contains system configuration information that frequently changes.

10. d. *split –n outfile* separates a file into multiple output files, each with *n* lines, and names them *outfileaa*, *outfileab*, and so on. Since the original file had 12 lines and Carolyn split it into sets of 4 lines, the result is three files named *glaa*, *glab*, and *glac*, each containing 4 lines.

11. c. CD-ROMs use the *iso9660* filesystem, which is the default for **mount**, but also indicated using –t. Without the assistance of an entry in */etc/fstab*, both the mount device (*/dev/cdrom*) and the mount point (*/mnt/cdrom*) must be provided.

12. b. The write will continue until the hard limit of 110 MB is reached, after which the write fails and data is lost.

13. b and d. Without user privilege to the file, *jdoe* cannot see the contents. However, as the file's owner, the mode can be changed to gain access. Everyone in *finance* is granted permission, but *jdoe* as the owner is denied.

14. b and c. **find** and **locate** do not search the contents of files. */etc/passwd* is not a script.

15. cmd1 | cmd2

16. a. The variable must be set and exported. The semicolon separates the two commands.

17. */etc/group*

18. a and c. */etc*, */lib*, */bin*, */sbin*, and */dev* must be in the */root* filesystem.

19. **cron.**

20. d. The first **echo** argument is unquoted and thus returns its contents, **ls**. The second is quoted with double quotes, which do not preserve the $, so it too returns **ls**. The third is quoted with single quotes, which do preserve the $, so it returns the string $MYVAR. The last argument is backquoted, which means that it returns the result of the command stored in $MYVAR. The command is **ls**, which displays the only file in the directory, *Afile1*.

21. e. Using the & character puts a program in the background.

22. d. The **tr** program translates characters from one group into another, including case.

23. b. **init**, the grandfather of all processes, always has PID 1.

24. c. The **g** indicates that we're operating on the group privilege, and the **+s** indicates that we should add the "set id" bit, which means that the SGID property will be applied.

25. a. User mode 7 is the same as u=rwx, group mode 5 is the same as g=rx, and other mode 4 is the same as o=r. The ~/ syntax implies the user's home directory.

26. **ln –s**

27. c. The octal dump program, when used with the **–t x** option, will output in hexadecimal notation.

28. d. The **-p**, or preserve, option is required to retain dates.

29. d. The [Ll] matches both letters.

30. a. **kill -9** is drastic but necessary for processes unable to respond to other signals.

31. e. **Ctrl-Z** stops the job and gives control back to the terminal. **bg** places the job into the background and restarts it.

32. **fdisk**

33. b. By default, files do not have the execute privilege, which rules out all responses containing odd numbers in the mode. They also do not by default have the sticky bit set, which eliminates response e. Response b is the result of masking initial bits 666 with **umask** 027, leaving 640, which is the same as 0640.

34. e. The script has an error and will not produce the expected output. In a **for** statement, the loop variable does not have the dollar sign. Changing line 2 to **for v1 in a1 a2** will correct the error and produce the output in answer B.

35. c. **tar** should be used with the extraction option **x** and a tape device, such as SCSI tape 0 */dev/st0*.

36. a. **cp** should be aliased to the interactive mode with the **–i** option in *.bashrc*. *.bash_profile* normally doesn't include aliases.

37. d. The **nl** command numbers lines.

38. b and e. The *users* option grants non-privileged users the right to mount and unmount the filesystem. */dev/fd0* is a floppy device.

39. d. Brackets ([]) are used to group a character set consisting of numbers 1–8 and characters A–Z and a–z. The ^ just inside the opening bracket negates the whole string, such that the string matches numbers 0, 9, and symbols.

40. d. The shadow password system has been implemented, placing all passwords in */etc/shadow* as denoted by the **x** following the username.

41. **init 1**. **telinit 1** would also work, as they are both links to the same file.

42. d. *The Linux System Administrators' Guide* is a free publication of the Linux Documentation Project (LDP) and is available online at *http://www.ibiblio.org/mdw/index.html*.

43. c. The sticky bit in the mode prevents deletion by non-owners, but *root* can still delete the file.

44. **PATH**.

45. a. The **which** command is used to search the directories specified in variable **PATH**.

46. c. The **runlevel** command yields the previous and present runlevels.

47. b. */etc/syslog.conf* is the configuration file for the Syslog daemon **syslogd**.

48. d. **pr** converts text files into paginated, columnar versions.

49. c. Since Dave is using a modular kernel, the network driver *3c509.o* is a kernel module. LILO can send kernel parameters but not module parameters. These are stored in */etc/conf.modules*.

50. c. While answers b and d are technically correct, answer c best describes */sbin*.

51. SUID.

52. **nice**.

53. a. **cat** concatenates files, and as a subset, will list one or more files to standard output. **tac** lists files in reverse order.

54. b. A metacharacter is a special character that is used to modify and control the interpretation of literals. File globbing is generally considered distinct but very similar to the use of regular expressions.

55. d. PCs usually have two IDE interfaces, each capable of handling two devices.

56. e. A filesystem without free inodes cannot create new objects until existing objects are removed.

57. c. This is an example line from the output of **df -h**, the "human-readable" mode of **df**.

58. d. The **shutdown –f** command configures the filesystem to skip the **fsck** checking. The **-F** option forces the check.

59. a. LILO can start the Windows NT boot loader and many other operating systems.

60. b. The > character opens and writes to a new file, while >> appends to an existing file, unless that file doesn't exist, in which case it is opened first.

Exam 101
Highlighter's Index

GNU and Unix Commands (Topic 1.3)

Objective 1: Work Effectively on the Unix Command Line

The interactive shell and shell variables

- A *shell* provides the command prompt and interprets commands.

- A *shell variable* holds a value that is accessible to shell programs.

- PATH is a shell variable that contains a listing of directories that hold executable programs.

- Commands must be **bash** built-ins, found in the PATH, or explicitly defined in order to succeed.

- When shell variables are *exported*, they become part of the *environment*.

Entering commands

- Commands are comprised of a valid command, with or without one or more options and arguments, followed by a carriage return.

- Interactive commands can include looping structures more often used in shell scripts.

Command history, editing, and substitution

- Shell sessions can be viewed as a conversation. History, expansion, and editing make that dialogue more productive.

- Commands can be reissued, modified, and edited. Examples are shown in Table 1-29.

- Command substitution allows the *result* of a command to be placed into a shell variable.

Table 1-29: Shell Expansion, Editing, and Substitution Examples

History Type	Examples
Expansion	! ! !n ^string1^string2
Editing	**Ctrl-P**, previous line **Ctrl-K**, kill to end of line **Ctrl-Y**, paste (yank) text
Substitution	VAR=$ (*command*)

Recursive execution

- Many commands contain either a **-r** or **–R** option for recursive execution through a directory hierarchy.

- The **find** command is inherently recursive, and is intended to descend through directories looking for files with certain attributes or executing commands.

Objective 2: Process Text Streams Using Text Processing Filters

The following programs modify or manipulate text from files and standard input:

cut [*files*]
Cut out selected columns or fields from one or more *files*.

expand *files*
Convert tabs to spaces in *files*.

fmt [*files*]
Format text in *files* to a specified width by filling lines and removing newline characters.

head [*files*]
Print the first few lines of *files*.

join *file1 file2*
Print a line for each pair of input lines, one each from *file1* and *file2*, that have identical *join fields*.

nl [*files*]
Number the lines of *files*, which are concatenated in the output.

od [*files*]
Dump *files* in octal, hexadecimal, ASCII, and other formats.

paste *files*
Paste together corresponding lines of one or more *files* into vertical columns.

pr [*file*]
> Convert a text *file* into a paginated, columnar version, with headers and page fills.

split [*infile*] [*outfile*]
> Split *infile* into a specified number of line groups; the output will go into a succession of files of *outfileaa*, *outfileab*, and so on.

tac [*file*]
> Print *file* to standard output in reverse line order.

tail [*files*]
> Print the last few lines of one or more *files*.

tr [*string1* [*string2*]]
> Translate characters by mapping from *string1* to the corresponding character in *string2*.

wc [*files*]
> Print counts of characters, words, and lines for *files*.

The stream editor, sed

sed is a popular text-filtering program found on nearly every Unix system; it has the following syntax:

sed *command* [*files*]

sed -e *command1* [-e *command2*] [*files*]

sed -f *script* [*files*]
> Execute **sed** *commands*, or those found in *script*, on standard input or *files*.

Objective 3: Perform Basic File Management

- Filesystem creation is called *formatting*, which prepares a disk partition for use. Linux usually uses the native *ext2* (second extended) filesystem.

- The Linux filesystem is arranged into a hierarchical structure anchored at the *root directory*, or /. Beneath this is a tree of directories and files.

- Identification information for a filesystem object is stored in its *inode*, which holds location, modification, and security information. Filesystems are created with a finite number of inodes.

File and directory management commands

The following commands are essential for the management of files and directories:

cp *file1 file2*

cp *files directory*
> Copy *file1* to *file2*, or copy *files* to *directory*.

mkdir *directories*
> Create one or more *directories*.

mv *source target*
> Move or rename files and directories.

rm *files*

> Delete one or more *files* from the filesystem. When used recursively (with the -r option), rm also removes directories.

rmdir *directories*

> Delete *directories*, which must be empty.

touch *files*

> Change the access and/or modification times of *files* by default to the present time.

File-naming wildcards

Wildcards (also called *file globs*) allow the specification of many files at once. A list of commonly used wildcards can be found in Table 1-30.

Table 1-30: File-Naming Wildcards

Wildcard	Function
*	Match zero or more characters.
?	Match exactly one character.
[characters]	Match any single character from among characters listed between brackets
[!characters]	Match any single character other than characters listed between brackets.
[a-z]	Match any single character from among the range of characters listed between brackets.
[!a-z]	Match any single character from among the characters not in the range listed between brackets.
{frag1, frag2, frag3, ...}	Brace expansion: create strings frag1, frag2, and frag3, etc., such that {file_one,two,three} yields file_one, file_two, and file_three.

Objective 4: Use Unix Streams, Pipes, and Redirects

- A central concept for Linux and Unix systems is that *everything is a file*.

- Many system devices are represented in the filesystem using a *device file*, such as */dev/ttyS0* for a serial port.

Standard I/O

- The shell provides the *standard I/O* capability, offering three default file descriptors to running programs.

- *Standard input* (*stdin*) is a text input stream, by default attached to the keyboard.

- *Standard output (stdout)* is an output stream for normal program output.

- *Standard error (stderr)* is an additional output stream meant for error messages.

Pipes and redirection

- It is possible to tie the output of one program to the input of another. This is known as a *pipe* and is created by joining commands using the pipe symbol (|).

- Pipes are a special form of *redirection*, which allows you to manage the origin of input streams and the destination of output streams. Redirection syntax for various shells differs slightly. See Table 1-31 for examples of common redirection operators.

Table 1-31: Common Redirection Operators

Redirection Function	Syntax for bash
Send *stdout* to *file*.	`$ cmd > file` `$ cmd 1> file`
Send *stderr* to *file*.	`$ cmd 2> file`
Send both *stdout* and *stderr* to *file*.	`$ cmd > file 2>&1`
Receive *stdin* from *fil.e*	`$ cmd < file`
Append *stdout* to *fil.e*	`$ cmd >> file` `$ cmd 1>> file`
Append *stderr* to *file*.	`$ cmd 2>> file`
Append both *stdout* and *stderr* to *file*.	`$ cmd >> file 2>&1`
Pipe *stdout* from *cmd1* to *cmd2*.	`$ cmd1	cmd2`
Pipe *stdout* and *stderr* from *cmd1* to *cmd2*.	`$ cmd1 2>&1	cmd2`
Pipe *stdout* from *cmd1* to *cmd2* while simultaneously writing it to *file1* using *tee*.	`$ cmd1 tee file1	cmd2`

Objective 5: Create, Monitor, and Kill Processes

- Processes have:
  - A lifetime.
  - A PID.
  - A UID.
  - A GID.
  - A parent process.
  - An environment.
  - A current working directory.

Monitoring commands

ps
> Generate a one-time snapshot of the current processes on standard output.

pstree
> Display a hierarchical list of processes in a tree format.

top
> Generate a continuous, formatted, real-time process activity display on a terminal or in a terminal window.

Signaling processes

- Processes listen for *signals* sent by the kernel or users using the **kill** command:

  kill *-sigspec* [*pids*]
  > Send *sigspec* to *pids*.

- Common **kill** signals are listed in Table 1-32.

Table 1-32: Common Signals

Signal	Number	Meaning
HUP	1	Hangup, reread configuration.
INT	2	Interrupt, stop running.
KILL	9	Stop immediately.
TERM	15	Terminate nicely.
TSTP	18	Stop executing, ready to continue.

Shell job control

Shells can run processes in the *background,* where they execute on their own, or in the *foreground,* attached to a terminal. Each process handled in this way is known as a *job.* Jobs are manipulated using job control commands:

bg [*jobspec*]
> Place *jobspec* in the background as if it had been started with **&**.

fg [*jobspec*]
> Place *jobspec* in the foreground, making it the current job.

jobs [*jobspecs*]
> List *jobspecs* on standard output.

Objective 6: Modify Process Execution Priorities

- A process' *execution priority* is managed by the kernel.

- You can bias the execution priority by specifying a *nice number* in the range of −20 to +19 (default is 0).

- Positive nice numbers reduce priority; negative nice numbers increase priority and are reserved for the superuser.

nice −*adjustment* [*command*]

Apply nice number *adjustment* to the process created to run *command*.

renice [+|−] *nicenumber targets*

Alter the *nicenumber*, and thus the scheduling priority, of one or more running *target* processes.

Objective 7: Perform Searches of Text Files Making Use of Regular Expressions

* *Regular expressions* are used to match text. The term is used to describe the loosely defined text-matching language as well as the patterns themselves. A regular expression is often called a *regex* or a *regexp*.

* Regular expressions are made up of *metacharacters* (with special meaning) and *literals* (everything that is not a metacharacter).

Position anchors

These operators match line position:

^

Match the beginning of a line.

$

Match the end of a line.

Character sets

These operators match text:

[abc]

[a−z]

Match any single character from among listed characters or from among the characters comprising a range.

[^abc]

[^a−z]

Match any single character not among listed characters or ranges.

\<*word*\>

Match *words* bounded by whitespace.

. *(A single period, or dot)*

Match any single character except a *newline*.

\

Turn off (escape) the special meaning of a metacharacter that follows.

Modifiers

These operators modify the way other operators are interpreted:

*

Match zero or more of the character that precedes it.

. ?

Match zero or one instance of the preceding *regex*.

+

Match one or more instances of the preceding *regex*.

\{*n*, *m*\}

Match a range of occurrences of the single character or *regex* that precedes this construct.

|

Match the character or expression to the left or right of the vertical bar.

Devices, Linux Filesystems, and the Filesystem Hierarchy Standard (Topic 2.4)

Objective 1: Create Partitions and Filesystems

Disk drives and partitions

- IDE disks are known as */dev/hda*, */dev/hdb*, */dev/hdc*, and */dev/hdd*.

- SCSI disks are known as */dev/sda*, */dev/sdb*, */dev/sdc*, and so on.

- Three types of partitions:

  Primary
  Filesystem container. At least one must exist, and up to four can exist on a single physical disk. They are identified with numbers 1 to 4, such as */dev/hda1*, */dev/hda2*, and so on.

  Extended
  A variant of a primary partition but it cannot contain a filesystem. Instead, it contains one or more *logical partitions*. Only one extended partition may exist, and it takes one of the four possible spots for primary partitions.

  Logical
  Created *within* the extended partition. From 1 to 12 logical partitions may be created. They are numbered from 5 to 16, such as */dev/hda5*, */dev/hda10*, and so on.

- Up to 15 partitions with filesystems may exist on a single physical disk.

The root filesystem and mount points

- The top of the filesystem tree is occupied by the *root filesystem*. Other filesystems are mounted under it, creating a unified filesystem.

- */etc*, */lib*, */bin*, */sbin*, and */dev* must be part of the root filesystem.

Partition and filesystem management commands

The following commands are commonly used to repair and manage filesystems:

fdisk [*device*]

> Manipulate or display the partition table for *device* using a command-driven interactive text interface. *device* is a physical disk such as */dev/hda*, not a partition such as */dev/hda1*.

mkfs *device*

> Make a filesystem on *device*.

mkswap *device*

> Prepare a partition for use as swap space.

Objective 2: Maintain the Integrity of Filesystems

These commands are commonly used in day-to-day filesystem maintenance:

df [*directories*]

> Display overall disk utilization information for mounted filesystems on *directories*.

du [*directories*]

> Display disk utilization information for *directories*.

fsck *filesystems*

> Check *filesystems* for errors and optionally correct them.

Objective 3: Control Filesystem Mounting and Unmounting

Managing the filesystem table

- */etc/fstab* contains mount information for filesystems. Each line contains a single filesystem entry made up of six fields, shown in Table 1-33.

Table 1-33: Fields Found in the /etc/fstab File

Entry	Description
Device	The device file for the partition holding the filesystem.
Mount point	The directory upon which the filesystem is to be mounted.
Filesystem type	A filesystem type, such as *ext2*.
Mount options	A comma-separated list.
Dump frequency	For use with *dump*.
Pass number for **fsck**	Used at boot time.

Mounting and unmounting

The following commands are used to mount and unmount filesystems:

mount *device*
mount *directory*
mount *device directory*

> Mount filesystems onto the hierarchy. The first and second forms consult */etc/fstab* for additional information.

Devices, Linux Filesystems, and the Filesystem Hierarchy Standard (Topic 2.4)

umount *device*
umount *directory*
　　Unmount the filesystem on *device* or mount it on *directory*.

Filesystem types

Common filesystem types compatible with Linux include:

ext2
　　The standard Linux filesystem.

iso9660
　　The standard CD-ROM format.

msdos
　　The MS-DOS FAT filesystem.

nfs
　　Remote servers.

proc
　　The *proc* filesystem, which is a system abstraction for access to kernel parameters.

swap
　　Swap partitions.

vfat
　　Virtual FAT, used instead of *msdos*.

Objective 4: Set and View Disk Quota

• 　Quotas are used to enforce a disk space or an inode maximum on individuals, groups, or both.

• 　These types of quota limits can be set:

Per-user hard
　　The maximum size for an individual.

Per-user soft
　　A warning threshold.

Per-group hard
　　The maximum size for a group.

Per-group soft
　　A warning threshold.

Grace period
　　A time restriction on the soft limit.

• 　These commands manipulate quotas:

quota *user*
quota –g *group*
　　Display quota limits on *user* or *group*.

quotaon [*filesystems*]
　　Enable previously configured disk quotas on one or more *filesystems*.

quotaoff [*filesystems*]
> Disable disk quotas on one or more *filesystems*.

quotacheck [*filesystems*]
> Examine filesystems and compile quota databases. Usually run via **cron**.

edquota *names*
> Modify user or group quotas by spawning a text editor.

repquota *filesystems*
> Display a summary report of quota status for *filesystems*, or use –a for all filesystems:

NOTE

Enabling quotas requires **usrquota** and/or **grpquota** options in */etc/fstab*, creation of *quota.user* and *quota.group* files at the top of the filesystem, a **quotacheck**, and a **quotaon**.

Objective 5: Use File Permissions to Control Access to Files

Access control

- Access control is implemented using a set of properties called the *access mode*, stored in the inode. Three classes of user are defined:

  User
  > The user that owns the file.

  Group
  > The group that owns the file.

  Other
  > All other users on the system.

- Three permissions are either granted or not granted to each class of user:

  Read (r)
  > Allows access to file contents and listing of directory contents.

  Write (w)
  > Allows writing a file or creating files in a directory.

  Execute (x)
  > Allows execution of a file and read/write files in a directory.

- These comprise nine bits in the mode User **rwx**, Group **rwx**, and Other **rwx**.

- Three additional mode bits are defined:

  SUID
  > To grant processes the rights of an executable file's owner.

  SGID
  > To grant processes the rights of an executable file's group.

  Sticky bit
  > Prohibits file deletion by nonowners.

- These 12-mode bits are often referred to in octal notation as well as with mnemonic constructs.
- Mode bits are displayed using such commands as **ls** and **stat**.

Setting access modes

- New files receive initial access mode as described by the **umask**.
- The **umask** strips specified bits from the initial mode settings. Typical **umasks** are 002 and 022.
- Existing file modes are changed using **chmod** with either symbolic or octal mode specifications:
  - Symbolic:
    ```
    [ugoa][-+=][rwxXst]
    ```
  - Octal bits:
    ```
    user r, w, x, group r, w, x, other r, w, x
    rwxrwxrwx = 111111111 = 777
    rwxr-xr-- = 111101100 = 751
    ```

chmod uses the following syntax:

chmod *mode files*
> Modify the access mode on *files* using a symbolic or octal *mode*.

Objective 6: Manage File Ownership

- Access modes are tied to file ownership.
- Files have both individual and group ownership:

  chown *user-owner.group-owner files*
  > Change the owner and/or group of *files* to *user-owner* and/or *group-owner*.

  chgrp *group-owner files*
  > Change the group ownership of *files* to *group-owner*.

- **chgrp** functionality is included in **chown**.

Objective 7: Create and Change Hard and Symbolic Links

- A link is a pseudonym for another file.
- Links take very little space in the filesystem.
- A *symbolic link* is a tiny file that contains a pointer to another file. Symbolic links can span filesystems.
- A *hard link* is a copy of a file's directory entry. Both directory entries point to the same inode and thus the same data, ownership, and permissions.

ln has the following syntax:

> **ln** *file link*
> **ln** *files directory*

Create *link* to *file* or in *directory* for all *files*. Symbolic links are created with the -s option.

Objective 8: Find System Files and Place Files in the Correct Location

- The FHS is used by Linux distributions to standardize filesystem layout. It defines two categories of data use, each with opposing subtypes:

  - Data sharing: sharable data can be used by multiple host systems on a network. Non-sharable data is unique to one particular host system.

  - Data modification: variable data is changed continually by naturally occurring (i.e., frequent) processes. Static data is left alone, remaining unchanged over extended periods of time.

- The FHS seeks to define the filesystem contents in these terms and locate information accordingly.

The directory hierarchy

- The root filesystem:

  - Must contain utilities and files sufficient to boot the operating system, including the ability to mount other filesystems.

  - Should contain the utilities needed by the system administrator to repair or restore a damaged system.

  - Should be relatively small.

- */usr* contains system utilities and programs that do not appear in the */root* partition. It includes directories such as */bin*, */lib*, */local*, and */src*.

- */var* contains varying data such as printer spools and log files, including directories such as *log*, *mail*, and *spool*.

Locating files

- Various methods can be used to locate files in the filesystem:

  which *command*
  Determine the location of *command* and display the full pathname of the executable program that the shell would launch to execute it.

  find *paths expression*
  Search for files that match *expression* starting at *paths* and continuing recursively.

  locate *patterns*
  Locate files whose names match one or more *patterns* by searching an index of files previously created.

  updatedb
  Refresh (or create) the *slocate* database, usually via **cron**.

whatis *keywords*
apropos *keywords*
> Search the **whatis** database for *keywords*. **whatis** finds only exact matches, while **apropos** finds partial word matches.

Boot, Initialization, Shutdown, and Runlevels (Topic 2.6)

Objective 1: Boot the System

LILO, the Linux loader

- LILO is a utility designed to load a Linux kernel (or another operating system) into memory and launch it. It has two parts:

The boot loader.
> A two-stage program intended to find and load a kernel. The first stage resides in the disk boot sector and is started by the system BIOS. It locates and launches a second, larger stage residing elsewhere on disk.

The lilo command
> The map installer, used to install and configure the LILO boot loader. It reads */etc/lilo.conf* and writes a corresponding map file.

- The */etc/lilo.conf* file contains options and kernel image information. Popular directives are:

boot
> The name of the hard disk partition that contains the boot sector.

image
> Refers to a specific kernel file.

install
> The file installed as the new boot sector.

label
> Provides a label, or name, for each image.

map
> Directory where the *map* file is located.

prompt
> Prompts the user for input (such as kernel parameters or runlevels) before booting and without a keystroke from the user.

read-only
> The root filesystem should initially be mounted read-only.

root
> Used following each image, this specifies the device that should be mounted as *root*.

timeout
> The amount of time, in tenths of a second, the system waits for user input.

Kernel parameters and module configuration

- LILO can pass kernel parameters using *name=value* pairs.

- Linux kernels are modular, with portions of kernel functionality compiled as modules to be used as needed.

- Parameters to modules can be specified in */etc/conf.modules*.

Boot-time messages

- The kernel gives detailed status information as it boots. This information can also be found in system logs such as */var/log/messages* and from the **dmesg** command.

Objective 2: Change Runlevels and Shutdown or Reboot System

- Runlevels specify how a system is used by controlling which services are running.

- Runlevels are numbered 0 through 6, as well as with a few single characters.

- Runlevel 0 implies system shutdown.

- Runlevel 6 implies system reboot.

- The intermediate runlevels differ in meaning among distributions.

- Runlevel 1 (also s or S) is usually single-user (maintenance) mode.

- Runlevels 2 through 5 usually define some kind of multiuser state, including an X login screen.

Single-user mode

- Runlevel 1 is a bare-bones operating environment intended for maintenance. Remote logins are disabled, networking is disabled, and most daemons are shut down.

- Single-user mode can be entered with the *single*, or simply *1*, parameter at the LILO prompt.

- Switching to single-user mode is done using *init 1*.

The /etc/rc.d directory

- The */etc/rc.d* file contains initialization scripts and links controlling the boot process for many Linux distributions:

    rc.sysinit
    > The startup script launched by **init** at boot time.

    rc.local
    > A script for local startup customizations, started automatically after the system is running.

    rc
    > A script used to change runlevels.

init.d
> The directory containing scripts to start and stop system services.

rc0.d through rc6.d
> Links to scripts in *init.d*.

- Names of the links are [*K*| *S*][*nn*][*init.d_name*]:

  - *K* and *S* prefixes mean *kill* and *start*, respectively.

  - *nn* is a sequence number controlling startup or shutdown order.

  - *init.d_name* is the name of the script being linked.

Default runlevel, determining runlevel, changing runlevels

- The default runlevel is located in */etc/inittab* on the line containing *initdefault*:

  id:*n*:initdefault:
  > *n* is a valid runlevel number such as 3.

- Runlevel is determined by the **runlevel** command, which displays the previous and current runlevels. An *N* for previous runlevel indicates that the runlevel has not changed since startup.

- Runlevels can be changed using **init**:

  init *n*
  > Change to runlevel *n*.

- System shutdown can also be initiated using **shutdown**:

  shutdown *time*
  > Bring the system down in a secure, organized fashion. *time* is mandatory, in the form of *hh:mm*, *now*, or *+n* for *n* minutes.

Documentation (Topic 1.8)

Objective 1: Use and Manage Local System Documentation

Text and paging

- In the context of Linux systems, *plain text* means files or streams of both printable characters and control characters, using a standard encoding scheme such as ASCII.

- Differentiating text from nontext isn't obvious, but the *file* command examines a file given as its argument and offers a response that indicates the file type.

- A *pager* is a program intended to offer a quick and simple interface for viewing text files, one screen at a time.

- **more** is a popular pager available on most Unix systems.

- **less** is a full-featured text pager, which emulates **more** and offers significant advantages. Common **less** commands are listed in Table 1-34.

Table 1-34: Common less Commands

less Command	Description
Space	Scroll forward one screen.
D	Scroll forward one-half screen.
Return	Scroll forward one line.
B	Scroll backward one screen.
U	Scroll backward one-half screen.
Y	Scroll backward one line.
g	Go to the beginning of the text (could be slow with large amounts of text).
G	Go to the end of the text (could be slow with large amounts of text).
/*pattern*	Search forward for *pattern*, which can be a regular expression.
?*pattern*	Search backward for *pattern*, which can be a regular expression.
H	Display a help screen.
:n	Display next file from command line (two-character command).
:p	Display previous file from command line (two-character command).

- A pager such as **less** is used by the **man** facility.

The man facility

- A *manpage* exists for most commands and is viewed using **man**:

  man [*section*] *command*
  > Format and display manpages from the manual *section* based on the topic of *command* using a pager.

- Manpages are usually found in the */usr/man* directory, but they can also be found elsewhere in the filesystem. The manpage location can be found in */etc/man.config*, along with the paging program to use and other information about the manpages.

/usr/doc

- Many documents for Linux systems are available in */usr/doc*. Included here are package-related documents, FAQs, HOWTOs, and so on.

The info facility

- The Free Software Foundation provides the **info** documentation format.
- GNU software comes with **info** documentation.
- The documentation is viewed with the **info** command, which displays a full-screen editor-like paging system. Common **info** commands are listed in Table 1-35.

Table 1-35: Common info Commands

info Command	Description
Tab	Move among hypertext links.
Enter	Follow hypertext links.
d	Return to the top (directory node) of the menu.
?	List all **info** commands.
p and n	Move to previous and next pages, respectively.
u	Move up one level in the Texinfo hierarchy.
q	Terminate the system.
h	Give a primer for first-time users.
/*string*	Enter a *string*.
/*pattern*	Search forward for *pattern*, which can be a regular expression.

Objective 2: Find Linux Documentation on the Internet

Linux Documentation Project

- A loosely knit team of writers, proofreaders, and editors who work together to create the definitive set of documentation for Linux. The Linux Documentation Project can be found online at *http://www.linuxdoc.org*.
- The LDP has a wide range of documents, from complete books to personal accounts of problem-solving techniques.

Other sources

- Many Usenet newsgroups, such as *comp.os.linux*, *comp.os.linux.advocacy*, *comp.os.linux.development*, and others, are dedicated to Linux.
- Mailing lists offered by many Linux groups serve to keep members informed through email distribution of information.

Objective 3: Write System Documentation

- System manpages are an excellent place to create local documentation.
- Raw **man** files are usually processed using **nroff** for display purposes. You can use this format or simply create a text file and store it in the appropriate **cat** directory.
- Local manpages will probably go in */usr/local/man*.

Administrative Tasks (Topic 2.11)

Objective 1: Manage Users and Group Accounts and Related System Files

passwd and group

- User account information is stored in */etc/passwd*.
- Each line in */etc/passwd* contains a username, password, UID, GID, user's name, home directory, and default shell.
- Group information is stored in */etc/group*.
- Each line in */etc/group* contains a group name, group password, GID, and group member list.
- *passwd* and *group* are world-readable.

Shadow files

- To prevent users from obtaining encrypted passwords from *passwd* and *group*, shadow files are implemented.
- Encrypted passwords are moved to a new file, which is readable only by *root*.
- The shadow file for */etc/passwd* is */etc/shadow*.
- The shadow file for */etc/group* is */etc/gshadow*.

User and group management commands

The following commands are commonly used for manual user and group management:

useradd *user*
  Create the account *user*.

usermod *user*
  Modify the *user* account.

userdel *user*
  Delete the *user* account.

groupadd *group*
  Add *group*.

groupmod *group*
  Modify the parameters of *group*.

groupdel *group*
  Delete *group*.

passwd *username*
  Interactively set the password for *username*.

gpasswd *groupname*
  Interactively set the password for *groupname*.

pwconv

> Convert a standard password file to a shadow configuration.

pwunconv

> Revert from a shadow password configuration.

grpconv

> Convert a standard group file to a shadow configuration.

grpunconv

> Revert from a shadow group configuration.

chage *user*

> Modify password aging and expiration settings for *user*.

Objective 2: Tune the User Environment and System Environment Variables

Configuration scripts

- The **bash** shell uses system-wide configuration scripts—such as */etc/profile* and */etc/bashrc*—when it starts.

- Commands in */etc/profile* are executed at login time.

- Commands in */etc/bashrc* are executed for each invocation of **bash**.

- Changes to these system-wide files affect all users on the system.

New account home directories

- New user directories are populated automatically by copying */etc/skel* and its contents.

- The system administrator may add, modify, and delete files in */etc/skel* as needed for the local environment.

Objective 3: Configure and Use System Log Files to Meet Administrative and Security Needs

Syslog

- The **syslog** system displays and records messages describing system events.

- Messages can be placed on the console, in log files, and on the text screens of users.

- **syslog** is configured by */etc/syslog.conf* in the form *facility.level action:*

  facility

  > The creator of the message, selected from among *auth, authpriv, cron, daemon, kern, lpr, mail, mark, news, syslog, user,* or *local0* through *local7.*

level

    Specifies a severity threshold beyond which messages are logged and is one of (from lowest to highest severity) *debug, info, notice, warning, err, crit, alert,* or *emerg.* The special level *none* disables a facility.

action

    The destination for messages that correspond to a given selector. It can be a filename, *@hostname,* a comma-separated list of users, or an asterisk, meaning all logged-in users.

- Together, *facility.levels* comprise the *message selector.*
- Most *syslog* messages go to */var/log/messages.*

Log file rotation

- Most system log files are *rotated* to expire old information and prevent disks from filling.
- *logrotate* accomplishes log rotation and is configured using */etc/logrotate.conf.*

Examining log files

- Files in */var/log* (such as *messages*) and elsewhere can be examined using utilities such as *tail, less,* and *grep.*
- Information in *syslog* log files includes date, time, origin hostname, message sender, and descriptive text.
- To debug problems using log file information, first look at the hostname and sender, then at the message text.

Objective 4: Automate System Administration Tasks by Scheduling Jobs to Run in the Future

- Both **cron** and at can be used to schedule jobs in the future.
- Scheduled jobs can be any executable program or script.

Using cron

- The **cron** facility consists of **crond**, the cron daemon, and *crontab* files containing job-scheduling information.
- **cron** is intended for the execution of commands on a periodic basis.
- **crond** examines all *crontab* files every minute.
- Each system user has access to **cron** through a personal *crontab* file.
- The **crontab** command, shown here, allows the *crontab* file to be edited and viewed:

crontab

    View, or with **-e**, edit *crontab* files.

- Entries in the *crontab* file are in the form of:

    minute hour day month dayofweek command

- Asterisks in any of the time fields match all possible values.

- In addition to personal *crontab* files, the system has its own *crontab* files: */etc/ crontab* as well as files in */etc/cron.d*.

Using at

- The **at** facility, shown here, is for setting up one-time future command execution:

  at *time*
  > Enter an interactive session with **at**, where commands may be entered. *time* is of the form *hh:mm, midnight, noon*, and so on.

User access

- Access to **cron** can be controlled using lists of users in *cron.allow* and *cron.deny*.

- Access to **at** can be controlled using lists of users in *at.allow* and *at.deny*.

Objective 5: Maintain an Effective Data Backup Strategy

- System backup provides protection against disk failures, accidental file deletion, accidental file corruption, and disasters.

- System backup provides access to historical data.

- Full backups save all files.

- Differential backups save files modified or created since the last full backup.

- Incremental backups save files modified or created since the last full or incremental backup.

- A full backup will be coupled with either differential or incremental backups, but not both.

- Backup media are rotated to assure high-quality backups.

- Backup media must be verified to assure data integrity.

- Backup is often performed using **tar** and **mt**, as follows:

  tar *files*
  > Archive or restore files recursively, to tape or to a tarfile.

  mt *operation*
  > Control a tape drive, including skipping over multiple archives on tape, rewinding, and ejecting. *operations* include *fsf, bsf, rewinde*, and *offline* (see the manpage for a complete list).

- Backup should include everything necessary to restore a system to operation in the event of a disaster. Examples include */etc, /home, /var/log*, and */var/ spool*, though individual requirements vary.

PART 2

General Linux Exam 102

Part 2 covers the Topics and Objectives for the LPI's General Linux Certification for Exam 102 and includes the following sections:

- Exam 102 Overview
- Exam 102 Study Guide
    - Hardware and Architecture
    - Linux Installation and Package Management
    - Kernel
    - Text Editing, Processing, and Printing
    - Shells, Scripting, Programming, and Compiling
    - X
    - Networking Fundamentals
    - Networking Services
    - Security
- Exam 102 Review Questions and Exercises
- Exam 102 Practice Test
- Exam 102 Highlighter's Index

Exam 102
Overview

LPI Exam 102 is the second of two exams required for the LPI's Level 1 certification. This exam tests your knowledge on 9 of the 14 major Topic areas specified for LPIC Level 1.

Exam Topics are numbered using a *level.topic* notation (i.e., 1.1, 2.2, etc.). In the LPI's early stages of development, Topics were assigned to exams based on a different scheme than we see today. When the scheme changed, the Topics were redistributed to Exams 101 and 102, but the pairing of Topic numbers to exams was dropped. As a result, we have 1.x and 2.x Topics in both Level 1 Exams.

The Level 1 Topics are distributed between the two exams to create tests of similar length and difficulty without subject matter overlap. As a result, there's no requirement or advantage to taking the exams in sequence.

Each Topic contains a series of Objectives covering specific areas of expertise. Each of these Objectives is assigned a numeric weight, which acts as an indicator of the importance of the Objective. Weights run between 1 and 10, with higher numbers indicating more importance. An Objective carrying a weight of 1 can be considered relatively unimportant and isn't likely to be covered in much depth on the exam. Objectives with larger weights are sure to be covered on the exam, so you should study these topics closely. The weights of the Objectives are provided at the beginning of each Topic section.

The Topics for Exam 102 are listed in Table 2-1.

Table 2-1: LPI Topics for Exam 102

Name	Number of Objectives	Description
Hardware and Architecture (Topic 1.1)	3	Covers PC architecture issues, such as IRQs, I/O addresses, SCSI BIOS, NICs, modems, and sound cards.
Linux Installation and Package Management (Topic 2.2)	6	Covers hard disk layout, LILO, making and installing programs from source, managing shared libraries, and using Red Hat and Debian packages.
Kernel (Topic 1.5)	2	Covers kernel module management, as well as building and installing a custom kernel.
Text-Editing, Processing, and Printing (Topic 1.7)	4	Covers **vi** and printer management.
Shells, Scripting, Programming, and Compiling (Topic 1.9)	2	Covers the shell and its startup files and writing **bash** scripts. Despite the name, compiling programs from source is not included (it's covered in Topic 2.2).
X (Topic 2.10)	4	Includes an overview of XFree86, using XDM, and customizing a window manager.
Networking Fundamentals (Topic 1.12)	3	Explores TCP/IP, network interfaces, DHCP, and PPP and includes trouble-shooting commands.
Networking Services (Topic 1.13)	5	Covers **inetd** and basic **sendmail**, Apache, NFS, Samba, and DNS configuration.
Security (Topic 1.14)	3	Covers security issues such as package verification, SUID issues, shadow passwords, and user limits.

As you can see from Table 2-1, the Topic numbers assigned by the LPI are not sequential, due to various modifications made by the LPI to their exam program as it developed. In particular, in Exam 102 two last-minute Objectives covering Red Hat and Debian package management were added to Topic 2.2. Regardless, the Topic numbers serve only as a reference and are not used on the exam.

Exam 102 lasts a maximum of 90 minutes and contains approximately 72 questions. The exam is administered using a custom application on a PC in a private room with no notes or other reference material. About 90 percent of the exam is made up of multiple-choice single-answer questions. These multiple-choice questions have only one correct answer, which are answered using radio buttons. A few of the questions present a scenario needing administrative action. Others seek the appropriate commands for performing a particular task or for proof of understanding of a particular concept.

The exam also includes a few multiple-choice multiple-answer questions, which are answered using checkboxes. These questions can have multiple correct responses, each of which must be checked. These are probably the most difficult type of question to answer because the possibility of multiple answers increases the likelihood of mistakes. An incorrect response on any one of the possible answers causes you to miss the entire question.

The exam also has some fill-in-the-blank questions. These questions provide a one-line text area input box for you to fill in your answer. These questions check your knowledge of concepts such as important files, commands, or well-known facts that you are expected to know.

Exam 102
Study Guide

Part 2 of this book contains a section for each of the nine Topics found on Exam 102 for LPIC Level 1 certification. Each of the following nine sections detail the Objectives described for the corresponding Topic on the LPI web site, *http:// www.lpi.org/p-obj-102.html.*

Exam Preparation

LPI Exam 102 is thorough, but if you have a solid foundation in Linux concepts as described here, you should find it straightforward. If you've already taken Exam 101, you'll find that 102 contains 20 percent more questions and covers a broader range of Linux administration skills. Included are basics such as PC architecture and Linux installation, and more advanced topics such as GUI (X Windows), customization, and networking. Exam 102 is quite specific on some Topics, such as package managers. However, you won't come across questions intended to trick you, and you're unlikely to find questions that you feel are ambiguous.

For clarity, this material is presented in the same order as the LPI Topics and Objectives. It may be helpful to devise a sequence of study in some areas. For example, working on "Networking Fundamentals" (Topic 1.12) prior to "Networking Services" (Topic 1.13) may be helpful. However, other Topics stand alone, and you may choose to study the Topics in any order. To assist you with your preparation, Table 2-2 through Table 2-10 provide a complete listing of the Topics and Objectives for Exam 102. After you complete your study of each Objective, simply check it off here to measure and organize your progress.

Table 2-2: Hardware and Architecture (Topic 1.1)

Objective	Weight	Description
1	3	Configure Fundamental System Hardware (see page 258)
2	4	Set Up SCSI and NIC Devices (see page 262)
3	3	Configure Modems and Sound Cards (see page 267)

Table 2-3: Linux Installation and Package Management (Topic 2.2)

Objective	Weight	Description
1	2	Design a Hard Disk Layout (see page 271)
2	2	Install a Boot Manager (see page 274)
3	2	Make and Install Programs from Source (see page 277)
4	3	Manage Shared Libraries (see page 284)
5	5	Use Debian Package Management (see page 287)
6	8	Use Red Hat Package Manager (RPM) (see page 293)

Table 2-4: Kernel (Topic 1.5)

Objective	Weight	Description
1	3	Manage Kernel Modules at Runtime (see page 300)
2	4	Reconfigure, Build, and Install a Custom Kernel and Modules (see page 310)

Table 2-5: Text Editing, Processing, and Printing (Topic 1.7)

Objective	Weight	Description
1	2	Perform Basic File Editing Operations Using vi (see page 320)
2	2	Manage Printers and Print Queues (see page 324)
3	1	Print Files (see page 331)
4	3	Install and Configure Local and Remote Printers (see page 332)

Study Guide
102

Table 2-6: Shells, Scripting, Programming, and Compiling (Topic 1.9)

Objective	Weight	Description
1	4	Customize and Use the Shell Environment (see page 340)
2	5	Customize or Write Simple Scripts (see page 351)

Table 2-7: X (Topic 2.10)

Objective	Weight	Description
1	4	Install and Configure XFree86 (see page 368)
2	1	Set Up xdm (see page 380)
3	1	Identify and Terminate Runaway X Applications (see page 383)
4	4	Install and Customize a Window Manager Environment (see page 384)

Table 2-8: Networking Fundamentals (Topic 1.12)

Objective	Weight	Description
1	4	Fundamentals of TCP/IP (see page 389)
2	NA	**Superseded by information from other Topics**
3	10	TCP/IP Troubleshooting and Configuration (see page 400)
4	4	Configure and Use PPP (see page 414)

Table 2-9: Networking Services (Topic 1.13)

Objective	Weight	Description
1	5	Configure and Manage inetd and Related Services (see page 425)
2	5	Operate and Perform Basic Configuration of sendmail (see page 429)
3	3	Operate and Perform Basic Configuration of Apache (see page 432)
4	4	Properly Manage the NFS, SMB, and NMB Daemons (see page 434)
5	3	Set Up and Configure Basic DNS Services (see page 439)

Table 2-10: Security (Topic 1.14)

Objective	Weight	Description
1	4	Perform Security Administration Tasks (see page 446)
2	4	Set Up Host Security (see page 458)
3	2	Set Up User-Level Security (see page 460)

Hardware and Architecture
(Topic 1.1)

This brief Topic requires general knowledge of fundamental PC architecture facts, necessary before attempting any operating system installation. It includes these Objectives:

Objective 1: Configure Fundamental System Hardware
This Objective includes PC basics such as BIOS configuration, interrupt request (IRQ) assignments, and I/O addresses. Weight: 3.

Objective 2: Set Up SCSI and NIC Devices
This Objective covers the setup of Small Computer System Interface (SCSI) controllers and network interfaces. Weight: 4.

Objective 3: Configure Modems and Sound Cards
Hardware compatibility can be a significant consideration for modems under Linux, particularly with low-cost PCs. This Objective covers modem and sound issues. Weight: 3.

Objective 1: Configure Fundamental System Hardware

Setting up a PC for Linux (or any other operating system) requires some familiarity with the devices installed in the system and their configuration. Items to be aware of include installed modems, serial and parallel ports, network adapters, SCSI (pronounced "scuzzy") adapters, and sound cards. Many of these devices, particularly older ones, require manual configuration of some kind to avoid conflicting resources. The rest of the configuration for the system hardware is done in the PC's firmware, or BIOS.

BIOS

The firmware located in a PC, commonly called the Basic Input/Output System, or BIOS, is responsible for bringing all of the system hardware to a state at which it is ready to boot an operating system. Systems vary, but this process usually includes system initialization, the testing of memory and other devices, and ultimately locating an operating system from among several storage devices. In addition, the BIOS provides a low-level system configuration interface, allowing the user to choose such things as boot devices and resource assignments. Quite a few vendors of BIOS firmware provide customized versions of their products for various PC system architectures.[*] Due to these variations, it's impossible to test specifics, but the LPIC Level 1 exams do require an understanding of the basics.

At boot time, most PCs display a method of entering the BIOS configuration utility, usually by entering a specific keystroke during startup. Once the utility is started, a menu-based screen in which system settings can be configured appears. Depending on the BIOS vendor, these will include settings for disks, memory behavior, onboard ports (such as serial and parallel ports), the clock, as well as many others.

Date and time

One of the basic functions of the BIOS is to manage the onboard hardware clock. This clock is initially set in the BIOS configuration by entering the date and time in the appropriate fields. Once set, the internal clock keeps track of time and makes the time available to the operating system. The operating system can also set the hardware clock, which is often useful if an accurate external time reference is available on the network while the system is running.

Disks and boot devices

Another fundamental configuration item required in BIOS settings is the selection of storage devices. Modern PCs can contain a variety of removable and fixed media, including floppy disks, hard disks, CD-ROMs, CD-RWs, DVD-ROMs, and Zip and/or Jaz drives. Newer systems are able to detect and properly configure much of this hardware automatically. However, older BIOS versions require manual configuration. This may include the selection of floppy disk sizes and disk drive parameters.

Most PCs have at least three bootable media types: an internal hard disk (IDE or SCSI, or perhaps both), a CD-ROM drive (again IDE or SCSI), and a floppy disk. After initialization, the BIOS seeks an operating system (or an operating system loader such as the Linux Loader, LILO) on one or more of these media. By default,

---

[*] For example, a laptop BIOS may differ significantly from a desktop system of similar capability from the same manufacturer.

many BIOS configurations enable booting from the floppy or CD-ROM first, then the hard disk, but the order is configurable in the BIOS settings.

On the Exam

You should be familiar with the general configuration requirements and layout of the BIOS configuration screens for a typical PC.

Resource Assignments

Some of the details in the BIOS configuration pertain to the internal resources of the PC architecture, including selections for *interrupts* (or IRQs), I/O Addresses, and Direct Memory Access (DMA) Channels. Interrupts are electrical signals sent to the PC's microprocessor, instructing it to stop its current activity and respond to an asynchronous event (a keystroke, for example). Modern devices in PCs often share interrupts, but older hardware requires manual verification that interrupt settings are unique to avoid conflicts with other devices.

I/O addresses are locations in the microprocessor's *memory map* (a list of defined memory addresses) reserved for input/output devices such as network interfaces. The microprocessor can write to the devices in the same way it writes to memory, which simplifies the device interface. If multiple devices inadvertently share the same I/O address, the system might behave oddly or crash.

DMA allows some devices to work directly with memory through a DMA "channel," freeing the microprocessor for other tasks. Without DMA, data must be read from I/O ports for a device and stored in memory—all by the microprocessor. A device that has DMA capabilities has direct access to memory and writes its own data there when the microprocessor is busy with computation. This can improve performance.

All of these are finite resources, and it is important to avoid conflicting settings. Common devices such as serial and parallel ports have standard assignments, as shown in Table 2-11.

Table 2-11: Common Device Settings

Device	I/O Address	IRQ	DMA
ttyS0 (COM1)	3f8	4	NA[1]
ttyS1 (COM2)	2f8	3	NA
ttyS2 (COM3)	3e8	4	NA
ttyS3 (COM4)	2e8	3	NA
lp0 (LPT1)	378–37f	7	NA
lp1 (LPT2)[2]	278–27f	5	NA

Table 2-11: Common Device Settings (continued)

Device	I/O Address	IRQ	DMA
fd0, fd1 (floppies 1 and 2)	3f0–3f7	6	2
fd2, fd3 (floppies 3 and 4)	370–377	10	3

1. NA: not applicable.

2. *lp1* uses IRQ 5. Some older PC audio devices commonly use this interrupt, which could be a problem if two parallel ports are required.

Most PCs don't contain all of these devices. For example, a typical configuration includes two serial ports, *ttyS0* and *ttyS1*. These two ports can be used to attach external modems or terminals and occupy interrupts 4 and 3, respectively. For systems with additional serial ports installed, *ttyS0* and *ttyS2* share interrupt 4, and *ttyS1* and *ttyS3* share interrupt 3. However, the system design does not allow these ports to concurrently share the interrupt and exchange serial data. Otherwise, communications would fail if both ports from either pair were to be used together.

On the Exam

You don't have to memorize all the possible device settings for the PC architecture, but you should be ready to answer specific questions regarding some of the more common ones, such as interrupt settings for serial and parallel ports. You should also be able to identify conflicting I/O and IRQ assignments given a scenario.

1024-Cylinder Limit

With most PC operating systems, data loaded by the BIOS to boot the operating system is found at the beginning of the disk in the Master Boot Record, or MBR. Windows users rarely have to think about the MBR because there is no alternate location for the boot record. With Linux, however, the user can place the boot loader (LILO) into either the MBR or the root partition. This flexibility can lead to a problem for the BIOS and LILO and cause a failure at boot time. The failure can occur because the BIOS must load LILO into memory and start it, but the BIOS can't always access portions of the disk beyond the 1024th cylinder. If the BIOS can't read all of LILO, the boot fails. Also, older versions of LILO must have a kernel image located within the first 1024 cylinders for similar reasons. These limitations aren't significant, but do require planning during the partitioning of disks at installation time. This Topic is discussed further in "Part 2: *Linux Installation and Package Management (Topic 2.2)*, Objective 2: Install a Boot Manager."

On the Exam

Be aware that LILO and kernels should be installed below cylinder 1024 on larger disks.

Objective 2: Set Up SCSI and NIC Devices

As described in Objective 1, when you add hardware to a PC you must accommodate the resource requirements of all installed devices. Some devices, in particular SCSI controllers and older network interfaces, require special configuration. This Objective describes in general terms some of these considerations.

NICs

More than ever before, today's PCs are expected to be connected to a network. This means that some form of *network interface card* (or NIC) is used to make the connection between the computer and the network. Older hardware, particularly Industry Standard Architecture (ISA) bus hardware, requires manual configuration. Exam 102 requires familiarity with these configuration problems.

Generally speaking, we may think about device configuration methodologies from one of three general eras:

Jumper era
> This hardware was constructed in such a way that settings were controlled by changing the position of shorting jumpers on terminal strips. This method is inconvenient in that it requires internal access to the PC as well as available documentation on the jumper locations. On the other hand, it is a hardware-only solution, and the settings are obvious to the observer. Many such devices are still in service on older PCs.

Nonvolatile era
> These more recent hardware designs abandoned jumpers in favor of settings that, while still manually set, are stored in a nonvolatile memory space. This design eliminated the physical access problem with jumpered hardware, but introduced a requirement that custom configuration programs be written, supported, and provided to consumers by hardware vendors. This software was almost always based on MS-DOS. Using these configuration tools to program a card for use under Linux may require a working MS-DOS machine to provide initial configuration.

Modern era
> Most recent NICs work with the PCI bus to automatically configure themselves. The settings are done during system initialization, prior to loading the operating system. This automation eliminates manual configuration and frees the user from worrying about device conflicts.

To configure an older NIC, you may need to set jumpers or possibly run MS-DOS and a proprietary configuration utility. More often than not, factory default settings can be used with the Linux networking drivers. However manual configuration is accomplished, you'll need to be sure that you don't have conflicts with IRQs, I/O addresses, and possibly DMA channel assignments.

Using the /proc filesystem

When adding new hardware to an existing Linux system, you may wish to verify which resources the existing devices are using. The */proc* filesystem, the kernel's status repository, contains this information. The *proc* files—*interrupts*, *dma*, and *ioports*—show how system resources are currently utilized. Here is an example of */proc/interrupts* from a dual-CPU system with an Adaptec dual-AIC7895 SCSI controller:

```
# cat /proc/interrupts
           CPU0        CPU1
   0:   98663989           0       XT-PIC     timer
   1:      34698       34858       IO-APIC-edge   keyboard
   2:          0           0       XT-PIC     cascade
   5:       7141        7908       IO-APIC-edge   MS Sound System
   6:          6           7       IO-APIC-edge   floppy
   8:   18098274    18140354       IO-APIC-edge   rtc
  10:    3234867     3237313       IO-APIC-level  aic7xxx, eth0
  11:         36          35       IO-APIC-level  aic7xxx
  12:     233140      216205       IO-APIC-edge   PS/2 Mouse
  13:          1           0       XT-PIC     fpu
  15:      44118       43935       IO-APIC-edge   ide1
 NMI:          0
 ERR:          0
```

In this example, you can see that interrupt 5 is used for the sound system, thus it isn't available for a second parallel port. The two SCSI controllers are using interrupts 10 and 11, respectively, while the Ethernet controller shares interrupt 10. You may also notice that only one of the two standard IDE interfaces is enabled in the system BIOS, freeing interrupt 14 use for another device.

Here are the */proc/dma* and */proc/ioports* files from the same system:

```
# cat /proc/dma
 0: MS Sound System
 1: MS Sound System
 2: floppy
 4: cascade
# cat /proc/ioports
0000-001f : dma1
0020-003f : pic1
0040-005f : timer
0060-006f : keyboard
0070-007f : rtc
0080-008f : dma page reg
00a0-00bf : pic2
00c0-00df : dma2
00f0-00ff : fpu
0170-0177 : ide1
02f8-02ff : serial(auto)
0370-0371 : OPL3-SAx
0376-0376 : ide1
0388-0389 : mpu401
03c0-03df : vga+
03f0-03f5 : floppy
03f7-03f7 : floppy DIR
03f8-03ff : serial(auto)
0530-0533 : WSS config
0534-0537 : MS Sound System
```

```
e800-e8be : aic7xxx
ec00-ecbe : aic7xxx
ef00-ef3f : eth0
ffa0-ffa7 : ide0
ffa8-ffaf : ide1
```

On the Exam

You should be aware of the default resource assignments listed in Table 2-11. You should also know how to examine a running Linux system's resource assignments using the */proc* filesystem.

SCSI

SCSI is an interface for streaming devices and block storage devices such as tape drives, hard disks, CD-ROMs, and other peripheral instruments. SCSI is the standard interface on server-style PCs, Unix workstations, and many older Apple models (mostly 604 and earlier systems). Desktop PCs and newer Apple systems (G3 and above) usually opt for the IDE (ATA)-style disk interfaces because they are less expensive. The advantage that SCSI has over IDE is that it offers much more flexibility and expandability, as well as faster throughput.

SCSI defines a *bus* to which multiple devices are connected. The medium is a high-quality cable or a series of cables connected to daisy-chained devices in series. One of the devices in the chain is the *SCSI controller*, which is the host interface to the other connected SCSI devices. The controller and all of the other devices on the bus are assigned a permanent *SCSI address*, also known as the *SCSI ID*, which defines each SCSI device uniquely on the bus. The controller can access devices individually by using the unique SCSI address to access a specific device.

SCSI types

The world of SCSI can be a little confusing, despite the standards set by ANSI. The original SCSI-1 interface is a 5-MBps (megabytes per second) 8-bit interface. It uses a 50-pin Centronics connector, similar to but larger than those found on most printers. This interface is still in popular use today, although the connector is usually replaced by a 50-pin micro-D connector. (This connector is similar to the DB-25 used for serial ports but has a much higher pin density.) As performance demands escalated, manufacturers began offering enhanced products with faster data transfer rates:

SCSI-1
   The original: 8-bit, 5-MBps Centronics 50 connector.

SCSI-2
   8-bit, 5-MBps Micro-D 50-pin connector. Interchangeable with SCSI-1. This interface is still adequate for low-end to midrange tape drives but is too slow for current technology disks.

Wide SCSI
   16-bit, 10-MBps, Micro-D 68-pin connector. This standard uses a wider cable to support 16-bit transfers, obtaining faster throughput using the same clock rate.

Fast SCSI
> 8-bit, 10-MBps, Micro-D 50-pin connector. Higher throughput is obtained by doubling the original clock rate.

Fast Wide SCSI
> 16-bit, 20-MBps, Micro-D 68-pin connector. This interface combines both the higher clock rate and the wider bus.

Ultra SCSI
> 8-bit, 20-MBps, Micro-D 50-pin connector. Additional changes to clocking yield still better performance.

Ultra Wide SCSI (also known as SCSI-3)
> 16-bit, 40-MBps.

Ultra2
> 8-bit, 40-MBps.

Wide Ultra2
> 16-bit, 80-MBps.

Recent developments have yielded additional SCSI interface types with up to 160 MBps throughput, and efforts continue to keep SCSI competitive with other technologies. As performance increases, however, constraints on cabling and connectors become more significant. Such constraints are a major factor in deploying large SCSI-based systems. Also, with the variety of connectors, cables, and transfer rates available in the SCSI standards, it's important to plan carefully. The other inhibiting factor, at least on the consumer level, is that SCSI hard drives tend to cost two to three times the amount of a similar-sized IDE drive.

SCSI IDs

Each device on a SCSI bus, including the controller, has an address based on a binary reading of the address lines. The 8-bit SCSI buses have three address lines and thus will accommodate $2^3=8$ devices, including the controller. For the 16-bit busses, there are four address lines resulting in a possible $2^4=16$ devices. This results in a maximum of 7 and 15 devices, respectively. These addresses can be configured using jumpers (typical for disk drives) or switches. SCSI addresses run from 0 to 7 for 8-bit buses and from 0 to 15 for 16-bit buses. It is customary for the controller to occupy address 7 for both bus widths. Disks and other devices must be assigned a unique address on the bus, and they must be provided with proper *termination*, discussed later in this section.

SCSI logical unit numbers

Some SCSI devices, such as RAID controllers, appear to the SCSI controller as a disk drive with a single SCSI address. In order for the controller to access multiple logical devices using a single SCSI address, an accompanying *logical unit number* (LUN), is reported to the controller. Single disks and tape drives don't usually use the LUN or report LUN zero.

Linux SCSI disk device files

On Linux systems, IDE disk devices are known as */dev/hda*, */dev/hdb*, */dev/hdc*, and */dev/hdd*. For SCSI, a similar pattern emerges, with */dev/sda*, */dev/sdb*, and so on. The first partition on disk */dev/sda* will be */dev/sda1*—but remember that the partition number has nothing to do with the SCSI ID. Instead, the letter names of the Linux SCSI devices start with *sda* and proceed across all SCSI IDs and LUNs. The numbers are sequentially assigned to partitions on a single ID/LUN combination.

For example, a SCSI-2 bus with two disks, a tape drive, a RAID controller with two LUNs, and the SCSI controller might be assigned addresses as shown in Table 2-12.

Table 2-12: Sample SCSI Configuration

Device	SCSI Address	LUN	Linux Device
Disk 0	0	-	*/dev/sda*
Disk 1	1	-	*/dev/sdb*
Tape drive	5	-	*/dev/st0*
RAID controller device 0	6	0	*/dev/sdc*
RAID controller device 1	6	1	*/dev/sdd*
Controller	7	-	-

If a disk on the SCSI bus is to be bootable, you may need to configure the SCSI controller's BIOS with the disk's address. By default, address 0 is expected to be a bootable disk.

Termination

Another facet of SCSI that can be confusing is termination. A SCSI bus can be considered a cable with devices connected along its length, but not at the ends. Instead of devices, the ends of the SCSI bus have terminators, which are simple electrical devices that condition the signal and reduce electrical noise on the bus. However, most external terminators look like a bare connector at the end of a SCSI cable. Without a terminator, a SCSI bus can be marginally functional, but it's more likely that it will fail completely, so proper termination is extremely important. Termination can be particularly problematic if you attempt to mix 8- and 16-bit devices on a single bus and use an 8-bit terminator, leaving half of the 16-bit SCSI bus unterminated.

External terminators are straightforward because they are visible. Most device manufacturers include termination circuitry on their devices, so the application of an external terminator device is not always necessary. SCSI controllers can terminate one end of the SCSI bus while an external terminator or a disk's internal terminator is used on the other end. Whichever type of terminator is being used, you must be sure that exactly one terminator is placed at each end of the SCSI bus (for a total of exactly two terminators), otherwise the bus may fail.

SCSI controllers on PCs

Most PCs don't come with integrated SCSI controllers, but a number of add-on cards are available. SCSI controllers have their own firmware installed along with an accompanying BIOS, which has its own configuration menus. If you're using SCSI on a PC, it's important to be able to manipulate these settings appropriately.

Like the BIOS, a SCSI controller BIOS usually has a keyboard combination, announced at boot time, to enter the setup utility. Once the utility is launched, you can control a number of aspects of the controller, including:

Controller SCSI address
> The default controller address is usually 7, but you may use any address.

Default boot device
> Typically this is set to address 0 for a hard disk.

Onboard termination
> Depending upon how a controller is utilized (internal or external bus, or both) you may elect to turn on the controller's terminator.

SCSI bus speed
> Most SCSI adapters that are capable of higher speeds (Ultra SCSI, for example) can be manually set to lower speeds to accommodate older devices or longer cable lengths.

On the Exam

Be sure to be familiar with SCSI IDs, termination, the SCSI BIOS, and Linux SCSI device naming for the 102 exam.

Objective 3: Configure Modems and Sound Cards

Like NICs and SCSI adapters, modems and sound adapters have a few special considerations during installation. This Objective covers some of these issues.

Modems

A modem (a word derived from *mo*dulate and *dem*odulate) is that familiar device that modulates a digital signal into an analog signal for transmitting information via telephone lines. A modem on the other end of the connection demodulates the signal back into its digital form. Modems can also add digital compression and error correction capabilities to increase speed and reliability.

Modem types

Modems are serial devices, where data enters and exits one bit at a time. Traditionally, modems were external devices attached via cable to industry standard RS-232 serial ports, such as those still found on most PCs. This arrangement continues to work well, because the data rates of telephone connections are still below the maximum rate of the serial ports. As a result, external devices yield solid performance. Internal modems (ISA or PCI bus cards that reside inside a PC) were developed to reduce costs associated with external modems (namely, the case, power supply, and shipping charges) and offer the same functionality as an external modem.

Most internal modems present themselves to the PC as a standard serial port. In a typical PC with the first two serial ports built in (*/dev/ttyS0* and */dev/ttyS1*), an internal modem will appear as the third port (*/dev/ttyS2*). This means that from a programming point of view, internal modems are indistinguishable from external modems. While there is some variation in modem configuration across manufacturers, the differences are small, and most serial-port-style modems will work with Linux. One exception is a modem designed specifically to work with the Windows operating system. These so-called *WinModems* rely on the CPU and a special software driver to handle some of the communications processing, thus lack the full hardware capabilities of standard modems. As such, WinModems are not compatible with Linux unless a Linux-specific driver is available. Information on such support is available from *http://www.linmodems.org*. One example of such support is an effort by IBM to support *Mwave* WinModems installed in its laptop line.[*]

Modem hardware resources

As with any add-on card, particularly cards configured manually, the user must be careful to avoid resource conflicts. Modems shouldn't cause much difficulty since they're simple serial ports. However, you should confirm that the correct interrupt and I/O addresses are set on your modem. If the modem shares an interrupt with another serial port, that port cannot be used at the same time as the modem.

On the Exam

Watch out for WinModems, which often don't work with Linux. Remember that PC serial ports may share an interrupt (but not an I/O port).

This Objective requires knowledge regarding the setup of a modem for outbound dialup. For this information, see "Part 2: *Networking Fundamentals (Topic 1.12),* Objective 4: Configure and Use PPP."

Sound Devices

Nearly every laptop and desktop PC shipped today includes a sound device. Fortunately, Linux sound drivers are available for most sound chipsets, including the industry standard chipset originally defined by Creative Labs with its

---

[*] A search for "mwave" on *http://oss.software.ibm.com* should yield information on the WinModem driver.

SoundBlaster series. Part of the configuration for a sound card involves correctly specifying the sound card's resources to the sound driver, which is a kernel module.

On the Exam

Be aware that the sound driver is a kernel module that has its settings stored in */etc/modules.conf.*

Linux Installation and Package Management (Topic 2.2)

Many resources describe Linux installation.[*] Despite its title, however, this section's Topic and Objectives do not provide an overview for the installation of any particular Linux distribution. Rather, they focus on four installation topics and two packaging tools as required for LPI Exam 102:

Objective 1: Design a Hard Disk Layout
The layout and partitioning of disks is a fundamental concept for almost all computer platforms. Unlike other operating systems though, Linux uses multiple partitions in a unified filesystem. This Objective covers this file-system layout. Weight: 2.

Objective 2: Install a Boot Manager
Booting Linux is a process started by a *boot manager*. This Objective covers the use of LILO. Weight: 2.

Objective 3: Make and Install Programs from Source
The unique advantages of open source software allow the distribution of programs in source code form. This Objective covers compiling and installing programs from source code. (Objectives 5 and 6 deal with binary package management.) Weight: 2.

Objective 4: Manage Shared Libraries
One of the efficiencies of modern operating systems is the concept of *shared libraries* of system software. This Objective provides an overview of shared libraries and their configuration. Weight: 3.

Objective 5: Use Debian Package Management.
This topic covers the management of Debian Linux binary packages. Weight: 5.

Objective 6: Use Red Hat Package Manager (RPM)
This topic covers the management of RPM binary packages. Weight: 8.

---

[*] One excellent resource is *Running Linux, Third Edition*, by Matt Welsh, Matthias Kalle Dalheimer, and Lar Kaufman (O'Reilly & Associates).

Objective 1: Design a Hard Disk Layout

Part of the installation process for Linux is the design of the hard disk partitioning scheme. If you're used to systems that reside on a single partition, this step may seem to complicate installation. However, there are advantages to splitting the filesystem into multiple partitions, potentially on multiple disks. Details about disks, partitions, and Linux filesystem top-level directories are provided in Part 1, *Devices, Linux Filesystems, and the Filesystem Hierarchy Standard (Topic 2.4)*. This Topic covers considerations for implementing Linux disk layouts.

System Considerations

A variety of factors influence the choice of a disk layout plan for Linux, including:

- The amount of disk space
- The size of the system
- What the system will be used for
- How and where backups will be performed

Limited disk space

Except for read-only filesystems (such as CD-ROMs or a shared */usr* partition), most Linux filesystems should have some free space available. Filesystems holding user data should be maintained with a generous amount of free space to accommodate user activity. Unfortunately, if there are many filesystems and all of them contain free space, a significant portion of disk space could be considered wasted. This presents a tradeoff between the number of filesystems in use and the availability of free disk space. Finding the right configuration depends on system requirements and available disk resources.

When disk space is limited, it is desirable to reduce the number of filesystems, thereby combining free space into a single contiguous pool. For example, installing Linux on a PC with only 1 GB of available disk space might best be implemented using only a few partitions:

/boot
50 MB. A small */boot* filesystem in the first partition ensures that all kernels are below the 1024-cylinder limit.

/swap
100 MB.

/
850 MB. A large root partition holds everything on the system that's not in */boot*.

The */boot* partition could be combined with the root partition as long as the entire root partition fits within the 1024-cylinder limit (see "Part 2: *Hardware and Architecture (Topic 1.1)*, Objective 1: Configure Fundamental System Hardware").

On older systems with smaller hard drives, Linux is often installed by spreading the directory tree across multiple physical disks. This is no different in practice than using multiple partitions on a single disk and often encourages the reuse of older hardware. An additional disk might be dedicated to */home* in order to allow a larger work area for the users' home directories.

Larger systems

On larger platforms, functional issues such as backup strategies and required file-system sizes can dictate disk layout. For example, suppose a file server is to be constructed serving 100 GB of executable datafiles to end-users via NFS. Such as system will have enough resources to compartmentalize various parts of the directory tree into separate filesystems and might look like this:

/boot
> 50 MB. Keep kernels under the 1024-cylinder limit.

/swap
> 100 MB.

/
> 100 MB.

/usr
> 1 GB. All of the executables in */usr* are shared to workstations via read-only NFS.

/var
> 500 MB. By placing log files in their own partition, they won't threaten system stability if the filesystem is full.

/tmp
> 100 MB. By placing temporary files in their own partition, they won't threaten system stability if the filesystem is full.

/home
> 98 GB. This is the big filesystem, offered to users for their home directories.

On production servers, much of the system is often placed on redundant media, such as mirrored disks. Large filesystems, such as */home*, may be stored on some form of disk array using a hardware controller.

System role

The role of the system also can dictate disk layout. In a traditional Unix-style network with NFS file servers, most of the workstations won't necessarily need all of their own executable files. In the days when disk space was at a premium, this represented a significant savings in disk space. While space on workstation disks isn't the problem it once was, keeping executables on a server still eliminates the administrative headache of distributing updates to workstations.

Backup

Some backup schemes use disk partitions as the basic unit of system backup. In such a scenario, each of the filesystems listed in */etc/fstab* is backed up separately, and they are arranged so that each filesystem fits within the size of the backup media. For this reason, the available backup device capabilities can play a role in determining the ultimate size of partitions.

Swap Space

When you install Linux, you're asked to configure a *swap*, or *virtual memory*, partition. This special disk space is used to temporarily store portions of main memory containing programs or program data that is not needed constantly, allowing more processes to execute concurrently. An old rule of thumb for Linux is to set the size of the system's swap space to be equal to the amount of physical RAM in the machine. For example, if your system has 64 MB of RAM, it would be reasonable to set your swap size to at least 64 MB. Another rule of thumb that predates Linux says swap space should equal three times the main memory size. These are just guidelines, of course, because a system's utilization of virtual memory depends on what the system does and the number and size of processes it runs. Using the size of main memory, or thereabouts, is a good starting point.

Spreading swap space across multiple disk drives can allow better swap performance because multiple accesses can occur concurrently when multiple devices are used. For even better performance, place those disks on separate controllers, increasing bandwidth. For example, you could place half of your planned swap space on each of two IDE disks in your system. Those disks could be attached to the two separate IDE interfaces.

General Guidelines

Here are some guidelines for partitioning a Linux system:

- Keep the root filesystem (/) small by distributing larger portions of the directory tree to other partitions. A small root filesystem is less likely to be corrupted than a large one.

- Separate a small */boot* partition below cylinder 1024 for kernels.

- Separate */var*. Make certain it is big enough to handle your logs and their rotation scheme, but not so large that disk space is wasted when the rotation is filled.

- Separate */tmp*. Its size depends on the demands of the applications you run. It should be large enough to handle temporary files for all of your users simultaneously.

- Separate */usr* and make it big enough to accommodate kernel building. Making it standalone allows you to share it read-only via NFS.

- Separate */home* for machines with multiple users. For production use, put it on a disk array subsystem.

- Set swap space around the same size as the main memory. If possible, try to split the swap space across multiple disks and controllers.

On the Exam

Since a disk layout is the product of both system requirements and available resources, no single example can represent the best configuration. Factors to remember include placing the kernel below cylinder 1024, ways to effectively utilize multiple disks, sizing of partitions to hold various directories such as */var* and */usr*, the importance of the root filesystem, and swap space size. Also remember the trick of splitting swap space across multiple physical disks to increase virtual memory performance.

Objective 2: Install a Boot Manager

While it is possible to boot Linux from a floppy disk, most Linux installations boot from the computer's hard disk.* This is a two-step process that begins after the system BIOS is initialized and ready to run an operating system. Starting Linux consists of the following two basic phases:

Run lilo from the boot disk
> It is Linux loader's (LILO's) job to find the selected kernel and get it loaded into memory, including any user-supplied options.

Launch the Linux kernel and start processes
> LILO starts the loaded kernel. LILO's job at this point is complete and the hardware is placed under the control of the running kernel, which sets up shop and begins running processes.

LILO

The Linux Loader (LILO) is a small utility designed to load the Linux kernel (or the boot sector of another operating system) into memory and start it. A program that performs this function is commonly called a boot loader. While other boot loaders exist, LILO is the most popular and is installed as the default boot loader on most Linux distributions. LILO consists of two parts:

The boot loader
> This part of LILO is a two-stage program intended to find and load a kernel.†
> The first stage of LILO usually resides in the Master Boot Record (MBR) of the hard disk. This is the code that is started at boot time by the system BIOS. It locates and launches a second, larger stage of the boot loader that resides

---

* This isn't to say that you can't boot from other media such as floppies—many people do.

† It's a two-stage operation because the boot sector of the disk is too small to hold the entire boot loader program. The code located in the boot sector is compact because its only function is to launch the second stage, which is the interactive portion.

---

elsewhere on disk. The second stage offers a user prompt to allow boot-time and kernel image selection options, finds the kernel, loads it into memory, and launches it.

The lilo command

Also called the *map installer*, **lilo** is used to install and configure the LILO boot loader. The **lilo** command reads a configuration file, which describes where to find kernel images, video information, the default boot disk, and so on. It encodes this information along with physical disk information and writes it in files for use by the boot loader.

The boot loader

When the system BIOS launches, LILO presents you with the following prompt:

```
LILO:
```

The LILO prompt is designed to allow you to select from multiple kernels or operating systems installed on the computer and to pass parameters to the kernel when it is loaded. Pressing the **Tab** key at the LILO prompt yields a list of available kernel images. One of the listed images will be the default as designated by an asterisk next to the name:

```
LILO: <TAB>
linux*    linux_586_smp   experimental
```

Under many circumstances, you won't need to select a kernel at boot time because LILO will boot the kernel configured as the default during the install process. However, if you later create a new kernel, have special hardware issues, or are operating your system in a dual-boot configuration, you may need to use some of LILO's options to load the kernel or operating system you desire.

The LILO map installer and its configuration file

Before any boot sequence can complete from your hard disk, the boot loader and associated information must be installed by the LILO map installer utility. The **lilo** command writes the portion of LILO that resides in the MBR, customized for your particular system. Your installation program will do it, then you'll repeat it manually if you build a new kernel yourself.

lilo

Syntax

```
lilo [options]
```

The **lilo** map installer reads a configuration file and writes a map file, which contains information needed by the boot loader to locate and launch Linux kernels or other operating systems.

Frequently used options

–C *config_file*

Read the *config_file* file instead of the default */etc/lilo.conf*.

–m *map_file*

Write *map_file* in place of the default as specified in the configuration file.

-q

    Query the current configuration.

-v

    Increase verbosity.

LILO's configuration file contains options and kernel image information. An array of options is available. Some are global, affecting LILO overall, while others are specific to a particular listed kernel image. Most basic Linux installations use only a few of the configuration options. Example 2-1 shows a simple LILO configuration file.

Example 2-1: Sample /etc/lilo.conf File

```
boot = /dev/hda
timeout = 50
prompt
read-only
map=/boot/map
install=/boot/boot.b
image = /boot/vmlinuz-2.2.5-15
  label = linux
  root = /dev/hda1
```

Each of these lines is described in the following list:

boot

    The boot directive tells **lilo** the name of the hard disk partition device that contains the boot sector. For PCs with IDE disk drives, the devices will be */dev/hda*, */dev/hdb*, and so on.

timeout

    The timeout directive sets the timeout in tenths of a second (deciseconds) for any user input from the keyboard. To enable an unattended reboot, this parameter is required if the **prompt** directive is used.

prompt

    This directive instructs the boot loader to prompt the user. This behavior can be stimulated without the prompt directive if the user holds down the **Shift**, **Ctrl**, or **Alt** key when LILO starts.

read-only

    This directive specifies that the root filesystem should initially be mounted read-only. Typically, the system startup procedure will remount it later as read/write.

map

    The map directive specifies the location of the map file, which defaults to */boot/map*.

install

    The install directive specifies the file to install as the new boot sector, which defaults to */boot/boot.b*.

`image`

An image line specifies a kernel image to offer for boot. It points to a specific kernel file. Multiple image lines may be used to configure LILO to boot multiple kernels and operating systems.

`label`

The optional label parameter is used after an image line and offers a label for that image. This label can be anything and generally describes the kernel image. Examples include `linux`, or perhaps `smp` for a multiprocessing kernel.

`root`

This parameter is used after each image line and specifies the device to be mounted as root for that image.

There is more to configuring and setting up *LILO*, but a detailed knowledge of LILO is not required for this LPI Objective. It is important to review one or two sample LILO configurations to make sense of the boot process. A discussion on using LILO to boot multiple kernels is presented in Part 2, *Kernel (Topic 1.5)*.

LILO locations

During installation, LILO can be placed either in the boot sector of the disk or in your root partition. If the system is intended as a Linux-only system, you won't need to worry about other boot loaders, and LILO can safely be placed into the boot sector. However, if you're running another operating system such as Windows, you should place its boot loader in the boot sector.[*]

On the Exam

It is important to understand the distinction between lilo, the map installer utility run interactively by the system administrator, and the boot loader, which is launched by the system BIOS at boot time. Both are parts of the LILO package.

Study Guide
102

Objective 3: Make and Install Programs from Source

Open source software is credited with offering value that rivals or even exceeds that of proprietary vendors' products. While binary distributions make installation simple, you sometimes won't have access to a binary package. In these cases, you'll have to compile the program from scratch.

---

[*] Multiple-boot and multiple-OS configurations are beyond the scope of the LPIC Level 1 exams.

Getting Open Source and Free Software

Source code for the software that makes up a Linux distribution is available from a variety of sources. Your distribution media contain both source code and compiled binary forms of many software projects. Since much of the code that comes with Linux originates from the Free Software Foundation (FSF), the GNU web site contains a huge array of software.* Major projects, such as Apache (*http://www.apache.org*), distribute their own code. Whatever outlet you choose, the source code must be packaged for your use, and among the most popular packaging methods for source code is the tarball.

What's a tarball?

Code for a significant project that a software developer wishes to distribute is originally stored in a hierarchical tree of directories. Included are the source code (in the C language), a *Makefile*, and some documentation. In order to share the code, the entire tree must be encapsulated in a way that is efficient and easy to send and store electronically. A common method of doing this is to use **tar** to create a single *tarfile* containing the directory's contents, and then use **gzip** to compress it for efficiency. The resulting compressed file is referred to as a *tarball*. This method of distribution is popular because both **tar** and **gzip** are widely available and understood, ensuring a wide audience. A tarball is usually indicated by the use of the multiple extensions *.tar* and *.gz*, put together into *.tar.gz*. A combined single extension of *.tgz* is also popular.

Opening a tarball

The contents of a tarball is obtained through a two-step process. The file is first uncompressed with **gzip** and then extracted with **tar**. Following is an example, starting with *tarball.tar.gz*:

```
# gzip -d tarball.tar.gz
# tar xvf tarball.tar
```

The **-d** option to **gzip** indicates "decompress mode." If you prefer, you can use **gunzip** in place of **gzip -d** to do the same thing:

```
# gunzip tarball.tar.gz
# tar xvf tarball.tar
```

You can also avoid the intermediate unzipped file by piping the output of **gzip** straight into **tar**:

```
# gzip -dc tarball.tar.gz | tar xv
```

---

* Not just for Linux, either. Although Linux distributions are largely made up of GNU software, that software runs on many other Unix and Unix-like operating systems, including the various flavors of BSD (e.g., FreeBSD, NetBSD, and OpenBSD).

In this case, the –c option to **gzip** tells it to keep the compressed file in place. By avoiding the full-sized version, disk space is saved. For even more convenience, avoid using **gzip** entirely and use the decompression capability in **tar:***

```
# tar zxvf tarball.tar.gz
```

On the Exam

All of these methods achieve the same result. Be sure you understand that **tar** can archive directly to files (not just to a tape drive) and that a compressed version of a tarfile is made with **gzip**. Be familiar with the various ways you could extract files from a tarball, including **gzip –d**; **tar**, **gunzip**; **tar**, **gzip –d | tar**; and **tar z**. You should be comfortable using **tar** and **gzip** and their more common options.

Compiling Open Source Software

Once you've extracted the source code, you're ready to compile it. You'll need to have the appropriate tools available on your system, namely a **configure** script, the GNU C compiler, **gcc**, and the dependency checker, **make**.

configure

Most larger source code packages include a **configure** script[†] located at the top of the source code tree. This script needs no modification or configuration from the user. When it executes, it examines your system to verify the existence of a compiler, libraries, utilities, and other items necessary for a successful compile. It uses the information it finds to produce a custom *Makefile* for the software package on your particular system. If **configure** finds that something is missing, it fails and gives you a terse but descriptive message. **configure** succeeds in most cases, leaving you ready to begin the actual compile process.

make

make is a utility for compiling software. When multiple source-code files are used in a project, it is rarely necessary to compile all of them for every build of the executable. Instead, only the source files that have changed since the last compilation really need to be compiled again.

make works by defining *targets* and their *dependencies*. The ultimate target in a software build is the executable file or files. They depend on object files, which in turn depend on source-code files. When a source file is edited, its date is more recent than that of the last compiled object. **make** is designed to automatically handle these dependencies and do the right thing.

---

* GNU **tar** offers compression; older **tar** programs didn't.

† **configure** is produced for you by the programmer using the **autoconf** utility. **autoconf** is beyond the scope LPIC Level 1 exams.

To illustrate the basic idea, consider this trivial and silly example. Suppose you're writing a program with code in two files. The C file, *main.c*, holds the `main()` function:

```
int main() {
  printit();
}
```

and *printit.c* contains the `printit()` function, which is called by `main()`:

```
#include <stdio.h>
void printit() {
  printf("Hello, world\n");
}
```

Both source files must be compiled into objects *main.o* and *printit.o*, and then linked together to form an executable application called **hw**. In this scenario, **hw** depends on the two object files, a relationship that could be defined like this:

```
hw: main.o printit.o
```

Using this syntax, the dependency of the object files on the source files would look like this:

```
main.o: main.c
printit.o: printit.c
```

With these three lines, there is a clear picture of the dependencies involved in the project. The next step is to add the commands necessary to satisfy each of the dependencies. Compiler directives are added next:

```
gcc -c main.c
gcc -c printit.c
gcc -o hw main.o printit.o
```

To allow for a change of compilers in the future, a variable can be defined to hold the actual compiler name:

```
CC = gcc
```

To use the variable, use the syntax $(*variable*) for substitution of the contents of the variable. Combining all this, the result is:

```
CC = gcc

hw: main.o printit.o
        $(CC) -o hw main.o printit.o

main.o: main.c
        $(CC) -c main.c

printit.o: printit.c
        $(CC) -c printit.c
```

This illustrates a simple *Makefile*, the default control file for **make**. It defines three targets: **hw** (the application), and *main.o* and *printit.o* (the two object files). A full compilation of the **hw** program is invoked by running **make** and specifying **hw** as the desired target:

```
# make hw
gcc -c main.c
gcc -c printit.c
gcc -o hw main.o printit.o
```

make automatically expects to find its instructions in *Makefile*. If a subsequent change is made to one of the source files, **make** will handle the dependency:

```
# touch printit.c
# make hw
gcc -c printit.c
gcc -o hw main.o printit.o
```

This trivial example doesn't illustrate a real-world use of **make** or the *Makefile* syntax. **make** also has powerful rule sets that allow commands for known dependency relationships to be issued automatically. These rules would shorten even this tiny *Makefile*.

Installing the compiled software

Most mature source-code projects come with a predetermined location in the filesystem for the executable files created by compilation. In many cases, they're expected to go to */usr/local/bin*. To facilitate installation to these default locations, many *Makefiles* contain a special target called *install*. By executing the **make install** command, files are copied and set with the appropriate attributes.

WARNING

The default installation directory included in a project's *Makefile* may differ from that defined by your Linux distribution. If you upgrade software you are already using, this could lead to confusion over versions.

On the Exam

A basic understanding of **make** is sufficient for Exam 102. In addition, be prepared to add to or modify the contents of variables in a *Makefile*, such as *include* directories or paths. This could be necessary, for example, if additional libraries must be included in the compilation or if a command must be customized.

Example: Compiling bash

GNU's **bash** shell is presented here as an example of the process of compiling. You can find a compressed tarball of the **bash** source at the GNU FTP site, *ftp:// ftp.gnu.org/gnu/bash/*. Multiple versions might be available. Version 2.03 is used in this example (you will find more recent versions). The compressed tarball is *bash-2.03.tar.gz*. As you can see by its name, it is a *tar* file that has been compressed with **gzip**. To uncompress the contents, use the compression option in **tar**:

```
# tar zxvf bash-2.03.tar.gz
bash-2.03/
bash-2.03/CWRU/
bash-2.03/CWRU/misc/
bash-2.03/CWRU/misc/open-files.c
bash-2.03/CWRU/misc/sigs.c
bash-2.03/CWRU/misc/pid.c
... (extraction continues) ...
```

Next move into the new directory, take a look around, and read some basic documentation:

```
# cd bash-2.03
# ls
AUTHORS        NEWS
CHANGES        NOTES
COMPAT         README
COPYING        Y2K
CWRU           aclocal.m4
INSTALL        alias.c
MANIFEST       alias.h
Makefile.in    ansi_stdlib.h
... (listing continues) ...
# less README
```

The build process for **bash** is started by using the *dot-slash* prefix to launch **configure**:

```
# ./configure
creating cache ./config.cache
checking host system type... i686-pc-linux-gnu
Beginning configuration for bash-2.03 for i686-pc-linux-gnu
checking for gcc... gcc
checking whether the C compiler (gcc  ) works... yes
checking whether the C compiler (gcc  ) is a
  cross-compiler... no
checking whether we are using GNU C... yes
checking whether gcc accepts -g... yes
checking whether large file support needs explicit
  enabling... yes
checking for POSIXized ISC... no
checking how to run the C preprocessor... gcc -E # make
... (configure continues) ...
```

Next, compile:

```
# make
/bin/sh ./support/mkversion.sh -b -s release -d 2.03 \
  -p 0 -o newversion.h && mv newversion.h version.h
```

```
**********************************************************
*                                                        *
* Making Bash-2.03.0-release for a i686 running linux-gnu
*                                                        *
**********************************************************

rm -f shell.o
gcc  -DPROGRAM='"bash"' -DCONF_HOSTTYPE='"i686"' \
  -DCONF_OSTYPE='"linux-gnu"' -DCONF_MACHTYPE='"i686
-pc-linux-gnu"' -DCONF_VENDOR='"pc"' -DSHELL \
  -DHAVE_CONFIG_H -D_FILE_OFFSET_BITS=64  -I.  -I. -I./
lib -I/usr/local/include -g -O2 -c shell.c
rm -f eval.o
... (compile continues) ...
```

If the compile yields fatal errors, **make** terminates and the errors must be addressed before installation. Errors might include problems with the source code (unlikely), missing header files or libraries, and other problems. Error messages will usually be descriptive enough to lead you to the source of the problem.

The final step of installation requires that you are logged in as *root* in order to copy the files to the system directories:

```
# make install
/usr/bin/install -c -m 0755 bash /usr/local/bin/bash
/usr/bin/install -c -m 0755 bashbug /usr/local/bin/bashbug
( cd ./doc ; make \
        man1dir=/usr/local/man/man1 man1ext=1 \
        man3dir=/usr/local/man/man3 man3ext=3 \
        infodir=/usr/local/info install )
make[1]: Entering directory `/home/ftp/bash-2.03/doc'
test -d /usr/local/man/man1 || /bin/sh ../support/mkdirs /usr/local/man/
man1
test -d /usr/local/info || /bin/sh ../support/mkdirs
  /usr/local/info
/usr/bin/install -c -m 644 ./bash.1
  /usr/local/man/man1/bash.1
/usr/bin/install -c -m 644 ./bashbug.1
  /usr/local/man/man1/bashbug.1
/usr/bin/install -c -m 644 ./bashref.info
  /usr/local/info/bash.info
if /bin/sh -c 'install-info --version'
  >/dev/null 2>&1; then \
  install-info --dir-file=/usr/local/info/dir
  /usr/local/info/bash.info; \
else true; fi
make[1]: Leaving directory `/home/ftp/bash-2.03/doc'
```

The installation places the new version of **bash** in */usr/local/bin*. Now, two working versions of **bash** are available on the system:

```
# which bash
/bin/bash
# /bin/bash -version
```

```
GNU bash, version 1.14.7(1)
# /usr/local/bin/bash -version
GNU bash, version 2.03.0(1)-release (i686-pc-linux-gnu)
Copyright 1998 Free Software Foundation, Inc.
```

On the Exam

Familiarize yourself with the acquisition, configuration, compilation, and installation of software from source. Be prepared to answer questions on **make** and *Makefile*, the function of the **configure** utility, **gzip**, and **tar**.

Objective 4: Manage Shared Libraries

When a program is compiled under Linux, many of the functions required by the program are linked from system *libraries* that handle disks, memory, and other functions. For example, when printf() is used in a program, the programmer doesn't provide the printf() source code, but instead expects that the system already has a library containing such functions. When the compiler needs to link the code for printf(), it can be found in a system library and copied into the executable. A program that contains executable code from these libraries is said to be *statically linked* because it stands alone, requiring no additional code at runtime.

Statically linked programs can have a few liabilities. First, they tend to get large, because they include executables for all of the library functions linked into them. Also, memory is wasted when many different programs running concurrently contain the same library functions. To avoid these problems, many programs are *dynamically linked*. Such programs utilize the same routines but don't contain the library code. Instead, they are linked into the executable at runtime. This dynamic linking process allows multiple programs to use the same library code in memory and makes executable files smaller. Dynamically linked libraries are shared among many applications and are thus called *shared libraries*. A full discussion of libraries is beyond the scope of the LPIC Level 1 exams. However, a general understanding of some configuration techniques is required.

Shared Library Dependencies

Any program that is dynamically linked will require at least a few shared libraries. If the required libraries don't exist or can't be found, the program will fail to run. This could happen, for example, if you attempt to run an application written for the GNOME graphical environment but haven't installed the required GTK+ libraries. Simply installing the correct libraries should eliminate such problems. The **ldd** utility can be used to determine which libraries are necessary for a particular executable.

---

ldd

Syntax

ldd *programs*

Description

Display shared libraries required by each of the *programs* listed on the command line. The results indicate the name of the library and where the library is expected to be in the filesystem.

Example

In Objective 3, a trivial executable called **hw** was created. Despite its small size, however, **hw** requires two shared libraries:

```
# ldd /home/jdean/hw
/home/jdean/hw:
    libc.so.6 => /lib/libc.so.6 (0x40018000)
    /lib/ld-linux.so.2 => /lib/ld-linux.so.2 (0x40000000)
```

The **bash** shell requires three shared libraries:

```
# ldd /bin/bash
/bin/bash:
    libtermcap.so.2 => /lib/libtermcap.so.2 (0x40018000)
    libc.so.6 => /lib/libc.so.6 (0x4001c000)
    /lib/ld-linux.so.2 => /lib/ld-linux.so.2 (0x40000000)
```

Linking Shared Libraries

Dynamically linked executables are examined at runtime by the shared object dynamic linker, *ld.so*. This program looks for dependencies in the executable being loaded and attempts to satisfy any unresolved links to system-shared libraries. If *ld.so* can't find a specified library, it fails, and the executable won't run.

To illustrate this, let's assume that the printit() function from the **hw** example in Objective 3 is moved to a shared library instead of being compiled into the program. The custom library is called *libprintit.so* and stored in */usr/local/lib*. **hw** is reconfigured and recompiled to use the new library.* By default, *ld.so* doesn't expect to look in */usr/local/lib* for libraries, and fails to find printit() at runtime:

```
# ./hw
./hw: error in loading shared libraries: libprintit.so:
    cannot open shared object file: No such file or directory
```

To find the new library, *ld.so* must be instructed to look in */usr/local/lib*. There are a few ways to do this. One simple way is to add a colon-separated list of directories to the shell environment variable LD_LIBRARY_PATH, which will prompt *ld.so* to look in any directories it finds there. However, this method may not be appropriate for system libraries, because users might not set their LD_LIBRARY_PATH correctly.

---

* Though not complicated, the compilation of *libprintit.so* and **hw** is beyond the scope of the LPIC Level 1 exams.

To make the search of */usr/local/lib* part of the default behavior for *ld.so*, files in the new directory must be included in an index of library names and locations. This index is */etc/ld.so.cache*. It's a binary file, which means it can be read quickly by *ld.so*. To add the new library entry to the cache, its directory is first added to the *ld.so.conf* file, which contains directories to be indexed by the **ldconfig** utility.

ldconfig

Syntax

```
ldconfig [options] lib_dirs
```

Description

Update the *ld.so* cache file with shared libraries specified on the command line in *lib_dirs*, in trusted directories */usr/lib* and */lib*, and in the directories found in */etc/ld.so.conf*.

Frequently used options

-p

Display the contents of the current cache instead of recreating it.

-v

Verbose mode. Display progress during execution.

Example 1

Examine the contents of the *ld.so* library cache:

```
# ldconfig -p
299 libs found in cache `/etc/ld.so.cache' (version 1.7.0)
    libzvt.so.2 (libc6) => /usr/lib/libzvt.so.2
    libz.so.1 (libc6) => /usr/lib/libz.so.1
    libz.so.1 (ELF) => /usr/i486-linux-libc5/lib/libz.so.1
    libz.so (libc6) => /usr/lib/libz.so
    libx11amp.so.0 (libc6) => /usr/X11R6/lib/libx11amp.so.0
    libxml.so.0 (libc6) => /usr/lib/libxml.so.0
(... listing continues ...)
```

Example 2

Look for a specific library entry in the cache:

```
# ldconfig -p | grep "printit"
    libprintit.so (libc6) => /usr/local/lib/libprintit.so
```

Example 3

Rebuild the cache:

```
# ldconfig
```

After */usr/local/lib* is added, *ld.so.conf* might look like this:

```
/usr/lib
/usr/i486-linux-libc5/lib
/usr/X11R6/lib
/usr/local/lib
```

Next, **ldconfig** is run to include libraries found in */usr/local/lib* in */etc/ld.so.cache*:

```
# ldconfig
# ./hw
Hello, world
```

Now the **hw** program can execute correctly because *ld.so* can find *libprintit.so* in */usr/local/lib*. It is important to run **ldconfig** after any changes in system libraries to be sure that the cache is up-to-date.

Objective 5: Use Debian Package Management

The Debian package management system is a versatile and automated suite of tools used to acquire and manage software packages for Debian Linux. The system automatically handles many of the management details associated with interdependent software running on your system.

Debian Package Management Overview

Each Debian package contains program and configuration files, documentation, and noted dependencies on other packages. The names of Debian packages have three common elements, including:

Package name
> A Debian package name is short and descriptive. When multiple words are used in the name, they are separated by hyphens. Typical names include *binutils*, *kernel-source*, and *telnet*.

Version number
> Each package has a version number. Most package versions are the same as that of the software they contain, thus the format of package versions varies from package to package. Most are numeric, with major, patch, and release numbers, but other information may appear as well. Typical versions are *0.6.7-7*, *0.96a-14*, *6.05*, *80b2-8*, and *2.0.7.19981211*. The version is separated from the package name with an underscore.

A file extension
> By default, all Debian packages end with *.deb* file extension.

Figure 2-1 illustrates a Debian package name.

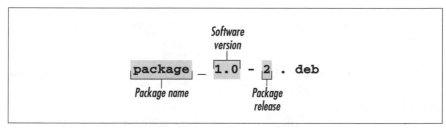

Figure 2-1: The structure of a Debian GNU/Linux package name

Managing Debian Packages

The original Debian package management tool is **dpkg**, which operates directly on *.deb* package files and can be used to automate the installation and maintenance of software packages. The alternative **apt-get** tool operates using package names, obtaining them from a predefined source (such as CD-ROMs, FTP sites, etc.). Both tools work from the command line.

The **dselect** command offers an interactive menu that allows the administrator to select from a list of available packages and mark them for subsequent installation. The **alien** command allows the use of non-Debian packages, such as the Red Hat RPM format.

For complete information on Debian package management commands, see details in their respective manpages.

---

dpkg

Syntax

    dpkg [*options*] action

Description

The Debian package manager command, **dpkg**, consists of an *action* that specifies a major mode of operation as well as zero or more *options*, which modify the action's behavior.

The **dpkg** command maintains package information in */var/lib/dpkg*. Two files located there of particular interest are:

available
> The list of all available packages.

status
> Contains package attributes, such as whether it is installed or marked for removal.

These files are modified by **dpkg**, **dselect**, and **apt-get**, and it is unlikely that they will ever need to be edited.

Frequently used options

–E
> Using this option, **dpkg** will not overwrite a previously installed package of the same version.

–G
> Using this option, **dpkg** will not overwrite a previously installed package with an older version of that same package.

–R *(also* --**recursive***)*
> Recursively process package files in specified subdirectories. Works with –i, --**install**, --**unpack**, and so on.

Frequently used actions

--configure *package*
> Configure an unpacked package. This involves setup of configuration files.

-i *package_file (also* **--install** *package_file)*
> Install the package contained in *package_file*. This involves backup of old files, unpacking and installation of new files, and configuration.

-l *[pattern] (also* **--list** *[pattern])*
> Display information for installed package names that match *pattern*.

-L *package (also* **--listfiles** *package)*
> List files installed from *package*.

--print-avail *package*
> Display details found in */var/lib/dpkg/available* about *package*.

---purge *package*
> Remove everything for *package*.

-r *package (also* **--remove** *package)*
> Remove everything except configuration files for *package*.

-s *package (also* **--status** *package)*
> Report the status of *package*.

-S *search_pattern (also* **--search** *search_pattern)*
> Search for a filename matching *search_pattern* from installed packages.

--unpack *package_file*
> Unpack *package_file,* but don't install the package it contains.

Example 1

Install a package using dpkg -i with the name of an available package file:

```
# dpkg -i ./hdparm_3.3-3.deb
(Reading database ... 54816 files and directories
   currently installed.)
Preparing to replace hdparm 3.3-3 (using hdparm_3.3-3.deb)
Unpacking replacement hdparm ...
Setting up hdparm (3.3-3) ...
```

Alternatively, use **apt-get install** with the name of the package. In this case, the package comes from the location or locations configured in */etc/apt/sources.list*. For this example, the location is *http://http.us.debian.org*:

```
# apt-get install elvis
Reading Package Lists... Done
Building Dependency Tree... Done
The following extra packages will be installed:
   libncurses4 xlib6g
The following NEW packages will be installed:
   elvis
2 packages upgraded, 1 newly installed, 0 to remove
   and 376 not upgraded.
```

```
Need to get 1678kB of archives. After unpacking 2544kB
  will be used.
Do you want to continue? [Y/n] y
Get:1 http://http.us.debian.org stable/main
  libncurses4 4.2-9 [180kB]
Get:2 http://http.us.debian.org stable/main
  xlib6g 3.3.6-11 [993kB]
Get:3 http://http.us.debian.org stable/main
  elvis 2.1.4-1 [505kB]
Fetched 1678kB in 4mlls (6663B/s)
(Reading database ... 54730 files and directories
  currently installed.)
Preparing to replace libncurses4 4.2-3 (using
  .../libncurses4_4.2-9_i386.deb) ...
Unpacking replacement libncurses4 ...
(installation continues...)
```

Example 2

Upgrading a package is no different from installing one. However, you should use the **–G** option when upgrading with **dpkg** to ensure that the installation won't proceed if a newer version of the same package is already installed.

Example 3

Use **dpkg -r** or **dpkg --purge** to remove a package:

```
# dpkg --purge elvis
(Reading database ... 54816 files and directories
  currently installed.)
Removing elvis ...
(purge continues...)
```

Example 4

Use the **dpkg -S** command to find a package containing specific files. In this example, **apt-get** is contained in the **apt** package:

```
# dpkg -S apt-get
apt: /usr/share/man/man8/apt-get.8.gz
apt: /usr/bin/apt-get
```

Example 5

Obtain package status information, such as version, content, dependencies, integrity, and installation status, using **dpkg -s**:

```
# dpkg -s apt
Package: apt
Status: install ok installed
Priority: optional
Section: admin
Installed-Size: 1388
(listing continues...)
```

Example 6

List the files in a package using **dpkg -L** and process the output using **grep** or **less**:

```
# dpkg -L apt | grep '^/usr/bin'
/usr/bin
/usr/bin/apt-cache
/usr/bin/apt-cdrom
/usr/bin/apt-config
/usr/bin/apt-get
```

Example 7

List the installed packages using **dpkg -l**; if you don't specify a pattern, all packages will be listed:

```
# dpkg -l xdm
ii  xdm              3.3.2.3a-11    X display manager
```

Example 8

Use **dpkg -S** to determine the package from which a particular file was installed with the filename:

```
# dpkg -S /usr/bin/nl
textutils: /usr/bin/nl
```

---

apt-get

Syntax

```
apt-get [options] [command] [package_name ...]
```

Description

The **apt-get** command is part of the Advanced Package Tool (APT) management system. It does not work directly with *.deb* files like **dpkg**, but uses package names instead. **apt-get** maintains a database of package information that enables the tool to automatically upgrade packages and their dependencies as new package releases become available.

Frequently used options

-d

Download files, but do not install. This is useful when you wish to get a large number of package files but delay their installation to prevent installation errors from stopping the download process.

-s

Simulate the steps in a package change, but do not actually change the system.

-y

Automatically respond "yes" to all prompts, instead of prompting you for a response during package installation/removal.

Frequently used commands

dist–upgrade

> This command is used to automatically upgrade to new versions of Debian Linux.

install

> The **install** command is used to install or upgrade one or more packages by name.

remove

> This command is used to remove the specified packages.

update

> Running **apt-get update** fetches a list of currently available packages. This is typically done before any changes are made to existing packages.

upgrade

> The **upgrade** command is used to safely upgrade a system's complete set of packages to current versions. It is conservative and will not process upgrades that could cause a conflict or break an existing configuration; it also will not remove packages.

Additional commands and options are available. See the **apt-get** manpage for more information.

apt-get uses */etc/apt/sources.list* to determine where packages should be obtained. This file is not in the Objectives for Exam 102.

Example

Remove the *elvis* package using *apt-get*.

```
# apt-get remove elvis
Reading Package Lists... Done
Building Dependency Tree... Done
The following packages will be REMOVED:
  elvis
0 packages upgraded, 0 newly installed, 1 to remove
  and 376 not upgraded.
Need to get 0B of archives. After unpacking 1363kB
  will be freed.
Do you want to continue? [Y/n] y
(Reading database ... 54816 files and directories
  currently installed.)
Removing elvis ...
(removal continues...)
```

In this example, the user is required to respond with **y** when promted to continue. Using the **-y** option to **apt-get** would eliminate this interaction.

---

dselect

Syntax

```
dselect
```

Description

dselect is an interactive, menu-driven, frontend tool for dpkg and is usually invoked without parameters. The dselect command lets you interactively manage packages by selecting them for installation, removal, configuration, and so forth. Selections are made from a locally stored list of available packages, which may be updated while running dselect. Package actions initiated by dselect are carried out using dpkg.

alien

Syntax

```
alien [--to-deb] [--patch=patchfile] [options] file
```

Description

Convert to or install a non-Debian (or "alien") package. Supported package types include Red Hat *.rpm*, Stampede *.slp*, Slackware *.tgz*, and generic *.tar.gz* files. rpm must also be installed on the system in order to convert an RPM package into a *.deb* package. The alien command produces an *output package* in Debian format by default after conversion.

Frequently used option

-i

Automatically install the output package and remove the converted package file.

Example

Install a non-Debian package on Debian system using alien with the -i option:

```
alien -i package.rpm
```

On the Exam

dselect, apt-get, and alien are important parts of Debian package management, but detailed knowledge of dpkg is of primary importance for Exam 102.

Objective 6: Use Red Hat Package Manager (RPM)

The Red Hat Package Manager is among the most popular methods for the distribution of software for Linux and is installed by default on many distributions. It automatically handles many of the management details associated with interdependent software running on your system.

RPM Overview

RPM automates the installation and maintenance of software packages. Built into each package are program files, configuration files, documentation, and dependencies on other packages. Package files are manipulated using the **rpm** command, which maintains a database of all installed packages and their files. Information from new packages is added to this database, and it's consulted on a file-by-file basis for dependencies when packages are removed, queried, and installed.

As with Debian packages, RPM filenames have three common elements:

Name

An RPM package name is short and descriptive. If multiple words are used, they are separated by hyphens (not underscores, as you might expect). Typical names include *binutils, caching-nameserver, cvs, gmc, kernel-source,* and *telnet.*

Version

Each package has a version. Most package versions are the same as that of the software they contain, thus the format of package versions varies from package to package. Most are numeric, with major, patch, and release numbers, but other information may appear as well. Typical versions are *3.0beta5-7, 1.05a-4, 2.7-5, 1.10.5-2, 1.1.1pre2-2, 1.14r4-4, 6.5.2-free3-rsaref,* and *0.9_alpha3-6.* The version is separated from the name by a hyphen.

Architecture

Packages containing binary (compiled) files are by their nature specific to a particular type of system. For PCs, the RPM architecture designation is *i386,* meaning the Intel 80386 and subsequent line of microprocessors and compatibles. For Sun and Sun-compatible processors, the architecture is *sparc.* The architecture is separated from the version with a dot.

A .rpm extension

All RPM files end with *.rpm* extension by default.

An RPM filename is constructed by tying these elements together in one long string, as shown in Figure 2-2.

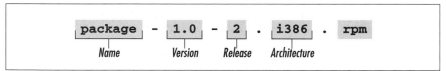

Figure 2-2: The structure of an RPM package name

As you can see, there are three uses for hyphens in RPM filenames. They appear as word separators in package names, as a delimiter between names and versions, and as part of the version. This may be confusing at first, but the version is usually obvious, making the use of hyphens unambiguous.[*]

---

[*] Perhaps this won't be clear at first glance, but once you're used to RPM names you'll know what to expect.

Running rpm

The **rpm** command provides for the installation, removal, upgrade, verification, and other management of RPM packages and has a bewildering array of options. Some are of the traditional single-letter style, while others are the *--option* variety. In most cases, both styles exist and are interchangeable. At first glance, configuring **rpm** may appear to be a bit daunting. However, its operation is segmented into *modes*, which are enabled using one (and only one) of the *mode options*. Within a mode, additional mode-specific options become available to modify the behavior of **rpm**. The major modes of **rpm** and some of the most frequently used mode-specific options follow. For complete information on how to use and manage RPM packages, see the **rpm** manpage or the synopsis offered by **rpm** **--help**.

rpm

Syntax

> *rpm* –*i* (also *rpm* – – *install*),
> *rpm* –*U* (also *rpm* – – *upgrade*)
> *rpm* –*e* (also – – *uninstall*)
> *rpm* –*q* (also – – *query*)
> *rpm* – *V*

Install/Upgrade mode

The *install mode* (**rpm -i**) is used to install new packages. A variant of install mode is the *upgrade mode* (**rpm -U**), where an installed package is upgraded to a more recent version.

Frequently used install- and upgrade-mode options

--force

> This option allows the replacement of existing packages and of files from previously installed packages; for upgrades, it allows the replacement of a newer package with an older one.

-h *(also --hash)*

> This option adds a string of 50 hash marks (#) during installation as a sort of progress indicator.

--nodeps

> **rpm** will skip dependency checking with this option enabled. This allows you to install a package without regard to dependencies.

--test

> This option will run through all the motions except for actually writing files; it's useful to verify that a package will install correctly prior to making the attempt. Note that verbose and hash options cannot be used with **--test**, but **-vv** can.

-v

> This option sets verbose mode.

-vv

> This sets really verbose mode. The manpage describes this as "print lots of ugly debugging information."

Study Guide 102

Example 1

To install a new package, simply use the **rpm -i** command with the name of a package file. If the new package depends upon another package, the install fails, like this:

```
# rpm -iv netscape-communicator-4.72-3.i386.rpm
error: failed dependencies:
        netscape-common = 4.72 is needed by
        netscape-communicator-4.72-3
```

To correct the problem, the dependency must first be satisfied. In this example, *netscape-communicator* is dependent on *netscape-common*, which is installed first:

```
# rpm -iv netscape-common-4.72-3.i386.rpm
netscape-common
# rpm -iv netscape-communicator-4.72-3.i386.rpm
netscape-communicator
```

Example 2

Upgrading an existing package to a newer version can be done with the -U option. Upgrade mode is really a special case of the install mode, where existing packages can be superseded by newer versions. Using -U, a package can be installed even if it doesn't already exist, in which case it behaves just like -i:

```
# rpm -U netscape-common-4.72-3.i386.rpm
```

Uninstall mode

This mode is used to remove installed packages from the system. By default, **rpm** uninstalls a package only if no other packages are dependent on it.

Frequently used uninstall-mode options

--nodeps
> **rpm** skips dependency checking with this option enabled.

--test
> This option runs through all the motions except for actually uninstalling things; it's useful to verify that a package can be uninstalled correctly without breaking other dependencies prior to making the attempt. Note that verbose and hash options cannot be used with --**test**, but -vv can.

Example

Package removal is the opposite of installation and has the same dependency constraints:

```
# rpm -e netscape-common
error: removing these packages would break dependencies:
        netscape-common = 4.72 is needed by
        netscape-communicator-4.72-3
```

Query mode

Installed packages and raw package files can be queried using the **rpm -q** command. Query-mode options exist for package and information selection.

Frequently used query-mode package selection options

-a *(also* --all*)*

> Display a list of all packages installed on the system. This is particularly useful when piped to **grep** if you're not sure of the name of a package or when you want to look for packages that share a common attribute.

-f *filename (also* --file*)*

> Display the package that contains a particular file.

-p *package_filename*

> Query a package file. Most useful with –i, described next.

Frequently used query-mode information selection options

-c *(also* --configfiles*)*

> List only configuration files.

-d *(also* --docfiles*)*

> List only documentation files.

-i *package*

> Not to be confused with the *install mode.* Display information about an installed package, or when combined with **-p**, about a package file. In the latter case, *package* is a filename.

-l *package (also* --list*)*

> List all of the files contained in *package.* When used with **-p**, the *package* is a filename.

-R *(also* --requires*)*

> List packages on which this package depends.

Example 1

To determine the version of the software contained in an RPM file, use the query and package information options:

```
# rpm -qpi xv-3.10a-13.i386.rpm | grep Version
Version    : 3.10a              Vendor: Red Hat Software
```

For installed packages, omit the **-p** option and specify a package name instead of a package filename:

```
# rpm -qi kernel-source | grep Version
Version    : 2.2.5              Vendor: Red Hat Software
```

Example 2

Enter query mode and list the files contained in a package:

```
# rpm -qlp gnucash-1.3.0-1.i386.rpm
/usr/bin/gnc-prices
/usr/bin/gnucash
/usr/bin/gnucash.gnome
/usr/doc/gnucash
/usr/doc/gnucash/CHANGES
  (...output continues ...)
```

For an installed package, enter query mode and use the –l option along with the package name:

```
# rpm -ql kernel-source
/usr/src/linux-2.2.5/COPYING
/usr/src/linux-2.2.5/CREDITS
/usr/src/linux-2.2.5/Documentation
/usr/src/linux-2.2.5/Documentation/00-INDEX
/usr/src/linux-2.2.5/Documentation/ARM-README
(...output continues ...)
```

Example 3

List the documentation files in a package:

```
# rpm -qd at
/usr/doc/at-3.1.7/ChangeLog
/usr/doc/at-3.1.7/Copyright
/usr/doc/at-3.1.7/Problems
/usr/doc/at-3.1.7/README
/usr/doc/at-3.1.7/timespec
/usr/man/man1/at.1
/usr/man/man1/atq.1
/usr/man/man1/atrm.1
/usr/man/man1/batch.1
/usr/man/man8/atd.8
/usr/man/man8/atrun.8
```

Use –p for package filenames.

Example 4

List configuration files or scripts in a package:

```
# rpm -qc at
/etc/at.deny
/etc/rc.d/init.d/atd
```

Example 5

Determine the package from which a particular file was installed. Of course, not all files originate from packages:

```
# rpm -qf /etc/issue
file /etc/issue is not owned by any package
```

Those that are package members look like this:

```
# rpm -qf /etc/aliases
sendmail-8.9.3-10
```

Example 6

List the packages that have been installed on the system (all or a subset):

```
# rpm -qa
(... hundreds of packages are listed ...)
```

To search for a subset with *kernel* in the name, pipe the previous command to **grep**:

```
# rpm -qa | grep kernel
kernel-headers-2.2.5-15
kernel-2.2.5-15
kernel-pcmcia-cs-2.2.5-15
kernel-smp-2.2.5-15
kernel-source-2.2.5-15
kernelcfg-0.5-5
kernel-ibcs-2.2.5-15
kernel-doc-2.2.5-15
```

Verify mode

Files from installed packages can be compared against their expected configuration from the RPM database by using **rpm -V**. The output is described in "Part 2: *Security (Topic 1.14)*, Objective 1: Perform Security Administration Tasks."

Frequently used verify-mode options

--nofiles
> Ignores missing files.

--nomd5
> Ignores MD5 checksum errors.

--nopgp
> Ignores PGP checking errors.

Additional operational modes

There are also modes in RPM for building, rebuilding, signing, and checking the signature of RPM files; however, these are beyond the scope of the LPIC Level 1 exams.

On the Exam

Make certain that you are aware of RPM's major operational modes and their commonly used mode-specific options. Knowledge of specific options will be necessary. Read through the **rpm** manpage at least once.

Kernel
(Topic 1.5)

In the early days of personal computing, operating systems were simple interfaces, designed to provide access to a rudimentary filesystem and to launch
programs. Once a program was running, it had full control of the system. This
made the system simple but also contributed to instability, because a single
program failure could cause the entire system to crash. To run a computer in an
organized and reliable fashion, it is important to isolate physical hardware
resources from the software running on the system. In Linux, the *kernel* is the core
software that owns and manages your system. It controls hardware, memory, and
process scheduling, and provides an interface for programs to indirectly access
hardware resources.

This Topic on the Linux kernel has two Objectives:

Objective 1: Manage Kernel Modules at Runtime
    This Objective covers kernel modules and the commands for managing them.
    Weight: 3.

Objective 2: Reconfigure, Build, and Install a Custom Kernel and Modules
    This Objective describes the creation of new kernels using your existing
    kernel source code as provided in your Linux distribution. Weight: 4.

Objective 1: Manage Kernel Modules at Runtime

With Linux, code for system devices can be compiled into the kernel. Because the
kernel already has built-in support for most devices, it is said to be *monolithic*, as
the kernel manages all system hardware by itself. Monolithic kernels aren't very
flexible because a new kernel build is necessary for new peripheral devices to be
added to the system. Monolithic kernels also have the potential to be "bloated" by
drivers for hardware that isn't physically installed. Instead, most users run *modular*

kernels, in which device drivers are inserted into the running kernel as needed. Modular configurations can adapt to changes in the hardware and provide a convenient way of upgrading driver software while a system is running.

Module Files

Linux kernel modules are object files (*.o*) produced by the C compiler but not linked into a completed executable (in this case, the kernel executable file). Most modules are distributed with the kernel and compiled along with it. Because they are so closely related to the kernel, separate sets of modules are installed when multiple kernels are installed. This reduces the likelihood that a kernel module will be inserted into the wrong kernel version.

Modules are stored in a directory hierarchy headed by */lib/modules/kernel-version*, where *kernel-version* is the string reported by **uname -r**, such as 2.2.5-15smp. In this example, the modules directory would be */lib/modules/ 2.2.5-15smp*. Multiple module hierarchies may be available under */lib/modules* if multiple kernels are installed.

Subdirectories that contain modules of a particular type exist beneath the */lib/ modules/kernel-version* directory. For example, for kernel *2.2.5-15smp*, network interface modules are stored in subdirectory */lib/modules/2.2.5-15smp/ net*. This grouping is convenient for administrators but also facilitates important functionality to the **modprobe** command. Typical module subdirectories are:

block
: Modules for a few block-specific devices such as RAID controllers or IDE tape drives.

cdrom
: Device driver modules for nonstandard CD-ROM devices.

fs
: Contains drivers for filesystems such as MS-DOS (the *msdos.o* module).

ipv4
: Includes modular kernel features having to do with IP processing, such as IP masquerading.

misc
: Anything that doesn't fit into one of the other subdirectories ends up here. Note that no modules are stored at the top of this tree.

net
: Network interface driver modules.

scsi
: Contains driver modules for the SCSI controller.

video
: Special driver modules for video adapters.

Module directories are also referred to as *tags* in the context of module manipulation commands.

Manipulating Modules

A module is dynamically linked into the running kernel when it is loaded. Much of Linux kernel module handling is done automatically. However, there may be times when it is necessary for you to manipulate the modules yourself, and you may come across the manipulation commands in scripts. For example, if you're having difficulty with a particular driver, you may need to get the source code for a newer version of the driver, compile it, and insert the new module in the running kernel. The commands listed in this section can be used to list, insert, remove, and query modules.

lsmod

Syntax

    lsmod

Description

For each kernel module loaded, display its name, size, use count, and a list of other referring modules. This command yields the same information as is available in */proc/modules*.

Example

Here, **lsmod** shows that quite a few kernel modules are loaded, including file-system (*vfat*, *fat*), networking (*3c59x*), and sound (*soundcore*, *mpu401*, etc.) modules, among others:

```
# lsmod
Module          Size    Used by
vmnet           9688    2
vmppuser        5020    0  (unused)
parport_pc      5044    0  [vmppuser]
parport         7712    0  [vmppuser parport_pc]
vmmon           14100   1
nls_iso8859-1   2020    1  (autoclean)
nls_cp437       3548    1  (autoclean)
ide-floppy      8396    1  (autoclean)
vfat            11612   1  (autoclean)
fat             25856   1  (autoclean) [vfat]
nfsd            151192  8  (autoclean)
lockd           31336   1  (autoclean) [nfsd]
sunrpc          53572   1  (autoclean) [nfsd lockd]
3c59x           18984   1  (autoclean)
opl3            11208   0  (unused)
opl3sa2         3720    0
ad1848          15984   0  [opl3sa2]
mpu401          18576   0  [opl3sa2]
sound           59064   0  [opl3 opl3sa2 ad1848 mpu401]
soundlow        304     0  [sound]
soundcore       2788    7  [sound]
aic7xxx         107024  8
```

insmod

Syntax

insmod [*options*] *module*

Description

Insert a module into the running kernel. The module is located automatically and inserted. You must be logged in as the superuser to insert modules.

Frequently used options

−s

Display results on *syslog* instead of the terminal.

−v

Set verbose mode.

Example

The *msdos* filesystem module is installed into the running kernel. In this example, the kernel was compiled with modular support for the *msdos* filesystem type, a typical configuration for a Linux distribution for i386 hardware. To verify that you have this module, check for the existence of */lib/modules/kernel-version/fs/ msdos.o*:

```
# insmod msdos
/lib/modules/2.2.5-15smp/fs/msdos.o: unresolved symbol fat_add_cluster_
Rsmp_eb84f594
/lib/modules/2.2.5-15smp/fs/msdos.o: unresolved symbol fat_cache_inval_
inode_Rsmp_6da1654e
/lib/modules/2.2.5-15smp/fs/msdos.o: unresolved symbol fat_scan_Rsmp_
d61c58c7
     ( ... additional errors omitted ... )
/lib/modules/2.2.5-15smp/fs/msdos.o: unresolved symbol fat_date_unix2dos_
Rsmp_83fb36a1
# echo $?
1
```

This **insmod msdos** command yields a series of unresolved symbol messages and an exit status of 1. This is the same sort of message that might be seen when attempting to link a program that referenced variables or functions unavailable to the linker. In the context of a module insertion, such messages indicate that the functions are not available in the kernel. From the names of the missing symbols, you can see that the *fat* module is required to support the *msdos* module, so it is inserted first:

```
# insmod fat
```

Now the *msdos* module can be loaded:

```
# insmod msdos
```

Use the **modprobe** command to automatically determine these dependencies and install prerequisite modules first.

rmmod

Syntax

rmmod [*options*] *modules*

Description

Unless a module is in use or referred to by another module, the **rmmod** command is used to remove modules from the running kernel. You must be logged in as the superuser to remove modules.

Frequently used options

-a

> Remove all unused modules.

-s

> Display results on *syslog* instead of the terminal.

Example

Starting with both the *fat* and *msdos* modules loaded, remove the *fat* module (which is used by the *msdos* module):

```
# lsmod
Module                 Size  Used by
msdos                  8348  0   (unused)
fat                    25856 0   [msdos]
# rmmod fat
rmmod: fat is in use
```

In this example, the **lsmod** command fails because the *msdos* module is dependent on the *fat* module. So, in order to unload the *fat* module, the *msdos* module must be unloaded first:

```
# rmmod msdos
# rmmod fat
```

The **modprobe -r** command can be used to automatically determine these dependencies and remove modules and their prerequisites.

---

modinfo

Syntax

modinfo [*options*] *module_object_file*

Description

Display information about a module from its *module_object_file*. Some modules contain no information at all, some have a short one-line description, and others have a fairly descriptive message.

Options

-a

> Display the module's author.

-d

Display the module's description.

-p

Display the typed parameters that a module may support.

Examples

In these examples, **modinfo** is run using modules compiled for a multiprocessing (*smp*) kernel Version 2.2.5. Your kernel version, and thus the directory hierarchy containing modules, will be different.

```
# modinfo -d /lib/modules/2.2.5-15smp/misc/zftape.o
zftape for ftape v3.04d 25/11/97 - VFS interface for the
        Linux floppy tape driver. Support for QIC-113
        compatible volume table and builtin compression
        (lzrw3 algorithm)
```

```
# modinfo -a /lib/modules/2.2.5-15smp/misc/zftape.o
(c) 1996, 1997 Claus-Justus Heine
        (claus@momo.math.rwth-aachen.de)
```

```
# modinfo -p /lib/modules/2.2.5-15smp/misc/ftape.o
ft_fdc_base int, description "Base address of FDC
        controller."
Ft_fdc_irq int, description "IRQ (interrupt channel)
        to use."
ft_fdc_dma int, description "DMA channel to use."
ft_fdc_threshold int, description "Threshold of the FDC
        Fifo."
Ft_fdc_rate_limit int, description "Maximal data rate
        for FDC."
ft_probe_fc10 int, description "Tf non-zero, probe for a
        Colorado FC-10/FC-20 controller."
ft_mach2 int, description "If non-zero, probe for a
        Mountain MACH-2 controller."
ft_tracing int, description "Amount of debugging output,
        0 <= tracing <= 8, default 3."
```

modprobe

Syntax

modprobe [*options*] *module* [*symbol=value* ...]

Description

Like **insmod**, **modprobe** is used to insert modules.* However, **modprobe** has the ability to load single modules, modules and their prerequisites, or all modules stored in a specific directory. The **modprobe** command can also remove modules when combined with the **-r** option.

---

* In fact, **modprobe** is a wrapper around **insmod** and provides additional functionality.

A module is inserted with optional *symbol=value* parameters (see more on parameters in the discussion on the module configuration file, later in this section). If the module is dependent upon other modules, they will be loaded first. The **modprobe** command determines prerequisite relationships between modules by reading *modules.dep* at the top of the module directory hierarchy (i.e., */lib/modules/2.2.5-15smp/modules.dep*).

You must be logged in as the superuser to insert modules.

Frequently used options

-a

> Load all modules. When used with the -t *tag*, "all" is restricted to modules in the *tag* directory. This action probes hardware by successive module-insertion attempts for a single type of hardware, such as a network adapter (in which case the *tag* would be net, representing */lib/modules/kernel-version/net*). This may be necessary, for example, to probe for more than one kind of network interface.

-c

> Display a complete module configuration, including defaults and directives found in */etc/modules.conf* (or */etc/conf.modules*, depending on your distribution). The -c option is not used with any other options.

-l

> List modules. When used with the -t *tag*, list only modules in directory *tag*. For example, if *tag* is net, then modules in */lib/modules/kernel-version/net* are displayed.

-r

> Remove *module*, similar to **rmmod**. Multiple modules may be specified.

-s

> Display results on *syslog* instead of the terminal.

-t *tag*

> Attempt to load multiple modules found in the directory *tag* until a module succeeds or all modules in *tag* are exhausted. This action "probes" hardware by successive module-insertion attempts for a single type of hardware, such as a network adapter (in which case *tag* would be net, representing */lib/modules/kernel-version/net*).

-v

> Set verbose mode.

Example 1

Install the *msdos* filesystem module into the running kernel:

```
# modprobe msdos
```

Module *msdos* and its dependency, *fat*, will be loaded. **modprobe** determines that *fat* is needed by *msdos* when it looks through *modules.dep*. You can see the dependency listing using **grep**:

```
# grep /msdos.o: /lib/modules/2.2.5-15smp/modules.dep
/lib/modules/2.2.5-15smp/fs/msdos.o:
        /lib/modules/2.2.5-15smp/fs/fat.o
```

Example 2

Remove *fat* and *msdos* modules from the running kernel, assuming *msdos* is not in use:

```
# modprobe -r fat msdos
```

Example 3

Attempt to load available network modules until one succeeds:

```
# modprobe -t net
```

Example 4

Attempt to load all available network modules:

```
# modprobe -at net
```

Example 5

List all modules available for use:

```
# modprobe -l
/lib/modules/2.2.5-15smp/fs/vfat.o
/lib/modules/2.2.5-15smp/fs/umsdos.o
/lib/modules/2.2.5-15smp/fs/ufs.o
( ... listing continues ... )
```

Example 6

List all modules in the *net* directory for 3Com network interfaces:

```
# modprobe -lt net | grep 3c
/lib/modules/2.2.5-15smp/net/3c59x.o
/lib/modules/2.2.5-15smp/net/3c515.o
/lib/modules/2.2.5-15smp/net/3c509.o
/lib/modules/2.2.5-15smp/net/3c507.o
/lib/modules/2.2.5-15smp/net/3c505.o
/lib/modules/2.2.5-15smp/net/3c503.o
/lib/modules/2.2.5-15smp/net/3c501.o
```

On the Exam

Familiarize yourself with modules on a nonproduction Linux system, and explore the */lib/modules* hierarchy. Review the *modules.dep* file. Be aware of what a module is, how and why it is inserted, what it means to "probe" with multiple modules, and how to determine if a module is dependent on other modules. Pay special attention to **modprobe**.

Configuring Modules

You may sometimes need to control elements of a module such as hardware interrupt assignments or Direct Memory Access (DMA) channel selections. Other situations may dictate special procedures to prepare for, or clean up after, a module insertion or removal. This type of special control of modules is implemented in the configuration file */etc/conf.modules* (or in */etc/modules.conf,* depending on your distribution), which controls the behavior of **modprobe**. The */etc/conf.modules* file can contain the following information:

Comments
> Blank lines and lines beginning with # are ignored.

keep
> The keep parameter, when found before any path directives, causes the default paths to be retained and added to any paths specified.

depfile=*full_path*
> This directive overrides the default location for the modules dependency file, *modules.dep* (described in the next section). For example:
>
> ```
> depfile=/lib/modules/2.2.14/modules.dep
> ```

path=*path_directory*
> This directive specifies a directory to search for modules.

options *module opt1=val1 opt2=val2 ...*
> Options for modules can be specified using the options configuration line in *conf.modules* or on the **modprobe** command line. The command line overrides configurations in the file. *module* is the name of a single module without the *.so* extension. Options are specified as *name=value* pairs, where the *name* is understood by the module and reported using **modinfo -p**. For example:
>
> ```
> options opl3 io=0x388
> ```

alias
> Aliases can be used to associate a generic name with a specific module. For example:
>
> ```
> alias scsi_hostadapter aic7xxx
> alias eth0 3c59x
> alias parport_lowlevel parport_pc
> ```

pre-install *module command*
> This directive causes some shell *command* to be executed prior to insertion of *module*. For example, PCMCIA services need to be started prior to installing the *pcmcia_core* module:
>
> ```
> pre-install pcmcia_core /etc/rc.d/init.d/pcmcia start
> ```

install *module command*
> This directive allows a specific shell *command* to override the default module-insertion command.

post-install *module*
> This directive causes some shell *command* to be executed after insertion of *module*.

pre-remove *module*
> This directive causes some shell *command* to be executed prior to removal of *module*.

remove *module*

> This directive allows a specific shell *command* to override the default module-removal command.

post-remove *module*

> This directive causes some shell *command* to be executed after removal of *module*.

The following is an example the */etc/conf.modules* file:

```
alias scsi_hostadapter aic7xxx
alias eth0 3c59x
alias parport_lowlevel parport_pc
pre-install pcmcia_core /etc/rc.d/init.d/pcmcia start
alias sound opl3sa2
pre-install sound insmod sound dmabuf=1
alias midi opl3
options opl3 io=0x388
options opl3sa2 mss_io=0x530 irq=5 dma=0 dma2=1
        mpu_io=0x388 io=0x370
```

On the Exam

Remember that the files *conf.modules* and *modules.conf* are the same file, depending on distribution. Also, while it is important for you to understand the configuration lines */etc/conf.modules*, detailed module configuration is beyond the scope of the LPIC Level 1 exams.

Module Dependency File

modprobe can determine module dependencies and install prerequisite modules automatically. To do this, **modprobe** scans the first column of */lib/modules/* kernel-version/*modules.dep* to find the module it is to install. Lines in *modules.dep* are in the following form:

> *module_name.o: dependency1 dependency2 ...*

A typical dependency looks like this:

```
/lib/modules/2.2.5-15smp/fs/msdos.o:
        /lib/modules/2.2.5-15smp/fs/fat.o
```

Here, the *msdos* module is dependent upon *fat*.

All of the modules available on the system are listed in the *modules.dep* file and are referred to with their full path and filenames, including their *.o* extension. Those that are not dependent on other modules are listed, but without dependencies. Dependencies that are listed are inserted into the kernel by **modprobe** first, and when all of them are successfully inserted, the subject module itself can be loaded.

The *modules.dep* file must be kept current to ensure the correct operation of **modprobe**. If module dependencies were to change without a corresponding modification to *modules.dep*, then **modprobe** may fail, because a dependency could be missed. As a result, *modules.dep* is created each time the system is booted. On most distributions, the **depmod -a** command is called during *rc.sysinit*:

```
echo "Finding module dependencies"
/sbin/depmod -a
```

The **depmod -a** command recreates and overwrites *modules.dep* each time the system is booted. This procedure is also necessary after any change in module dependencies. (The **depmod** command is actually a link to the same executable as **modprobe**. The functionality of the command differs depending on which name is used to call it.) The **depmod** command is not specifically called out in the LPIC Level 1 Objectives, but it is important to understand how the command works since it generates *modules.dep*.

On the Exam

Be sure you know what is in *modules.dep*, as well as what the file is used for, how it is created, and when it is created. Be prepared to cite the consequences of a missing or obsolete *modules.dep* file.

Objective 2: Reconfigure, Build, and Install a Custom Kernel and Modules

Because Linux is an open source operating system, you are free to create a customized Linux kernel that suits your specific needs and hardware. For example, you may wish to create a kernel for your system if your distribution installed a generic kernel that was compiled using the 80386 instruction set. Such a kernel will run on any compatible processor but may not utilize some of the capabilities of newer processors. Running a kernel optimized for your particular CPU can enhance its performance.

You can also install new kernels to add features, fix bugs, or experiment with kernels still under development. While the compilation of such kernels isn't much of a leap beyond recompiling your existing version, it's beyond the scope of the LPIC Level 1 exams.

Kernel Background

If you are new to the idea of building a custom kernel, don't feel intimidated. Linux developers have created a simple and reliable process that you can follow, and everything you need is available in your Linux distribution.

Kernel versions

Nearly all software projects, even small ones, use a numerical versioning scheme to describe each successive release. Kernel versions are numbered using the following convention:

`major.minor.patchlevel`

Major release

> Increments in the major release indicate major developmental milestones in the kernel. The present release is 2.x.x (don't let the low major release number fool you—there have been plenty of developmental milestones in the Linux kernel's history).

Minor release

> The minor release indicates significant changes and additions, which taken together will culminate in a new major release. The Linux kernel minor release numbers fall into one of the following categories:
>
> *Even-numbered releases*
>
> > Kernels with even-numbered kernel versions (2.0, 2.2, 2.4, and so on) are considered stable.
>
> *Odd-numbered releases*
>
> > Kernels with odd-numbered minor release versions (2.1, 2.3, and so on) are in development and are primarily used by kernel developers. When goals for the development of a minor release are met and testing shows that the kernel is stable, a new even-numbered minor release is created. This is how development kernels are released as production kernels.

Patch level

> As bugs are found and corrected or as planned features are added, the kernel patch level is incremented (2.2.15, 2.3.38, and so on). Generally speaking, it is safest to run the latest patch level of the kernel to be assured of having the most current bug fixes. In reality, it is more important to track kernel development and upgrade your kernel only if your existing version is found to have a serious problem or if you are already experiencing difficulty.

Required tools and software

To compile a custom kernel, you need development tools including a C compiler, assembler, linker, and the **make** utility. If you selected a kernel development option when you installed Linux, you should already have these tools on your system. The C compiler is the program that translates C source code into the binary form used by your system. The standard compiler on most Linux systems is the GNU C Compiler, **gcc**. The assembler and linker are needed for some portions of the kernel compilation.

The compilation process is controlled by **make**, a utility that executes commands such as **gcc** as directed by a list of dependency rules. These rules are stored in the *Makefile*. A brief introduction to **make** is provided in "Part 2: *Linux Installation and Package Management (Topic 2.2)*, Objective 3: Make and Install Programs from Source."

Of course, you also need the kernel source code. Your Linux distribution will come with one or more packages containing everything you need. For example, on a Red Hat system, use the following two RPM packages (listed here without their version numbers):

kernel-source

> This package contains the C language source code for the kernel and modules.

kernel-headers

> This package contains C language header files for the kernel. The header files define structures and constants that are needed for building most C programs, as well as the kernel itself.

On most systems, the kernel's source code can be found in */usr/src/linux*, which should be a symbolic link to the specific version of the kernel you're using. For example, here is the */usr/src* directory for a system with several kernel versions:

```
# ls -l /usr/src
lrwxrwxrwx  1 root   root        12  Feb 16 04:19
        linux -> linux-2.3.45
drwxr-xr-x 15 root   root      1024  Jan 29 01:13 linux-2.2.14
drwxr-xr-x 17 root   root      1024  Feb 16 03:00 linux-2.2.5
drwxr-xr-x 14 root   root      1024  Feb 16 04:35 linux-2.3.45
```

In this example, symbolic link */usr/src/linux* points to the directory hierarchy for development kernel 2.3.45. The */usr/src/linux* link is important when you work with multiple kernels, as it is assumed that the link will be manually removed before installing new kernel source trees. For the purposes of Exam 102, you need to be concerned only with the kernel source installed by your distribution.

On the Exam

You will need to know where the kernel source code is stored (e.g., */usr/ src/linux*). Explore the kernel source tree to familiarize yourself with its contents. Pay particular attention to *.config* and the *Makefile*.

Compiling a Custom Kernel

This section provides an overview of kernel compilation and installation by way of example. This example uses kernel Version 2.2.5, and our objective is to create a single-processor 2.2.5 kernel for a Pentium system with IDE disks* to replace a generic kernel that came with the distribution.

Assume that the development environment—including compiler, **make**, kernel source code, and kernel headers—is installed. The *root* account will be used to create and install the kernel, although any user can compile a kernel given the appropriate filesystem permissions. Before building a customized kernel, you should read */usr/doc/HOWTO/Kernel-HOWTO* and */usr/src/linux/README*.

---

* A system that boots from a SCSI disk and has the SCSI driver compiled as a module requires the use of an initial RAM disk, which is not covered here.

Creating a kernel configuration

The first step in creating a kernel is configuration. There are more than 500 options for the kernel, such as filesystem, SCSI, and networking support. Many of the options list kernel features that can be either compiled directly into the kernel or compiled as modules. During configuration, you indicate for each option whether you want that feature:

- Compiled into the kernel (*"yes"* response)

- Compiled as a module (**module** response)

- Don't want the feature at all (*"no"* response)

Some selections imply a group of other selections. For example, when you indicate that you wish to include SCSI support, additional options become available for specific SCSI drivers and features. The results from all of these choices are stored in the kernel configuration file */usr/src/linux/.config*, which is a plain text file that lists the options as shell variables set to one of *y*, *m*, or *n* in accordance with your response for each item.

To begin, set the current working directory to the top of the source tree:

```
# cd /usr/src/linux
```

There are several ways to set up *.config*. Although you can do so, you should not edit the file manually. Instead, you may select from three interactive approaches. An additional option is available to construct a default configuration. Each is started using **make**.

---

make config

Syntax

```
make config
```

Description

Running **make config** is the most rudimentary of the automated kernel-configuration methods and does not depend on any form of display capability on your terminal. In response to **make config**, the system presents you with a question in your console or window for each kernel option. You respond to the questions with *y*, *m*, or *n* for *yes*, *module*, or *no*, respectively. This method can admittedly get a bit tedious and has the liability that you must answer all the questions before being asked if you wish to save your *.config* file and exit. However, it is helpful if you do not have sufficient capability to use one of the menu-based methods (described next). A **make config** session looks like this:

```
# make config
rm -f include/asm
( cd include ; ln -sf asm-i386 asm)
/bin/sh scripts/Configure arch/i386/config.in
#
# Using defaults found in arch/i386/defconfig
#
*
* Code maturity level options
*
```

```
Prompt for development and/or incomplete code/drivers
(CONFIG_EXPERIMENTAL) [Y/n/?]Y
```

Each option is offered in this manner.

make menuconfig

Syntax

```
make menuconfig
```

Description

This configuration method is more intuitive and can be used as an alternative to
make config. It creates a text-mode-windowed environment where you may use
up/down/left/right and other keys to configure the kernel. The menu depends on
the ability of your terminal or terminal window to use *curses*, a standard library of
terminal cursor manipulation instructions. If your terminal does not support curses
(though most do), you must select another method. The **make menuconfig**
window is illustrated in Figure 2-3 in an **xterm**.

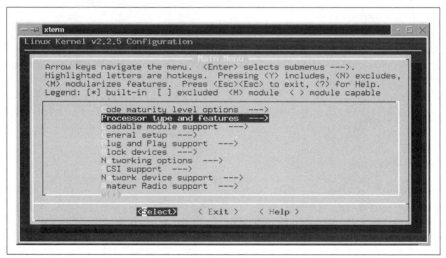

Figure 2-3: The make menuconfig menu display

make xconfig

Syntax

```
make xconfig
```

Description

If you are running the X Window System, the **make xconfig** configuration method
presents a GUI menu with radio buttons to make the selections. It is the most
appealing visually but requires a graphical console or X display. Figure 2-4 shows
the top-level **make xconfig** window.

The options presented in each case are the same, as is the outcome.

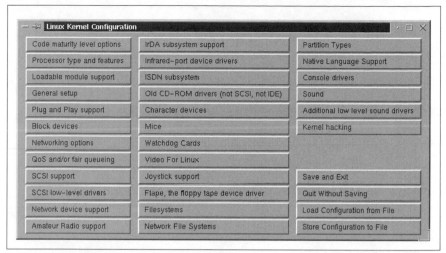

Figure 2-4: The make xconfig menu display

make oldconfig

Syntax

```
make oldconfig
```

Description

make oldconfig can create a default *.config* file. This method sets up a default *.config* file without interaction from the user. This is convenient if you need a starting point and your distribution did not install a default *.config* file. This method will also build a new *.config* file from one customized for a previous kernel release, but this is beyond the scope of Exam 102.

NOTE

In the absence of user responses, **menuconfig** and **xconfig** will create a default *.config* file, equivalent to the one created by **oldconfig**.

Example

To create the *.config* file for this example, the target processor is set as Pentium. Using **make xconfig**, the selection looks like the window shown in Figure 2-5.

By setting the *Processor family* parameter to *Pentium/K6/TSC* and saving the configuration, the following revised configuration lines are written in *.config*:

```
# Processor type and features
#
# CONFIG_M386 is not set
# CONFIG_M486 is not set
# CONFIG_M586 is not set
```

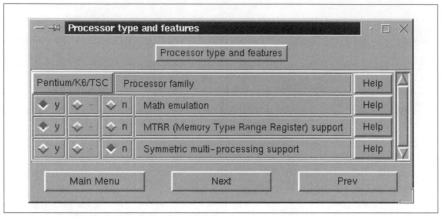

Figure 2-5: The make xconfig processor-selection window

```
CONFIG_M586TSC=y
# CONFIG_M686 is not set
CONFIG_X86_WP_WORKS_OK=y
CONFIG_X86_INVLPG=y
CONFIG_X86_BSWAP=y
CONFIG_X86_POPAD_OK=y
CONFIG_X86_TSC=y
CONFIG_MATH_EMULATION=y
CONFIG_MTRR=y
# CONFIG_SMP is not set
```

The complete *.config* file will contain approximately 800 lines. You should look through the other kernel options with one of the windowed selectors first to familiarize yourself with what is available before making your selections.

Now that *.config* is created, one small change is made to *Makefile* to differentiate our new custom kernel from the generic one. Examining */usr/src/linux/Makefile*, the first four lines look like this:

```
VERSION = 2
PATCHLEVEL = 2
SUBLEVEL = 5
EXTRAVERSION = -15
```

You can see that the kernel version is 2.2.5 and that an additional version number is available. In this case, the generic kernel had the extra version suffix of -15, yielding a complete kernel version number 2.2.5-15. This EXTRAVERSION parameter can be used to indicate just about anything. In this example it denotes the 15th build of kernel 2.2.5, but –pentium is added to the end for our custom version. Edit *Makefile* and change EXTRAVERSION as follows:

```
EXTRAVERSION = -15-pentium
```

This change completes the configuration for this example.

Compiling the kernel

Once the *.config* and *Makefile* files are customized, the new kernel can be compiled by running the following commands:

1. **make dep**

   In this step, source files (*.c*) are examined for dependencies on header files. A file called *.depend* is created in each directory containing source files to hold the resulting list, with a line for each compiled object file (*.o*). The *.depend* files are automatically included in subsequent **make** operations to be sure that changes in header files are compiled into new objects. Since kernel code isn't being developed here, no header file changes are needed. Nevertheless, **make dep** is an essential first step in the compilation process.

2. **make clean**

   The "clean" operation removes old output files that may exist from previous kernel builds. These include core files, system map files, and others. They must be removed in order to compile a new, clean kernel.

3. **make bzImage**

   The *bzImage* file is our ultimate goal, a bootable kernel image file, compressed using the *bzip2* utility.* It is created in this step along with some additional support files needed for boot time.

4. **make modules**

   Device drivers and other items that were configured as modules are compiled in this step.

5. **make modules_install**

   All of the modules compiled during **make modules** are installed under */lib/modules/kernel-version* in this step. A directory are created there for each kernel version, including various extraversions.

The *bzImage* and *modules* portions of the kernel-compilation process will take the most time. Overall, the time required to build a kernel depends on your system's capabilities.

After completing this series of **make** processes, compilation is complete. The new kernel image is now located in */usr/src/linux/arch/i386/boot/bzImage*.

Installing the new kernel and configuring LILO

Now that the new kernel has been compiled, the system can be configured to boot it:

1. The first step is to put a copy of our new *bzImage* on the root partition so it can be booted by LILO. The copy is named just as it was named during compilation, including the extraversion:

   ```
   # cp -p /usr/src/linux/arch/i386/boot/bzImage
         /boot/vmlinuz-2.2.5-15-pentium
   ```

---

* bzip2 is a compression utility similar to the more familiar **gzip**. **bzip2** uses a different compression algorithm that generally produces better compression results. See the **bzip2** manpage for more information.

2. Now, a listing of kernels should show at least your default kernel and your new one, *vmlinuz-2.2.5-15-pentium*:

```
# ls -l /boot/vmlinuz*
/boot/vmlinuz
/boot/vmlinuz-2.2.14
/boot/vmlinuz-2.2.5-15
/boot/vmlinuz-2.2.5-15-pentium
/boot/vmlinuz-2.2.5-15smp
/boot/vmlinuz-2.3.45
```

3. Next, add a new image section to the bottom of */etc/lilo.conf*:

```
image=/boot/vmlinuz-2.2.5-15-pentium
     label=linux-pentium
     root=/dev/sda1
     read-only
```

4. Finally, **lilo** (the map installer) is run again to incorporate the new kernel:

```
# lilo
Added linux-smp *
Added linux-up
Added latest
Added linux-pentium
```

It's not uncommon to forget the execution of **lilo**. If you do forget, **lilo** won't know about the new kernel you've installed despite the fact that it's listed in the *lilo.conf* file. This is because *lilo.conf* is not consulted at boot time.

If everything has gone according to plan, it's time to reboot and attempt to load the new kernel.

NOTE

As you review the *README* file that comes with the kernel source, you may see suggestions for overwriting your existing kernel, perhaps with a generic name such as *vmlinuz*, and reusing your existing LILO configuration unaltered (i.e., without changing *lilo.conf*). Unless you're absolutely sure about what you are doing, overwriting a known-good kernel is a bad idea. Instead, keep the working kernel around as a fallback position in case there's a problem with your new one.

Examine the new modules

Now that the new kernel is installed, you should take a look at */lib/modules*, which now has a new directory for the new kernel:

```
# ls -1 /lib/modules
2.2.14
2.2.5-15
2.2.5-15-pentium
2.2.5-15smp
2.3.45
```

On the Exam

Remember the series of **make** steps required to build the kernel: **config** (or
menuconfig or **xconfig**), **dep**, **clean**, **bzImage**, **modules**, and **modules-install**.
Be aware of where the kernel source code is installed. Also, note that you
need to copy the kernel image file (*bzImage*) to the root filesystem and that
you must rerun **lilo** before you can boot it. By all means, practice compiling
and installing a kernel at least once before taking Exam 102.

Text-Editing, Processing, and Printing (Topic 1.7)

Two general areas of text handling under Linux are described in this section: editing with **vi** and printing. The **vi** editor is important for everyone, because it is available with just about every Linux distribution. Also, despite new automated Linux configuration tools, proficiency with at least one text editor is extremely important for system administration. Printing is covered from an installation and management perspective. This section includes four Objectives:

Objective 1: Perform Basic File Editing Operations Using vi
No matter what your opinion on what the best text editor is, **vi** is available everywhere, and administrators must be familiar with it in order to pass the exam. This Objective covers **vi** basics. Weight: 2.

Objective 2: Manage Printers and Print Queues
Printer management can be easy given a general understanding of **lpq**, **lprm**, and **lpc**. Weight: 2.

Objective 3: Print Files
This Objective is short, covering only **lpr**. Weight: 1.

Objective 4: Install and Configure Local and Remote Printers
This Objective involves the installation of **lpd** and related utilities, filters, and remote printers. Weight: 3.

Objective 1: Perform Basic File Editing Operations Using vi

When working on multiple systems, the availability of a text editor may be of prime importance. Since an editor is an essential configuration tool for Linux, learning at least the basics of the resident editor is a requirement. For Linux and nearly all other Unix systems, the universally available editor is **vi**. This Objective covers **vi** basics.[*]

Invoking vi

The **vi** editor has two modes of operation: *command* or *insert*. In command mode, **vi** allows you to navigate around your file and enter commands. To enter new text, put **vi** into insert mode. In command mode, the keyboard keys are interpreted as **vi** commands instead of text. The convenience of being able to manipulate the editor without moving your hands from the keyboard is considered one of **vi**'s strengths.

To start **vi**, simply provide one or more text files on the command line:

```
$ vi file1.txt file2.txt
```

You are presented with a main window showing the contents of *file1.txt*, or if the specified files don't already exist, a blank screen with tilde (~) characters running the length of the left column (they indicate areas of the screen containing no text, not even blank lines).

Commands are brief, case-sensitive combinations of one or more letters. For example, to switch from command to insert mode, press the i key. To terminate insert mode, press the **Escape** key (**Esc**), which puts you back in command mode.

Terminating vi

Once you've started **vi**, the first thing you need to know is how to stop it. When in command mode, you can use any of the key sequences shown in Table 2-13. If you're in insert mode, you must first switch back to command mode in order to exit, by pressing the **Esc**.

Table 2-13: Common Commands for Exiting vi

Key Command	Description
:n	Next file; when multiple files are specified for editing, this command loads the next file.
:q	Quit without saving changes.
:q!	Quit without saving changes and without confirmation.
:wq	Write the file contents (if changed) and quit.
:x	Write the file contents (if changed) and quit (the **ex** equivalent of ZZ).
ZZ	Write the file contents (if changed) and quit.

---

[*] Some Linux systems come with a newer version of **vi**, called **vim**, which is an open source **vi** clone, with improvements. Additional information on **vim** can be found online at *http://www.vim.org*.

Basic Navigation Commands

While in command mode, you can move around your file by character, word, sentence, paragraph, and major section. You can position the cursor at various places in lines or relative to the screen. Table 2-14 lists some of the most frequently used navigation commands.

Table 2-14: Commands for Moving Around in vi

Key Command	Description
Ctrl–b	Move up one screen.
Ctrl–f	Move down one screen.
0 *(zero)*	Move to the beginning of the current line.
^	Move to the first non-whitespace character on the current line.
$	Move to the end of the current line.
b	Move backward one word.
G	Move to the end of the file.
h	Move left one character.
H	Move to the top of the screen.
j	Move down one line.
k	Move up one line.
l	Move right one character.
L	Move to the bottom of the screen.
w	Move forward one word.

Basic Editing Commands

To edit in **vi**, you use one of its text-editing commands, including those that enter insert mode, copy and paste, and search for text. Here are some of the frequently used editing commands, grouped by category:

Inserting

To insert new text, first navigate to the location where the text belongs, then enter insert mode and begin typing:

i

Enter insert mode to place text before the cursor.

a

Enter insert mode to append, or place text after the cursor.

Editing

Here are a few handy editing commands:

C

Delete to end-of-line and enter insert mode.

R

Enter *replace mode* (a variant of insert mode) and overwrite existing characters.

Deleting

Delete a text block defined by a movement command relative to the location where the command started:

dl

Delete the next character.

dw

Delete the current word.

dG

Delete to end-of-file.

dd

Delete the entire current line.

D

Delete to end-of-line (same as **d$**).

Copy and paste

The **yank*** command is used to copy a text block defined by a movement command relative to the location where the command started:

yl

Yank forward one character.

yw

Yank forward one word.

yG

Yank to end-of-file.

yy

Yank the entire current line.

Paste operations insert text that was previously cut:

P

Paste text one line above the cursor.

p

Paste text one line below the cursor.

Find

The following commands can be used to search for text:

/pattern

Search forward for *pattern*.

?pattern

Search backward for *pattern*.

---

* Emacs users should be careful not to confuse the **vi** definition of **yank** (copy) with that of Emacs (paste).

n

    Repeat the last search.

N

    Repeat the last search in the opposite direction.

On the Exam

You'll need to be familiar with **vi**'s command and insert modes, how to switch between them, and how to perform basic navigation and editing tasks.

Objective 2: Manage Printers and Print Queues

Printing documents is a slow and error-prone process. Printers accept data in small amounts; they run out of paper, jam, and go offline for other reasons. Printers also must accept requests from multiple system users. As a result, by design, the end user is isolated from printing functions on most computer systems. This isolation comes in the form of a *print queue*, which holds print requests until the printer is ready for them. It also manages the order in which print jobs are processed.

Many Unix and Linux systems use printing utilities developed for Berkeley Unix, commonly known as **lpd**. This objective describes printer management using **lpd**. The companion commands **lpr**, **lpq**, and **lprm** are SUID programs, which run with privileges of the superuser.* This is necessary to allow their use by all users, because they manipulate files in the protected print spooling directories. **lpr** is covered in "Objective 3: Print Files." **lpd**, filters, spool directories, and */etc/printcap* is covered in "Objective 4: Install and Configure Local and Remote Printers."

Linux Printing Overview

On Linux, the default printing system is derived from a standard developed for Unix systems. It consists of the following elements:

lpd

    The **lpd** daemon is started at boot time and runs constantly, listening for print requests directed at multiple printers. When a job is submitted to a print queue, **lpd** forks a copy of itself to handle jobs on that queue. The copy exits when the queue is emptied. Thus, during idle periods, one **lpd** process will be running on your system. When printing is active, one additional **lpd** process will be running for each active queue.

---

* SUID means "set user ID" root; see "Part 1: *Devices, Linux Filesystems, and the Filesystem Hierarchy Standard (Topic 2.4)*, Objective 5: Use File Permissions to Control Access to Files."

/etc/printcap

The *printcap* file (short for "printer capabilities") contains printer names, parameters, and rules; it is used by **lpd** when spooling print jobs. See Objective 4 for additional information on the */etc/printcap* file.

lpr

The **lpr** (short for "line print") program submits both files and information piped to its standard input to print queues.

lpq

The **lpq** program queries and displays the status and contents of print queues.

lprm

lprm removes print jobs from print queues.

lpc

The superuser administers print queues with **lpc** (line printer control).

Filters

When a printer lacks the ability to directly render a print job, software filters are used to transform the origin data into something the printer can handle. A common example is the conversion from PostScript to PCL for laser printers without native PostScript capability.

Spool directories

The **lpd** daemon uses */var/spool/lpd* for the spooling of data awaiting printing. This directory contains a subdirectory for each printer configured on the system (both local and remote). For example, the default locally attached printer on most Linux systems is simply called **lp** (for "line printer"), and all of its control files and queued jobs are stored in directory */var/spool/lpd/lp*.

Print jobs

Each submitted print request is spooled to a queue and assigned a unique number. The numbered print jobs can be examined and manipulated as needed.

Managing Print Queues

As a system administrator, you'll be asked to manage and manipulate printer queues more often than you'd like. On Linux, the **lpq**, **lprm**, and **lpc** commands are your tools.

lpq

Syntax

```
lpq [options] [users] [job#s]
```

Description

Query a print queue. If numeric *job#s* are included, only those jobs are listed. If *users* are listed, only jobs submitted by those users are listed.

Options

-l

Long output format. This option results in a multiline display for each print job.

-P*name*

This specifies the print queue *name*. In the absence of **-P**, the default printer is queried.

Example 1

Examine active jobs:

```
$ lpq
lp is ready and printing
Rank   Owner    Job  Files              Total Size
active root     193  filter             9443 bytes
1st    root     194  resume.txt         11024 bytes
2nd    root     196  (standard input)   18998 bytes
```

Here, *filter* is currently being printed. *resume.txt* is up next, followed by the 18,998 bytes of data that was piped into **lpr**'s standard input.

Example 2

Examine queue **lp**, which turns out to be empty:

```
$ lpq -Plp
no entries
```

Example 3

Examine those same jobs using the long format:

```
$ lpq -l
lp is ready and printing

root: active                        [job 193AsJRzIt]
         filter                     9443 bytes

root: 1st                           [job 194AMj9lo9]
         resume.txt                 11024 bytes

root: 2nd                           [job 196A6rUGu5]
         (standard input)           18998 bytes
```

Example 4

Examine jobs owned by *bsmith*:

```
$ lpq bsmith
Rank   Owner    Job  Files              Total Size
7th    bsmith   202  .bash_history      1263 bytes
9th    bsmith   204  .bash_profile      5676 bytes
```

Using the job numbers reported by **lpq**, any user may remove her own print jobs from the queue, or the superuser may remove any job.

lprm

Syntax

```
lprm [-Pname] [users] [job#s]
lprm -
```

Description

Remove jobs from a print queue. In the first form, remove jobs from queue *name* or from the default queue if -**P** is omitted. If *users* or *job#s* are specified, only those jobs will be removed. In the second form, all of a normal user's jobs will be omitted; for the superuser, the queue will be emptied.

Example 1

As a normal user, remove all of your print jobs:

```
$ lprm -
```

Example 2

As the superuser, remove all jobs from queue **ps**:

```
# lprm -Pps -
```

You may occasionally be surprised to see a no entries response from **lpq**, despite observing that the printer is dutifully printing a document. In such cases, the spool has probably been emptied into the printer's buffer memory, and the result is that the job is no longer under the control of the printing system. To kill such jobs, you need to use the printer's controls (or its power switch!) to stop and delete the job from memory.

Managing print queues with lpc

Printer control on Linux includes the oversight of three distinct and independently controlled activities managed by the **lpd** daemon:

Job queuing
> Turn new print jobs on and off.

Printing
> Turn on and off the transfer of data to your printer.

lpd *child processes*
> Force the per-queue **lpd** subprocesses to exit and restart.

lpc can be used in either interactive or command-line form. If **lpc** is entered without any options, it enters interactive mode and displays its own prompt where **lpc** commands may then be entered. For example:

```
# lpc
lpc> help
Commands may be abbreviated.  Commands are:

abort   enable  disable help    restart status  topq    ?
clean   exit    down    quit    start   stop    up
lpc>
```

If valid commands are included on the command line, **lpc** responds identically but returns control to the terminal:

```
# lpc help
Commands may be abbreviated.  Commands are:

abort    enable   disable help    restart status  topq    ?
clean    exit     down    quit    start   stop    up
#
```

For the discussion that follows, **lpc** commands are shown as entered on the command line, but results in interactive mode are identical.

---

lpc

Syntax

```
lpc
lpc [command]
```

Description

In the first form, enter interactive mode and accept **lpc** commands. In the second form, submit *command* for processing directly from the command line. **lpc** has no command-line options. Instead, it has commands (see Table 2-15), which are separated here into two groups—those that affect print queues and those that don't. Most of the commands require a single argument: either the word `all` (meaning all printers) or a specific printer name.[*]

Table 2-15: Commands for lpc

Command	Description
abort {all|*printer*}	This command works like **stop** but terminates printing immediately, even in the middle of a job. The job is retained for reprint when the printer is again **started**.
disable {all|*printer*} enable {all|*printer*}	These two commands control the queuing of new print jobs. With a queue disabled but printing started, printing continues but new jobs are rejected.
down {all|*printer*} [*message*]	**disable**, **stop**, and store the free-form *message* for display by **lpr**, informing the user why the printer is unavailable.
exit or quit	Terminate **lpc**'s interactive mode.
help	Display help information on commands, as shown earlier.
restart {all|*printer*}	This command kills and restarts a child **lpd**, or starts one when none was previously running.

---

[*] For this reason, `all` would be a bad choice for a print queue name!

Table 2-15: Commands for lpc (continued)

Command	Description
start {all|*printer*} stop {all|*printer*}	These two commands control printing and the child **lpd** processes. When a **stop** command is issued, the current print job is allowed to complete. Then the child daemon is stopped and further printing is disabled. **start** enables printing and starts the child **lpd** if jobs are pending. The print queues remain active.
status [all|*printer*]	Display queue status. The all|*printer* argument is optional for this command.
topq *name jobs*	Place *jobs* at the top of queue *name*, behind any active jobs.
up {all|*printer*}	**enable** and **start**.

Example 1

Use the status command to display current printing activity:

```
# lpc status
lp:
queuing is enabled
printing is enabled
2 entries in spool area
lp is ready and printing
```

Example 2

Suppose user *jdean* has submitted two important print jobs, 206 and 207, and that he needs job 207 to be moved to the top of the queue, followed immediately by 206 (see the emphasized lines in the **lpq** output). First, examine the existing jobs:

```
# lpq
Rank    Owner     Job  Files              Total Size
active  root      203  filter             9443 bytes
1st     root      204  status             25 bytes
2nd     root      205  (standard input)   6827 bytes
3rd     jdean     206  (standard input)   403 bytes
4th     jdean     207  cert1.txt          4865 bytes
```

Now modify the position of print jobs 206 and 207:

```
# lpc topq lp 207 206
lp:
moved cfA206AlIwYoh
moved cfA207Ad6utse
```

Finally, verify the results:

```
# lpq
Rank    Owner     Job  Files              Total Size
1st     jdean     207  cert1.txt          4865 bytes
2nd     jdean     206  (standard input)   403 bytes
3rd     root      203  filter             9443 bytes
4th     root      204  status             25 bytes
5th     root      205  (standard input)   6827 bytes
```

With this reconfiguration, printing continues with jobs 207 and 206 first, and then reverts to jobs 203 through 205.

Example 3

Disable and enable print queue **lp**, to allow current printing to complete while rejecting new jobs:

```
# lpc disable lp
lp:
queuing disabled
# lpc enable lp
lp:
queuing enabled
```

Example 4

Stop and restart printing on the printer attached to queue **lp**, but allow new jobs to be queued for future printing:

```
# lpc stop lp
lp:
printing disabled
# lpc start lp
lp:
printing enabled
daemon started
```

If no jobs are pending, a child **lpd** will not start immediately in response to **start**, though the `daemon started` message is still displayed. Note also that when a child **lpd** process is stopped, its subprocesses (such as filters) are also stopped.

Example 5

Abandon all printing activity on the print queue **lp**. Note that a printer with data in its print buffer may continue to print even after an **abort**:

```
# lpc abort lp
lp:
printing disabled
daemon (pid 2012) killed
```

On the Exam

You'll need to know the function of each of the **lpq**, **lprm**, and **lpc** commands as well as their options. Note that **lpq** and **lprm** (along with **lpr**, described later) share the –**P** option to specify a printer. Pay special attention to **lpc**'s syntax, including the `all` or `printer` arguments (without one of these, **lpc** won't do anything). Remember that **lpc** commands `disable/enable` handle queues, `stop/start` handle printing and child **lpd**s, and `down/up` handle all three. Also remember that **lpc** commands can be entered on the command line or interactively.

Queuing and printing control details

Though it is beyond the scope of the LPIC Level 1 exams, it's interesting to note that **lpd** uses a crude but tricky way to log the status of queuing and printing. In the spool directory for each print queue, a **lock** file is written that contains the PID of the child **lpd** process handling the queue. Normally, this file has permissions 644:

```
# cd /var/spool/lpd/lp
# ls -l lock
-rw-r--r--   1 root      root               5 Mar 18 19:50 lock
```

When printing is stopped, the user's execute permission bit is set on this file:

```
# lpc stop lp
# ls -l lock
-rwxr--r--   1 root      root               5 Mar 18 19:50 lock
```

When queuing is disabled, the group's execute bit is also set:

```
# lpc disable lp
lp:
        queuing disabled
# ls -l lock
-rwxr-xr--   1 root      root               5 Mar 18 19:50 lock
```

These bits act as flags to indicate the status of printing and queuing.

Objective 3: Print Files

The **lpr** command ("line print") is used to send jobs to the **lpd** daemon for printing.

lpr

Syntax

```
lpr [options] [files]
```

Description

Send *files* or standard input to a print queue. A copy of the input source is placed in the spool directory under */var/spool/lpr* until the print job is complete.

Frequently used options

-#count
> Send *count* copies of the print job to the printer.

-Pname
> Specify the print queue *name*. In the absence of **-P**, the default printer is queried.

-s

> Instead of copying a file to the print spooling area, make a symbolic link to the file instead, thereby eliminating transfer time and storage requirements in */var/spool/lpr* for very large files.

Example 1

Print the file */etc/lilo.conf* on the default print queue:

```
# lpr /etc/lilo.conf
```

Example 2

Print a manpage by piping to **lpr**'s standard input:

```
# man -t 5 printcap | lpr
```

Example 3

Disable a print queue:

```
# lpc disable lp
```

Then attempt to print three copies of a file to the disabled queue as superuser:

```
# lpr -#3 /etc/lilo.conf
```

Success, despite the disabled printer queue. Now try as a regular user:

```
$ lpr -#3 ~/resume.txt
lpr: Printer queue is disabled
```

As expected, normal users can't print to the disabled queue.

NOTE

Objective 3 suggests that examinees should be familiar with the conversion of plain text (ASCII) files to PostScript format. One popular way to accomplish this is using the **a2ps** software package available from *http://www.gnu.org/directory/a2ps.html*. While not specifically required for Exam 102, **a2ps** can be helpful for creating formatted hardcopy of text and other files.

On the Exam

You must be familiar with **lpr** and its use with both files and standard input. Also remember that **lpr** doesn't send data to the printer, but to **lpd**, which handles sending it to the printer.

Objective 4: Install and Configure Local and Remote Printers

If you've been able to run the commands listed in Objectives 2 and 3, you already have the printing system installed on your system. However, if you don't have the package, you can get the source code from MetaLab (*ftp://ibiblio.org/pub/linux/system/printing*), along with the other software mentioned later in this Objective. You should be able to build the software simply using **make** followed by **make install**.

The printing system implemented by the **lpd** suite is primitive by today's standards. It provides for queuing, administrative control, and some handling of special file formats but doesn't directly address the recent trend away from character-oriented printers to more programmable machines. Fortunately, the software is modular, making its foundation easy to build upon, making it sufficient for most printing situations.

/etc/printcap

The printing process on Linux systems is governed by the "printer capability" file /etc/printcap. This text file defines all of the system's available print queues and their characteristics. The file is parsed by **lpd**, which ignores blank lines and comments beginning with a pound sign (#). Each printer definition in the file comprises one logical line, which is often broken up among multiple physical lines in the file using the \ line-continuation character. The definition itself is made up of fields delimited by colons. The first field, which begins in the first column of the file, holds the system name for the printer, such as **lp**. This field may contain aliases for the printer name separated by vertical bars. The rest of the fields in the definition hold mnemonics providing control flags and printer parameters. A basic *printcap* file defining a single printer is shown in Example 2-2.

Example 2-2: A Basic /etc/printcap File
```
# A basic /etc/printcap
#
lp|ljet:\
        :sd=/var/spool/lpd/lp:\
        :mx#0:\
        :sh:\
        :lp=/dev/lp0:\
        :if=/var/spool/lpd/lp/filter:
        :lf=/var/spool/lpd/lp/log:
```

In this example, printer `lp` is defined with the alias `ljet`. Either name could be used to print with this printer, using **lpr –Plp** or **lpr –Pljet**. `lp` is the default printer unless the user overrides it by placing a different name in the PRINTER environment variable. Note that the name of the printer has a trailing colon, followed by the line-continuation character. The subsequent lines contain printer attributes inside colon pairs. Some of the frequently used attributes are:

if=*input_filter*
> Input filter (see the next section "Filters," for additional information).

lp=*printer_device*
> Local printer device, such as */dev/lp0*.

lf=*log_file*
> Error message log file.

mx=*max_size*
> Maximum size of a print job in blocks. A maximum size of #0 indicates no limit.

sd=*spool_directory*
   Spool directory under */var/spool/lpd*.

sh
   Suppress header pages for a single printer definition.

Both locally attached and remote printers will have queues defined in */etc/printcap*.

On the Exam

Familiarize yourself with the */etc/printcap* file and the attribute variables. Remember that a single printer definition can have multiple names and that multiple printer definitions can refer to the same hardware.

Filters

The printing process involves the rendering of various data formats by a single hardware device. Considering the wide range of possible formats (plain text, HTML, PostScript, troff, TeX, and graphics files such as JPEG and TIFF, just to name a few), affordable printers can't be expected to natively handle them all. Instead, Linux systems use a two-step transformation process:

1. Raw input data is translated by a *filter* program into a standard Page Description Language (PDL), which is a form of PostScript for Linux. PostScript data is not printed itself but is interpreted as a program to be executed by a Post-Script interpreter. PostScript can handle images, fonts, and complex page layout.

2. The PostScript program is sent to the Ghostscript utility (**gs**) from Aladdin Enterprises.* Ghostscript is a PostScript interpreter that contains a number of specific printer drivers. As a result, it can translate PostScript into a printer-specific format and send it to the printer.

This translation process and its intermediate data formats are depicted in Figure 2-6.

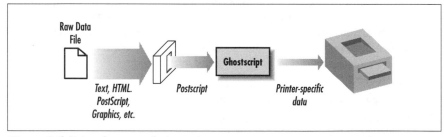

Figure 2-6: Print data translation steps

---

* A GPL'd version of **gs** is offered for free by Aladdin, which makes it appropriate for inclusion in Linux distributions.

Each print queue found in */etc/printcap* can use a different input filter, as directed by the if=*filter* specification.

This data translation process sometimes isn't necessary. For example, plain text can be printed directly by most printers, making the translation to PostScript and subsequent Ghostscript invocation unnecessary for basic output. Many printers, particularly laser printers, have a built-in PostScript interpreter, making Ghostscript unnecessary. These situations are detected and controlled by the filter program.

A filter can be very simple. For example, you may have implemented a filter yourself by using a utility like **pr** to add a margin to a plain text print job before piping it into **lpr**. In practice, filters are conceptually similar, but are more complex and capable than this and usually handle multiple input formats. They do this by looking at the *magic number* at the beginning of the data file to be printed.* As a result, the filters are referred to as *magic filters*. Two such filters are **APSfilter** and **magicfilter**. Your familiarity with both filters is required for Exam 102.

APSfilter

This popular filter program accepts files in the PostScript, TeX DVI, ASCII, PCL, GIF, TIFF, Sun Raster files, FIG, PNM (pbmplus), HTML, and PDF formats. As mentioned earlier, **APSfilter** and the other software discussed here can be found at MetaLab. After downloading **APSfilter**, the compressed tarball should be unpacked in */usr/lib*. Then, simply invoke **cd apsfilter** and run the installer, **./SETUP**. This interactive program presents a menu-based installation, where you direct such things as the Ghostscript printer driver selection, the choice of printer interface (such as */dev/lp0*), the default print resolution, the use of color, and the output paper format. It then creates new printer entries in */etc/printcap*, as well as creates new printer spool directories, and sets file permissions and ownership. It also compiles a few utilities necessary for the proper use of the filter. Once **APSfilter** is installed, your */etc/printcap* will look something like that shown in Example 2-3.†

Example 2-3: The APSfilter /etc/printcap Description

```
# apsfilter setup Tue Mar 21 02:38:48 EST 2000
#
ascii|lp1|ljet3d-letter-ascii-mono|ljet3d ascii mono:\
        :lp=/dev/lp0:\
        :sd=/var/spool/lpd/ljet3d-letter-ascii-mono:\
        :lf=/var/spool/lpd/ljet3d-letter-ascii-mono/log:\
        :af=/var/spool/lpd/ljet3d-letter-ascii-mono/acct:\
        :if=/usr/lib/apsfilter/filter/\
aps-ljet3d-letter-ascii-mono:\
        :mx#0:\
        :sh:
#
```

---

* See the **file** command's manpage for more information on *magic* and *magic numbers*.

† *SETUP* makes a backup copy of */etc/printcap* called */etc/printcap.orig* before creating its new *printcap* file.

Example 2-3: The APSfilter /etc/printcap Description (continued)

```
lp|lp2|ljet3d-letter-auto-mono|ljet3d auto mono:\
        :lp=/dev/lp0:\
        :sd=/var/spool/lpd/ljet3d-letter-auto-mono:\
        :lf=/var/spool/lpd/ljet3d-letter-auto-mono/log:\
        :af=/var/spool/lpd/ljet3d-letter-auto-mono/acct:\
        :if=/usr/lib/apsfilter/filter/\
aps-ljet3d-letter-auto-mono:\
        :mx#0:\
        :sh:
#
raw|lp3|ljet3d-letter-raw|ljet3d auto raw:\
        :lp=/dev/lp0:\
        :sd=/var/spool/lpd/ljet3d-raw:\
        :lf=/var/spool/lpd/ljet3d-raw/log:\
        :af=/var/spool/lpd/ljet3d-raw/acct:\
        :if=/usr/lib/apsfilter/filter/\
aps-ljet3d-letter-raw:\
        :mx#0:\
        :sh:
```

As you can see, the installation creates three printer definitions, each with multiple aliases and each using the same output device. This allows some degree of control over the filter, because the selection of the queue implies specific print parameters. The first definition (ascii) is intended to allow the user to force the printing of plain text even if the data is a PostScript program. The second entry (lp, the default) is the standard magic **APSfilter**, which tries to identify the data type itself. The last definition allows users to force **APSfilter** to send raw data directly to the printer with no intervention. This can be useful, for example, if you wish to print a PostScript file's programming instructions. **APSfilter** also configures logging and accounting for each printer queue. Finally, the setup routine optionally prints a graphical test page to verify your installation.

After **APSfilter** is installed, you must restart **lpd** to enable the new print queues:

```
# lpc restart all
```

or:

```
# /etc/rc.d/init.d/lpd stop
# /etc/rc.d/init.d/lpd start
```

APSfilter allows for some controls in */etc/apsfilterrc* (and the user file *~/.apsfilterrc*). Examples of these controls are configuration for Ghostscript features, special control sequences for printers, and configuration for the use of a particular filter method. While this file is beyond the scope of LPIC Level 1 Objectives, you should be familiar with it and its purpose.

On the Exam

You should install **APSfilter** to become familiar with the software and its setup.

Magicfilter

Another filter you may wish to try is **magicfilter**, which can also be obtained from MetaLab. Unlike **APSfilter**, which is implemented as scripts, **magicfilter** is compiled from C and comes with a traditional **configure, make, make install** procedure.[*] Building and installing **magicfilter** is straightforward and shouldn't cause any difficulty. However, the installation does not automatically create print queues in */etc/printcap*, although you can easily define one by setting the input filter to */usr/local/bin/magicfilter*, as shown in Example 2-4.

Example 2-4: The magicfilter Print Queue

```
lp|lpmagic:\
        :sd=/var/spool/lpd/lp:\
        :mx#0:\
        :sh:\
        :lp=/dev/lp0:\
        :if=/usr/local/bin/magicfilter:
```

Multiple filters

When a filter is installed, it is placed in a directory where it can be called from as needed. The printer definitions in */etc/printcap* put the filter into service. Because you can create as many printer definitions as you like, it is possible to have multiple filters in place at the same time.

On the Exam

You should have a working knowledge of the printing process, the role of filters, the role of Ghostscript, and where PostScript data is used. Also remember that PostScript is rendered directly on some printers, eliminating the need for Ghostscript.

Remote lpd and Samba Printers

Configuring your system to use a remote Linux printer (or other **lpd** device, such as a network-attached printer) can be as simple as adding a local printer. Two additional configuration variables are added to the printer definition in */etc/printcap* to specify the remote host and the queue name on that host. For example:

```
rlp:\
        :sd=/var/spool/lpd/rlp:\
        :rm=lphost:\
        :rp=rlp:\
        :mx#0:\
        :sh:\
        :if=/usr/local/bin/magicfilter:
```

---

[*] See "Part 2: *Linux Installation and Package Management (Topic 2.2)*, Objective 3: Make and Install Programs from Source," for additional information on how to install software.

Here, this local print queue will send jobs to printer `rlp` residing on `lphost`. Since remote printers still have local queues, you must create the spool directory, in this example, */var/spool/lpd/rlp*.

Configuring a remote printer that's on a Windows network is also straightforward. (The Windows printer must be properly shared and you must have Samba installed and running.) First, a local spool directory is created as usual—for example, */var/spool/lpd/winpr*. Next, an */etc/printcap* entry is added that looks something like this:

```
winpr:\
        :sd=/var/spool/lpd/winpr:\
        :mx#0:\
        :sh:\
        :if=/usr/bin/smbprint:
```

The input filter for this printer is `smbprint`, a utility from the Samba software suite. Finally, a *.config* file is created in the spool directory, which contains:

* The NetBIOS name of the Windows machine with the printer

* The service name that represents the printer

* The password used to access that service

The service name and password are set in the Sharing dialog box on the Windows machine. The *.config* file might look similar to the following:

```
server=WINBOX
service=WINPR
password=""
```

After restarting **lpd**, you should be able to print text documents to the Windows printer.

On the Exam

Remember the **rm** and **rp** printer configuration variables for remote **lpd** printers. For Samba printing on Windows clients, remember to use the **smbprint** input filter and to create the *.config* file in the local spool directory.

Shells, Scripting, Programming,
and Compiling
(Topic 1.9)

Depending upon the computing environments you're used to, the concepts of shells and shell programs (usually called *scripts*) may be a little foreign. In the Windows world, for example, native scripting capabilities are limited to the command interpreter's simple batch command language. This facility has only the most primitive automation capabilities, and many extensions and alternatives have appeared on the market to fill the void. If you've used an AS/400 system, you had similar limitations for scripting. On Linux systems, shells and their scripting languages are fundamental concepts used throughout the system and they have widely ranging capabilities.

This chapter covers *Shells, Scripting, Programming, and Compiling* and its two Objectives:

Objective 1: Customize and Use the Shell Environment
    This Objective covers your shell and basic scripting concepts, including environment variables, functions, and script files that control the login environment. Weight: 4.

Objective 2: Customize or Write Simple Scripts
    Customization of the many scripts found on a Linux system is important for its management and automation. Topics for this Objective include shell syntax, checking the status of executed programs, and issues surrounding the properties of script files. Weight: 5.

It is important for Linux administrators to become comfortable with at least one shell and its programming language. This can be an area of some concern to those used to graphics-only environments, where the use of a command interpreter is not a daily activity. As you'll see, becoming adept at working with your favorite shell will empower you and will allow you to let your computer carry a larger share of your daily responsibilities.

Objective 1: Customize and Use the Shell Environment

This Objective could be considered a brief "getting started with shells" overview because it details many of the basic concepts necessary to utilize the shell environment on Linux. These concepts are fundamental and very important for system administrators working on Linux and Unix systems. If you're new to shells and shell scripting, take heart. You can think of it as a combination of computer interaction (conversation) and computer programming (automation). It is nothing more than that, but the result is far more than this simplicity implies. If you're an old hand with shell programming, you may want to skip ahead to brush up on some of the particulars necessary for Exam 102.

An Overview of Shells

A shell is a fundamental and important part of your Linux computing environment. Shells are user programs not unlike other text-based programs and utilities. They offer a rich customizable interface to your system. Some of the main items provided by your shell are:

An interactive textual user interface to the operating system
> In this the role, the shell is a command interpreter and display portal to the system. It offers you a communications channel to the kernel and is often thought of as the "shell around the kernel." That's where the name *shell* originates and is a good metaphor for conceptualizing how shells fit into the overall Linux picture.

An operating environment
> Shells set up an *environment* for the execution of other programs, which affect the way some of them behave. This environment consists of any number of *environment variables*, each of which describes one particular environment property by defining a *name=value* pair. Other features such as *aliases* enhance your operating environment by offering shorthand notations for commonly used commands.

A facility for launching and managing commands and programs
> Shells are used not only by users but also by the system to launch programs and support those programs with an operating environment.

A programming language
> Shells offer their own programming languages. At its simplest, this feature allows user commands to be assembled into useful sequences. At the other end of the spectrum, complete programs can be written in shell languages, with loop control, variables, and all of the capabilities of Linux's rich set of operating system commands.

On a Linux system, you have a choice of at least five different shells. There are two basic families:

Bourne-derived shells

Many shells are related to the *Bourne shell*, **sh**, named for creator Steve Bourne. **sh** is the oldest of the currently available shells and lacks several features considered necessary for modern interactive use. However, it is well understood, is used regularly for programming, and can be found on nearly every Unix or Unix-like system. One of the descendants of **sh** is **bash**, which is described in the next section.

C-shells

For interactive use, many people like to use the C-shell, **csh**, or its descendant, **tcsh**. These shells have some elements in their associated programming language syntax that are similar to the C language. Despite this, many feel that programming in the C-shell is less than satisfactory due to some missing features. Additional shells include **zsh** and **ksh**.

All of the shells share some common concepts:

- They are all distinct from the kernel and run as user programs.

- Each shell can be customized by tuning the shell's operating environment.

- Shells are run for both interactive use by end users and noninteractive use by the system.

- A shell can be run from within another shell, enabling you to try a shell other than your default shell. To do this, you simply start the other shell from the command line of your current shell. In fact, this happens constantly on your system as scripts are executed and programs are launched. The new shell does not replace the shell that launched it. Instead, the new shell is a process running with the original shell as a parent process. When you terminate the child shell, you go back to the original one.

- Shells use a series of *configuration files* to establish their operating environment.

- Shells pass on environment variables to child processes.

The bash Shell

To enhance the Bourne shell while retaining its programming constructs, a few descendants have been written over the years. Among those descendants is **bash**, which stands for Bourne-again shell, from the Free Software Foundation (the FSF is famous for tongue-in-cheek command names). While there are a number of shells available to choose from on a Linux system, **bash** is very popular and powerful, and is the default shell for new accounts. Exam 102 concentrates on its use and configuration. The next few sections deal with general shell concepts, but the examples are specific to **bash**.

Shell and environment variables

Many programs running under Linux require information about you and your personal preferences to operate sensibly. While you could instruct each program you run with important details it needs to proceed, much of the information you'd convey would be redundant because you'd be telling every command you enter the same ancillary information at each invocation. For example, you'd need to tell your paging program about the size and nature of your terminal or terminal window each time you use it. You would also need to give fully qualified directory names for the programs you run.

Rather than force users to include so much detail to issue commands, the shell handles much of this information for you automatically. You've already seen that the shell creates an operating environment for you. That environment is made up of a series of *variables*, each of which has a value that is used by programs and other shells. There are two types of variables used by most shells:

Environment variables

These variables can be thought of as *global variables* because they are passed on to all processes started by the shell, including other shells. This means that child processes inherit the environment. By convention, environment variables are given uppercase names.* Your shell maintains many environment variables, including the following examples:

PATH

A list of directories through which the shell looks for executable programs as you enter them on the command line. All of the directories that contain programs that you'll want to execute are stored together in the PATH environment variable. Your shell looks through this list in sequence, from left to right, searching for each command you enter. Your PATH may differ from the PATHs of other users on your system because you may use programs found in different locations or you may have a local directory with your own custom programs that need to be available. The PATH variable can become quite long as more and more directories are added.

HOME

Your home directory, such as */home/bsmith*.

USERNAME

Your username.

TERM

The type of terminal or terminal window you are running. This variable is likely to have a value such as *xterm* or *xterm-color*. If you are running on a physical VT100 (or compatible) terminal, TERM is set to *vt100*.

Shell variables

These variables can be thought of as *local* because they are specific only to the current shell. Child processes do not inherit them. Some shell variables are automatically set by the shell and are available for use in shell scripts. By convention, shell variables are given lowercase names.

In the **csh** and **tcsh** shells, environment variables and shell variables are differentiated by their case, and shell variables are always local while environment variables are always global. In **bash**, this distinction is blurred somewhat, because variables are shell variables until they are *exported to the environment*, making them

---

* **bash** doesn't require the case convention; it's intended for clarity to humans.

environment variables that will be passed on to child shells and programs. In addition, nearly all the shell and environment variables you'll encounter in **bash** will be uppercase.

To create a new **bash** shell variable, simply enter a *name=value* pair on the command line:

```
# PI=3.14
```

To see that this value is now assigned to the local variable PI, use the **echo** command to display its contents:

```
# echo $PI
3.14
```

The dollar sign preceding the variable name indicates that the name will be replaced with the variable's value. Without the dollar sign, **echo** would just return the text that was typed, which in this case is the variable name PI. At this point, PI is a local variable and is not available to child shells or programs. To make it available to other shells or programs, the variable must be exported to the environment:

```
# export PI
```

Aliases

Among the features missing from **sh** was the ability to easily make new commands or modify existing commands. **bash** has the ability to set an **alias** for commonly used commands or sequences of commands. For example, if you habitually call for the older pager **more** but actually prefer **less**, an alias can be handy to get the desired behavior, regardless of the command you use:

```
$ alias more='less'
```

This has the effect of intercepting any command entries for **more**, substituting **less** instead. The revised command is passed along to the shell's command interpreter.

Another common use for an alias is to modify a command slightly so that its default behavior is more to your liking. Many people, particularly when operating with superuser privileges, will use this alias:

```
$ alias cp='cp -i'
```

With this alias in effect, the use of the **cp** (copy) command becomes safer, because with the -i option always enforced by the alias, **cp** prompts you for approval before overwriting a file of the same name. Additional options you enter on the command line are appended to the end of the new command, such that **cp -p** becomes **cp -i -p** and so on.

If the righthand side of the aliased command is bigger than a single word or if it contains multiple commands (separated by semicolons, **bash**'s command terminator), you probably need to enclose it in single quotation marks to get your point across. This is because you need to prevent the shell in which you're working (your current **bash** process) from interpreting file globbing or other characters that might be part of your alias value. For example, suppose you wished to use a single alias to pair two simple commands:

```
$ alias lsps=ls -l;ps
```

Your current **bash** process will interpret this command not as a single alias but as two separate commands. First the alias **lsps** will be created for **ls -l**, and then a **ps** command will be added for immediate execution. What you really want is:

```
$ alias lsps='ls -l;ps'
```

Now, entering the command **lsps** will be aliased to **ls -l; ps**, and will correctly generate **ls** output immediately followed by **ps** output, as this example shows:

```
$ lsps
total 1253
drwx------  5 root  root    1024 May 27 17:15 dir1
drwxr-xr-x  3 root  root    1024 May 27 22:41 dir2
-rw-r--r--  1 root  root   23344 May 27 22:44 file1
drwxr-xr-x  2 root  root   12288 May 25 16:13 dir3
  PID TTY          TIME CMD
  892 ttyp0    00:00:00 bash
 1388 ttyp0    00:00:00 ps
```

Admittedly, this isn't a very useful command, but it is built upon in the next section.

After adding aliases, it may become easy to confuse which commands are aliases or native. To list the aliases defined for your current shell, simply enter the **alias** command by itself. This results in a listing of all the aliases currently in place:

```
$ alias
alias cp='cp -i'
alias lsps='ls -l;ps'
alias mv='mv -i'
alias rm='rm -i'
```

Note that aliases are local to your shell and are not passed down to programs or to other shells. You'll see how to ensure that your aliases are always available in the section on configuration files.

Aliases are mainly used for simple command replacement. The shell inserts your aliased text in place of your alias name before interpreting the command. Aliases don't offer logical constructs and are limited to a few simple variable replacements. Aliases can also get messy when the use of complicated quoting is necessary, usually to prevent the shell from interpreting characters in your alias.

Functions

In addition to aliases, **bash** also offers *functions*. They work in much the same way as aliases, in that some function name of your choosing is assigned to a more complex construction. However, in this case that construction is a small program rather than a simple command substitution. Functions have a simple syntax:

```
$ [ function ] NAME () { COMMAND-LIST; }
```

This declaration defines a function called NAME. The word `function` is optional, and the parentheses after NAME are required if `function` is omitted. The body of the function is the COMMAND-LIST between the curly brackets ({ and }). This list is a series of commands, separated by semicolons or by new lines. The series of commands are executed whenever **NAME** is specified as a command. The simple **lsps** alias shown earlier could be implemented as a function like this:

```
$ lsps () { ls -l; ps; }
```

Using this new function as a command yields exactly the same result the alias did. However, by implementing this command using a function, parameters can be added to the command. Here is a new version of the same function, this time entered on multiple lines (which eliminates the need for semicolons within the function):

```
$ lsps () {
> ls -l $1
> ps -aux | grep `/bin/basename $1`
> }
```

The > characters come from **bash** during interactive entry, indicating that **bash** is awaiting additional function commands or the } character, which terminates the function definition. This new function allows us to enter a single *argument* to the function, which is inserted everywhere $1 is found in the function. These arguments are called *positional parameters* because each one's number denotes its position in the argument list. This example uses only one positional parameter; there can be many, and the number of parameters is stored for your use in a special variable $#.

The command implemented in the previous example function now returns a directory listing and process status for any program given as an argument. For example, if the Apache web server is running, the command:

```
$ lsps /usr/sbin/httpd
```

yields a directory listing for */usr/sbin/httpd* and also displays all currently running processes that match **httpd**:

```
-rwxr-xr-x  1 root root 165740 Apr  7 17:17 /usr/sbin/httpd
root    3802 0.0  3.8 2384 1192 ?      S 16:34 0:00 httpd
nobody 3810 0.0  4.2 2556 1292 ?      S 16:34 0:00 httpd
nobody 3811 0.0  4.2 2556 1292 ?      S 16:34 0:00 httpd
nobody 3812 0.0  4.2 2556 1292 ?      S 16:34 0:00 httpd
nobody 3813 0.0  4.2 2556 1292 ?      S 16:34 0:00 httpd
nobody 3814 0.0  4.2 2556 1292 ?      S 16:34 0:00 httpd
root    3872 0.0  1.4 1152 432 ttyp0 S 16:45 0:00 grep httpd
```

Configuration files

It's a good assumption that every Linux user will want to define a few aliases, functions, and environment variables to suit his needs. However, it's undesirable to manually enter them upon each login or for each new invocation of **bash**. In order to set up these things automatically, **bash** uses a number of configuration files to set its operating environment when it starts. Some of these files are used only upon initial log in, while others are executed for each instance of **bash** you start, including login time. Some of these configuration files are system-wide files for all users to use, while others reside in your home directory for your use alone.

bash configuration files important to Exam 102 are listed in Table 2-16.

Table 2-16: bash Configuration Files

File	Description
/etc/profile	This is the systemwide initialization file, executed during log in. It usually contains environment variables, including an initial PATH, and startup programs.
/etc/bashrc	This is another systemwide initialization file that may be executed by a user's *.bashrc* for each **bash** shell launched. It usually contains functions and aliases.
~/.bash_profile	If this file exists, it is executed automatically after */etc/profile* during log in.
~/.bash_login	If *.bash_profile* doesn't exist, this file is executed automatically during log in.
~/.profile	If neither *.bash_profile* nor *.bash_login* exist, this file is executed automatically during log in. Note that this is the original bourne shell configuration file.
~/.bashrc	This file is executed automatically when **bash** starts. This includes login, as well as subsequent interactive and noninteractive invocations of **bash**.
~/.bash_logout	This file is executed automatically during log out.
~/.inputrc	This file contains optional key bindings and variables that affect how **bash** responds to keystrokes. By default, bash is configured to respond like the Emacs editor.

In practice, users will generally (and often unknowingly) use the systemwide */etc/profile* configuration file to start. In addition, they'll often have three personal files in their home directory: *~/.bash_profile*, *~/.bashrc*, and *~/.bash_logout*. The local files are optional, and **bash** does not mind if one or all of them are not available in your directory.

NOTE

The syntax ~/ refers to **bash**'s "home directory." While this shortcut may not represent much of a savings in typing, some Linux configurations may place users' directories in various and sometimes nonobvious places in the filesystem. Using the tilde syntax reduces the need for you to know exactly where a user's home directory is located.

Each of these configuration files consists entirely of plain text. They are typically simple, often containing just a few commands to be executed in sequence to prepare the shell environment for the user. Since they are evaluated by **bash** as lines of program code, they are said to be *sourced*, or interpreted, when **bash** executes them.

Like most programming languages, shell programs allow the use of comments. Most shells including **bash** consider everything immediately following the hash (#)

character on a single line to be a comment.[*] Comments can span an entire line or share a line by following program code. All of your shell scripts and configuration files should use comments liberally.

Files sourced at login time are created mainly to establish default settings. These settings include such things as where to search for programs requested by the user (the PATH) and creation of shortcut names for commonly used tasks (aliases and functions). After login, files sourced by each subsequent shell invocation won't explicitly need to do these things again because they *inherit* the environment established by the login shell. Regardless, it isn't unusual to see a user's *.bashrc* file filled with all of their personal customizations. It also doesn't hurt anything, provided the *.bashrc* file is small and quick to execute.

While it is not necessary to have detailed knowledge of every item in your shell configuration files, Exam 102 requires that you understand them and that you can edit them to modify their behavior and your resulting operating environment. The following examples are typical of those found on Linux systems and are annotated with comments. Example 2-5 shows a typical Linux system-wide *profile*. This file is executed by every user's **bash** process at login time. A few environment variables and other parameters are set in it.

Example 2-5: An Example System-wide bash profile

```
# /etc/profile
# System-wide environment and startup programs
# Functions and aliases go in system wide /etc/bashrc

# PATH was already set, this is an extension
PATH="$PATH:/usr/X11R6/bin"

# Set a default prompt string
PS1-"[\u@\h \W]\\$ "

# Set an upper limit for "core" files
ulimit -c 1000000

# Set a default umask, used to set default file permissions
if [ `id -gn` = `id -un` -a `id -u` -gt 14 ]; then
    umask 002
else
    umask 022
fi

# Set up some shell variables
USER=`id -un`
LOGNAME=$USER
MAIL="/var/spool/mail/$USER"
HOSTNAME=`/bin/hostname`
HISTSIZE=1000
```

---

[*] An important exception is the $# *variable*, which has nothing to do with comments but contains the number of positional parameters passed to a function.

Customize and Use the Shell Environment   347

Example 2-5: An Example System-wide bash profile (continued)

```
HISTFILESIZE=1000
INPUTRC=/etc/inputrc

# Make all these into environment variables
export PATH PS1 HOSTNAME HISTSIZE HISTFILESIZE
    USER LOGNAME MAIL INPUTRC

# Execute a series of other files
for i in /etc/profile.d/*.sh ; do
    if [ -x $i ]; then
        . $i
    fi
done

unset I       # Clean up the variable used above
```

Example 2-6 shows a system-wide *.bashrc* file. This file is not sourced by default when **bash** starts. Instead, it is optionally sourced by users' local *.bashrc* files.

Example 2-6: An Example System-wide .bashrc File

```
# /etc/bashrc

alias more='less'                   # prefer the "less" pager
alias lsps='ls -l;ps'               # a dubious command
```

Example 2-7 shows an example user's local *.bash_profile*. Note that this file sources the system-wide */etc/bashrc*, then goes on to local customizations.

Example 2-7: An Example User .bash_profile File

```
# .bash_profile

# Get the aliases and functions from the systems administrator
if [ -f ~/.bashrc ]; then
    . ~/.bashrc
fi

# User specific environment and startup programs

PATH=$PATH:$HOME/bin  # Add my binaries directory to the path
EDITOR=emacs            # Set my preferred editor to Emacs
VISUAL=emacs            # Set my preferred editor to Emacs
PAGER=less              # Set my preferred pager to less

# Make my variables part of the environment
export PATH EDITOR VISUAL PAGER
```

Example 2-8 shows an individual's *.bashrc* file. Like the *.bash_profile* earlier, this file also sources the system-wide */etc/bashrc*.

Example 2-8: An Example User's .bashrc File

```
# .bashrc

# User-specific aliases and functions

# Source global definitions
if [ -f /etc/bashrc ]; then
    . /etc/bashrc
fi

alias rm='rm -i'                    # Add a safety net to rm
alias cp='cp -i'                    # Add a safety net to cp
alias mv='mv -i'                    # Add a safety net to mv

lsps() {                           # Define a personal function
    ls -l $1
    ps -aux | grep `/bin/basename $1`
}
```

Example 2-9 shows a short, simple, and not uncommon *.bash_logout* file. Probably the most likely command to find in a logout file is the **clear** command. Including a **clear** in your logout file is a nice way of being certain that whatever you were doing just before you log out won't linger on the screen for the next user to ponder. This file is intended to execute commands for a logout from a text session, such as a system console or terminal. In a GUI environment where logout and login are handled by a GUI program, *.bash_logout* may not be of much value.

Example 2-9: A Simple .bash_logout File

```
# .bash_logout
# This file is executed when a user logs out of the system
/usr/bin/clear          # clear the screen
/usr/games/fortune      # print a random adage
```

On the Exam

Make certain that you understand the difference between execution at login and execution at shell invocation, as well as which of the startup files serve each of those purposes.

Inputrc

Among the many enhancements added to **bash** is the ability to perform as if your history of commands is the buffer of an editor. That is, your command history is available to you, and you may cut, paste, and even search among command lines entered previously. This powerful capability can significantly reduce typing and increase accuracy. By default, **bash** is configured to emulate the Emacs editor, but a **vi** editing interface is also available.

The portion of **bash** that handles this function, and in fact handles all of the line input during interactive use, is known as *readline*. Readline may be customized by putting commands into an initialization file, which by default is in your home directory and called *.inputrc*.* For example, to configure **bash** to use **vi**-style editing keys, add this line to *.inputrc*:

```
set editing-mode vi
```

The default editing facilities enabled in **bash** are extensive and are beyond the scope of this section and Exam 102. However, you need to understand the concepts of adding your own custom key bindings to the *.inputrc* file and how they can help automate common keystrokes unique to your daily routine for the test.

For example, suppose you often use **top** to watch your system's activity (**top** is a useful process-monitoring utility that is described in Part 1, *GNU and Unix Commands (Topic 1.3)*):

```
$ top -Ssd1
```

If you do this often enough, you'll get tired of typing the command over and over and will eventually want an alias for it. To create the alias, simply alias this command to **top**:

```
$ alias top='/usr/bin/top -Ssd1'
```

Better yet, you can use *.inputrc* to create a key binding that will enter it for you. Here's how the *.inputrc* file would look if you were to bind your **top** command to the key sequence **Ctrl-t**:

```
# my .inputrc file
Control-t: "top -Ssd1 \C-m"
```

The lefthand side of the second line indicates the key combination you wish to use (**Ctrl-t**). The righthand side indicates what you wish to bind to that key sequence. In this case, **bash** outputs **top -Ssd1** and a carriage return, denoted here by \C-m (**Ctrl-m**), when **Ctrl-t** is pressed.

Through modifications of your local configuration files, you can customize your environment and automate many of your daily tasks. You may also override system-wide settings in your personal files simply by setting variables, aliases, and functions.

On the Exam

You won't need to have detailed knowledge of this key-binding syntax, but be aware of the *.inputrc* file and the kinds of things it enables **bash** to do.

---

* You may also set the INPUTRC variable to the name of another file if you prefer. On your system, this variable may be set to */etc/initrc* by default, which would override any settings you put into a local *.initrc*. To use your own file, you must first explicitly place unset INPUTRC in your *.bash_profile*.

Objective 2: Customize or Write Simple Scripts

You've seen how the use of **bash** configuration files, aliases, functions, variables, and key bindings can customize and make interaction with your Linux system efficient. The next step in your relationship with the shell is to use its natural programming capability, or *scripting language*. The scripting language of the original Bourne shell is found throughout a Linux system, and **bash** is fully compatible with it. This section covers essential **bash** scripting language concepts as required for Exam 102.

In order to have a full appreciation of shell scripting on Linux, it's important to look at your Linux system as a collection of unique and powerful tools. Each of the commands available on your Linux system, along with those you create yourself, has some special capability. Bringing these capabilities together to solve problems is among the basic philosophies of the Unix world.

Script Files

Just as the configuration files discussed in the last section are plain text files, so are the scripts for your shell. In addition, unlike compiled languages such as C or Pascal, no compilation of a shell program is necessary before it is executed. You can use any editor to create script files, and you'll find that many scripts you write are portable from Linux to other Unix systems.

Creating a simple bash script

The simplest scripts are those that simply string together some basic commands and perhaps do something useful with the output. Of course, this can be done with a simple alias or function, but eventually you'll have a requirement that exceeds a one-line request, and a shell script is the natural solution. Aliases and functions have already been used to create a rudimentary new command, **lsps**. Now let's look at a shell script (Example 2-10) that accomplishes the same thing.

Example 2-10: The lsps Script

```
# a basic lsps command script for bash
ls -l $1
ps -aux | grep `/bin/basename $1`
```

As you can see, the commands used in this simple script are identical to those used in the alias and in the function created earlier. To make use of this new file, instruct your currently running **bash** shell to source it, giving it an option for the $1 positional parameter:

$ **source ./lsps /usr/sbin/httpd**

If you have */usr/sbin/httpd* running, you should receive output similar to that found previously for the alias. By replacing the word **source** with a single dot, you can create an alternate shorthand notation to tell **bash** to source a file, as follows:

$ **. ./lsps /usr/sbin/httpd**

Another way to invoke a script is to start a new invocation of **bash** and tell that process to source the file. To do this, simply start **bash** and pass the script name and argument to it:

```
$ /bin/bash ./lsps /usr/sbin/httpd
```

This last example gives us the same result; however, it is significantly different from the alias, the function, or the sourcing of the **lsps** file. In this particular case, a new invocation of **bash** was started to execute the commands in the script. This is important, because the environment in which the commands are running is distinct from the environment where the user is typing. This is described in more detail later.

NOTE

The ./ syntax indicates that the file you're referring to is in the current working directory. To avoid specifying ./ for users other than the super-user, put the directory . in the PATH. The PATH of the superuser should not include the current working directory, as a security precaution against Trojan horse–style attacks.

Thus far, a shell script has been created and invoked in a variety of ways, but it hasn't been made into a command. A script really becomes useful when it can be called by name like any other command.

Executable files

On a Linux system, programs are said to be *executable* if they have content that can be run by the processor (native execution) or by another program such as a shell (interpreted execution). However, in order to be eligible for execution when called at the command line, the files must have attributes that indicate to the shell that they are executable. Conspicuously absent is anything in the filename that indicates that the file is executable, such as the file extension of *.exe* found on MS-DOS and Windows applications. It would be possible to name our example file *lsps.exe* if desired, or for that matter *lsps.sh* or *lsps.bin*. None of these extensions has any meaning to the shell, though, and the extension would become part of the command entered when executing the program. For this reason, most executable Linux programs and scripts don't have filename extensions. To make a file execut-able, it must have at least one of its *executable bits* set. To turn our example script from a plain text file to an executable program, that bit must be set using the **chmod** command:

```
$ chmod a+x lsps
```

Once this is done, the script is executable by owner, group members, and everyone else on the system. At this point, running the new command from the **bash** prompt yields the familiar output:

```
$ ./lsps /usr/sbin/httpd
```

When **lsps** is called by name, the commands in the script are interpreted and executed by the **bash** shell. However, this isn't ultimately what is desired. In many cases, users will be running some other shell interactively but will still want to program in **bash**. Programmers also use other scripting languages such as Perl. To have our scripts interpreted correctly, the system must be told which program should interpret the commands in our scripts.

She-bang!

There are many kinds of script files found on a Linux system, and each interpreted language comes with a unique and specific command structure. There needs to be a way to tell Linux which interpreter to use. This is accomplished by using a special line at the top of the script naming the appropriate interpreter. Linux examines this line and launches the specified interpreter program, which then reads the rest of the file. The special line must begin with #!, a construct often called "she-bang." For **bash**, the she-bang line is:

```
#!/bin/bash
```

This command explicitly states that the program named **bash** can be found in the */bin* directory and designates **bash** to be the interpreter for the script. You'll also see other types of lines on script files, including:

#!/bin/sh
> The bourne shell.

#!/bin/csh
> The C-shell.

#!/bin/tcsh
> The enhanced C-shell.

#!/bin/sed
> The stream editor.

#!/usr/bin/awk
> The awk programming language.

#!/usr/bin/perl
> The Perl programming language.

Each of these lines specifies a unique command interpreter use for the script lines that follow.[*]

On the Exam

An incorrectly stated she-bang line can cause the wrong interpreter to attempt to execute commands in a script.

---

[*] **bash** is fully backward compatible with **sh**; **sh** is just a link to **bash** on Linux systems.

The shell script's environment

When running a script with #!/bin/bash, a new invocation of **bash** with its own environment is started to execute the script's commands as the parent shell waits. Exported variables in the parent shell are copied into the child's environment; the child shell executes the appropriate shell configuration files (such as .bash_profile). Because configuration files will be run, additional shell variables may be set and environment variables may be overwritten. If you are depending upon a variable in your shell script, be sure that it is either set by the shell configuration files or exported into the environment for your use, but not both.

Another important concept regarding your shell's environment is *one-way inheritance*. Although your current shell's environment is passed *into* a shell script, that environment is *not passed back* to the original shell when your program terminates. This means that changes made to variables during the execution of your script are not preserved when the script exits. Instead, the values in the parent shell's variables are the same as they were before the script executed. This is a basic Unix construct; inheritance goes from parent process to child process, and not the other way around.

On the Exam

It is important to remember how variables are set, how they are inherited, and that they are inherited only from parent process to child process.

Location, ownership, and permissions

The ability to run any executable program, including a script, under Linux depends in part upon its location in the filesystem. Either the user must explicitly specify the location of the file to run or it must be located in a directory known by the shell to contain executables. Such directories are listed in the PATH environment variable. For example, the shells on a Linux system (including **bash**) are located in */bin*. This directory is usually in the PATH, because you're likely to run programs that are stored there. When you create shell programs or other utilities of your own, you may want to keep them together and add the location to your own PATH. If you maintain your own *bin* directory, you might add the following line to your .bash_profile:

```
PATH=$PATH:$HOME/bin
```

This statement modifies your path to include your */home/bin* directory. If you add personal scripts and programs to this directory, **bash** finds them automatically.

Execute permissions (covered in "Part 1: *Devices, Linux Filesystems, and the Filesystem Hierarchy Standard (Topic 2.4)*, Objective 5: Use File Permissions to Control Access to Files") also affect your ability to run a script. Since a script is just a text file, execute permission must be granted to them before they are considered executable, as shown earlier.

You may wish to limit access to the file from other users using:

```
$ chmod 700 ~/bin/lsps
```

This prevents anyone but the owner from making changes to the script.

The issue of file ownership is dovetailed with making a script executable. By default, you own all of the files you create. However, if you are the system administrator, you'll often be working as the superuser and will be creating files with username *root* as well. It is important to assign the correct ownership and permission to scripts to ensure that they are secured.

SUID and GUID rights

On rare occasions, it may become necessary to allow a user to run a program under the name of a different user. This is usually associated with programs run by nonprivileged users who need special privileges to execute correctly. Linux offers two such rights, known as *set user ID* (SUID) and *set group ID* (SGID).

When an executable file is granted the SUID right, processes created to execute it are owned by the user who owns the file instead of the user who launched the program. This is a security enhancement in that the delegation of a privileged task or ability does not imply that the superuser password must be widely known. On the other hand, any process whose file is owned by root and which has the SUID set will run as root for everyone. This could represent an opportunity to break the security of a system if the file itself is easy to attack (as a script is). For this reason, Linux systems will ignore SUID and SGID attributes for script files. Setting SUID and SGID attributes is detailed in "Part 1: *Devices, Linux Filesystems, and the Filesystem Hierarchy Standard (Topic 2.4)*, Objective 5: Use File Permissions to Control Access to Files."

On the Exam

Be sure to think through any questions that require you to determine a user's right to execute a file. Consider location, ownership, execute permissions, and SUID/SGID rights together. Also, watch for new scripts that haven't been granted any execute privileges.

Basic bash Scripts

Now that some of the requirements for creating and using executable scripts are established, some of the features that make them so powerful can be introduced. This section contains basic information needed to customize and create new **bash** scripts.

Return values

As shell scripts execute, it is important to confirm that their constituent commands complete successfully. Most commands offer a *return value* to the shell when they terminate. This value is a simple integer and has meaning specific to the program you're using. Almost all programs return the value 0 when they are successful, and return a nonzero value when a problem is encountered. The value is stored in the special bash variable `$?`, which can be tested in your scripts to check for successful command execution. This variable is reset for every command executed by the shell, so you must test it immediately after execution of the command you're verifying. As a simple example, try using the **cat** program on a nonexistent file:

```
$ cat bogus_file
cat: bogus_file: No such file or directory
```

Then immediately examine the status variable twice:

```
$ echo $?
1
$ echo $?
0
```

The first **echo** yielded 1 (failure) because the **cat** program failed to find the file you specified. The second **echo** yielded 0 (success) because the first **echo** command succeeded. A good script makes use of these status flags to exit gracefully in case of errors.

If it sounds backward to equate zero with success and nonzero with failure, consider how these results are used in practice:

Error detection

Scripts that check for errors include *if-then* code to evaluate a command's return status:

```
command
if (failure_returned) {
  ...error recovery code...
}
```

In a **bash** script, `failure_returned` is simply the `$?` variable, which contains the result of the command's execution.

Error classification

Since commands can fail for multiple reasons, many return more than one failure code. For example, **grep** returns 0 if matches are found and 1 if no matches are found; it returns 2 if there is a problem with the search pattern or input files. Scripts may need to respond differently to various error conditions.

On the Exam

Make certain you understand the meaning of return values in general and that they are stored in the `$?` variable.

File tests

During the execution of a shell script, specific information about a file—such as whether it exists, is writable, is a directory or a file, and so on—may sometimes be required. In **bash**, the built-in command **test** performs this function.* **test** has two general forms:

test *expression*
>   In this form, **test** and an *expression* are explicitly stated.

[*expression*]
>   In this form, **test** isn't mentioned; instead, the *expression* is enclosed inside brackets.

The *expression* can be formed to look for such things as empty files, the existence of files, the existence of directories, equality of strings, and others. (See the more complete list with their operators in the next section.)

When used in a script's **if** or **while** statement, the brackets ([and]) may appear to be grouping the test logically. In reality, [is simply another form of the test command, which requires the trailing]. A side effect of this bit of trickery is that the spaces around [and] are mandatory, a detail that is sure to get you into trouble eventually. See the later section, "Abbreviated bash command reference," for some of the available tests.

Command substitution

Bash offers a handy ability to do *command substitution*. This feature allows you to replace $(*command*) with the result of *command*, usually in a script. That is, wherever $(*command*) is found, its output is substituted prior to interpretation by the shell. For example, to set a variable to the number of lines in your *.bashrc* file, you could use **wc -l**:

```
$ RCSIZE=$(wc -l ~/.bashrc)
```

An older form of command substitution encloses *command* in *backquotes*:

```
$ RCSIZE=`wc -l ~/.bashrc`
```

The result is the same, except that the backquote syntax allows the backslash character to escape the dollar symbol ($), the backquote (`), and another backslash (\). The $(*command*) syntax avoids this nuance by treating all characters between the parentheses literally.

Mailing from scripts

The scripts you write will often be rummaging around your system at night when you're asleep or at least while you're not watching. Since you're too busy to check on every script's progress, a script will sometimes need to send some mail to you or another administrator. This is particularly important when something big goes wrong or when something important depends on the script's outcome. Sending mail is as simple as piping into the **mail** command:

```
echo "Backup failure 5" | mail -s "Backup failed" root
```

---

* There is also a standalone executable version of **test** available in */usr/bin* for non-**bash** shells.

The -s option indicates that a quoted subject for the email follows. The recipient could be yourself, root, or if your system is configured correctly, any Internet email address. If you need to send a log file, redirect the input of mail from that file:

```
mail -s "subject" recipient < logfile
```

Sending email from scripts is easy and makes tracking status easier than reviewing log files every day. On the downside, having an inbox full of "success" messages can be a nuisance too, so many scripts are written so that mail is sent only in response to an important event, such as a fatal error.

Abbreviated bash command reference

This section lists some of the important **bash** built-in commands used when writing scripts. Please note that not all of the *bash* commands are listed here; for a complete overview of the **bash** shell, see *Learning the bash Shell* by Cameron Newham and Bill Rosenblatt (O'Reilly & Associates).

---

break

Syntax

```
break [n]
```

Description

Exit from the innermost (most deeply nested) *for*, *while*, or *until* loop or from the *n* innermost levels of the loop.

---

case

Syntax

```
case string
in
    regex1)
    commands1
    ;;
    regex2)
    commands2
    ;;
    ...
esac
```

Description

Choose *string* from among a series of possible regular expressions. If *string* matches regular expression *regex1*, perform the subsequent *commands1*. If string matches *regex2*, perform *commands2*. Proceed down the list of regular expressions until one is found. To catch all remaining strings, use *)* at the end.

---

continue

Syntax

```
continue [n]
```

Description

Skip remaining commands in a *for, while,* or *until* loop, resuming with the next iteration of the loop (or skipping *n* loops).

echo

Syntax

```
echo [options] [string]
```

Description

Write *string* to standard output, terminated by a newline. If no *string* is supplied, echo only a newline.

Frequently used options

-e

Enables interpretation of escape characters.

-n

Suppresses the trailing newline in the output.

\a

Sounds an audible alert.

\b

Inserts a backspace.

\c

Suppresses the trailing newline (same as -n).

\f

Form feed.

exit

Syntax

```
exit [n]
```

Description

Exit a shell script with status *n*. The value for *n* can be 0 (success) or nonzero (failure). If *n* is not given, the exit status is that of the most recent command.

Example

```
if ! test -f somefile
then
   echo "Error: Missing file somefile"
```

```
    exit 1
fi
for x [in list]
do
    commands
done
```

---

for

Syntax

```
for x in list
do
    commands
done
```

Description

Assign each word in *list* to *x* in turn and execute *commands*. If *list* is omitted, it is assumed that positional parameters from the command line, which are stored in $@, are to be used.

Example

```
for filename in bigfile*
{
  echo "Compressing $filename"
  gzip $filename
}
```

---

function

Syntax

```
function name
{
    commands
}
```

Description

Define function *name*. Positional parameters ($1, $2, ...) can be used within *commands*.

Example

```
# function myfunc
{
  echo "parameter is $1"
}
# myfunc 1
parameter is 1
# myfunc two
parameter is two
```

getopts

Syntax

```
getopts   string name  [args]
```

Description

Process command-line arguments (or *args*, if specified) and check for legal options. The **getopts** command is used in shell script loops and is intended to ensure standard syntax for command-line options. The *string* contains the option letters to be recognized by **getopts** when running the script. Valid options are processed in turn and stored in the shell variable *name*. If an option letter is followed by a colon, the option must be followed by one or more arguments when the command is entered by the user.

if

Syntax

```
if expression1
then
    commands1
elif expression2
then
    commands2
else
    commands
fi
```

Description

The **if** command is used to define a conditional statement. There are three possible formats for using the **if** command:

```
if-then-fi
if-then-else-fi
if-then-elif-then-...fi
```

The *expressions* are made up of tests (or [] commands).

kill

Syntax

```
kill [options]  IDs
```

Description

Send signals to each specified process or job *ID*, which you must own unless you are a privileged user. The default signal sent with the **kill** command is TERM, instructing processes to shut down.

Options

–l

    List the signal names.

–s *signal or* –**signal**

    Specifies the signal number or name.

---

read

Syntax

    read [*options*] *variable1* [*variable2*...]

Description

Read one line of standard input, and assign each word to the corresponding *variable*, with all remaining words assigned to the last variable.

Example

```
echo -n "Enter last-name, age, height, and weight > "
read lastname everythingelse
echo $lastname
echo $everythingelese
```

The name entered is placed in variable $lastname; all of the other values, including the spaces between them, are placed in $everythingelse.

---

return

Syntax

    return [*n*]

Description

This command is used inside a function definition to exit the function with status *n*. If *n* is omitted, the exit status of the previously executed command is returned.

---

shift

Syntax

    shift [*n*]

Description

Shift positional parameters down *n* elements. If *n* is omitted, the default is 1, so $2 becomes $1, $3 becomes $2, and so on.

---

source

Syntax

    source *file* [*arguments*]
    . *file* [*arguments*]

Description

Read and execute lines in *file*. The *file* does not need to be executable but must be in a directory listed in PATH. The "dot" syntax is equivalent to stating **source**.

test

Syntax

```
test expression
[ expression ]
```

Description

Evaluate the conditional *expression* and return a status of 0 (true) or 1 (false). The first form explicitly calls out the **test** command. The second form implies the test command. The spaces around *expression* are required in the second form. *expression* is constructed using options.

Frequently used options

-d *file*
> True if *file* exists and is a directory

-e *file*
> True if *file* exists

-f *file*
> True if *file* exists and is a regular file

-L *file*
> True if *file* exists and is a symbolic link

-n *string*
> True if the length of *string* is nonzero

-r *file*
> True if *file* exists and is readable

-s *file*
> True if *file* exists and has a size greater than zero

-w *file*
> True if *file* exists and is writable

-x *file*
> True if *file* exists and is executable

-z *string*
> True if the length of *string* is zero

file1 -ot *file2*
> True if *file1* is older than *file2*

string1 = *string2*
> True if the strings are equal

string1 != *string2*
> True if the strings are not equal

Example

To determine if a file exists and is readable, use the **-r** option:

```
if test -r file
then
    echo "file exists"
fi
```

Using the [ ] form instead, the same test looks like this:

```
if [ -r file ]
then
    echo "file exists"
fi
```

---

until

Syntax

```
until
    test-commands
do
    commands
done
```

Description

Execute *test-commands* (usually a test command) and if the exit status is nonzero (that is, the test fails), perform *commands*; repeat. Opposite of **while**.

---

while

Syntax

```
while
    test-commands
do
    commands
done
```

Description

Execute *test-commands* (usually a test command) and if the exit status is zero, perform *commands*; repeat. Opposite of **until**.

Example

Example 2-11 shows a typical script from a Linux system. This example is */etc/rc.d/ init.d/sendmail*, which is the script that starts and stops sendmail. This script demonstrates many of the built-in commands referenced in the last section.

Example 2-11: Sample sendmail Startup Script

```
#!/bin/sh
#
# sendmail     This shell script takes care of starting
#              and stopping sendmail.
#
# chkconfig: 2345 80 30
# description: Sendmail is a Mail Transport Agent, which
#              is the program that moves mail from one
#              machine to another.
# processname: sendmail
# config: /etc/sendmail.cf
# pidfile: /var/run/sendmail.pid

# Source function library.
. /etc/rc.d/init.d/functions

# Source networking configuration.
. /etc/sysconfig/network

# Source sendmail configuration.
if [ -f /etc/sysconfig/sendmail ] ; then
  . /etc/sysconfig/sendmail
else
  DAEMON=yes
  QUEUE=1h
fi

# Check that networking is up.
[ ${NETWORKING} = "no" ] && exit 0

[ -f /usr/sbin/sendmail ] || exit 0

# See how we were called.
case "$1" in
  start)
  # Start daemons.
  echo -n "Starting sendmail: "
  /usr/bin/newaliases > /dev/null 2>&1
  for i in virtusertable access domaintable mailertable ; do
    if [ -f /etc/mail/$i ] ; then
      makemap hash /etc/mail/$i < /etc/mail/$i
    fi
  done
  daemon /usr/sbin/sendmail $([ "$DAEMON" = yes ] \
    && echo -bd) $([ -n "$QUEUE" ] && echo -q$QUEUE)
  echo
  touch /var/lock/subsys/sendmail
  ;;
```

Example 2-11: Sample sendmail Startup Script (continued)

```
stop)
# Stop daemons.
echo -n "Shutting down sendmail: "
killproc sendmail
echo
rm -f /var/lock/subsys/sendmail
;;

restart)
$0 stop
$0 start
;;

status)
status sendmail
;;

*)
echo "Usage: sendmail {start|stop|restart|status}"
exit 1
esac

exit 0
```

On the Exam

You should be familiar with a script's general structure, as well as the use of she-bang, *test*, *if* statements and their syntax (including the trailing *fi*), return values, exit values, and so on.

X
(Topic 2.10)

Unix has a long history of utility that predates the popular demand for a graphical user interface (GUI). However, a GUI is an essential part of running small systems today, and the standard GUI on Linux systems is the X Window System, or more simply, X. Originally developed at MIT and Digital Equipment Corporation, X's current release is Version 11 Release 6. This version is more commonly referred to as *X11R6*, or just *X11*. X is a complete windowing GUI and is distributable under license without cost. The implementation of X for Linux is *XFree86* (*http://www.xfree.org*), which is available for multiple computer architectures and is released under the GNU Public License. This section covers these four Objectives on XFree86 for LPI Exam 102:

Objective 1: Install and Configure XFree86
Most distributions install XFree86 when Linux is installed, but a number of the configuration details are important for Exam 102. This Objective covers X servers, fonts, and automated XFree86 configuration tools. Weight: 4.

Objective 2: Set Up xdm
This Objective covers the X display manager, a graphical login system. Weight: 1.

Objective 3: Identify and Terminate Runaway X Applications
Sometimes an X application becomes unresponsive or fails to terminate normally. This Objective mentions methods to cope with these situations. Weight: 1

Objective 4: Install and Customize a Window Manager Environment
This Objective covers the selection and customization of X window managers, including menus, X terminals, X library issues, and a number of control files. Weight: 4.

An Overview of X

X is implemented using a client/server model. X servers and clients can be located on the same computer or separated across a network, so that computation is handled separately from display rendering. While X servers manage hardware, they do not define the look of the display and they offer no utilities to manipulate clients. The X server is responsible for rendering various shapes and colors on screen. Examples of X Servers include:

- Software from XFree86, which controls your Linux PC's video card.

- XFree86 software on a separate networked system, displaying output from a program running on your system.

- Other networked Unix systems running their own X server software.

- X implementations for other operating systems, such as Microsoft Windows.

- An *X Terminal*, which is a hardware device with no computational ability of its own, built solely for display purposes.

X clients are user programs, such as spreadsheets or CAD tools, which display graphical output. Examples of X clients are:

- A browser, such as Netscape Navigator.

- A mail program, such as Evolution or Kmail.

- Office applications, such as StarOffice, Gnumeric, or AbiWord.

- A terminal emulator, such as *xterm*, running within an X window.

A special client program called a *window manager* is responsible for these functions and provides windows, window sizing, open and close buttons, and so forth. The window manager controls the other clients running under an X server. Multiple window managers are available for XFree86, allowing you to choose an interface style that suits your needs and personal taste.

A few complete graphical *desktop environments* are also available. These packages can include a window manager and additional applications that work together to create a complete, unified working environment. Most Linux distributions ship with either the KDE or GNOME, or both, along with a number of standalone window managers. There is no standard window manager or environment for Linux—the selection is entirely up to the user.

Objective 1: Install and Configure XFree86

Most Linux distributions install and automatically configure XFree86, freeing users from much of its installation and configuration. However, Exam 102 requires specific knowledge of some of the underpinnings of X configuration.

WARNING

Be careful about installing an X server on a system that already has X installed. A backup should be made prior to the installation.

Selecting and Configuring an X Server

The XFree86 project provides support for an amazing array of graphics hardware. This outcome is possible partly due to cooperation by manufacturers through public release of graphics device documentation and driver software, and partly due to the tenacity of the XFree86 developers. Fortunately, many manufacturers who were historically uninterested in offering technical information to the XFree86 project have become cooperative. The result is that most recent video hardware is well-supported by XFree86.

Supported video hardware

To avoid problems, it is important to verify XFree86 compatibility with your hardware prior to installation. At the very least, you should be aware of these items:

Your XFree86 version
> As with any software, improvements in XFree86 are made over time, particularly in support for hardware devices. You should choose a version of XFree86 that offers a good balance between the video support and stability you require. To determine the version of X you're running, simply issue the following command:

> ```
> $ /usr/X11R6/bin/X -version
> XFree86 Version 4.0.1a / X Window System
> ```

The video chipset
> XFree86 video drivers are written for graphics chipsets, not the video cards they're installed on. Multiple video cards from a variety of manufacturers can carry the same chipset, making those cards nearly identical in function. You must verify that the chipset on your video card is supported by XFree86 to use advanced graphics features.

Monitor type
> XFree86 can be configured to handle just about any monitor, particularly the newer and very flexible multisync monitors sold today, which can handle preset configurations provided in the XFree86 configuration utilities. However, if you have a nonstandard monitor, you need to know some parameters describing its capabilities before configuring X, including your monitor's horizontal sync frequency (in kHz), vertical refresh frequency (in Hz), and resolution (in pixels). These items can usually be found in your monitor's documentation, but since most monitors conform to standard display settings such as *XGA* (1024×768 pixels at 60 Hz vertical refresh), you should be able to use a preset configuration.

As an example of these considerations, suppose you're using a Number Nine video chipset in your system.* If you examine the chipset support information included with XFree86 Version 3.3.6, you'll find that the I128 driver handles your chipset. However, XFree86 Version 4.0.1 does not, so v4.0.1 is not a viable choice. Your chipset must be supported by the version of XFree86 you're installing. Check the XFree86 release notes for specific information on supported chipsets.

---

* Number Nine was the manufacturer of some popular PC video hardware. The company is now out of business.

Installing XFree86 from packages

The procedures for installation vary depending on the release of X you're using. For example, with versions prior to 4.0, a specific X server is required to match your chipset in order to use modes other than standard VGA. For versions after 4.0, a newer modular design allows a single server program to manage all supported chipsets by calling driver modules. In addition, the type of XFree86 distribution you're using affects installation. XFree86 is available as source code, in precompiled binary form, or as an RPM or Debian package. (Because of the precompiled and package options, there's little reason to compile from scratch.)

If you're going to use a version of XFree86 that came with a Linux distribution, simply use the package installation tools from your distribution with the XFree86 packages. For example, on a Red Hat 6.0 system with XFree86 v3.3.3.1, the following components of XFree86 were installed by the RPM package:*

```
XFree86-SVGA-3.3.3.1-49
X11R6-contrib-3.3.2-6
Xconfigurator-4.2.3-1
XFree86-3.3.3.1-49
XFree86-75dpi-fonts-3.3.3.1-49
XFree86-libs-3.3.3.1-49
XFree86-xfs-3.3.3.1-49
XFree86-XF86Setup-3.3.3.1-49
```

The first item in this list is the SVGA X server (*XFree86-SVGA-3.3.3.1-49*), which supports a number of video chipsets (other server programs, packaged separately, may be needed to support other video chipsets). The XFree86 package (*XFree86-3.3.3.1-49* in the list) is the core of XFree86. The other items are either required or recommended packages. Such recommendations can come from the installation program or from notes accompanying the package. For example, the XFree86 package indicates that:

> In addition to installing the [XFree86] package, you will need to install the *XFree86* package [that] corresponds to your video card, the *X11R6-contrib* package, the *Xconfigurator* package, and the *XFree86-libs* package. You may also need to install one of the XFree86 fonts [*sic*] packages.

Using a packaged installation targeted for your particular Linux distribution will probably be the simplest method.

Installing XFree86 from precompiled binaries

You may wish to try a version of XFree86 that is more recent than available packaged versions. In this case, you may wish to install a precompiled binary from the XFree86 project. To get the files needed to install the latest version, consult the XFree86 web site or one of the many mirror sites listed there.

---

* In this example, all of the package names are followed by a version number. Here, XFree86 v3.3.3.1 is installed.

The first step in deploying a precompiled XFree86 binary is to get the configuration program, **Xinstall.sh.*** Using the **–check** option, this utility can determine which precompiled binary distribution is right for your system:

```
# ./Xinstall.sh -check
Checking which OS you're running...
uname reports 'Linux' version '2.2.5-15smp',
  architecture 'i686'.
Object format is 'ELF'.  libc version is '6.1'.
Binary distribution name is 'Linux-ix86-glibc21'
```

The last line directs us to the appropriate binary distribution, which in this case is *Linux-ix86-glibc21* (your results will differ). Next we need to get the files for that distribution. Some, such as fonts and extra programs, are optional. Details on exactly which files to get are available in the *Install* document, which may be retrieved along with **Xinstall.sh**. The files listed in Table 2-17 are mandatory for use with v4.0.1.

Table 2-17: Files Necessary for Use with XFree86 v4.0.1

Filename	Description
Xinstall.sh	The installer script
extract	The utility for extracting tarballs
Xbin.tgz	X clients/utilities and runtime libraries
Xlib.tgz	Some data files required at runtime
Xman.tgz	Manual pages
Xdoc.tgz	XFree86 documentation
Xfnts.tgz	Base set of fonts
Xfenc.tgz	Base set of font-encoding data
Xetc.tgz	Runtime configuration files
Xvar.tgz	Runtime data
Xxserv.tgz	XFree86 X server
Xmod.tgz	XFree86 X server modules

After you have retrieved these files, simply run **Xinstall**.sh as *root* to begin installation as described in the *Install* document.

Configuring an X server and the XF86Config file

XFree86 configuration differs slightly among versions and among Linux distributions, but essentially involves the creation of the *XF86Config* file customized for your system. The X server uses this configuration file as it starts to set such things as keyboard and mouse selections, installed fonts, and screen resolutions.

---

* It's important to use binary-mode FTP to get this program. Browsers may not transfer the program correctly.

XF86Config contains technical details concerning the capabilities of system hardware, which can be intimidating for some users. For this reason, automated configuration tools are available that will generate the file for you:

xf86config

> This program is distributed with XFree86. It is a simple text-mode program that requests information about the system from the user and then writes a corresponding *XF86Config* file. This utility does not use information stored in an existing configuration file, so its utility is limited. (Remember that **xf86config** is a binary program that writes the *XF86Config* text file.)

XF86Setup

> This program is distributed with XFree86. **XF86Setup** is a graphical program that starts a VGA X server, which should run on most PC hardware. It allows you to select the graphics chipset, monitor, mouse, and keyboard device types and writes the appropriate configuration file for you.

xf86cfg

> This program is distributed with XFree86 v4.0. Like **XF86Setup**, it is a graphical tool; however, **xf86cfg**'s interface is slightly different. Whereas other tools offer a menu-based approach, **xf86cfg** offers a block diagram of the system, including a monitor, video device, keyboard, and mouse. The user configures each element by manipulating its properties. When the user is happy with the configuration, the tool writes the *XF86Config* file.

Distribution-specific tools

> Various Linux distributors provide their own configuration utilities. For example, **Xconfigurator** is distributed by Red Hat Software. It is menu-based, provides for automated probing of graphics chipsets and capabilities, and uses a list of known monitors to retrieve timing information.

Example 2-12 contains an abbreviated *XF86Config* file created using the Red Hat **Xconfigurator** tool for XFree86 v3.3.3.[*]

Example 2-12: A sample XF86Config File for XFree86 v3.3.3

```
# File generated by XConfigurator.

Section "Files"
    RgbPath     "/usr/X11R6/lib/X11/rgb"
    FontPath    "unix/:-1"
EndSection

Section "ServerFlags"
EndSection

Section "Keyboard"
    Protocol    "Standard"
    AutoRepeat  500 5
```

---

[*] The *XF86Config* files shown here are examples and are not intended for use on your system.

Example 2-12: A sample XF86Config File for XFree86 v3.3.3 (continued)

```
    LeftAlt     Meta
    RightAlt    Meta
    ScrollLock  Compose
    RightCtl    Control
    XkbDisable
    XkbKeycodes     "xfree86"
    XkbTypes        "default"
    XkbCompat       "default"
    XkbSymbols      "us(pc101)"
    XkbGeometry     "pc"
    XkbRules        "xfree86"
    XkbModel        "pc101"
    XkbLayout       "us"
EndSection

Section "Pointer"
    Protocol    "PS/2"
    Device      "/dev/mouse"
    Emulate3Buttons
    Emulate3Timeout     50
EndSection

Section "Monitor"
    Identifier  "My Monitor"
    VendorName  "Unknown"
    ModelName   "Unknown"
    HorizSync   31.5 - 64.3
    VertRefresh 50-90
    # 1280x1024 @ 61 Hz, 64.2 kHz hsync
    Mode "1280x1024"
        DotClock    110
        Htimings    1280 1328 1512 1712
        Vtimings    1024 1025 1028 1054
    EndMode
EndSection

Section "Device"
    Identifier  "My Video Card"
    VendorName  "Unknown"
    BoardName   "Unknown"
    VideoRam    16256
EndSection

Section "Screen"
    Driver      "svga"
    Device      "My Video Card"
    Monitor     "My Monitor"
    Subsection "Display"
        Depth       32
        Modes       "1280x1024"
```

Example 2-12: A sample XF86Config File for XFree86 v3.3.3 (continued)

```
        ViewPort     0 0
    EndSubsection
EndSection
```

Under v3.3.3, the default location for the *XF86Config* file is in */etc/X11*. The file contains the following sections:

Files

> This section is used to specify the default font path and the path to the RGB database. Using the FontPath "*path*" directive multiple times creates a list of directories that the X server will search for fonts. The RGB database is an equivalence table of numeric red/green/blue color values with names. Here's a short excerpt of the RGB database:

```
255 228 196            bisque
255 218 185            peach puff
255 218 185            PeachPuff
255 222 173            navajo white
```

> Hundreds of these names are defined and may be used in the configuration of X applications where color names are required.

ServerFlags

> This section allows customization of X server options such as the handling of hotkeys.

Keyboard

> This section is used to specify the keyboard input device, its parameters, and default keyboard-mapping options.

Pointer

> This section is used to define the pointing device (mouse).

Monitor

> Multiple Monitor sections are used to define the specifications of monitors and a list of video modes they can handle.

Device

> Multiple Device sections are used to define video hardware (cards) installed.

Screen

> The Screen section ties together a Device with a corresponding Monitor and includes some configuration settings for them.

On the Exam

You don't need to memorize details about *XF86Config*, but it is an important file, and your familiarity with it will be tested. In particular, be aware of what each of the sections does for the X server, and remember that the Screen section ties together a Device and a Monitor.

The *XF86Config* file format was modified slightly for XFree86 v4.0. In particular, a new ServerLayout section has been added; it ties the Screen, Pointer, and

Keyboard sections together. Example 2-13 contains an abbreviated *XF86Config* file created using the bundled **xf86cfg** tool from the XFree86 project.

Example 2-13: A Sample XF86Config File for XFree86 v4.0.1

```
Section "ServerLayout"
    Identifier      "XFree86 Configured"
    Screen      0   "Screen0" 0 0
    InputDevice     "Mouse0" "CorePointer"
    InputDevice     "Keyboard0" "CoreKeyboard"
EndSection

Section "Files"
EndSection

Section "InputDevice"
    Identifier  "Keyboard0"
    Driver      "keyboard"
EndSection

Section "InputDevice"
    Identifier  "Mouse0"
    Driver      "mouse"
    Option      "Protocol" "PS/2"
    Option      "Device" "/dev/mouse"
EndSection

Section "Monitor"
    Identifier  "Monitor0"
    VendorName  "Monitor Vendor"
    ModelName   "Monitor Model"
    HorizSync   31.5 - 64.3
    VertRefresh 50.0    90.0
EndSection

Section "Device"
    Identifier  "Card0"
    Driver      "nv"
    VendorName  "NVidia"
    BoardName   "Riva TNT"
    ChipSet     "RIVATNT"
    BusID       "PCI:1:0:0"
EndSection

Section "Screen"
    Identifier      "Screen0"
    Device          "Card0"
    Monitor         "Monitor0"
    DefaultDepth 24
    SubSection "Display"
        Depth       24
    EndSubSection
EndSection
```

Under v4.0, the default location for the *XF86Config* file is in */etc/X11*. The file contains the following sections:

ServerLayout

This section ties together Screen with one or more InputDevices. Multiple ServerLayout sections may be used for multiheaded configurations (i.e., systems with more than one monitor).

Files

This section is used to add paths to fonts and color information, just as it is in XFree86 v3.3.3.

InputDevice

Multiple InputDevice sections should be used to include at least a keyboard and mouse. Subsections within InputDevice in v4.0 replace the Pointer and Keyboard sections for XFree86 v3.3.3.

Monitor

This section is similar to the Monitor section for XFree86 v3.3.3, except that mode specifications are not usually necessary. The X server is already aware of standard VESA video modes and chooses the best mode based on the horizontal sync and vertical refresh rates.

Device

This section specifies the modular driver for the X server. Multiple Device sections can be included to handle multiple graphics devices.

Screen

This section ties together a Monitor with a Device and is specified in the ServerLayout. Multiple Screen sections can be included to handle multiple monitor/device pairs.

On the Exam

As already mentioned, you don't need to worry about details in *XF86Config*. However, you should be aware of the major differences in the configuration files for XFree86 Versions 3.3 and 4.0.

X Fonts

XFree86 is distributed with a collection of fonts for most basic purposes, including text displays in terminal windows and browsers. For many users, the default fonts are adequate, but others may prefer to add additional fonts to their system. A variety of fonts are available, both free and commercially, from many sources, such as Adobe. Some very creative fonts are created by individuals and distributed on the Internet (a search engine should return some useful links to a query such as "*XFree86 fonts*").

XFree86 makes fonts that it finds in the *font path* available to client programs. A basic font path is compiled into the X server, but you can specify your own font path using the FontPath directive in the *Files* section of *XF86Config*. The simple syntax is:

```
FontPath "path"
```

For example:

```
Section "Files"
    RgbPath     "/usr/X11R6/lib/X11/rgb"
    FontPath    "/usr/X11R6/lib/X11/fonts/misc"
    FontPath    "/usr/X11R6/lib/X11/fonts/Type1"
    FontPath    "/usr/X11R6/lib/X11/fonts/Speedo"
    FontPath    "/usr/X11R6/lib/X11/fonts/100dpi"
    FontPath    "/usr/X11R6/lib/X11/fonts/75dpi"
    FontPath    "/usr/X11R6/lib/X11/fonts/local"
EndSection
```

This group of `FontPath` directives creates a font path consisting of six directories, all under */usr/X11R6/lib/X11/fonts*. When XFree86 starts, it parses these font directories and includes their contents in the list of fonts available during the X session.

Installing fonts

Adding new fonts is straightforward.[*] First, a suitable directory should be created for the new fonts, such as */usr/X11R6/lib/X11/local* or */usr/local/fonts*. You may wish to separate your own fonts from the default XFree86 directories to protect them during upgrades. After the fonts are installed in the new directory, the **mkfontdir** utility is run to catalog the new fonts in the new directory. New entries are added to the *XF86Config* file to include the path for new fonts. For example:

```
FontPath    "/usr/local/fonts"
```

At this point, the X server can be restarted to recognize the new fonts, or the fonts can be dynamically added using the **xset** command:

```
# xset fp+ /usr/local/fonts
```

xset is beyond the scope of the LPIC Level 1 exams.

On the Exam

Be sure you understand how the X font path is created and how to extend it to include additional directories. Knowledge of the internal details of font files is not necessary.

The X font server

On a network with multiple workstations, managing fonts manually for each system can be time consuming. To simplify this problem, the administrator can install all of the desired fonts on a single system and then run **xfs**, the X fonts server, on that system. The X font server is a small daemon that sends fonts to clients on both local and remote systems. Some Linux distributions use **xfs** exclusively, without a

---

* For this brief discussion, we assume that we're working with Type 1 fonts. Other types, such as TrueType fonts, may require additional configuration depending on your version of XFree86.

list of directories in the manually created font path. To include **xfs** in your system's font path, add a `FontPath` directive like this:

```
Section "Files"
    RgbPath      "/usr/X11R6/lib/X11/rgb"

    FontPath     "unix/:-1"
EndSection
```

If you install **xfs** from a package from your distribution, it is probably automatically configured to start at boot time and run continually, serving fonts to local and remote client programs. To start **xfs** manually, simply enter the **xfs** command. For security purposes, you may wish to run **xfs** as a non-root user. **xfs** is configured using its configuration file, */etc/X11/fs/config*. Example 2-14 contains an example *config* file for **xfs**.

Example 2-14: Sample configuration File for xfs

```
# Allow a max of four clients to connect to this font server
client-limit = 4

# When a font server reaches its limit, start up a new one
clone-self = on

catalogue = /usr/X11R6/lib/X11/fonts/misc:unscaled,
        /usr/X11R6/lib/X11/fonts/75dpi:unscaled,
        /usr/X11R6/lib/X11/fonts/100dpi:unscaled,
        /usr/X11R6/lib/X11/fonts/misc,
        /usr/X11R6/lib/X11/fonts/Type1,
        /usr/X11R6/lib/X11/fonts/Speedo,
        /usr/X11R6/lib/X11/fonts/75dpi,
        /usr/X11R6/lib/X11/fonts/100dpi,
        /usr/share/fonts/ISO8859-2/100dpi,
        /usr/share/fonts/ISO8859-9/100dpi
        /usr/X11R6/lib/X11/fonts/local

# In 12 points, decipoints
default-point-size = 120

# 100 x 100 and 75 x 75
default-resolutions = 75,75,100,100

# How to log errors
use-syslog = on
```

As you can see, the *config* file contains the following *keyword=value* pairs:

catalogue
    This keyword holds a comma-separated list of directories containing fonts to be served by **xfs**. This is where new font directories are added.

alternate-servers (*strings*)
    This section contains a listing of alternate font servers that can be found on the local machine or on other machines.

`client-limit`
This shows the maximum number of client requests to be served.

`clone-self`
When on, the font server makes copies of itself if it reaches the `client-limit`.

You don't need to remember details about the contents of the **xfs** configuration file (*config*), but be aware of the use and general contents of the file. In particular, remember that the `catalogue` keyword is used similarly to `FontPath` in *XF86Config*.

On the Exam

Remember that **xfs** can take the place of the list of directories in a manually configured font path. However, running **xfs** doesn't replace the font path—**xfs** itself must be on that path as noted earlier in Example 2-12 with the *unix/:-1* entry.

Controlling X Applications with .Xresources

The X Window System also has many built-in customization features. Many X applications are programmed with a variety of *resources*, which are configuration settings that can be externally manipulated. Rather than have a configuration utility built into each application, applications can be written to examine the contents of a file in the user's home directory. The *.Xresources* file contains a line for each configured resource in the following form:

```
program*resource: value
```

This line can be translated as follows:

- *program* is the name of a configurable program, such as `emacs` or `xterm`.
- *resource* is one of the configurable settings allowed by the program, such as colors.
- *value* is the setting to apply to the resource.

For example, the following is an excerpt from *.Xresources* that configures colors for an `xterm`:

```
xterm*background: Black
xterm*foreground: Wheat
xterm*cursorColor: Orchid
xterm*reverseVideo: false
```

On the Exam

You should be aware of X resources and the function of the *.Xresources* file. In particular, you should understand that X applications will look in the *.Xresources* file for settings. You should also be able to construct a resource setting given a particular example, but you do not need to be able to generate a configuration file from scratch.

Objective 2: Set Up xdm

The X Display Manager, or **xdm**, is a tool to manage X sessions on physical displays both locally and across the network. Part of its job is to handle user authentication through a graphical login screen, which replaces the familiar text-mode login.

Configuring xdm

xdm is distributed as part of XFree86 and is configured by a series of files located in */etc/X11/xdm*. These files include:

Xaccess
> This file controls inbound requests from remote hosts.

Xresources
> This file is similar to *.Xresources*, discussed earlier. It holds configuration information for some **xdm** resources, including the graphical login screen. This file can be edited to modify the appearance of the **xdm** login screen.

Xservers
> This file associates the X display names (`:0`, `:1`, ...) with either the local X server software or a foreign display such as an X terminal.

Xsession
> This file contains the script **xdm** launches after a successful login. It usually looks for *.xsession* in the user's home directory and executes the commands found there. If such a file doesn't exist, *Xsession* starts a default window manager (or environment) and applications.

Xsetup_0
> This file is a script started before the graphical login screen. It often includes commands to set colors, display graphics, or run other programs. This script is executed as root.

xdm-config
> This file associates **xdm** configuration resources with the other files in this list. It usually isn't necessary to make changes in this file unless an expert administrator plans to customize **xdm** configuration.

Running xdm manually

xdm uses the X server to run on your local display. Therefore, you must have a working X configuration prior to using a display manager. Then, to start **xdm**, simply enter it as *root*:

```
# xdm
```

xdm launches the X server and display the graphical login, and you can log in as usual. **xdm** then starts your graphical environment. After you log out, **xdm** resets and again displays the login screen.

Most Linux distributions enable virtual consoles. You can switch among them using the key combinations **Ctrl–Alt–F1**, **Ctrl–Alt–F2**, and so on. Typically, the first six consoles are set up as text-mode screens, and X launches on console 7 (**Ctrl–Alt–F7**). This means that, as with **startx**, your original text-mode console remains unchanged after you manually start **xdm**. Therefore, you must log out of your text-mode console if you plan to leave the system unattended with **xdm** running manually.

If you want to stop **xdm**, you first must be sure that all of the X sessions under its management are logged out. Otherwise, they'll die when **xdm** exits and you could lose data. Then simply stop the **xdm** process using **kill** or **killall** from a text console:

```
# killall xdm
```

Of course, **xdm** isn't very useful for your local system if you must always start it manually. That's why most Linux distributions include a boot-time option to start **xdm** for you, eliminating the text-mode login completely.

Running xdm automatically

For Linux systems using the System-V-style initialization, a runlevel is usually reserved for login under **xdm**. This line at the bottom of */etc/inittab* instructs **init** to start **xdm** for runlevel 5:

```
# Run xdm in runlevel 5
x:5:respawn:/usr/X11R6/bin/xdm -nodaemon
```

Using this configuration, when the system enters runlevel 5, **xdm** starts and presents the graphical login as before. See "Part 1: *Boot, Initialization, Shutdown, and Runlevels (Topic 2.6),* Objective 2: Change Runlevels and Shutdown or Reboot the System," for more information on runlevels.

It's also possible to automatically start **xdm** simply by adding it to the end of an initialization script, such as *rc.local.* This method offers less control over **xdm** but may be adequate for some situations and for Linux distributions that don't offer runlevels.

Basic xdm customization

You may wish to personalize the look of **xdm** for your system. The look of the graphical login screen can be altered by manipulating the resources in */etc/X11/ xdm/Xresources.*[*] For example, the following excerpt shows settings to control the greeting (*Welcome to Linux on smp-pc*), other prompts, and colors:

```
! Xresources file
xlogin*borderWidth: 10
xlogin*greeting: Welcome to Linux on CLIENTHOST
xlogin*namePrompt: Login:\040
xlogin*fail: Login incorrect - try again!
xlogin*failColor: red
xlogin*Foreground: Yellow
xlogin*Background: MidnightBlue
```

---

[*] Note that *Xresources* uses ! to initiate comments.

You can also include command-line options to the X server in */etc/X11/xdm/ Xservers* if you wish to override those found in *XF86Config*. For example, to change the default color depth, add the **-bpp** (bits per pixel) option for the local display:

```
# Xservers file
:0 local /usr/X11R6/bin/X -bpp 24
```

To include additional X programs or settings on the graphical login screen, put them in */etc/X11/xdm/Xsetup 0*. In this example, the background color of the X display is set to a solid color (in hexadecimal form), and a clock is added at the lower righthand corner of the screen:

```
#!/bin/sh
# Xsetup
/usr/X11R6/bin/xsetroot -solid "#356390"
/usr/X11R6/bin/xclock -digital -update 1 -geometry -5-5 &
```

Note that in this example, **xsetroot** exits immediately after it sets the color, allowing the *Xsetup_0* script to continue. **xclock**, however, does not exit and must be put into the background using an & at the end of the command line. If such commands are not placed into the background, the *Xsetup_0* script hangs, and the login display does not appear.

X Stations

X stations, also known as *X terminals*, sadly are a vanishing breed of low-cost display devices for X. They are usually diskless systems that implement an X server and drive a monitor. Such devices can be configured to access a remote host to find an **xdm** daemon or will broadcast to the entire network looking for a "willing host" to offer **xdm** services. The selected system will run an X session across the network with the X terminal as the target display. With this setup, a large number of relatively inexpensive X terminals can make use of a few high-powered host systems to run graphical clients.

xdm for X terminals

To use an X terminal with your host, **xdm** must first be running on the host machine. The host listens for inbound connections from the X terminals using *XDMCP*, the **xdm** Control Protocol (the default port for *xdmcp* is 177). When a request is received, **xdm** responds with the same graphical login screen that's used on the local system. The difference is that the X server is implemented in the X terminal hardware, not in the XFree86 software on the **xdm** host, and all of the graphics information is transmitted over the network.

You can configure access to your system's **xdm** daemon in the */etc/X11/xdm/ Xaccess* file. This file is a simple list of hosts that are to be restricted or enabled. To enable a host, simply enter its name. To restrict a host, enter its name with an exclamation point (!) before it. The * wildcard is also allowed to handle groups of devices.

The following example allows access to all X terminals on the local domain but prohibits access from `xterm1` on an outside domain:

```
*.localdomain.com
!xterm1.outsidedomain.com
```

Objective 3: Identify and Terminate Runaway X Applications

This short Objective highlights what can be a frustrating aspect of working with X. You're likely to sometimes experience problems with X, perhaps even an X server crash. Usually the applications that were running during the X session exit immediately. However, some X client programs may leave processes running after the X server terminates. These programs may consume resources on your system and need to be identified.

As an example of this behavior, it's possible for the Netscape browser to remain after an X session crash. If this happens, you'll probably note that your system is sluggish. Use the **top** utility to identify the offending program and **kill** or **killall** to terminate it.

If your X session hangs completely, you can use a virtual terminal* to log in again and kill runaway processes or even the X server. Use **Ctrl-Alt-F2** or **Ctrl-Alt-F3** to switch to terminals 2 or 3, respectively.

---

* Virtual terminals are configured in */etc/inittab*. Most Linux distributions preconfigure six virtual terminals.

Study Guide
102

Objective 4: Install and Customize a Window Manager Environment

The selection of a desktop environment for X is a personal decision. At a minimum, you need a window manager such as **twm** to provide basic window frames, menus, and controls. On the more elaborate side, an integrated working environment such as KDE or GNOME offers a rich set of applications. Regardless of how you configure your desktop, it's important to understand some basic customization techniques.

Starting X and a Default Window Manager

Starting XFree86 can be as simple as issuing the **X** command as *root*. However, **X** alone doesn't give you a working environment. At the very least, you also need to start a window manager and an application and set up basic X access authority.* You may also wish to choose from among multiple desktop environments and window managers installed on your system.

The XFree86 startup process

Assuming for the moment that we're not using **xdm**, the process of starting X goes like this:

1. The user issues the **startx** command. This is a script provided by XFree86 and often modified by distributors and administrators. **startx** is intended as a frontend to **xinit**.

2. **startx** calls **xinit** with two main arguments:

    a. An *Xinitrc* script, which contains X programs to run. This script could be *.xinitrc* from the user's home directory, or if that doesn't exist, a system-wide default found in */etc/X11/xinit/xinitrc*.

    b. Server options, such as X authority information.

3. **xinit** launches XFree86 and the chosen *Xinitrc* script.

4. XFree86 starts. Note that X itself does not provide any applications. They appear only as the result of the commands found in the *Xinitrc* script.

5. Client programs and a window manager found in the *Xinitrc* script start.

The contents of **startx** and the system default */etc/X11/xinit/xinitrc* can vary from distribution to distribution and can be changed by administrators to suit local needs. They may also reference additional files, such as */etc/X11/xinit/Xclients,* to determine which programs and window manager to run. Example 2-15 shows the contents of */etc/X11/xinit/xinitrc*, a modified version of the original distributed with XFree86.

---

* X authority configuration is beyond the scope of the LPIC Level 1 certification and is not covered in this book.

Example 2-15: A System Default xinitrc

```
#!/bin/sh
# $XConsortium: xinitrc.cpp,v 1.4 91/08/22 rws Exp $

userresources=$HOME/.Xresources
usermodmap=$HOME/.Xmodmap
sysresources=/usr/X11R6/lib/X11/xinit/.Xresources
sysmodmap=/usr/X11R6/lib/X11/xinit/.Xmodmap

# merge in defaults and keymaps

if [ -f $sysresources ]; then
    xrdb -merge $sysresources
fi

if [ -f $sysmodmap ]; then
    xmodmap $sysmodmap
fi

if [ -f $userresources ]; then
    xrdb -merge $userresources
fi

if [ -f $usermodmap ]; then
    xmodmap $usermodmap
fi

# start some nice programs

(sleep 1; xclock -geometry 50x50-1+1) &
(sleep 1; xterm -geometry 80x50+494+51) &
(sleep 1; xterm -geometry 80x20+494-0) &
exec twm
```

In this example, resource and keyboard mappings are set, a few applications are launched, and the **twm** window manager is started. **twm** is installed as a basic default window manager on most distributions.

Customizing twm

Each of the window managers and desktop environments has its own style of configuration. In the case of **twm**, a single file called *.twmrc* in the user's home directory is used. If *.twmrc* doesn't exist, the system-wide default */etc/X11/twm/ system.twmrc* is used. The file can include:

- Font selections
- Color selections
- Bindings between actions (such as mouse clicks) and **twm** responses
- Menu definitions

Even for a basic window manager such as **twm**, a wide array of configuration options is available to tailor the window manager to your personal taste.

Example 2-16 contains parts of *system.twmrc*, which defines a default options menu, defops, and a submenu that starts various X terminals.

Example 2-16: Menu Configuration in system.twmrc

```
menu "defops"
{
"Twm"          f.title
"Netscape"     f.exec "netscape &"
"Terminals"    f.menu "Terms"
}

menu "Terms"
{
"Aterm"        f.exec "exec aterm &"
"Kvt"          f.exec "exec kvt &"
"Xterm"        f.exec "exec xterm &"}
```

For complete information on **twm**, see its manpage (**man twm**).

On the Exam

This Objective requires that you have a general understanding of the configuration of menus for a window manager. You will not be required to generate window manager configuration files for the test, but you should be aware of the need to edit and modify them.

---

xterm et al.

One of the most important applications available to a system administrator working in a graphical environment is a *terminal emulator*. The standard terminal emulator distributed with X is **xterm**, which understands DEC VT and Tektronix graphics terminal protocols. The VT behavior that is emulated includes cursor positioning, character effects, and reverse video, among others. In essence, an **xterm** is a direct replacement for a hardware terminal.

xterm has a large resource configuration file located in */usr/lib/X11/app-defaults/XTerm* that contains configurable menus, fonts, colors, and actions. You may customize this file to alter the default behavior of **xterm** on your system. These settings can also be overridden by resource settings contained in your own *.Xdefaults* file, located in your home directory.

On the Exam

You should be familiar with at least one of the popular X terminal programs available on your Linux system. Remember that some programs have system-wide configuration files that can be used to fine-tune their behavior and appearance.

X Libraries

Just as many executable programs are dependent upon shared system libraries for their execution, most X applications require a number of X-specific libraries. XFree86 comes bundled with the necessary set of libraries for traditional X applications. However, many graphical programming projects are created using toolkits whose libraries are not included in the XFree86 distribution. In these cases, you need to install the required libraries before programs requiring them will compile or execute.

For example, the GIMP Toolkit (GTK) is used to build much of the GNOME desktop environment. This means that GTK must be installed on the system in order to run GNOME applications, including The GIMP (*http://www.gimp.org*).

Library dependency issues typically occur when you try new software. Either the compiler fails as you attempt to build the program, or the loader fails when you try to run a precompiled dynamic binary. In either case, you need to locate the correct version of the libraries and install them. It should be relatively easy to find recent versions of the popular libraries in your distribution's package format by visiting web sites of the library distributor or your Linux distribution.

To manually check for library dependencies, you may use the **ldd** utility, described fully in "Part 2: *Linux Installation and Package Management (Topic 2.2),* Objective 4: Manage Shared Libraries."

Remote X Clients

One of the fundamental design elements of the X Window System is that it is a network protocol, which allows for displays to occur remotely across a network. Many sites employ high-powered systems for computation and use desktop X servers (X terminals or Linux systems, for example) for display rendering.

To send the output from an X application to a remote machine, you need to set the display environment variable.[*] This variable contains a description of the output destination and has three components.

> [*host*]:*display*[.*screen*]

host
> This part of the description specifies the remote hostname on the network. It can be any valid hostname, fully qualified domain name, or IP address. host is optional; the local system is used if the host is not specified.

display
> This specifies which display the output should be directed toward. A single system can manage many displays. Note that the colon is required even if the host is omitted.

screen
> This optional parameter is used for multiheaded systems (i.e., systems with more than one monitor) and specifies on which output screen the application will appear.

---

[*] Many X programs also include a command-line option to select the display.

Setting `display` to "point to" a remote host display causes all subsequent X applications to be displayed there. For example:

```
# export DISPLAY=yourhost:0.0
# xterm
```

In this example, the **xterm** is displayed on the first display on *yourhost*.[*]

Examples

The default display on the local host:

```
:0
```

The default display on a remote host:

```
yourhost:0
```

Display programs on the first screen of the second display found on the machine located at 192.168.1.2:

```
192.168.1.2:1.0
```

Display programs on the first screen of the third display on *yourhost*:

```
yourhost:2.0
```

On the Exam

You must be familiar with the `display` environment variable and how to use it to direct X client applications to remote X servers.

---

[*] This example ignores X authentication issues.

Networking Fundamentals
(Topic 1.12)

While it is not necessary for you to be a networking expert to pass the LPIC Level 1 exams, you must be familiar with networking, network-related vocabulary, and Linux networking configuration. This section introduces fundamental networking, troubleshooting, and dialup concepts specifically included in the exams. However, it is not a complete introductory treatment, and you are encouraged to review additional material for more depth. This section covers these three Objectives:

Objective 1: Fundamentals of TCP/IP
    This Objective includes TCP/IP basics such as network masks, ports, and utility programs. Weight: 4.

Objective 2: (Superseded by LPI.)
    An Objective 2 was originally included by the LPI in this Topic, but was later superseded by other Objectives. It remains in place to keep Objective numbering historically consistent and is likewise included here.

Objective 3: TCP/IP Troubleshooting and Configuration
    This Objective describes how to configure Linux network interfaces, including DHCP. Weight: 10.

Objective 4: Configure and Use PPP.
    This Objective includes the description of PPP client and server configuration. Weight: 4.

What follows is not a complete treatment of TCP/IP, but rather a refresher of its core concepts as they apply to Exam 102.

Objective 1: Fundamentals of TCP/IP

The TCP/IP suite of protocols was adopted as a military standard in 1983 and has since become the world standard for network communications on the Internet and on many LANs, replacing proprietary protocols in many cases. Much has been written about TCP/IP and the history of the Internet. This section includes only material cited by LPI Objectives.

Addressing and Masks

The early specification of the Internet Protocol (IP) recognized that it would be necessary to divide one's given allotment of IP addresses into manageable subnetworks. Such division allows for distributed management, added security (fewer hosts can potentially snoop network traffic), and the use of multiple networking technologies (Ethernet, Token Ring, ATM, etc.). IP also enables convenient partitioning of the physical portions of a network across physical and geographical boundaries. To provide the capability to locally define networks, IP addresses are considered as having two distinct parts: the part that specifies a *subnet* and the one that specifies a network interface.* The boundary between the network and host portions of an IP address is delineated by a *subnet mask*, required by the TCP/IP configuration of any network interface. Like the IP address, the subnet mask is simply a 32-bit number specified in four 8-bit segments using *dotted quad* decimal notation. The familiar class A, B, and C networks have these subnet masks:

Class A: 255.0.0.0 (binary 11111111.00000000.00000000.00000000)
   8-bit network address and 24-bit host address

Class B: 255.255.0.0 (binary 11111111.11111111.00000000.00000000)
   16-bit network address and 16-bit host address

Class C: 255.255.255.0 (binary 11111111.11111111.11111111.00000000)
   24-bit network address and 8-bit host address

When logically AND'd with an IP address, the bits set to 0 in the subnet mask obscure the host portion of the address. The remaining bits represent the *network address*. For example, a host on a class C network might have an IP address of 192.168.1.127. Applying the class C subnet mask 255.255.255.0, the network address of the subnet would be 192.168.1.0, and the host address would be 127, as depicted in Figure 2-7.

Address	192.168.1.127	11000000.10101000.00000001.01111111
Mask	255.255.255.0	11111111.11111111.11111111.00000000
Network Address	192.168.1.0	11000000.10101011.00000001.00000000
Host Interface Address	127	01111111

Figure 2-7: Host interface address calculation

While it is typical to use the predefined classes (A, B, and C), the boundary can be moved left or right in the IP address, allowing for fewer or more subnets, respectively. For example, if a single additional bit were added to the class C subnet mask, its IP address would be:

---

* Remember that IP addresses are assigned to network interfaces, not host computers, which can have multiple interfaces. For this discussion, however, we assume a 1:1 relationship between hosts and interfaces.

255.255.255.128 (binary 11111111.11111111.11111111.10000000)
   25-bit network address and 7-bit host address

With such a subnet defined on an existing class C network such as 192.168.1.0, the 256-bit range is split into two subnets, each with seven host bits. The first of the two subnets begins at 192.168.1.0 (the subnet address) and continues through 192.168.1.127 (the subnet broadcast address). The second subnet runs from 192.168.1.128 through 192.168.1.255. Each of the two subnets can accommodate 126 hosts. To extend this example, consider two additional bits:

255.255.255.192 (binary 11111111.11111111.11111111.11000000)
   26-bit network address and 6-bit host address

When applied to a class C network, four subnets are created, each with six host bits. Just as before, the first subnet begins at 192.168.1.0 but continues only through 192.168.1.63. The next subnet runs from 192.168.1.64 through 192.168.1.127 and so on. Each of the four subnets can accommodate 62 hosts. Table 2-18 shows more detail on class C subnets, considering only the host portion of the address.

Table 2-18: Class C IP Subnet Detail

Subnet Mask	Number of Subnets	Network Address	Broadcast Address	Minimum IP Address	Maximum IP Address	Number of Hosts	Total Hosts
128	2	0	127	1	126	126	
		128	255	129	254	126	252
192	4	0	63	1	62	62	
		64	127	65	126	62	
		128	191	129	190	62	
		192	255	193	254	62	248
224	8	0	31	1	30	30	
		32	63	33	62	30	
		64	95	65	94	30	
		96	127	97	126	30	
		128	159	129	158	30	
		160	191	161	190	30	
		192	223	193	222	30	
		224	255	225	254	30	240

On the Exam

Be prepared to define network and host addresses when provided an IP address and a subnet mask. Practice with a few subnet sizes within at least one classification (A, B, or C). Also, because the use of decimal notation can cloud human interpretation of IP addresses and masks, be ready to do binary-to-decimal conversion on address numbers.

As you can see, as the number of subnets increases, the total number of hosts that can be deployed within the original class C address range reduces. This is due to the loss of both broadcast addresses and network addresses to the additional subnets.

Protocols

TCP/IP is a suite of protocols, including the Transmission Control Protocol (TCP), Internet Protocol (IP), User Datagram Protocol (UDP), and Internet Control Message Protocol (ICMP), among others. Some protocols use *handshaking* (the exchange of control information among communicating systems) to establish and maintain a connection. Such a protocol is said to be *connection-oriented* and *reliable*, because the protocol itself is responsible for handling transmission errors, lost packets, and packet arrival order. A protocol that does not exchange control information is said to be *connectionless* and *unreliable*. In this context, "unreliable" simply means that the protocol doesn't handle transmission problems itself; they must be corrected in the application or system libraries. Connectionless protocols are simpler and have less overhead than connection-oriented protocols. TCP/IP is often said to be a *stack* of protocols, because protocols are built in a hierarchy of *layers*. Low-level protocols are used by higher-level protocols on adjacent layers of the protocol stack:

TCP

TCP is a connection-oriented transport agent used by applications to establish a network connection. TCP transports information across networks by handshaking and retransmitting information as needed in response to errors on the network. TCP guarantees packet arrival and provides for the correct ordering of received packets. TCP is used by many network services, including FTP, Telnet, and SMTP. By using TCP, these applications don't need to establish their own error-checking mechanisms, thus making their design simpler and easier to manage.

IP

IP[*] can be thought of as the fundamental building block of the Internet. IP, which is connectionless, defines datagrams (the basic unit of transmission), establishes the addressing scheme (the IP address), and provides for the routing of datagrams between networks.[†] IP is said to provide a *datagram delivery service*. Other higher-level protocols use IP as an underlying carrier.

UDP

UDP is a connectionless transport agent. It provides application programs direct access to IP, allowing them to exchange information with a minimum of protocol overhead. On the other hand, because UDP offers no assurance that packets arrive at destinations as intended, software must manage transmission errors and other problems such as missing and incorrectly ordered packets. UDP is used by applications such as DNS and NFS.

---

[*] IP is not specifically mentioned in this LPI Objective, but its fundamental importance warrants its mention here.

[†] This is an oversimplification of IP, of course, but you get the idea.

ICMP

ICMP is a connectionless transport agent that is used to exchange control information among networked systems. It uses IP datagrams for the following control, error-reporting, and informational functions:

Flow control

Sometimes inbound traffic becomes too heavy for a receiving system to process. In such cases, the receiving system can send a message via ICMP to the source instructing it to temporarily stop sending datagrams.

Detecting unreachable destinations

Various parts of network infrastructure are capable of detecting that a network destination is unreachable. In this case, ICMP messages are sent to the requesting system.

Redirecting routes

ICMP is used among network components to instruct a sender to use a different gateway.

Checking remote hosts

Hosts can transmit echo messages via ICMP to verify that a remote system's Internet Protocol is functioning. If so, the original message is returned. This is implemented in the **ping** command.

PPP

PPP is used for TCP/IP dialup network access via modem. The configuration and use of PPP is described later in Objective 4.

On the Exam

You will need a general understanding of the control messages sent via ICMP. In particular, note that ICMP does not transmit data and that it is used by **ping**.

TCP/IP Services

When an inbound network request is made, such as that from a web browser or *FTP* client, it is sent to the IP address of the server. In addition, the request carries inside it a *port number* (or just *port*), which is a 16-bit value placed near the beginning of a network packet. The port number defines the type of server software that should respond to the request. For example, by default, web browsers send requests encoded for port 80.* Web servers "listen" to port 80 and respond to incoming requests. The encoded port can be considered part of the address of a request. While the IP address specifies a particular host,† the port specifies a specific service available on that host. Many port numbers are predefined, and the list is expanded as needed to accommodate new technologies. The official list of

---

* Port numbers are usually referred to in decimal notation.

† Well, actually a particular interface.

---

port number assignments is managed by the Internet Assigned Numbers Authority (IANA). The ports known by your system are listed in */etc/services.*

Port numbers 1 through 1023 are often referred to as *privileged ports* because the services that use them often run with superuser authority. Many of these, such as ports used for FTP (21), Telnet (23), and HTTP (80), are often referred to as *well-known ports* because they are standards. Port numbers from 1024 through 65535 (the maximum) are *unprivileged ports* and can be used by applications run by ordinary system users.

During the initial contact, the client includes a local, randomly selected, unprivileged port on the client machine for the server to use when responding to the request. Client-to-server communications use the well-known port and the server-to-client communications use the randomly selected port. This Objective requires you to be familiar with the privileged port numbers detailed in Table 2-19.

Table 2-19: Common Privileged Port Numbers

Port Number	Assigned Use	Description
20	FTP data	When an FTP session is opened, the binary or ASCII data flows to the server using port 20, while control information flows on port 21. During use, both ports are managed by an *ftp daemon*, such as **wu-ftpd** or **PROftpd**.
21	FTP control	
23	Telnet server	Inbound Telnet requests are sent to server port 23 and processed by **telnetd**.
25	SMTP server	This port is used by mail transfer agents (MTAs) such as sendmail.
53	DNS server	Used by the Domain Name System server, **named**.
67	BOOTP/DHCP server	A BOOTP, or the more commonly used, DHCP server.
68	BOOTP/DHCP client	The client side for BOOTP/DHCP.
80	HTTP server	Web servers, such as Apache (**httpd**), usually listen in on this port.
110	POP3	The Post Office Protocol (POP) is used by mail client programs to transfer mail from a server.
119	NNTP Server	This port is used by news servers for Usenet news.
139	NetBIOS	Reserved for Microsoft's LAN network manager.
143	IMAP	An alternate to POP3, IMAP is another type of mail server.
161	SNMP	Agents running on monitored systems use this port for access to the Simple Network Management Protocol.

This list is a tiny fraction of the many well-known ports, but it may be necessary for you to know them both by name and by number.

On the Exam

You should commit the list of ports in Table 2-19 to memory so you can recognize a type of network connection solely by its port number. Your exam is likely to have at least one question on how a specific port is used.

TCP/IP Utilities

The following popular applications, while not strictly a part of TCP/IP, are usually provided along with a TCP/IP implementation.

---

dig

Syntax

dig *hostname*

Description

dig obtains information from DNS servers. Note that additional command-line arguments and options are available for **dig** but are beyond the scope of Exam 102.

Example

```
$ dig redhat.com

; <<>> DiG 8.2 <<>> redhat.com any
;; res options: init recurs defnam dnsrch
;; got answer:
;; ->>HEADER<<- opcode: QUERY, status: NOERROR, id: 6
;; flags: qr rd ra; QUERY: 1, ANSWER: 6, AUTHORITY: 4,
;; ADDITIONAL: 5 QUERY SECTION:
;;      redhat.com, type = ANY, class = IN

;; ANSWER SECTION:
redhat.com.             22h36m45s IN NS  ns.redhat.com.
redhat.com.             22h36m45s IN NS  ns2.redhat.com.
redhat.com.             22h36m45s IN NS  ns3.redhat.com.
redhat.com.             22h36m45s IN NS  speedy.redhat.com.
redhat.com.             23h48m10s IN MX  10 mail.redhat.com.
redhat.com.             23h48m10s IN A   207.175.42.154

;; AUTHORITY SECTION:
redhat.com.             22h36m45s IN NS  ns.redhat.com.
redhat.com.             22h36m45s IN NS  ns2.redhat.com.
redhat.com.             22h36m45s IN NS  ns3.redhat.com.
redhat.com.             22h36m45s IN NS  speedy.redhat.com.

;; ADDITIONAL SECTION:
ns.redhat.com.          1d23h48m10s IN A   207.175.42.153
```

```
ns2.redhat.com.          1d23h48m10s IN A  208.178.165.229
ns3.redhat.com.          1d23h48m10s IN A  206.132.41.213
speedy.redhat.com.       23h48m10s IN A  199.183.24.251
mail.redhat.com.         23h48m10s IN A  199.183.24.239

;; Total query time: 81 msec
;; FROM: smp to SERVER: default -- 209.195.201.3
;; WHEN: Wed Apr  5 03:15:03 2000
;; MSG SIZE  sent: 28  rcvd: 275
```

ftp

Syntax

```
ftp [options] host
...interactive commands...
```

Description

Establish an interactive File Transfer Protocol (FTP) connection with *host* in order to transfer binary or text files. FTP creates an interactive dialog and allows for two-way file transfer. The dialog includes username/password authentication, user commands, and server responses.

Frequently used options

–i

Turns off interactive prompting during multiple file transfers (also see the **prompt** command).

–v

Sets verbose mode, displays server responses and transfer statistics.

Frequently used commands

ascii, binary

Establish the transfer mode for files. ASCII mode is provided to correctly transfer text among computer architectures where character encoding differs.

get *file*

Receive a single *file* from the server.

mget *files*

Receive multiple *files* from the server.

ls [*files*]

Obtain a directory listing from the server, optionally listing *files*.

put *file*

Send a single *file* to the server

mput *files*

Send multiple *files* to the server.

prompt

Toggle on and off interactive prompting during **mget** and **mput** (also see the –i option).

pwd

Print the working remote directory.

quit, exit

Cleanly terminate the *FTP* session.

Example 1

Get a file from machine **smp**:

```
$ ftp -v smp
Connected to smp.
220 smp FTP server (Version wu-2.4.2-VR17(1)
Mon Apr 19 09:21:53 EDT 1999) ready.
Name (smp:root): jdean
331 Password required for jdean.
Password:<password here>
230 User jdean logged in.
Remote system type is UNIX.
Using binary mode to transfer files.
ftp> ls myfile
200 PORT command successful.
150 Opening ASCII mode data connection for /bin/ls.
-rw-r--r--   1 jdean     jdean          29 Jan 24 01:28 myfile
226 Transfer complete.
ftp> binary
200 Type set to I.
ftp> get myfile
local: myfile remote: myfile
200 PORT command successful.
150 Opening BINARY mode data connection for myfile
(29 bytes).
226 Transfer complete.
29 bytes received in 0.000176 secs (1.6e+02 Kbytes/sec)
ftp> quit
221-You have transferred 29 bytes in 1 files.
221-Total traffic for this session was 773 bytes in 3 transfers.
221-Thank you for using the FTP service on smp.
221 Goodbye.
```

Example 2

Many FTP servers are set up to receive requests from nonauthenticated users. Such public access is said to be *anonymous*. Anonymous FTP is established just like any FTP connection, except that anonymous is used as the username. An email address is commonly used as a password to let the system owner know who is transferring files:

```
# ftp -v smp
Connected to smp.
220 smp FTP server (Version wu-2.4.2-VR17(1)
Mon Apr 19 09:21:53 EDT 1999) ready.
Name (smp:root): anonymous
```

```
331 Guest login ok, send your complete e-mail address as password.
Password: me@mydomain.com
230 Guest login ok, access restrictions apply.
Remote system type is UNIX.
Using binary mode to transfer files.
ftp> <commands follow...>
```

ping

Syntax

ping *hostname*

Description

The **ping** command is used to send an ICMP echo request to *hostname* and report
on how long it takes to receive a corresponding ICMP echo reply. Much like sonar
systems send a pulse (or "ping") to a target and measure transit time, **ping** sends a
network packet to test the availability of a network node. This technique is often
used as a basic debugging technique when network problems arise.

Example

Ping a remote host and terminate using **Ctrl-C** after five packets are transmitted:

```
$ ping lpi.org
PING lpi.org (209.167.177.93) from 192.168.1.30 :
   56(84) bytes of data.
64 bytes from new.lpi.org (209.167.177.93):
   icmp_seq=0 ttl=240 time=51.959 msec
64 bytes from new.lpi.org (209.167.177.93):
   icmp_seq=1 ttl=240 time=60.967 msec
64 bytes from new.lpi.org (209.167.177.93):
   icmp_seq=2 ttl=240 time=47.173 msec
64 bytes from new.lpi.org (209.167.177.93):
   icmp_seq=3 ttl=240 time=46.887 msec
64 bytes from new.lpi.org (209.167.177.93):
   icmp_seq=4 ttl=240 time=46.836 msec

--- lpi.org ping statistics ---
5 packets transmitted, 5 packets received, 0% packet loss
round-trip min/avg/max/mdev = 46.836/50.764/60.967/5.460 ms
```

telnet

Syntax

telnet [*host*] [*port*]

Description

Establish a connection to *host* (either a system name or IP address) using *port*. If a
specific *port* is omitted, the default port of 23 is assumed. If *host* is omitted, **telnet**
goes into an interactive mode similar to ftp.

traceroute

Syntax

```
traceroute hostname
```

Description

Attempt to display the route over which packets must travel to reach a destination *hostname*. It is included here because it is mentioned in this Objective, but Objective 3 also requires **traceroute**. See the synopsis in Objective 3 for full information.

whois

Syntax

```
whois   target[@server]
fwhois  target[@server]
```

Description

Query the **whois** database for *target*. Such a database contains information on domain names, assigned IP addresses, and people associated with them. In the early days of the Internet, when domain registration was handled solely by the Internet Network Information Center (InterNIC), *server* was understood to be that of the InterNIC. Additional registrars now exist to process domain registrations, some of which have their own **whois** databases for public access.

The version of **whois** provided with Linux is a link to **fwhois**. *target* is a domain name or user *handle*. *server* is a valid **whois** server, which defaults to *rs.internic.net*. The information returned includes contact information, domain names, IP addresses, and DNS servers. Note that many web sites are available for **whois** searches as well, particularly for checking on domain name availability.

Example

```
$ fwhois linuxdoc.org@whois.networksolutions.com
Registrant:
Linux Documentation Project (LINUXDOC-DOM)
    4428 NE 74th Ave.
    Portland, OR 97218
    US
    Domain Name: LINUXDOC.ORG
    Administrative Contact, Technical Contact, Zone Contact:

        Account, Hostmaster  (AH243-ORG)
          hostmaster@LINUXPORTS.COM
        Command Prompt Software
        4428 NE 74th Ave.
        Portland, OR 97218
        US
          (503)493-1611
    Billing Contact:
```

```
Account, Hostmaster   (AH243-ORG)
   hostmaster@LINUXPORTS.COM
Command Prompt Software
4428 NE 74th Ave.
Portland, OR 97218
US
   (503)493-1611
Record last updated on 15-Feb-2000
Record created on 20-Feb-1999
Database last updated on 5-Apr-2000 12:51:28 EDT
Domain servers in listed order:
NS1.OPENDOCS.ORG          209.102.107.110
NS1.INETARENA.COM         206.129.216.1
NS.UNC.EDU                152.2.21.1
```

On the Exam

You must have a working knowledge of when and how to use the **dig**, **ftp**, **ping**, **telnet**, **traceroute**, and **whois** commands. Practice using any that you are unfamiliar with by experimenting on a working networked system.

Objective 3: TCP/IP Troubleshooting and Configuration

Linux distributions offer various automation and startup techniques for networks, but most of the essential commands and concepts are not distribution-dependent. The exam tests fundamental concepts and their relationships to one another as well as to system problems. This Objective covers the configuration of TCP/IP on common network interfaces such as Ethernet.

Network Interfaces

A computer must contain at least one *network interface* to be considered part of a network. The network interface provides a communications link between the computer and external network hardware. This could mean typical network adapters such as Ethernet or Token Ring, PPP dialup connections, parallel ports, wireless, and other networking forms.

Configuration files

The following files contain important information about your system's network configuration:

/etc/hostname (or sometimes /etc/HOSTNAME)
   This file contains the local assigned hostname for the system.

/etc/hosts

This file contains simple mappings between IP addresses and names and is used for name resolution. For very small private networks, */etc/hosts* may be sufficient for basic name resolution. For example, this file associates the local address 192.168.1.30 with the system smp and also with smp.mydomain.com:

```
127.0.0.1       localhost       localhost.localdomain
192.168.1.1     gate
192.168.1.30    smp smp.mydomain.com
```

/etc/nsswitch.conf

This file controls the sources used by various system library lookup functions, such as name resolution. It allows the administrator to configure the use of traditional local files (*/etc/hosts*, */etc/passwd*), an NIS server, or DNS. *nsswitch.conf* directly affects network configuration (among other things) by controlling how hostnames and other network parameters are resolved. For example, this fragment shows that local files are used for password, shadow password, group, and hostname resolution; for hostnames, DNS is used if a search of local files doesn't yield a result:

```
passwd:     files nisplus nis
shadow:     files nisplus nis
group:      files nisplus nis
hosts:      files dns nisplus nis
```

For more information, view the manpage with **man 5 nsswitch**. The *nsswitch.conf* file supersedes *host.conf*.

/etc/host.conf

This file controls name resolution sources for pre-*glibc2* systems. It should contain:

```
order hosts,bind
multi on
```

This configuration has the resolver checking */etc/hosts* first for name resolution, then DNS. multi on enables multiple IP addresses for hosts. Newer Linux system libraries use */etc/nsswitch.conf* instead of */etc/host.conf*.

/etc/resolv.conf

This file controls the client-side portions of the DNS system, which is implemented in system library functions used by all programs to resolve system names. In particular, */etc/resolv.conf* specifies the IP addresses of DNS servers. For example:

```
nameserver 192.168.1.5
nameserver 192.168.250.2
```

Additional parameters are also available. For more information, view the manpage with **man 5 resolver**.

/etc/networks

Like */etc/hosts*, this file sets up equivalence between addresses and names, but here the addresses represent entire networks (and thus must be valid network addresses, ending in 0). The result is that you can use a symbolic name to refer to a network just as you would a specific host. This may be convenient (though not required) in NFS or routing configuration, for example, and will be shown in commands such as **netstat**. For example:

```
loopback    127.0.0.0
mylan       192.168.1.0
```

It's not unusual for */etc/networks* to be left blank.

On the Exam

Be familiar with all the files listed in this section; each contains specific information important for network setup. Watch for questions on */etc/ host.conf*, which is not used in newer *glibc2* libraries.

Configuration commands

The commands listed in this section are used to establish, monitor, and trouble-shoot a network configuration under Linux.

---

host

Syntax

host [*options*] *host* [*server*]

Description

Look up the system with IP address or name *host* on the DNS *server*.

Frequently used options

-l

List the entire domain, dumping all hosts registered on the DNS server (this can be very long).

-v

Set verbose mode to view output.

Example 1

```
$ host oreilly.com
oreilly.com has address 204.148.40.5
```

Example 2

```
$ host -v oreilly.com
Trying null domain
rcode = 0 (Success), ancount=1
The following answer is not authoritative:
The following answer is not verified as authentic by the server:
oreilly.com     17397 IN        A       204.148.40.5
For authoritative answers, see:
```

```
oreilly.com    168597 IN      NS      AUTH03.NS.UU.NET
oreilly.com    168597 IN      NS      NS.oreilly.com
Additional information:
AUTH03.NS.UU.NET        168838 IN      A       198.6.1.83
NS.oreilly.com  168597 IN      A       204.148.40.4 $
```

See also the **nslookup** command in the section "DNS query utilities," in "Part 2: *Networking Services (Topic 1.13)*, Objective 5: Set Up and Configure Basic DNS Services."

hostname, domainname, dnsdomainname

Syntax

hostname [*localname*]
domainname [*nisname*]
dnsdomainname

Description

Set or display the current host, domain, or node name of the system. This is a single program with links defining additional names. When called as **hostname**, the system's hostname is displayed. If *localname* is provided, the hostname is set. **domainname** displays or sets the NIS domain name. **dnsdomainname** displays the current DNS domain name but does not set it. See **man 1 hostname** for full information.

ifconfig

Syntax

ifconfig *interface parameters*

Description

Configure network interfaces. **ifconfig** is used to create and configure *interfaces* and their parameters, usually at boot time. Without *parameters*, the interface and its configuration are displayed. If *interface* is also omitted, a list of all active interfaces and their configurations is displayed.

Frequently used parameters

address
> The *interface*'s IP address.

netmask *mask*
> The *interface*'s subnet mask.

up
> Activate an *interface* (implied if **address** is specified).

down
> Shut down the driver for the *interface*.

Example 1

Display all interfaces:

```
# ifconfig
eth0      Link encap:Ethernet  HWaddr 00:A0:24:D3:C7:21
          inet addr:192.168.1.30  Bcast:192.168.1.255
          Mask:255.255.255.0
          UP BROADCAST RUNNING MULTICAST  MTU:1500  Metric:1
          RX packets:1521805 errors:37 dropped:0
          overruns:0 frame:37
          TX packets:715468 errors:0 dropped:0 overruns:0
          carrier:0
          collisions:1955 txqueuelen:100
          Interrupt:10 Base address:0xef00

lo        Link encap:Local Loopback
          inet addr:127.0.0.1  Mask:255.0.0.0
          UP LOOPBACK RUNNING  MTU:3924  Metric:1
          RX packets:366567 errors:0 dropped:0 overruns:0
          frame:0
          TX packets:366567 errors:0 dropped:0 overruns:0
          carrier:0
          collisions:0 txqueuelen:0
```

Example 2

Shut down eth0:

```
# ifconfig eth0 down
# ifconfig eth0
eth0      Link encap:Ethernet  HWaddr 00:A0:24:D3:C7:21
          inet addr:192.168.1.30  Bcast:192.168.1.255
          Mask:255.255.255.0
          BROADCAST MULTICAST  MTU:1500  Metric:1
          RX packets:1521901 errors:37 dropped:0
          overruns:0 frame:37
          TX packets:715476 errors:0 dropped:0 overruns:0
          carrier:0
          collisions:1955 txqueuelen:100
          Interrupt:10 Base address:0xef00
```

Note in the emphasized line the lack of the UP indicator, which is present in Example 1. The missing UP indicates that the interface is down.

Example 3

Configure eth0 from scratch:

```
# ifconfig eth0 192.168.1.100 netmask 255.255.255.0
     broadcast 192.168.1.255
```

---

netstat

Syntax

```
netstat [options]
```

Description

Depending on options, **netstat** displays network connections, routing tables, interface statistics, masquerade connections, netlink messages, and multicast memberships. Much of this is beyond the scope of the LPIC Level 1 exams, but you must be aware of the command and its basic use.

Frequently used options

-c

Continuous operation. This option yields a **netstat** display every second until interrupted with **Ctrl-C**.

-i

Display a list of interfaces.

-n

Numeric mode. Display addresses instead of host, port, and usernames.

-p

Programs mode. Display the PID and process name.

-r

Routing mode. Display the routing table in the format of the *route* command.

-v

Verbose mode.

Example

Display the interfaces table and statistics (the example output is truncated):

```
# netstat -i
Kernel interface table
Iface MTU  Met     RX-OK RX-ERR RX-DRP RX-OVR  TX-OK
eth0  1500 0     1518801     37      0      0 713297
lo    3924 0      365816      0      0      0 365816
```

ping

Syntax

ping [*options*] *destination*

Description

Send an ICMP ECHO_REQUEST datagram to *destination*, expecting an ICMP ECHO_RESPONSE. **ping** is frequently used to test basic network connectivity.

Frequently used options

-c *count*

Send and receive *count* packets.

-q

Quiet output. Display only summary lines when **ping** starts and finishes.

route

Syntax

```
route [options]
route add [options and keywords] target
route del [options and keywords] target
```

Description

In the first form, display the IP routing table. In the second and third forms, respectively add or delete routes to *target* from the table. *target* can be a numeric IP address, a resolvable name, or the keyword *default*. The **route** program is typically used to establish static routes to specific networks or hosts (such as the default gateway) after an interface is configured. On systems acting as routers, a potentially complex routing scheme can be established initially, but this is beyond the scope of the LPIC Level 1 exams.

Frequently used options and keywords

-v
> Verbose output.

-h
> Display a usage message.

-n
> Numeric mode; don't resolve hostnames.

-net
> Specify that *target* is a network. Mutually exclusive with **-host**.

-host
> Specify that *target* is a single host. Mutually exclusive with **-net**.

-F
> Display the kernel routing table (the default behavior without *add* or *delete* keywords).

-C
> Display the kernel routing cache.

netmask *mask*
> Specify the *mask* of the route to be added. Often, the netmask is not required because it can be determined to be class A, B, or C, depending on the *target* address.

gw *gateway*
> IP packets for *target* are routed through *gateway*, which must be reachable, probably through a static route to *gateway*, which is already established.

When used to display routes, the following routing table columns are printed:

Destination
> The destination network or host.

Gateway
> The gateway address. If no gateway is set for the route, an asterisk (*) is displayed by default.

Genmask

The netmask for the destination. 255.255.255.255 is used for a host and 0.0.0.0 is used for the default route.

Route status flags

U

Route is up.

H

Target is a host.

G

Use gateway.

R

Reinstate route for dynamic routing.

D

Dynamically installed by daemon or redirect.

M

Modified from routing daemon or redirect.

!

Reject route.

Metric

The distance in hops to the target.

Ref

Number of references to this route. This is displayed for compatibility with other route commands but is not used in the Linux kernel.

Use

A count of lookups for the route. Depending on the use of **-F** and -C, the Use is either route cache misses (**-F**) or hits (-C).

Iface

The interface to which packets for this route are sent.

Example 1

Display the current routing table for a workstation:

```
# route
Kernel IP routing table
Destination  Gateway Genmask          Flags Met Ref Use Iface
192.168.1.30 *       255.255.255.255  UH    0   0     0 eth0
192.168.1.0  *       255.255.255.0    U     0   0     0 eth0
10.0.0.0     -       255.0.0.0        !     0   -     0 -
127.0.0.0    *       255.0.0.0        U     0   0     0 lo
default      gate    0.0.0.0          UG    0   0     0 eth0
```

In this example, the route to the local host 192.168.1.30 uses interface eth0. Note the mask 255.255.255.255 is used for host routes. The route to the local subnet 192.168.1.0 (with corresponding class C mask 255.255.255.0) is also through eth0. The route to 10.0.0.0 is rejected as indicated by the ! flag. The class A loopback network route uses device lo. The last route shows the *default gateway* route, which is used when no others match. This default uses eth0 to send data to router gate. The mask 0.0.0.0 is used for the default route.

Example 2

Display the current routing cache; the Metric (M) and Reference (R) columns are abbreviated here:

```
# route -C
Kernel IP routing cache
Source         Destination    Gateway        Flg M R Use Iface
smp            192.168.1.255 192.168.1.255 bl  0 0   1 eth0
192.168.1.102 192.168.1.255 192.168.1.255 ibl 0 0   0 lo
192.168.1.102 smp           smp            il  0 0   1 lo
192.168.1.50  smp           smp            il  0 0 224 lo
smp           192.168.1.102 192.168.1.102     0 1   0 eth0
smp           ns1.mynet.com gate              0 0   2 eth0
smp           192.168.1.50  192.168.1.50      0 1   0 eth0
localhost     localhost     localhost      1  0 0  15 lo
ns1.mynet.com smp           smp            1  0 0   6 lo
smp           ns1.mynet.com gate              0 0   6 eth0
```

Example 3

Add the default gateway 192.168.1.1 via eth0:

```
# route add default gw 192.168.1.1 eth0
```

---

traceroute

Syntax

```
traceroute [options] destination
```

Description

Display the route that packets take to reach *destination*, showing intermediate gateways (routers). There isn't a direct method to use to make this determination, so **traceroute** uses a trick to obtain as much information as it can. By using the *time-to-live* field in the IP header, **traceroute** stimulates error responses from gateways. The time-to-live field specifies the maximum number of gateway hops until the packet should expire. That number is decremented at each gateway hop, with the result that all packets will die at some point and not roam the Internet. To get the first gateway in the route, **traceroute** sets the time-to-live parameter to 1. The first gateway in the route to *destination* decrements the counter, and finding a 0 result, reports an ICMP TIME_EXCEEDED message back to the sending host. The second gateway is identified by setting the initial time-to-live value to 2 and so on. This continues until a PORT_UNREACHABLE message is returned, indicating that the host has been contacted. To account for the potential for multiple gateways at any one hop count, each probe is sent three times.

The display consists of lines showing each gateway, numbered for the initial time-to-live value. If no response is seen from a particular gateway, an asterisk is printed. This happens for gateways that don't return "time exceeded" messages, or do return them but set a very low time-to-live on the response. Transit times for each probe are also printed.

Frequently used options

-f *ttl*

> Set the initial probe's time-to-live value to *ttl*, instead of 1.

-n

> Display numeric addresses instead of names.

-v

> Use verbose mode.

-w *secs*

> Set the timeout on returned ICMP packets to *secs*, instead of 5.

Example

```
# traceroute www.lpi.org
traceroute to www.lpi.org (209.167.177.93),
 30 hops max, 40 byte packets
 1  gate (192.168.1.1)
        3.181 ms  1.200 ms  1.104 ms
 2  209.125.145.1 (209.125.135.1)
        16.041 ms  15.149 ms  14.747 ms
 3  a1-9-1-0-1.a01.phl1.us.io.net (137.94.47.1)
        84.132 ms  133.937 ms  77.865 ms
 4  ge-6-0.r01.phlapa01.us.io.net (126.250.29.17)
        22.450 ms  16.114 ms  16.051 ms
 5  p4-6-0-0.r01.nycmny01.us.bb.verio.net (129.250.3.126)
        18.043 ms  18.485 ms  18.175 ms
 6  nyc1.uunet.verio.net (129.250.9.62)
        19.735 ms  21.135 ms  19.212 ms
 7  105.ATM3-0.XR1.NYC1.ALTER.NET (146.188.177.154)
        20.237 ms  18.515 ms  18.712 ms
 8  295.ATM6-0.XR1.NYC4.ALTER.NET (146.188.178.90)
        26.855 ms  29.540 ms  35.908 ms
 9  189.ATM8-0-0.GW5.NYC4.ALTER.NET (146.188.179.225)
        36.541 ms  36.127 ms  30.849 ms
10  224.ATM1-0-0.BB1.TOR2.UUNET.CA.ALTER.NET (137.39.75.26)
        58.823 ms  68.675 ms  62.522 ms
11  f0-0-0.bb2.tor2.uunet.ca (205.150.242.110)
        336.310 ms  174.557 ms  394.909 ms
12  209.167.167.118 (209.167.167.118)
        56.027 ms  58.555 ms  56.289 ms
13  209.167.177.90 (209.167.177.90)
        59.349 ms  57.409 ms  57.993 ms
14  new.lpi.org (209.167.177.93)
        57.021 ms  56.162 ms  58.809 ms
```

In this example, there are 13 hops to *www.lpi.org*, reached with a time-to-live value of 14. All three probes of all time-to-live counts are successful.

Most of these commands will appear in system scripts used at boot and shutdown times. Such scripts differ among various Linux distributions but are usually found somewhere under */etc*, such as */etc/rc.d/init.d* or */etc/sysconfig*. You should review the networking scripts on a working Linux system to gain a perspective on how the various configuration commands are used together.

On the Exam

While the creation of complete network management scripts from scratch is beyond the LPIC Level 1 exams, you must be familiar with these commands individually, their functions, how they are used, as well as why they are used. For example, you must be familiar with route and its use in establishing routes to the loopback device, the localhost, the gateway machine, and the creation of the default gateway route. A general understanding of the routing table display is also required. Questions may ask you to determine the cause of a network problem based on the routing configuration (such as a missing default route).

Common manual network interface tasks

Network interfaces are established in the kernel at boot time through the probing of Ethernet hardware. As a result, these interfaces always exist unless the hardware or kernel module is removed. Other types of interfaces, such as PPP, are created by user programs. These interfaces are transient and exist only when they are in use.

To list interface parameters, use ifconfig with the interface name:

```
# ifconfig eth0
eth0      Link encap:Ethernet  HWaddr 00:A0:24:D3:C7:21
          inet addr:192.168.1.30  Bcast:192.168.1.255
          Mask:255.255.255.0
          UP BROADCAST MULTICAST  MTU:1500  Metric:1
          RX packets:1857128 errors:46 dropped:0
          overruns:0 frame:46
          TX packets:871709 errors:0 dropped:0
          overruns:0 carrier:0
          collisions:2557 txqueuelen:100
          Interrupt:10 Base address:0xef00
```

If you run ifconfig without any parameters, it displays all active interfaces, including the loopback interface lo and perhaps a PPP interface if a modem is dialed into a service provider.

To shut down a network interface that is currently running, simply use ifconfig with the down keyword:

```
# ifconfig eth0 down
```

When the interface goes down, any routes associated with it are removed from the routing table. For a typical system with a single Ethernet interface, this means that the routes to both the interface and the default gateway will be lost. Therefore, to start a previously configured network interface, ifconfig is used with up followed by the necessary route commands. For example:

```
# ifconfig eth0 up
# route add -host 192.168.1.30 eth0
# route add default gw 192.168.1.1 eth0
```

To reconfigure interface parameters, follow those same procedures and include the changes. For example, to change to a different IP address, the address is specified when bringing up the interface and adding the interface route:

```
# ifconfig eth0 down
# ifconfig eth0 192.168.1.60 up
# route add -host 192.168.1.60 eth0
# route add default gw 192.168.1.1 eth0
```

Your distribution probably supplies scripts to handle some of these chores. For example, Red Hat systems come with scripts like **ifup**, which handle all the details necessary to get an interface and its routes up and running.

On the Exam

Be prepared to answer questions on the use of **ifconfig** and **route** for basic interface manipulation. Also remember that scripts that use these commands, both manually and automatically, are usually available at boot time.

DHCP

The Dynamic Host Configuration Protocol (DHCP)[*] is a protocol extension of the BOOTP protocol, which provides automated IP address assignment (among other things) to client systems on a network. It handles IP address allocation in one of two ways:[†]

Dynamic allocation

In this scheme, a DHCP server maintains a preset list of IP addresses designated by the system administrator. IP addresses are assigned as clients request an address from the available addresses in the pool. The address can be used, or *leased*, for a limited period of time. The client must continually renegotiate the lease with the server to maintain use of the address beyond the allotted period. When the lease expires, the IP address is placed back into the pool for use by other requesting clients and a new IP address is assigned.

Manual allocation

The system administrator may wish to designate specific IP addresses to specific network interfaces (for example, to an Ethernet MAC address) while still using DHCP to deliver the address to the client. This allows the convenience of automated address setup and assures the same address each time.

DHCP can be configured to assign not only the IP address to the client but also such things as name servers, gateways, and architecture-specific parameters. Here's an overview of how it works:

1. A DHCP client sends a broadcast message to the network in order to discover a DHCP server.

---

[*] DHCP is a vendor-neutral protocol.

[†] If you read RFC 1531, you'll note that a third type of allocation, called *Automatic,* is mentioned. For the purposes of this discussion, consider *Automatic* and *Manual* to be equivalent methods.

2. One or more DHCP servers respond to the request via their own broadcast messages, offering an IP address to the client.

3. The client chooses one of the servers and broadcasts an acknowledgment, requesting the chosen server's identity.

4. The selected server logs the connection with the client and responds with an acknowledgement and possibly additional information. All of the other servers do nothing because the client declined their offer.

Subnets and relays

Since DHCP communications are initiated using broadcasts, they are normally confined to a single subnet. To accommodate DHCP clients and servers separated by one or more routers, a DHCP *relay* system can be established on subnets without DHCP servers. A relay system listens for DHCP client broadcasts, forwards them to a DHCP server on another subnet, and returns DHCP traffic back to the client. This configuration can centralize DHCP management in a large routed environment.

Leases

As already mentioned, when a client receives a dynamically assigned IP address from a DHCP server, the address is said to be *leased* for a finite duration. The length of a DHCP lease is configurable by the system administrator and typically lasts for one or more days. Shorter leases allow for faster turnover of addresses and are useful when the number of available addresses is small or when many transient systems (such as laptops) are being served. Longer leases reduce DHCP activity, thus reducing broadcast traffic on the network.

When a lease expires without being renegotiated by the client, it as assumed that the client system is unavailable, and the address is put back into the free pool of addresses. A lease may also be terminated by a client that no longer needs the IP address, in which case it is *released*. When this occurs, the DHCP server immediately places the IP address back in the free pool.

dhcpd

The DHCP server process is called **dhcpd**. It is typically started at boot time and listens for incoming DHCP request broadcasts. **dhcpd** can serve multiple subnets via multiple interfaces, serving a different pool of IP addresses to each.

dhcpd is configured using the text configuration file */etc/dhcpd.conf,* which contains one or more *subnet declarations.* These are text lines of the following form:

```
subnet network-address netmask subnet-mask {
    parameter. . .
    parameter. . .
    . . .
}
```

Each subnet declaration encloses parameters for each subnet between curly braces. Parameters include one or more ranges of IP addresses to serve, lease times, and optional items such as gateways (routers), DNS servers, and so forth. Each parameter line is terminated with a semicolon. For example:

```
subnet 192.168.1.0 netmask 255.255.255.0 {
    range 192.168.1.200 192.168.1.204;
    default-lease-time 600;
    option subnet-mask 255.255.255.0;
    option broadcast-address 192.168.1.255;
    option routers 192.168.1.1;
    option domain-name-servers 192.168.1.25;
}
```

In this example, the private class C network `192.168.1.0` is served five IP addresses, 200 through 204. The default DHCP lease is 600 seconds (10 minutes). Options are also set for the subnet mask, broadcast address, router (or gateway), and DNS server. For full information on *dhcp.conf,* see its manpage.

The preceding *option* lines are not required to create a minimal DHCP setup that simply serves IP addresses. Details on the daemon follow.

dhcpd

Syntax

dhcpd [*options*]

Description

Launch the DHCP server daemon. **dhcpd** requires that both its configuration file */etc/dhcpd.conf* and its lease log file */var/state/dhcp/dhcpd.leases* (or similar) exist. The daemon puts itself in the background and returns control to the calling shell.

Frequently used options

-cf *config-file*
    Use *config-file* instead of the default */etc/dhcpd.conf.*

-lf *lease-file*
    Use *lease-file* instead of the default to store lease information.

-q
    Use quiet mode. This option suppresses the default copyright message, keeping log files a little cleaner.

A full and detailed description of the configuration file syntax can be found in the *dhcpd.conf* manpage. When **dhcpd** runs, it sends output—including information on each transaction—to *syslog.* For example, this series of four log entries in */var/log/messages* shows a successful exchange between **dhcpd** and a requesting DHCP client:

```
Apr 24 02:27:00 rh62 dhcpd: DHCPDISCOVER
    from 00:60:97:93:f6:8a via eth0
Apr 24 02:27:00 rh62 dhcpd: DHCPOFFER
    on 192.168.1.200 to 00:60:97:93:f6:8a via eth0
```

```
Apr 24 02:27:01 rh62 dhcpd: DHCPREQUEST
   for 192.168.1.200 from 00:60:97:93:f6:8a via eth0
Apr 24 02:27:01 rh62 dhcpd: DHCPACK
   on 192.168.1.200 to 00:60:97:93:f6:8a via eth0
```

On the Exam

You must be able to configure a basic DHCP server. You should understand the basic syntax of the *dhcpd.conf* file and understand the sequence of events in a DHCP negotiation. You may be asked to locate a DHCP configuration problem given a particular scenario.

The use of DHCP relay systems and the detailed configuration of **dhcpd** are beyond the scope of Exam 102.

Objective 4: Configure and Use PPP

The Point-to-Point Protocol (PPP) is a method of constructing a network connection between two systems using a serial interface. Usually, this interface is a pair of modems connected by a telephone call over a switched voice network. However, PPP isn't specifically tied to the use of modems and can also work with a direct serial connection using a *null modem* cable (sometimes known as a *crossover* cable, which is not covered on LPI Exam 102). When PPP is implemented on a Linux system, it creates a new network interface, usually **ppp0**, which is configured for use with TCP/IP and an IP address.

In order to use PPP, your kernel must be compiled with PPP support. Most distributions include PPP support in the kernels they install, but if yours doesn't or if you build your own kernels, you must select *PPP Support* under *Network Device Support* in your kernel configuration (see "Part 2: *Kernel (Topic 1.5),* Objective 2: Reconfigure, Build, and Install a Custom Kernel and Modules," for information on compiling kernels).

Clients and servers

PPP is a peer-to-peer protocol, in which there is no technical difference between the two systems sharing a PPP link. When used for dialup communications, however, it is convenient to think of the system making the call as a PPP client and the system being called as a PPP server. Linux can do both jobs simultaneously if multiple serial interfaces are available, but this section covers only the client-side configuration as required by Exam 102.

Serial ports and modems

The only hardware required to create a PPP dialup connection are a serial interface and a modem. These may be separate devices, including an external modem device cabled to an internal serial interface. Internal modems implement both the port and the modem hardware on a single board, reducing costs. Serial ports are a standard item on most small computers and communicate using RS-232, an old standard for serial communications with terminals, modems, and other devices. On Linux, serial ports are accessed via device files, usually referred to as */dev/ttyS0* and */dev/ttyS1.*[*] In addition, a link for a default modem device, */dev/modem*, is often made to point to the serial port where a modem is attached. For example:

```
crw-------  1 root tty   Apr 25 18:28 /dev/ttyS0
crw-------  1 root tty   May  5  1998 /dev/ttyS1
lrwxrwxrwx  1 root root  Dec  7 23:04 /dev/modem -> ttyS0
```

Each byte of information to be sent through a serial interface is sent bit by bit at a periodic rate known as the *baud rate*. In the early days of modems, data was transmitted over the phone at the same baud rate as it was encoded by the serial port. However, modern modems compress data before transmitting it and can accommodate higher data rates from host systems. As a result, the serial port typically runs at its fastest speed, allowing the modem to independently set a line speed after negotiating with the server's modem. By keeping the data rate between computer and modem high, the modem has a constant stream of data ready for transmission, maximizing throughput.

Built into each serial interface is a data *buffer* capable of holding a finite amount of information. When serial data enters the buffer faster than it can be removed, a data overrun occurs unless the data flow is stopped through the use of a *flow control* signal. For example, when a system is sending data into a modem through a serial interface, the modem must send a stop signal when it has no more room in its buffer, and later send a start signal when the buffer again has free space. The result is that while the modem sends a constant stream to the other modem, the serial interface is running bursts of data managed by flow controls. In simple cases such as terminals, two flow control characters named XON and XOFF are transmitted in the serial data stream and are interpreted as controls to hardware. However, PPP uses the entire serial byte and is less efficient if control characters are allowed, so another means—known as *ready-to-send* (RTS) and *clear-to-send* (CTS)—is used for flow control. These signals are included in standard serial cables and allow *hardware flow control* between devices.

PPP overview

PPP connections are established through these general steps:

1. A serial connection is created with a remote PPP server. This involves setting local serial port parameters, setting local modem parameters, and instructing the modem to dial the telephone number of the PPP server. After the modem on the other end answers, the two modems negotiate the best possible link speed, depending on their capabilities and the quality of the telephone line.

2. User account authentication information is supplied to the PPP server. More than one method exists for this task, but in many cases, the PPP server simply provides clear text login and password prompts, and the client responds in the same way.

---

[*] These device names were */dev/cua0* and */dev/cua1* in previous Linux kernels. They're referred to as COM1: and COM2: in MS-DOS and Windows.

3. PPP is started on the client. Many servers automatically initiate PPP upon successful authentication, while others offer a sort of command-line interface where PPP can be started with a command.

4. The PPP server selects an IP address from a pool of addresses reserved for PPP connections and provides it to the client in plain text. The server then initiates a binary data stream to link the PPP client and server software.

5. The PPP client software uses the temporarily assigned IP address to configure the new interface and its required routes.* It then joins the server in establishing the PPP binary data stream.

Chat scripts

Most of this process requires a dialog between the calling computer and its modem, and subsequently the PPP server, including the interpretation of responses. For example, it's common to begin the entire process by instructing the modem to reset itself, ensuring that settings from previous communications sessions don't affect the current session. After the reset instruction is completed, the modem responds with OK on a line by itself. It would be impractical to proceed if the reset command fails, so the modem's response must be tested, and further modem commands presented only if the appropriate responses are received. This command/response dialog function is implemented using the **chat**† utility, intended specifically for use with modems. **chat** executes a script that contains lines of text to send to the modem as well as fragments of what to expect from the modem itself. The chat scripts also allow for default actions to typical modem responses, such as the ability to abort a call attempt if the modem reports a busy signal. Here is a typical chat script for a simple dialup configuration:

```
ABORT BUSY
ABORT ERROR
ABORT 'NO CARRIER'
ABORT 'NO DIALTONE'
ABORT 'Invalid Login'
ABORT 'Login incorrect'
'' ATZ
OK ATDT8005551212
CONNECT ''
ogin: jdoe
ssword: jdoepasswd
TIMEOUT 5
> ppp
```

In this chat script, the first six lines use the ABORT keyword to provide strings that **chat** should consider to be fatal errors, terminating the call attempt. Any of the modem or PPP server responses—BUSY, ERROR, NO CARRIER, NO DIALTONE, Invalid Login, and Login incorrect—will cause the script to terminate.

---

* Additional information beyond the IP address can be provided to clients using DHCP. Examples include the default gateway and DNS servers.

† The **chat** program is unrelated to the notion of Internet Relay Chat (IRC) and *chat rooms*.

Each subsequent line of this example is constructed using two items: an *expected response*, followed by a *send string*. Here, the first response is simply no response at all, indicated by the empty quotes, `""`. This causes **chat** to issue a send string consisting of the modem reset sequence ATZ without expecting any input. **chat** then waits for the next expected response, which should be an OK from the modem indicating a successful reset. After verifying that, the modem dials as a result of the ATDT command, and **chat** waits to receive a CONNECT response from the modem. If the modem returns BUSY instead of CONNECT, **chat** terminates as a result of the ABORT string at the top of the file. When CONNECT is received, **chat** simply sends a carriage return, indicated in the script by another set of empty quotes, to stimulate the PPP server to prompt for authentication (some PPP servers require this stimulation, others don't). Because this will be the first text from the server, it's possible that the first character could be garbled, so only the fragment ogin: is used to look for the login: prompt. In response, a username (*jdoe*) is sent, and then the user is prompted for a password. After successful authentication, this particular PPP server (a dedicated Cisco dialup server managed by an ISP) requires PPP to be started using the **ppp** command at the > prompt.

Note that strings with spaces or no characters are delimited with quotes and that a depiction of carriage returns isn't required. Neither must separate lines be used for each expect/send pair. This example could also look like this:

```
ABORT BUSY ABORT ERROR ABORT 'NO CARRIER'
ABORT 'NO DIALTONE' ABORT 'Invalid Login'
ABORT 'Login incorrect'
'' ATZ OK ATDT8005551212 CONNECT ''
ogin: jdoe ssword: jdoepasswd
TIMEOUT 5
> ppp
```

It's important that **chat** is given send/expect commands in pairs. Creating the file with separate lines for each pair makes for easy comprehension, but it isn't really necessary. Regardless of the chat script format, here's what the conversation looks like from **chat**'s point of view:

```
ATZ
OK
ATDT8005551212
CONNECT 31200/ARQ/V34/LAPM/V42BIS

User Access Verification

login:jdoe
Password:<jdoepasswd>

mxusw5>ppp
Entering PPP mode.
Async interface address is unnumbered (Loopback0)
Your IP address is 192.168.50.211. MTU is 1500 bytes

~ÿ}#.!}!C} }4}"}&} }*} } }%}&bGab}'}"}(}"V}?~~ÿ}#.!}!
4}"}&} }*} } }%}&bGab}'}"}(}".ÿ~~
```

The garbled text at the end is a terminal's attempt to render the binary PPP data as characters and is expected.

On the Exam

You should be able to create a basic chat script from scratch, providing basic login and PPP server information.

The PPP daemon

In addition to the kernel support mentioned at the beginning of this Objective, the PPP daemon (**pppd**) is required to run PPP on Linux. When used by a client computer to establish a dialup connection, **pppd** does not start at boot time and remain active as do many other daemons. Instead, it runs as directed by users or automatically when a network connection is required. **pppd** has a large number of available options, but only a general understanding is necessary for Exam 102.

---

pppd

Syntax

> pppd [*device*] [*speed*] [*options*]

Description

Start the PPP daemon on *device* with serial interface rate *speed*. The *speed* parameter is almost always set to the maximum speed of the serial interface (115200 bits per second) to allow the modem to keep data compression running at full capacity.

Frequently used options

asyncap *map*
> This option can be used to eliminate bits of the serial byte from use by **pppd**, preserving control characters. Each bit in *map* is excluded. It is common to set *map* to 00000000 to allow all 8 bits to be used.

connect *script-command*
> This option calls the script that handles the modem setup and authentication, usually **chat**. *script-command* is a complete command string that initiates the modem dialup sequence, including **chat**, its parameters and the chat script. Since it includes the **chat** command, options, and a script, the entire *script-command* should be quoted so that **pppd** does not attempt to interpret it as options.

crtscts
> This option instructs **pppd** to set the serial port to use hardware flow control (CTS/RTS).

debug
> This option turns on debugging. Information is logged to *syslog* and also to the calling terminal, unless **pppd** detached (see the **nodetach** option).

---

defaultroute

By setting this option, **pppd** creates a default route in the routing table for the new PPP device. This is a typical need for a dialup system without network access. Note, however, that a networked system that already has a default route to its network interface would then have two default routes, which doesn't make sense. In this case, the administrator must determine how best to configure the routing for PPP connections.

ipparam *name*

If this option is included, *name* is included as the sixth argument to */etc/ppp/ ip-up*, a script that handles a few logging and network details after the PPP link is established.

lock

This instructs **pppd** to establish a lock file to claim exclusive access to *device*.

nodetach

This option prevents **pppd** from putting itself in the background, instead remaining attached to the calling terminal. This is helpful for interactive use and debugging.

persist

In situations in which you want PPP to be constantly available (such as with dedicated modem links or direct system-to-system cable links), use the **persist** option. **pppd** attempts to reestablish a terminated PPP connection. This can protect your PPP link from modem power failure, line degradation, or line interruption. Note that this capability is specifically mentioned in Objective 4, and is likely to appear on Exam 102.*

On the Exam

You should have a firm understanding of **pppd** and the nature and form of its options. In particular, be familiar with the **persist** option.

Manual PPP connection

Here's a simple one-command example of a manual PPP connection, using the chat script presented earlier. In the **pppd** command, each option appears on a separate line for clarity, though this is not required in practice:

```
# /usr/sbin/pppd /dev/ttyS0 115200 \
    nodetach \
    lock \
    debug \
    crtscts \
    asyncmap 00000000
    connect "/usr/sbin/chat -vf \
        /etc/sysconfig/network-scripts/chat-ppp0"
```

---

* It is likely that your distribution's automated for PPP scripts are capable of reestablishing terminated PPP links, perhaps without the **persist** option. This can be achieved with the use of a while loop.

pppd first calls the chat script,[*] the results of which can be found in */var/log/messages*.[†]

```
kernel: PPP: version 2.3.3 (demand dialing)
kernel: PPP line discipline registered.
kernel: registered device ppp0
pppd[1291]: pppd 2.3.7 started by root, uid 0
chat[1295]: abort on (BUSY)
chat[1295]: abort on (ERROR)
chat[1295]: abort on (NO CARRIER)
chat[1295]: abort on (NO DIALTONE)
chat[1295]: abort on (Invalid Login)
chat[1295]: abort on (Login incorrect)
chat[1295]: send (ATZ^M)
chat[1295]: expect (OK)
chat[1295]: ATZ^M^M
chat[1295]: OK
chat[1295]:  -- got it
chat[1295]: send (ATDT8005551212^M)
chat[1295]: expect (CONNECT)
chat[1295]: ^M
chat[1295]: ATDT8005551212^M^M
chat[1295]: CONNECT
chat[1295]:  -- got it
chat[1295]: send (^M)
chat[1295]: expect (ogin:)
chat[1295]:  31200/ARQ/V34/LAPM/V42BIS^M
chat[1295]: ^M
chat[1295]: ^M
chat[1295]: User Access Verification^M
chat[1295]: ^M
chat[1295]: login:
chat[1295]:  -- got it
chat[1295]: send (jdow^M)
chat[1295]: expect (ssword:)
chat[1295]: jdoe^M
chat[1295]: Password:
chat[1295]:  -- got it
chat[1295]: send (<jdoepasswd>^M)
chat[1295]: timeout set to 5 seconds
chat[1295]: expect (>)
chat[1295]: ^M
chat[1295]: ^M
chat[1295]: ^M
chat[1295]: mxusw5>
chat[1295]:  -- got it
chat[1295]: send (ppp^M)
pppd[1291]: Serial connection established.
pppd[1291]: Using interface ppp0
```

---

[*] Your chat script location may vary; this example is from a Red Hat Linux system.

[†] **chat** logs output as a result of the **-v** option, as passed to **pppd** in the quoted **chat** command.

```
pppd[1291]: Connect: ppp0 <--> /dev/modem
pppd[1291]: local  IP address 192.168.100.202
pppd[1291]: remote IP address 192.168.100.1
```

The calling terminal, remaining attached to **pppd** due to the **nodetach** option, shows debugging information:

```
Serial connection established.
Using interface ppp0
Connect: ppp0 <--> /dev/ttyS0
sent [LCP ConfReq id=0x1 <asyncmap 0x0>
    <magic 0x5f6ecfaa> <pcomp> <accomp>]
rcvd [LCP ConfReq id=0x46 <asyncmap 0xa0000>
    <magic 0x77161be5> <pcomp> <accomp>]
sent [LCP ConfAck id=0x46 <asyncmap 0xa0000>
    <magic 0x77161be5> <pcomp> <accomp>]
rcvd [IPCP ConfReq id=0x3e <addr 192.168.100.1>]
sent [LCP ConfReq id=0x1 <asyncmap 0x0>
    <magic 0x5f6ecfaa> <pcomp> <accomp>]
rcvd [LCP ConfReq id=0x47 <asyncmap 0xa0000>
    <magic 0x7716279c> <pcomp> <accomp>]
sent [LCP ConfAck id=0x47 <asyncmap 0xa0000>
    <magic 0x7716279c> <pcomp> <accomp>]
rcvd [LCP ConfAck id=0x1 <asyncmap 0x0>
    <magic 0x5f6ecfaa> <pcomp> <accomp>]
sent [IPCP ConfReq id=0x1 <addr 192.168.1.30>]
rcvd [IPCP ConfReq id=0x3f <addr 192.168.100.1>]
sent [IPCP ConfAck id=0x3f <addr 192.168.100.1>]
rcvd [IPCP ConfRej id=0x1 <compress VJ 0f 01>]
sent [IPCP ConfReq id=0x2 <addr 192.168.1.30>]
rcvd [IPCP ConfNak id=0x2 <addr 192.168.100.96>]
sent [IPCP ConfReq id=0x3 <addr 192.168.100.96>]
rcvd [IPCP ConfAck id=0x3 <addr 192.168.100.96>]
local  IP address 192.168.1.220
remote IP address 192.168.1.1
Script /etc/ppp/ip-up started; pid = 3759
Script /etc/ppp/ip-up finished (pid 3759), status = 0x0
```

At this point, the PPP connection is up and these two new routes should appear in the routing table:

* A route to the new **ppp0** interface.

* A default route through the new **ppp0** interface.

For example (here, the Met and Ref columns, mentioned earlier, are deleted for clarity):

```
# route
Kernel IP routing table
Destination    Gateway        Genmask          Flags Use Iface
192.168.100.1  *              255.255.255.255 UH      0 ppp0
192.168.1.30   *              255.255.255.255 UH      0 eth0
192.168.1.0    *              255.255.255.0    U      0 eth0
127.0.0.0      *              255.0.0.0        U      0 lo
default        192.168.100.1  0.0.0.0          UG     0 ppp0
```

When your dialup session is complete, you can terminate **pppd** easily by entering **Ctrl-C** on the calling terminal:

```
^C
pppd[1291]: Terminating on signal 2.
pppd[1291]: Connection terminated.
pppd[1291]: Connect time 5.9 minutes.
pppd[1291]: Sent 22350 bytes, received 34553266 bytes.
pppd[1291]: Exit.
```

When **pppd** is running in the background, terminate a PPP link by sending a `SIGTERM` signal to the running **pppd**.

Authentication protocols

In the examples presented in this Objective, authentication with the PPP server is handled by means of a clear text username/password dialog and implemented using **chat**. This is a common setup, but three additional authentication techniques also exist. All of them embed the authentication information into the PPP data stream instead of using a clear text dialog prior to initiating PPP. These methods maintain authentication information, or *secrets*, in a file.

PAP

The Password Authentication Protocol (PAP) is initiated by the connecting client, which sends a username/password pair. Secret information is stored in */etc/ppp/pap-secrets*.

CHAP

The Challenge Handshake Authentication Protocol (CHAP) is initiated by the server, which sends a *challenge*. The challenge data contains the server's name, and the client must respond with its name plus a new value derived from the challenge information and the stored authentication information. For CHAP, this information is stored in */etc/ppp/chap-secrets*). CHAP may also include additional challenges over the life of the PPP connection.

MSCHAP

This is a Microsoft-specific variant of CHAP implemented on Windows NT systems using RAS. It is supported by **pppd**, although special provisions are required. See the *Linux PPP HOWTO* for more information if you're dialing into a Windows NT RAS server using MSCHAP.

The authentication information stored in the *secrets* files for PAP and CHAP has a common format but is beyond the scope of the Exam 102.

On the Exam

Be aware that PAP, CHAP, and MSCHAP exist and may be required for some dialup situations.

PPP over ISDN

Objective 4 makes casual mention of initiating ISDN connections using PPP over ISDN technology, but ISDN devices are beyond the scope of both LPIC Level 1 exams. That said, getting PPP running on an existing ISDN setup using supported hardware is very similar to a modem connection. Most ISDN terminal adapters supported by Linux behave much like modems, so the same connection methods may be employed. A chat script sets up the terminal adapter and instructs it to dial (probably with a special dial string that implies both ISDN BRI phone numbers), and **pppd** continues as usual. However, ISDN connections will likely require the use of one of the authentication protocols already mentioned. If PAP is used, the corresponding *pap-secrets* file is necessary. While creating this file is trivial (it just contains your username and password on two separate lines), this file and PAP are beyond the scope of the LPIC Level 1 exams.

Too many variables

Unfortunately, many of the elements involved in a dialup PPP connection lack specific standards:

- Modems from various manufacturers may require unique settings to be made prior to dialing the PPP server. This means that setup strings included in chat scripts may be hardware-specific. The *Linux Modem-HOWTO* contains information on modem requirements.

- Authentication and PPP startup schemes vary among ISPs and other PPP servers. Therefore, the configuration of a dialup interface depends on the server's requirements. Specific information from the PPP server provider is necessary.

- PPP automation techniques vary among Linux distributions. While **pppd** comes with a default configuration style, there's no guarantee that your distribution will fully utilize it. This is particularly true for systems that include custom configuration tools that may use special configuration files and scripts.

Study Guide 102

On the Exam

PPP setup can be confusing, particularly when your Linux distribution adds additional complexity in order to make dialup carefree. Be sure that you've been able to establish a PPP session with a server through both automated configuration and manual methods. You'll also need to understand how and why **chat** is used, how expect/send strings are constructed, how to get debugging information from **pppd**, and the routing implications of PPP (the default route). You don't need to memorize all of **pppd**'s many options or understand each script associated with automated startup of **pppd**, as these are beyond the scope of Exam 102. Nonchat authentication schemes and the setup of PPP servers are also beyond the scope of this exam.

Networking Services
(Topic 1.13)

Much of the success of Linux can be attributed to bundled networking services, such as the Apache web server, sendmail, NFS and Windows file sharing, and others. This section covers these five Objectives on networking services:

Objective 1: Configure and Manage inetd and Related Services
This Objective includes the so-called Internet superdaemon, or **inetd**. This single daemon manages other service-specific daemons, dispatching them as needed in response to inbound requests. Also included is the TCP wrappers facility for adding access control to **inetd**. Weight: 5.

Objective 2: Operate and Perform Basic Configuration of sendmail
sendmail is probably the most common mail transfer agent on the Internet. This Objective covers only the basics of sendmail configuration, including its alias feature. Weight: 5.

Objective 3: Operate and Perform Basic Configuration of Apache
Apache is the most popular HTTP server on the Internet and is the default web server for most Linux distributions. This Objective covers basic configuration of Apache. Weight: 3.

Objective 4: Properly Manage the NFS, smb, and nmb Daemons
This Objective covers file sharing using both NFS (Unix) and SMB (Samba, the open source file server for integrating Linux within a Windows network). Weight: 4.

Objective 5: Set Up and Configure Basic DNS Services
This Objective covers the basic configuration of DNS and address resolution settings. Weight: 3.

For systems deployed as servers, even in a small department, these Objectives cover some of most important system administration concepts to be performed for Linux.

Objective 1: Configure and Manage inetd and Related Services

Most network services execute as software *daemons*, which "listen" to a specific port for inbound requests from client software on the outside. (See "Part 2: *Networking Fundamentals (Topic 1.12)*, Objective 1: Fundamentals of TCP/IP," for a discussion on ports.) For example, the Telnet daemon, **telnetd**, listens on port 23 for inbound requests from Telnet clients. Each such request is handled by the daemon, which starts the login process for the client. If a single server were to offer many such services, many of the **telnetd** daemons would be running at any one time to handle multiple inbound Telnet requests.

In order to reduce the number of daemons necessary to service requests, the *Internet superdaemon*, or **inetd**, was created. Instead of running individual daemons for each service, **inetd** runs as a single service listening to all of the desired port numbers (23 for **telnet**, 21 for **ftp**, etc.). When an inbound request is received, it is handed off to the actual daemon for processing. With this scheme, the host daemons are still used as before, but they run only when needed and are started by **inetd**, freeing resources for other tasks.

This scheme also offers another convenience. Instead of launching the target daemons directly, **inetd** is usually configured to use the TCP wrappers access control facility. TCP wrappers, or **tcpd**, allows the administrator to define restrictions on the origin of inbound requests. TCP wrappers is described fully in "Part 2: *Security (Topic 1.14)*, Objective 1: Perform Security Administration Tasks."

inetd is well suited for services requested on a relatively infrequent basis, such as **telnet** and **ftp**. However, using **inetd** on services such as Apache would significantly impact the performance of a heavily used server under constant load. In such cases, it is common to simply configure the web server to handle its own connections.

The inetd Configuration File

inetd is usually started during system initialization and continues to run indefinitely (or until the process is stopped). When started (and later in response to signal SIGHUP), **inetd** reads its configuration file from */etc/inetd.conf*, which is nothing more than a plain text file that defines the services managed by **inetd**. (Commented lines begin with #.) Example 2-17 shows portions of an *inetd.conf*, with lines wrapped to fit the page (your *inetd.conf* will be different and should be configured with your security requirements in mind; more on this later).

Example 2-17: Sample inetd.conf File

```
# /etc/inetd.conf
# Internet server configuration database
# See inetd(8) for further information.
#
<service_name>  <socket_type>  <proto>  <flags>   <user>   <server_path>        <args>
#
ftp             stream         tcp      nowait    root     /user/sbin/tcpd      /user/sbin/in.ftpd
telnet          stream         tcp      nowait    root     /usr/sbin/tcpd       /usr/sbin/in.telnetd
#
pop-2           stream         tcp      nowait    root     /usr/sbin/tcpd       ipop2d
pop-3           stream         tcp      nowait    root     /usr/sbin/tcpd       ipop3d
imap            stream         tcp      nowait    root     /usr/sbin/tcpd       imapd
#
finger          stream         tcp      nowait    nobody   /usr/sbin/tcpd       /usr/sbin/in-fingerd
ident           stream         tcp      nowait    nobody   /usr/sbin/identd      identd -I
#
tftp            dgram          udp      wait      nobody   /usr/sbin/tcpd       /usr/sbin/in.tftpd /boot
bootps          dgram          udp      wait      root     /usr/sbin/bootpd      bootpd -i -t 120
```

Each noncommented line in *inetd.conf* must contain each of the following fields:

`service_name`
> This is the name of a service as defined in */etc/services*.

`socket_type`
> This entry specifies one of a few types of communications the service will use. It's usually `stream` or `dgram`.

`proto`
> This field specifies the service's protocol from among those in */etc/protocols*. For most services, it will be either `tcp` or `udp`, which correspond to the `stream` and `dgram` socket types.

`flags`
> The `wait/nowait` (`.max`) flag is used only for datagram services, where it helps to control the handling of inbound requests and is typically set to `wait`. It should be set to `nowait` for others. You can limit the number of server instances spawned by **inetd** within any 60-second interval by appending a dot and the maximum number (`.max`). For example, to limit the service to 20 instances, use `.20` after the `nowait` flag:
>
> `nowait.20`
> The default maximum is 40 instances (`.40`).

`user[.group]`
> This entry specifies the username (and optionally the group name) under which the service should execute, allowing them to be run with fewer permissions than *root*. A typical entry is the user `nobody`.

`server_path`
> This field is the full path to the executable daemon of the server program. When TCP wrappers is used, this entry specifies `tcpd`, as shown in Example 2-17.

`args`
> This last entry on the line may consist of multiple fields. It contains the name of the server daemon and all arguments that are to be passed to it.*

In many Linux installations, a majority of the lines in *inetd.conf* are commented out to increase security. The fewer services a system offers, the more likely it is to stand up to an attack. You should review your file to be certain that only necessary services are offered.

TCP wrappers with inetd

If you have a need to control access to **inetd**-managed services by IP address or by domain name, you may wish to configure TCP wrappers. For each inbound

---

* The daemon name is actually the first argument, or `argv[0]` from a programming point of view.

connection to a service protected by TCP wrappers, **tcpd** consults two files that define access:

/etc/hosts.allow
> If a rule in this file is met, access to the service is allowed.

/etc/hosts.deny
> If a rule in this file is met, access to the service is denied.

Rules in these files can be constructed to match all services or alternatively to match specific services. If no match occurs in the two files, access to the service (or services) is allowed. It is common to specify particular rules in the *.allow* file and provide a blanket denial in the *.deny* file, thereby limiting access to clients you specifically allow.

The language in the control files consists of a service list, followed by a colon, followed by a list of hosts. Hosts may be specified by name or by IP address. For example, to deny access to all service except inbound `ftp` from the local domain, these two simple files could be used:

hosts.allow
> This entry allows FTP access to clients in the local domain:
>
> ```
> ftp: LOCAL
> ```

hosts.deny
> This entry denies access to all services from all clients:
>
> ```
> ALL: ALL
> ```

The *hosts.deny* file is consulted after *hosts.allow*, enabling the administrator to define specific allow rules that will be matched prior to deny rules or a blanket denial.

Starting and Stopping Services

If **inetd** is not running, all of the services it manages are disabled. Likewise, if **inetd** is reconfigured, any changes to individual managed services take effect at the same time. To cause **inetd** to reread its configuration file, simply send it SIGHUP:

```
$ killall -HUP inetd
```

All **inetd** services that are commented out or missing from */etc/inetd.conf* will be disabled. However, a number of other services on Linux systems are managed through other means—typically through the runlevel system and the series of scripts and links in */etc/rc.d*. See "Part 1: *Boot, Initialization, Shutdown, and*

Runlevels (Topic 2.6), Objective 2: Change Runlevels and Shutdown or Reboot the System," for details on starting and stopping services such as Apache (**httpd**).

On the Exam

You must be generally familiar with the content and function of *inetd.conf*, *hosts.allow*, and *hosts.deny*. Memorizing configuration details is not necessary, but be prepared for questions on available services and the effect of TCP wrappers rules in the *hosts.allow* and *hosts.deny* files. Be sure you understand what happens to services that are commented out of *inetd.conf*, and that **inetd** must be signaled to reread the control file after any changes.

Objective 2: Operate and Perform Basic Configuration of sendmail

The sendmail Mail Transfer Agent (or MTA) is responsible for handling a large portion of email sent on the Internet and inside enterprises. It has broad capabilities to handle mail routing and can perform complex rewriting of email addresses. It also has a long history of deployment on early networked systems where I/O bottlenecks were significant. As a result of this history, sendmail's configuration file was constructed over the years to be succinct and small, allowing it to be read quickly by the sendmail daemon. Unfortunately, it can also appear to be somewhat cryptic to administrators, and detailed configuration of sendmail has become known as somewhat of an art.

Configuration details of sendmail are nontrivial and beyond the scope of the LPIC Level 1 exams. However, a basic sendmail configuration for a system in an established domain is relatively simple to implement and is covered in Exam 102.

Configuring sendmail

The sendmail configuration file is */etc/sendmail.cf*. This text file contains information to control the processing of mail on your system, and it is read at every invocation of sendmail. Each line in the file defines a configuration command, which begins with a short one- or two-letter command definition. The file can also contain comments beginning with #. To simplify a basic setup, example *sendmail.cf* files exist in most installations.

The smart host parameter

To enable mail transfer inside an established organization, you need to configure sendmail to transfer messages to a *smart host*, most likely the main mail-processing system in your domain. For example, if your enterprise's mail is handled by `mail.yourdomain.com`, you can configure your Linux systems to transfer all mail to that computer for further processing. To make this change, simply use the DS directive in *sendmail.cf*:

```
DSmail.yourdomain.com
```

Mail Aliases

Even on simple sendmail installations, it's useful to configure some of your system users to have their mail redirected to another user. For example, artificial users such as nobody shouldn't receive mail, so forwarding any mail received for that username to an administrator may help with problem solving. This forwarding is accomplished using *mail aliases*. A mail alias is simply a mapping from a username to one or more recipients in this form:

```
sysadmin:       jdean, bsmith
```

Aliases are defined in */etc/aliases*. Local mail intended for sysadmin is received by both jdean and bsmith on the local system, as shown in Example 2-18.

Example 2-18: A Typical /etc/aliases File

```
# Basic system aliases -- these MUST be present.
MAILER-DAEMON:  postmaster
postmaster:     root

# General redirections for pseudo accounts.
bin:            root
daemon:         root
games:          root
ingres:         root
nobody:         root
system:         root
toor:           root
uucp:           root

# Well-known aliases.
manager:        root
dumper:         root
operator:       root
webmaster:      root
abuse:          root
spam:           root

# Trap decode to catch security attacks
decode:         root

# Person who should get root's mail
root:           jdean

# Departmental accounts
sales:          bsmith
support:        jdoe
```

sendmail doesn't actually read the text aliases file, since it's not uncommon to find many aliases defined there. Instead, it reads a compiled database, */etc/aliases.db*, built from */etc/aliases*. Therefore, the database must be updated after any change is made to `aliases`, using the **newaliases** command; **newaliases** has no options and must be run as *root*.

Forwarding mail from your account to another account

In addition to permanently established mail aliases, individual users have the capability to create their own mail aliases on an as-needed basis by using a *forward* file in the home directory. Mail is sent to the alias by simply putting an email address on a line by itself in *.forward*.

On the Exam

Remember, the */etc/aliases* and *.forward* files define mail aliases, and the **newaliases** command must be executed after changing the aliases file to recreate the alias database.

Queued Mail

If sendmail cannot deliver mail immediately, such as on a system using an intermittent dialup connection, mail is queued for later processing. To see the mail queue, use the **mailq** command, like this:

```
$ mailq
Mail Queue (2 requests)
--Q-ID-- --Size-- -Priority- ---Q-Time--- -Sender/Recipient
WAA12372   3427      30043 Jul  4  2:19 bsmith
                (host map: lookup (mydom.com): deferred)
                                 jdean@mydom.com
WAA12384    313      30055 Jul  8 22:40 jdoe
                (host map: lookup (yourdom.com): deferred)
                                 you@yourdom.com
```

The first line printed for each message shows the internal identifier used on the local host for the message, the size of the message in bytes, the date and time the message was accepted into the queue, and the sender of the message. The second line shows the error message that caused this mail to be retained in the queue. Subsequent lines show message recipients. In this example, two outbound messages are queued because the DNS host lookups did not succeed.

On the Exam

Be aware that mail could be queued by sendmail and that **mailq** displays a list of those messages.

Study Guide
102

Starting and Stopping sendmail

sendmail is typically managed through the runlevel system and the series of scripts and links in */etc/rc.d*. See Part 1, *Boot, Initialization, Shutdown, and Runlevels (Topic 2.6)*, Objective 2," for details on starting and stopping services.

Objective 3: Operate and Perform Basic Configuration of Apache

Apache is a phenomenal open source success story. Despite the availability of commercial web servers, Apache continues to be the most popular web server on the Internet. It is also widely deployed inside corporate networks for managing internal communications. Apache is known as an HTTP daemon, or **httpd**.

Because it is so popular and likely to be found on just about every Linux server, understanding the basics of Apache administration is required for Exam 102.

Configuring Apache

Apache is configured using one or more text files. The names and locations of Apache configuration files vary by distribution. If you acquire Apache as source code, compile it, and install it, you get the default setup as provided with the software. If you use the preconfigured Apache version that came with a Linux distribution, things may be somewhat different. A typical Apache configuration is controlled by three files* located in */etc/httpd/conf* or */usr/local/apache/conf*, depending on how Apache is installed:

httpd.conf
> This file contains general attributes about the Apache server, such as the name of the administrator, the username under which the server should execute, how logging is handled, and others.

srm.conf
> This file is used to specify some local parameters about your system and your web site. Included here are definitions for the top of the HTML tree, where CGI programs are located, languages, and more.

access.conf
> This is a security definition file, which controls access to the server by client browsers.

Configuration is managed through *configuration directives*, one per line, in each of the files. The configuration files can also contain comments, which begin with a #. Directives are in the form:

```
DirectiveName [argument-list]
```

For example, the DocumentRoot directive, which tells Apache where the top of the HTML tree is located, might look like this:

---

* To simplify editing during Apache configuration, some distributions concatenate *httpd.conf*, *srm.conf*, and *access.conf* into a single *httpd.conf* file.

```
DocumentRoot /home/httpd/html
```

Here are some basic Apache configuration directives:

ServerType

> This directive can be either standalone or inetd. If you prefer to have inetd listen for inbound HTTP requests, set this to inetd and configure *inetd.conf* as needed. For web servers that see a significant amount of traffic, standalone is often specified, making Apache independent of inetd, and running indefinitely.

Port

> This parameter defines the port to which Apache listens. The default HTTP port is 80.

User *and* Group

> These two parameters determine the name and group, respectively, that Apache executes under. Typical examples are nobody, www, and httpd.

ServerAdmin

> This directive specifies the email address of the administrator, such as root@localhost.

DocumentRoot

> This directive tells Apache where to find the top of the HTML tree, such as */home/httpd/html.*

UserDir

> System users may use a standard personal subdirectory for their own HTML documents. This directive determines the name of that directory. It is often set to *public_html.* Files for user *jdean* would be accessed using a URL of *http://localhost/~jdean.*

Of course, there are many more, and additional syntax is used when necessary. In *access.conf,* groups can be delineated by keywords that look like HTML. Directives in such a group affect only a subset of the content served by Apache. For example, the following group of directives controls CGI execution in */home/httpd/cgi-bin:*

```
<Directory /home/httpd/cgi-bin>
AllowOverride None
Options ExecCGI
</Directory>
```

On the Exam

The LPI exam Objectives don't specify particular Apache configuration directives, but you should be prepared to interpret various configuration examples and have knowledge of the three configuration files and their likely locations.

Starting and Stopping Apache

Typically, Apache is managed through the runlevel system and the series of scripts and links in */etc/rc.d.* See *Part 1, Boot, Initialization, Shutdown, and Runlevels (Topic 2.6),* Objective 2," for information on starting and stopping services such as Apache.

Objective 4: Properly Manage the NFS, SMB, and NMB Daemons

Networked file and printer sharing is among the fundamental services offered by Linux and other operating systems. For years, the standard file sharing protocol for Unix has been the Network File System (NFS). Originally developed by Sun Microsystems, NFS has been implemented on many operating systems and is available in both commercial and free software implementations.

NFS

Any Linux system may act as both an NFS server and an NFS client. Clients use **mount** to attach remote filesystems from NFS servers to their local filesystem. Once mounted, the directory hierarchy mounted on the client appears to users as a local filesystem.

Exporting (sharing) local filesystems using NFS

To share a part of your system's filesystem, you must add a specification to */etc/exports.* Each line in this file describes a shared filesystem resource. The format of the file is:

```
directory    system(options) system(options) ...
```

directory is a local filesystem directory, such as */home.* Each of the space-separated **systems** describes clients by name or address, and the associated **options** control access. If the system name is omitted, no restriction is placed on which clients can connect. Typical options are:

ro
> Export with read-only attribute.

rw
> Export with read/write attribute, the default.

no_root_squash
> Allow access by GID 0, root.

noaccess
> Prohibit access below the named directory. This has the effect of pruning parts of other shared directories, perhaps for specific systems.

Example 2-19 shows three shared directories from an */etc/exports* file.

Example 2-19: Sample /etc/exports File

```
/               orion(rw,no_root_squash)
/usr            *.mydomain.com(ro) orion(rw)
```

Example 2-19: Sample /etc/exports File (continued)

```
/pub           (ro,insecure,all_squash)
/pub/private   factory*.mydomain.com(noaccess)
```

In this example, the entire filesystem (/) is shared with the system `orion` in read/write mode, and `root` access is accepted. The */usr* directory is shared as read-only (`ro`) to all systems in `mydomain.com` and read/write (`rw`) to `orion`. The */pub* directory is shared as read-only (`ro`) to any system, but `factory*.mydomain.com` systems cannot look into `/pub/private` because the `noaccess` option is used.

In order for new or revised entries to be incorporated in the NFS configuration, NFS daemons must be reconfigured or restarted (see "Starting and stopping NFS," later in this section).

On the Exam

Detailed configuration of NFS exports is beyond the scope LPIC Level 1 exams, but you must understand the contents of */etc/exports* and how to incorporate them into a running system.

Mounting remote NFS filesystems

Mounting an NFS volume requires the use of a local *mount point*, a directory in the filesystem over which the remote directory hierarchy will be placed. Once the directory exists, **mount** is used to create the NFS connection from the local client to the remote server. The syntax is similar to that used for local filesystems, with the addition of the NFS server name or address. For example, if `server1` is offering its */home* directory via NFS, it could be mounted locally as follows:

```
# mkdir /mnt/server1
# mount -t nfs server1:/home /mnt/server1
```

In this example, the **mount** command uses the `-t` option to specify mount type **nfs**. The second argument specifies the data source by concatenating the name of the NFS server (**server1**) with its exported directory (**/home**). The final argument is the directory name that will serve as the local mount point (**/mnt/server1**). After successfully mounting, */mnt/server1* appears to be a local filesystem.

This configuration could be incorporated into */etc/fstab* for automated mounting at boot time with a line like this:

```
server1:/home   /mnt/server1   nfs   defaults   0   0
```

In this example, `defaults` indicates that the filesystem should be mounted using the default options (see the manpage for **mount** for defaults). The two zeros indicate that the filesystem should not be backed up using **dump** and that it should not have a filesystem check at boot time.

Starting and stopping NFS

NFS consists of multiple daemons, which are typically managed through the runlevel system and the series of scripts and links in */etc/rc.d*. See *Part 1, Boot, Initialization, Shutdown, and Runlevels (Topic 2.6)*, Objective 2," for details on starting and stopping services such as the NFS family.

Samba and the SMB and NMB Daemons

Another extremely popular sharing mechanism is that used on Microsoft and IBM systems, called Server Message Block (SMB). It is implemented as free software as a suite of programs collectively known as *Samba*, which runs on a variety of operating systems including Linux. Samba consists of two daemons:

smbd

> This daemon handles file and printer sharing, as well as authentication.

nmbd

> This daemon implements the Windows Internet Name Service (WINS), which maps Windows system names to IP addresses.

On the Exam

It is the goal of the Samba team to eventually implement all of the services found on Windows servers, including Windows NT/2000 Domain Controller functionality. The LPI exam deliberately avoids specifics in this area, leaving only basic Samba configuration for the test.

Getting started

Your Linux distribution probably came with a recent version of Samba. If you already have Samba installed, setting up a basic configuration is easy. To check whether Samba is already installed on your system, issue the following command on the command line:

```
# smbd -h
```

If Samba is installed on your system, you should see a message similar to:

```
Usage: smbd [-D] [-p port] [-d debuglevel] [-l log basename]
   [-s services file]
Version 2.0.3
    -D                 become a daemon
    -p port            listen on the specified port
    -d debuglevel      set the debuglevel
    -l log basename.   Basename for log/debug files
    -s services file.  Filename of services file
    -P                 passive only
    -a                 append to log file (default)
    -o                 overwrite log file, don't append
    -i scope           NetBIOS scope to use (default none)
```

If not, you can get source or binary distributions for Samba from *http://www.samba.org*.

To begin using Samba, you must create its configuration file, *smb.conf.* Depending on how you acquired Samba, the default location for this file may be */etc* or */usr/ local/samba.* A basic *smb.conf* set up is shown in Example 2-20.

Example 2-20: Sample /etc/smb.conf File

```
[global]
workgroup = HOME
server string = LINUX
encrypt passwords = Yes
log file = /var/log/samba/log.%m
max log size = 50
socket options = TCP_NODELAY
printcap name = /etc/printcap
dns proxy = No
socket address = 192.168.1.30
wins support = no
wins server = 192.168.1.202
hosts allow = 192.168.1. 127.

[myshare]
path = /home/myshare
guest ok = yes
comment = My Shared Data
writeable = yes

[homes]
   comment = Home Directories
   browseable = no
   writable = yes

[printers]
   comment = All Printers
   printing = BSD
   print command = /usr/bin/lpr -r  %s
   path = /var/spool/samba
   guest ok = yes
   printable = yes
```

This example configuration allows Samba to participate in an SMB workgroup called HOME with a system name of LINUX. Hosts on the private network 192.168.1 as well as the loopback network (127.) are allowed to access shared resources. The default sections of Samba's */etc/smb.conf* file are as follows:

[global]
> The global section defines items applying to the entire system, such as the workgroup and system names.

[homes]
> A section that defines users' home directories to be shared.

[printers]
> This section shares all of the printers located in */etc/printcap* (provided that a BSD-style printer setup is in use).

Samba also has the following custom share section:

[myshare]
> This defines a shared directory myshare. The name myshare will appear as shared resources to clients. Users' home directories do not need to be explicitly shared if [homes] is used.

To use Samba, only the workgroup, server string, and a shared service such as [myshare] need to be configured.

See Samba's manpage for more detailed information on the *smb.conf* file.

WINS and browsing

Windows networks allow users to view available shared resources through *browsing*, a process by which one machine acts as a *browser* and is updated with information from other machines on the network.[*] Client machines can then obtain lists of resources on the entire network from that single browser machine. Samba's **nmbd** daemon implements WINS. To use Samba as a WINS client, you can specify the address of the WINS server on your network using the **wins server** directive, as shown in Example 2-18. Samba can also act as a WINS server itself, although this is beyond the scope of the LPIC Level 1 exams.

Using SWAT

Samba v2.0 and later comes with a web-based configuration tool called the Samba Web Administration Tool, or SWAT. To use **swat** with **inetd**, use a line similar to this in */etc/inetd.conf*:

```
swat    stream tcp nowait.400    root /usr/sbin/swat swat
```

On the Exam

You should be generally familiar with the *smb.conf* file and with the concepts of shared directories, shared printers, WINS, and SWAT. You don't need to worry about creating custom Samba configurations for Exam 102.

You can also run the **swat** daemon manually. In either case, you must list its port, 901, in */etc/services*. Once **swat** is configured, you can point your browser to *http://localhost:901* and log in using the root password; **swat** offers a convenient series of forms that you can fill in using the browser to configure Samba. When you commit changes, the *smb.conf* file is updated for your system.

---

[*] This *browser* has nothing to do with a web browser such as Netscape Navigator. Instead, it is a service of the operating system, or in the case of Samba, **nmbd**.

Objective 5: Set Up and Configure Basic DNS Services

The Domain Name Service (DNS) is the distributed database of name-to-IP-address translations. Technically, it isn't necessary to use host and domain names such as *www.lpi.org*, because it's the actual IP address that the computer requires to establish communications. DNS was created to allow the use of more convenient global domain names instead. For example, when a user enters a DNS name as part of a URL in a browser, the name portion is sent to a DNS server to be resolved into an IP address. Once the address is found, it is used to rewrite the URL and directly fetch the web page.

On the Exam

You must be familiar with the concept of name resolution on the Internet using DNS.

The server daemon that implements DNS is **named**, the *name daemon*, which is part of the Berkeley Internet Name Daemon package (BIND). It is **named**'s job to respond to requests from the resolver and return an IP address.

The resolver

The code that resolves names to IP addresses using DNS for client programs is implemented in system libraries collectively called the *resolver*. The resolver uses one of several means to determine an IP address from a hostname or domain name:

Static local files
> The local file */etc/hosts* can contain name-to-address mapping for a few systems on a network. However, for large enterprises, using static local files to manage IP address resolution is problematic due to the frequent changes required in the data. Updating all of the client systems would be impractical. This resolution method is sometimes referred to as the *files* method.

Network Information Service (NIS)
> Some private networks use a shared information service that can include address resolution. This is NIS, or a later version of it called NIS+, and is referred to as the nis method of resolution. Both services are beyond the scope of the LPIC Level 1 exams.

Domain Name Service (DNS)
> Because addresses and domains on the public Internet change frequently and are so numerous, static local files can't handle resolution far outside the enterprise. As already mentioned, DNS is a distributed database. That is, small portions of the DNS are managed by local authorities that are responsible only for their particular slice of the system. As you'd expect, using DNS for name resolution is called the dns method.

Study Guide
102

In most cases, */etc/hosts* will be used for name resolution of the local host and perhaps a few other nearby systems. DNS, perhaps together with NIS in enterprise environments, will handle everything else.

/etc/hosts and the other files used to configure the resolver are described in "Part 2: *Networking Fundamentals (Topic 1.12)*, Objective 3: TCP/IP Troubleshooting and Configuration," but here's a quick recap:

/etc/hosts
> This file lists statically defined name-to-address translations.

/etc/nsswitch.conf (or /etc/host.conf on older Linux systems)
> The "name service switch" file (*nsswitch.conf*) defines the order of name server methods to be used in succession by the resolver (it can also control other things such as passwords, but those don't apply here). Typically, this single entry is used to control name resolution:
>
> ```
> hosts:  files dns
> ```
>
> This entry instructs the resolver to resolve names using */etc/hosts* first, and if a match isn't found, to make a DNS query.

/etc/resolv.conf
> This file lists the IP addresses of name servers:
>
> ```
> nameserver 127.0.0.1
> nameserver 192.168.1.5
> nameserver 192.168.250.2
> ```

On the Exam

Be sure that you understand how */etc/nsswitch* controls the resolution order, that */etc/resolv.conf* identifies DNS servers by address, and that */etc/hosts* is for local, statically resolved addresses. Also remember that older versions of Linux used */etc/host.conf* to configure the resolution order instead of */etc/nsswitch.conf*.

When the resolver determines that a DNS query is required, it sends a request containing a domain name to one of the DNS servers listed in */etc/resolv.conf*. The DNS server uses its own records to find the domain or may resort to escalating to other DNS servers if the information isn't readily available. When a result is found by the DNS servers, the IP address corresponding to the requested name is returned to the originating client.

Domain registration

Domain names are assigned through a registration process with one of the domain name registrars available on the Internet (*http://rs.internic.net/regist.html*). Originally, a single authority managed domain names. As commercial uses for domain names spread, additional entities sought the ability to charge for the service of domain registration, and today there are a number of qualified registrars (a search for "domain registrar" on one of the popular search engines will yield a daunting list). Once a domain name is registered, it is listed in a worldwide database along

---

with contact information for the owners or their agents. The name servers that contain DNS information for the domain can go along with this record.

Most registrants offer a domain name search service, so you can test desired domain names for availability. If the domain name you're seeking is available, you can provide payment information to a registrant and purchase rights to use the name, usually for one or two years.

Using named as a local caching-only name server

named is often configured to serve DNS requests even when it does not have local information for a domain. Instead, it is used for its caching ability. When a client program requests an address resolution from the local **named**, the daemon first checks its local cache. If it doesn't find the domain there, it goes to other DNS servers as usual. If the cache does contain the domain, it is returned immediately to the client from the cache, which speeds the resolution process.

Some Linux distributions come with a caching-only **named** configuration pre-installed. If this isn't the case for you, simply follow the brief instructions in section 3 of the *DNS HOWTO* available from *http://www.linuxdoc.org* (or in your */usr/doc/HOWTO* directory). Part of the configuration includes setting your local system as the default DNS server in */etc/resolv.conf*:

```
nameserver 127.0.0.1
```

You can test the configuration using the **nslookup** utility:

```
# nslookup
Default Server:  localhost
Address:  127.0.0.1

> lpi.org
Server:  localhost
Address:  127.0.0.1

Name:    lpi.org
Address:  209.167.177.93

> lpi.org
Server:  localhost
Address:  127.0.0.1

Non-authoritative answer:
Name:    lpi.org
Address:  209.167.177.93

> exit
```

In this example, **nslookup** attaches to the default server `localhost` (`127.0.0.1`). In the first query for `lpi.org`, the local **named** must find the address from external DNS servers. However, the result is found in the cache on the second try, as indicated by the `Non-authoritative answer` response. If this behavior isn't seen, there may be a problem with the **named** configuration in */etc/named.conf*.

Some debugging information can be found in */var/log/messages*. For example, the highlighted line in this short excerpt shows an error in the configuration file:

```
smp named[216]: starting.  named
smp named[216]: cache zone "" (IN) loaded (serial 0)
smp named[216]: Zone "0.0.127.in-addr.arpa"
   (file named.local): No default TTL
   set using SOA minimum instead
smp named[216]: master zone "0.0.127.in-addr.arpa"
   (IN) loaded (serial 1997022700)
smp named[216]: /etc/named.conf:18: can't redefine
channel 'default_syslog'
smp named[216]: listening on [127.0.0.1].53 (lo)
smp named[216]: listening on [192.168.1.30].53 (eth0)
smp named[216]: listening on [172.16.132.1].53 (vmnet1)
smp named[216]: Forwarding source address is [0.0.0.0].1855
smp named[216]: Ready to answer queries.
```

Note that configuration of a caching-only name server is beyond the scope of the LPIC Level 1 exams but is a useful exercise in understanding the configuration of **named**.

DNS query utilities

A few tools exist to verify the operation of DNS name resolution. Here's a brief synopsis of **nslookup** and **host**, both specifically mentioned in this Objective. The **host** utility does not offer interactive mode but uses a syntax similar to **nslookup**.

nslookup

Syntax

```
nslookup host [dnsserver]
```

Description

Look up *host*, optionally specifying a particular *dnsserver*. **nslookup** can be used in either interactive or noninteractive modes. If *host* is provided on the command line, noninteractive mode is used. In interactive mode, a number of commands are available to control **nslookup** (the **ls** command to **nslookup** is used in the example). See the manpage for more details.

Noninteractive example

In this example, **nslookup** provides immediate results because *host*, in this case oreillynet.com, is provided on the command line:

```
# nslookup oreillynet.com 192.168.1.2
Server:  ns1.mydomain.com
Address:  192.168.1.2

Non-authoritative answer:
Name:    oreillynet.com
Address:  208.201.239.36
```

Interactive example

Here, **nslookup** is used interactively with DNS server `192.168.1.2` to find records from `yourdomain.com`:

```
# nslookup
Default Server:  localhost
Address:  127.0.0.1

> server 192.168.1.2
Default Server:  ns1.mydomain.com
Address:  192.168.1.2

> ls -a yourdomain.com
[ns1.mydomain.com]
$ORIGIN yourdomain.com.
ipass                    2D IN CNAME     snoopy
smtp                     2D IN CNAME     charlie
mail                     2D IN CNAME     charlie
pop                      2D IN CNAME     lucy
yourdomain               2D IN CNAME     charlie
ww2                      2D IN CNAME     linus
www                      2D IN CNAME     sally
> exit
```

host

Syntax

host [*options*] *host* [*dnsserver*]

Description

Look up *host*, optionally specifying a particular *dnsserver*.

Frequently used options

–d

Enable debugging, showing network transactions in detail.

–v

Use verbose mode. Results are displayed in the official domain master file format.

Example

```
# host -v oreillynet.com
Trying null domain
rcode = 0 (Success), ancount=1
The following answer is not authoritative:
oreillynet.com  1991 IN A      208.201.239.36
For authoritative answers, see:
oreillynet.com  167591 IN      NS      NS1.SONIC.NET
oreillynet.com  167591 IN      NS      NS.SONGLINE.COM
```

```
Additional information:
NS1.SONIC.NET    167591 IN       A       208.201.224.11
NS.SONGLINE.COM 167591 IN        A       208.201.239.31
```

On the Exam

Detailed knowledge of **nslookup** and **host** are not required, but you must be familiar with their purpose and basic operation.

Additional utilities, such as **dig** and **dnsquery**, also can help you with DNS queries, though they are not mentioned in this exam Objective.

BIND Version 4 versus Version 8 configuration files

It's likely that a Linux administrator will maintain or install systems running BIND v4.x as well as the newer v8.x. This LPI Objective requires an understanding of the differences between the configuration files for these two BIND versions. Under BIND v4, the configuration file was called */etc/named.boot*. Example 2-21 shows a trivial BIND v4 configuration file.

Example 2-21: BIND v4 named.boot File

```
directory                          /var/named
cache   .                          root.hints
primary 0.0.127.IN-ADDR.ARPA       127.0.0.zone
primary localhost                  localhost.zone
```

In BIND v8, the configuration file was renamed */etc/named.conf*. Example 2-22 shows the equivalent configuration in the BIND v8 format.

Example 2-22: BIND v8 named.conf File

```
// generated by named-bootconf.pl

options {
        directory "/var/named";
};

zone "." {
        type hint;
        file "root.hints";
};

zone "0.0.127.IN-ADDR.ARPA" {
        type master;
        file "127.0.0.zone";
};
```

Example 2-22: BIND v8 named.conf File (continued)

```
zone "localhost" {
        type master;
        file "localhost.zone";
};

    };
```

As you can see, the information contained in the files is largely the same, but the v8 format contains a more formal structure. For those upgrading to Version 8, the Perl script *named-bootconf.pl* is included in the v8 package to upgrade *named.boot* to *named.conf.*

On the Exam

You should be generally familiar with the structural differences between the configuration files for BIND v4 and v8. However, detailed **named** configuration is beyond the scope of the LPIC Level 1 exams.

Security
(Topic 1.14)

As with any multiuser-networked operating system, a secure environment is essential to system stability. This Topic covers basic Linux security administration. The following three Objectives are included:

Objective 1: Perform Security Administration Tasks
> This Objective includes the configuration of TCP wrappers (a facility that monitors inbound network connections), management of SUID and SGID properties, corrupted package files, management of user passwords, and the use of the secure shell (**ssh**). Weight: 4.

Objective 2: Set Up Host Security
> This Objective examines how to implement shadowed passwords, eliminate unnecessary network services, configure **syslogd**, and examine web sites with security information. Weight: 4.

Objective 3: Set Up User-Level Security
> This Objective covers the creation for user limits on logins, processes, and memory usage. Weight: 2.

Objective 1: Perform Security Administration Tasks

A good security policy includes such things as securing inbound network requests, verifying the authenticity of software packages to assure they are not hostile, and managing local security resources. This Objective details some of the most common of these activities that a system administrator performs.

TCP Wrappers

As a Linux system operates in a networked environment, it is constantly "listening" for inbound requests from the network. Many requests come into Linux on the same network interface, but they are differentiated from one another by their *port address*, a unique numeric designator used by network protocols. Each type of service listens on a different *port.* Established port numbers and their corresponding services are listed in */etc/services.* Here are some lines from that file:

```
# /etc/services:
#
ftp       21/tcp
ssh       22/tcp
ssh       22/udp
telnet    23/tcp
smtp      25/tcp
www       80/tcp
www       80/udp
```

The left column lists various services that could be provided by the system.[*] The right column lists the port numbers assigned to the services and the protocol (TCP or UDP) used by the service. For example, the **telnet** service uses port 23, and web servers use port 80. When a browser wishes to contact the web server on a specific IP address, it attempts to attach to port 80 at that address. Likewise, Telnet clients attach to port 23. If the appropriate service is listening, it responds and a new communications session is established. Linux networking software consults this table to determine port numbers.

On the attack

As the Internet has grown, the frequency of computer break-in attempts has kept pace. To gain entry to an unsuspecting host system, some intruders configure their systems to appear to target servers (that is, your servers) as trusted hosts. This could include a forged IP address or hostname, or the exploitation of aspects of the TCP protocol. Such attacks are carried out against multiple ports, sometimes in a *port scan* where multiple ports at a single IP address are attacked in succession.

In response to these threats, the *TCP wrapper* concept was created. The "wrappers" name comes from the idea that the services are "wrapped" in a protective layer. TCP wrappers consist of a single program, **tcpd**, which is called in place of actual services like **ftpd** or **telnetd**, among others. **tcpd** performs the following functions:

- Responds to network requests and does security tests on the information provided in the connection message

- Consults local configuration files (*/etc/host.allow* and */etc/host.deny*) to restrict access

- Provides detailed logging via the `authpriv` facility of **syslog** for connection requests

If a connection is approved, **tcpd** steps aside and allows the connection to be received by the true service. You could consider **tcpd** to be a gatekeeper of sorts, asking for identification at the door, and once satisfied, getting out of the way and allowing entry. By doing so, **tcpd** does not impact subsequent performance of the network connection. However, this aspect of **tcpd** prevents its use for services that

---

[*] Just being listed doesn't imply that a service is really active.

handle multiple clients at one time, such has NFS and **httpd**. Instead, services protected by **tcpd** include single-client programs such as **telnet** and **ftp**.

Configuring inetd and tcpd

"Part 2: *Networking Services (Topic 1.13),* Objective 1: Configure and Manage inetd and Related Services," examines **inetd** and its configuration file, */etc/inetd.conf.* Without **tcpd**, a typical service configuration looks like this:

```
telnet  stream  tcp  nowait  root  \
        /usr/sbin/in.telnetd   in.telnetd
```

In this example, */usr/sbin/in.telnetd* is the executable program that is called when a Telnet client tries to attach to the system on the Telnet port (23). With this configuration, *in.telnetd* responds directly and immediately to inbound requests. To enable the use of TCP wrappers for *in.telnetd*, it is specified that **tcpd** be called instead. Making this change yields this revised *inetd.conf* line:

```
telnet  stream  tcp  nowait  root  \
        /usr/sbin/tcpd   in.telnetd
```

Now, */usr/sbin/tcpd* is called in response to an inbound Telnet connection.

tcpd interacts with only the initial network connection. It does not interact with the client process (remote Telnet), the client user (the remote person initiating the Telnet session), or the server process (the local *in.telnetd*). Since it is autonomous, **tcpd** has these properties:

Application independence
   The same small **tcpd** program can be used on many different network services. This simplicity makes **tcpd** easy to install, configure, and upgrade.

Invisible from outside
   Anyone trying to gain access has no direct evidence that **tcpd** is in use.*

tcpd access control

tcpd provides a method of limiting access from external sources both by name and by address. After receiving a network request, **tcpd** first does its IP address and hostname checks. If those pass, **tcpd** then consults two control files, named *hosts.allow* and *hosts.deny*, for access control information. These are text files that contain rules (one per line) against which incoming network connections are tested:

/etc/hosts.allow
   tcpd consults this file first. When an incoming network request matches one of these rules, **tcpd** immediately grants access by passing the network connection over to the server daemon. If none of the rules are matched, the next file is consulted.

/etc/hosts.deny
   This file is consulted second. If a network request matches one of these rules, **tcpd** denies access to the service.

---

* However, it is customary for **tcpd** to be in use by default on modern Linux installations.

If no matches are made in either of the files, then the connection is allowed. This implies that missing *hosts.allow* and *hosts.deny* files means that no access control is implemented.

The form of the rules in these two files is simple:

```
service_list : foreign_host_list
```

The service list is made up of space-separated program names, such as *in.telnetd* and *in.ftpd*. The foreign host list can contain special codes, which can be used on both sides of the colon:

ALL

This is the universal wildcard, which always matches all requests. When used on the left side of a rule, ALL indicates every service protected by **tcpd**. On the right side, it means all possible hosts.

EXCEPT

In the context of:

```
list1 EXCEPT list2
```

this operator matches anything that matches list1 unless it also matches list2.

LOCAL

This wildcard matches machines on the local network—any host whose name does not contain a dot character.

KNOWN

This matches with a successful DNS lookup. Dependent on DNS servers.

PARANOID

This wildcard matches when a hostname lookup returns a different address than the inbound network connection is offering. **tcpd** must be compiled with the **DPARANOID** option to enable this capability. By default, connections in this category are dropped prior to testing against the rules in the control files.

UNKNOWN

Opposite of KNOWN. When a DNS lookup for a host fails, this wildcard matches. This could happen for valid reasons, such as a DNS server failure, so use this one with caution.

To create a system closed to all remote systems except those on the local network, the following line is placed in */etc/hosts.allow*:

```
ALL: LOCAL
```

This rule allows connections to ALL services from LOCAL machines. If LOCAL does not match, this single line in */etc/hosts.deny* is tested:

```
ALL : ALL
```

This rule denies ALL services from ALL machines anywhere. Remember that matches found in *hosts.allow* cause the search to stop, so that LOCAL machines are not tested against the rules in *hosts.deny*.

To enable access from systems in domain otherdom.com except its web server, and to allow access from systems in network 192.168.100.0, you could change the */etc/hosts.allow* file from the previous example to:

```
ALL: LOCAL
ALL: .otherdom.com EXCEPT www.otherdom.com
ALL: 192.168.100.
```

Note that the leading and trailing dots are significant. .otherdom.com matches any system in that domain, such as ftp.otherdom.com and lab1.otherdom.com. The address rule with 192.168.100. matches all of the addresses on that network, including 192.168.100.1, 192.168.100.2, 192.168.100.100, and so on.

On the Exam

Remember that *hosts.allow* is evaluated prior to *hosts.deny*. This means that if a match occurs in *hosts.allow*, the connection succeeds and any potential matches from *hosts.deny* are ignored. Also remember that, in the absence of control, file access is permitted.

Keep in mind that services that are not in use may have control settings. A configuration in */etc/hosts.allow* or */etc/hosts.deny* does not imply that listed services are actually running on the system. Evaluate the complete setup of *inetd.conf*, *hosts.allow*, and *hosts.deny* when answering questions about **tcpd**.

---

tcpd logging

When **tcpd** is enabled, it logs to the authpriv facility in **syslog** (**syslog** and its configuration are described in "Part 1: *Administrative Tasks (Topic 2.11),* Objective 3: Configure and Use System Log Files.") Check your */etc/syslog.conf* file to confirm where this facility will be logged on your system. For example, this */etc/syslog.conf* configuration line puts all authpriv messages in */var/log/secure*:

```
authpriv.*    /var/log/secure
```

Most system service daemons will do some logging on their own. For example, *in.telnetd* writes the following line to authpriv as the result of a Telnet connection:

```
Feb  8 17:50:04 smp login: LOGIN ON 0 BY jdean
         FROM 192.168.1.50
```

When **tcpd** is listening to the Telnet port in place of *in.telnetd*, it logs the request first, does its verifications, and then passes the connection on to *in.telnetd*, which then starts a login process as before. In this case, */var/log/secure* looks like this:

```
Feb  8 17:53:03 smp in.telnetd[1400]: connect
         from 192.168.1.50
Feb  8 17:53:07 smp login: LOGIN ON 0 BY jdean
         FROM 192.168.1.50
```

The first line was logged by **tcpd**. It indicates that a connection was received from `192.168.1.50` bound for the *in.telnetd* daemon.* As you can see, the **tcpd** report precedes the login report.

Finding Executable SUID Files

The set user ID (SUID) capability of the Linux *ext2* filesystem was covered in "Part 1: *Devices, Linux Filesystems, and the Filesystem Hierarchy Standard (Topic 2.4)*, Objective 5: Use File Permissions to Control Access to Files." In that section, the SUID property was described as both a security enhancement and a security risk. It can be considered an enhancement because it allows administrators to grant superuser privileges to specific, trusted programs that may be executed by anyone on the system. The example given is **lpr**, which needs special access to manipulate the print spools. Without using the SUID property, everyone on the system would need administrative rights to use **lpr**, which is clearly undesirable. It is also mentioned that an SUID capability that is granted unwisely can be a security risk, and all applications of SUID must be considered carefully. The reason for this concern is that the potential exists for an attacker to exploit the superuser privilege on an SUID file. For example, if the attacker is able to somehow overwrite the contents of **lpr**, he could effectively gain superuser access to the system by running an **lpr** of his own design that changes passwords, adds new accounts, or something else shady and unrelated to printing.

For systems on corporate networks and on the Internet, it is common to minimize the number of SUID files on the system and to regularly monitor the known list of programs for changes. In the event that a new SUID program is found that was not legitimately created or if an attribute of a known file changes, it could be a warning that system security has been compromised.

The **find** command can perform the searches for attributes such as SUID (see "Part 1: *GNU and Unix Commands (Topic 1.3)*, Objective 1: Work Effectively on the Unix Command Line," for details on **find**). In this example, a **find** command is constructed that searches the entire filesystem for files that have the SUID bit set; it avoids the */proc* filesystem (kernel information) to prevent permission problems. The example generates verbose output using **ls** to log detailed information about the SUID files found:

```
# find / \
        -path '/proc' -prune \
        -or \
        -perm -u+s \
        -exec ls -l {} \; \
     > /usr/local/etc/suid_list &
```

The first line calls the **find** program and indicates that the search should begin at the root directory `/`. The second line specifies a –path directive to match /proc utilizing the –prune modifier. This eliminates (or *prunes*) the */proc* directory from the search. The next line joins the –path directive to the –perm (permissions) directive with a logical –or, skipping execution of the –perm directive when –path matches /proc. The –perm directive uses a permission mode of –u+s,

Study Guide 102

---

* The **smp** on these example lines is the name of the host making the log entries.

which indicates "match SUID." The next line with the **–exec** directive indicates what **find** is to do for each SUID file found. Here, the **ls -l** command is invoked and fed the response from **find** to verbosely list the SUID file's attributes. The curly braces (**{ }**) are replaced with the matched text once for each match.* The final line redirects output from **find** into a new file and puts the command in the background with **&**.

Admittedly, **find** can get a bit long in the tooth but is nevertheless powerful. The result of this command is a listing of files on your system with the SUID property; the following is just a snippet of what that output would look like:

```
-rwsr-xr-x 1 root root  33120 Mar 21  1999 /usr/bin/at
-rwsr-xr-x 1 root root  30560 Apr 15  1999 /usr/bin/chage
-rwsr-xr-x 1 root root  29492 Apr 15  1999 /usr/bin/gpasswd
```

As you can see, the *s* bit is set on the user of the file, indicating SUID. Keeping this complete list in a file can be useful, because you'll want to check your system periodically for changes.

Verifying Packages

Package management systems provide a convenient method of managing software on Linux systems. The Red Hat Package Manager (RPM) not only can install package files but also can provide for the verification of package files and software installed on your system.

Checking installed packages

If an intruder were able to penetrate your system, it is likely that she would attempt to modify or replace executable files in order to grant herself special abilities. To check for such files, the verification option of the package manager can be used to check installed files. With RPM, it is possible to verify the installed files contained in a specific package like this:

```
# rpm -V apache
S.5....T c /etc/httpd/conf/httpd.conf
.......T c /etc/httpd/conf/srm.conf
missing    /home/httpd/html/index.html
missing    /home/httpd/html/poweredby.gif
```

In this example, **rpm** is reporting that four files do not match the original installed configuration. None is an executable file, and all are easy to explain, so no intruder is suspected here. If an executable file does turn up in the list, you may wish to investigate. For example:

```
# rpm -V XFree86-I128
S.5....T   /usr/X11R6/bin/XF86_I128
```

This shows that the file **XF86_I128** is not the same as the one originally installed. Unless you know why the file has changed, corrective action may be necessary to maintain security. In this case, the file in question is an X Server binary that was intentionally upgraded to a newer version than that supplied in the original package. Again, this is an expected result.

---

* Note that a backslash in front of the semicolon is required with **–exec**.

The output from **rpm –V** consists of an eight-character string, an optional **c** (indicating that the file is a configuration file), and the filename. Each column in the result string contains a dot when an attribute has not changed. The output codes listed in Table 2-20 can replace dots to indicate discrepancies.

Table 2-20: RPM Verification Codes

Dot Code	Description
5	The MD5 checksum, a sort of "fingerprint" for the file, is different.
S	The file size has changed.
L	Symlink attributes have changed.
T	The file's modification time (or *mtime*) has changed.
D	Device file has changed.
U	The file's user/owner has changed.
G	The file's group has changed.
M	The file's mode (permissions and file type) has changed.
?	Unknown or unexpected result.

It can be helpful to monitor all of the packages on your system and track changes to the resulting list on a regular basis. To check all installed packages, use the **a** verification option as follows:

```
# rpm -Va
S.5....T c /etc/exports
S.5....T c /etc/hosts.deny
S.5....T c /etc/printcap
S.5....T c /etc/services
.M......   /root
S.5....T c /usr/share/applnk/Multimedia/aktion.kdelnk
S.5....T c /etc/info-dir
..5....T c /etc/mime.types
S.5....T c /etc/httpd/conf/httpd.conf
.......T c /etc/httpd/conf/srm.conf
missing    /home/httpd/html/index.html
missing    /home/httpd/html/poweredby.gif
S.5....T c /etc/named.conf
S.5....T c /var/named/named.local
.M......   /dev/hdc
.M......   /dev/log
.M?....T   /dev/printer
.M......   /dev/pts
......G.   /dev/tty0
(... list continues ... )
```

This list will be large. As your system is configured, upgraded, and modified, you're likely to change many of the files from their original configurations. The important part is being able to explain changes that occur, particularly on executable files.

Checking packages prior to installation

From time to time, you may obtain precompiled software from various sources to add to your system. This may include updated versions of software you already have or new software you don't yet have. It's always best to obtain package files from a trusted source, such as the manufacturer or a well-known distributor. However, as an added safeguard. you may wish to verify that the packages you obtain have not been tampered with or otherwise corrupted. To check an RPM file, use the **--checksig** option:

```
# rpm --checksig --nopgp fileutils-4.0-1.i386.rpm
fileutils-4.0-1.i386.rpm: size md5 OK
```

The **size md5 OK** status indicates that "size" and "md5" checksum tests passed for the *.rpm* file. This means that the size of the file and its checksum* matched expected values. A **NOT OK** status could indicate a problem. In this example, the **--nopgp** option is also used to ignore PGP signatures, which may be necessary for you unless you have PGP installed and configured on your system.

SGID Workgroups

This Objective requires an understanding of the SGID (set group ID) mode bit and its application to a directory. When SGID is set on a directory, new files created within that directory are assigned the same group ownership as the directory itself. This is explored in detail in "Part 1: *GNU and Unix Commands (Topic 1.3)*, Objective 5: Create, Monitor, and Kill Processes." If you're currently preparing for Exam 102, be sure to refer back to Part 1 for a refresher on SGID.

Password Management

When a user calls saying he's forgotten his password, you need to use the super-user account to create a new one for him:

```
# passwd bsmith
Changing password for user bsmith
New UNIX password: (new password)
Retype new UNIX password: (new password again)
passwd: all authentication tokens updated successfully
```

Resist the temptation to use an easily guessed password, even if you expect the user to change it immediately.

Linux offers you the ability to set expiration dates on passwords. This is done to limit their lifetime, which presumably enhances security by forcing password changes. If a password has been discovered or broken, the password change will eventually correct the security lapse. The **chage** command configures password aging parameters on a per-user basis when using password aging. The following parameters are defined:

---

* A checksum is a calculated value based on the contents of a file (or other piece of information) used as a sort of "fingerprint."

Minimum password age
   The minimum number of days between password changes.

Maximum password age
   The maximum number of days between password changes. The user is forced to change his password before using the account after the number of days has elapsed without a password change.

Last password change
   The date on which the password was last changed.

Password expiration warning
   The number of days' warning that are issued in advance of a password expiration.

Password inactive
   The number of days of inactivity the system allows before locking a password. This is an automated way of avoiding stale but valid user accounts.

Account expiration date
   The date on which an account expires.

---

chage

Syntax

```
chage user
chage [options] user
```

Description

In the first form without options, **chage** is interactive. In the second form, **chage** may be used with parameters specified via options on the command-line.

Options

d *lastday*
   lastday is the number of days between the last password change and January 1, 1970. As an administrator, you may need to modify this value. *lastday* may also be specified as a date in /MM/DD/YY format.

-E *expiredate*
   expiredate is a date on which an account will no longer be accessible. Like *lastday*, it is stored as the number of days since January 1, 1970, and may be specified as a date in /MM/DD/YY format.

-I *inactive*
   inactive is the number of days of inactivity allowed after a password expires before an account is locked. A value of 0 disables the *inactive* feature.

-m *mindays*
   mindays is the minimum number of days between password changes. This prevents a user from making multiple password changes at one time.

-M *maxdays*

> *maxdays* is the maximum number of days that a password remains valid. This forces users to change their passwords periodically.

-W *warndays*

> *warndays* is the number of days before a password expires that the user is warned of the upcoming expiration.

Examples

User *bsmith* is to be provided with a password that cannot be changed more than once every 2 days, that must be changed at least every six months (180 days), that retains its default 7-day warning interval, that is set to lock after three weeks' of inactivity, and that expires altogether at the end of 2002. The following interactive session with **chage** makes these settings:

```
# chage bsmith
Changing the aging information for bsmith
Enter the new value, or press return for the default

        Minimum Password Age [0]: 2
        Maximum Password Age [99999]: 180
        Last Password Change (MM/DD/YY) [02/10/00]:<return>
        Password Expiration Warning [7]: <return>
        Password Inactive [0]: 21
        Account Expiration Date (MM/DD/YY)
            [12/31/69]: 12/31/2002
```

This creates the same settings using the command line:

```
# chage -m 2 -M 180 -I 21 -E 12/31/2002 bsmith
```

If you wish to set these parameters for groups of users or everyone on the system, you could create a simple shell script to loop over all users in */etc/passwd* and run the **chage** command with options.

The information on password aging is stored in either the */etc/passwd* file, or if shadow passwords are enabled, in the */etc/shadow* file.

The Secure Shell

Among the security issues surrounding networked computer systems is the problem of plain text communications. Much of the information traveling between systems is simply sent as text, including passwords at login time. If someone were able to capture the network packets of your communications without your knowledge, your passwords and other information could be compromised. While this may seem like a remote possibility, such activity has become much easier than it was just a few years ago, because low-cost hardware can be used to make a network analyzer for just this purpose.

In 1995, a researcher developed an application intended to replace some of the plain text communications programs such as **telnet**, **rlogin**, and **rsh**. The new application was titled Secure Shell, or SSH. This application may also be used to secure other communications such as the X Window System, though such use is beyond the requirements for the LPIC Level 1 exams. The following tutorial explains how to acquire, compile, install, and configure **ssh** for Linux, so that you can use it in place of Telnet.*

While you may find a precompiled package, it is a simple matter to compile and install **ssh** if you have a C compiler. SSH is available at *http://www.ssh.org* and at many mirror (copy) sites around the world. Using your browser or FTP client, download the latest version to your system and extract the tarball with the following command:

```
# tar zxvf ssh-2.0.13.tar.gz
```

The **z** option to **tar** instructs it to invoke **gzip** to decompress the archive before reading it. You now have a directory hierarchy called *ssh-2.0.13* (your version may be different). You should **cd** into the new directory and examine the documents you find there, then configure, compile, and install the software:

```
# cd ssh-2.0.13
# ./configure
# make
# make install
```

If you have a recent compiler such as **gcc**, you shouldn't have any difficulty with these steps. Configuration and compilation present typical output, so you won't see any surprises there if you've compiled software from source before. The installation, however, generates *keys* for the software to use in its encrypted communications. This process may take a few extra minutes.

Once SSH is installed, you may need to add */usr/local/bin* and */usr/local/sbin* to your PATH or use full pathnames. To enable login from remote systems using SSH, you must start **sshd**, which may be done simply by issuing the following command:

```
# sshd
```

Note that you do not need to put this command in the background, as it handles this detail itself. Once the **sshd** daemon is running, you may connect from another SSH-equipped system:

```
# ssh mysecurehost
```

The default configuration should be adequate for basic use of SSH. One common problem you may encounter is that a system may not be specifically listed by a DNS server. In this case, comment out (that is, put # in front of it using a text editor) the following line from */etc/ssh/sshd2_config*:

```
RequireReverseMapping           yes
```

This eliminates the DNS lookup and allow your configuration to function. If your systems are configured with a proper DNS server, this step should not be

---
* Licensing restrictions apply to the commercial use of SSH. Verify your intended use and license type.

necessary. If you have difficulty with SSH, examine the log for **syslog** facility **auth**, which is most likely */var/log/messages*, for information.

On the Exam

The Secure Shell (SSH) is an involved and highly configurable piece of software, and detailed knowledge of its setup is not required. However, SSH is an important part of the security landscape. Be aware that all communications using SSH are encrypted using public/private key encryption, which means that plain text passwords are unlikely to be compromised.

Objective 2: Set Up Host Security

Once a Linux system is installed and working, you may need to do nothing more to it. However, if you have specific security needs or just want to be cautious, you'll want to implement additional security measures on your system.

Shadow Passwords

The shadow password system enhances system security by removing encrypted passwords from the publicly available */etc/passwd* file and moving them to the secured */etc/shadow* file. This prevents users from running password-cracking programs against all of the encrypted passwords on your system.

Shadow passwords are covered in "Part 1: *Administrative Tasks (Topic 2.11),* Objective 1: Manage Users and Group Accounts," which describes user management. In order to secure a system, it is a good idea to implement shadow passwords if they aren't already. You can check this by looking for */etc/shadow* and verifying that the user list matches the one in */etc/passwd*. If shadow passwords are not enabled, you may enable them by entering the **pwconv** command with no arguments. In the unlikely event that you use group passwords, you should also enable group shadowing with **grpconv**.

inetd Minimalism

As mentioned in "Part 2: *Networking Services (Topic 1.13),* Objective 1: Configure and Manage inetd and Related Services," **inetd** and */etc/inetd.conf* (its configuration file) handle access to many system services. Despite the use of TCP wrappers on these services, the best security can be achieved by simply not offering services that aren't explicitly needed. Do this by removing or commenting out lines in *inetd.conf* for services that are unnecessary. For example, to eliminate the **talk** and **finger** servers from your system, comment their configuration lines:

```
#talk    dgram  udp wait    root /usr/sbin/tcpd  in.talkd
#ntalk   dgram  udp wait    root /usr/sbin/tcpd  in.ntalkd
#finger  stream tcp nowait root /usr/sbin/tcpd  in.fingerd
```

After making this change, you must instruct **inetd** to reconfigure itself. For example:

```
# finger root@localhost
[localhost]
Login: root                          Name: root
Directory: /root                     Shell: /bin/bash
On since Sat Feb 12 00:11 (EST) on tty1
     2 hours 48 minutes idle   (messages off)
On since Sat Feb 12 01:11 (EST) on ttyp1 (messages off)
No mail.
No Plan.
# vi /etc/inetd.conf
# killall -HUP inetd
# finger root@localhost
[localhost]
finger: connect: Connection refused
```

In this example, **finger** is first demonstrated to work. Then **inetd** is edited to disable **fingerd**, **inetd** is reconfigured, and **finger** stops working.

Logging and Superuser Mail

The **syslog** system is a constant companion to the security-conscious system administrator. Its logs are necessary to review security breaches and to trace possible perpetrators. The configuration of **syslog** is described in "Part 1: *Administrative Tasks (Topic 2.11)*, Objective 3: Configure and Use System Log Files."

Some system responses to security problems can come in the form of email to user *root*. You may wish to log in as *root* regularly to check its mail, but you can make such checking passive by instructing sendmail to forward *root*'s mail to administrators. To do so, add a line like this to */etc/aliases*:

```
root: jdoe, bsmith
```

Then execute the **newaliases** command to recompile the aliases database:

```
# newaliases
```

Now all email for *root* goes to both *jdoe* and *bsmith* (but not *root*), who will presumably act on important messages.

Watching for Security Announcements

Another important function of system administration is to keep on top of any new bugs and exploits in the software on your system. There are countless sites on the web you can watch to find announcements about such things, but two stand out and could be mentioned on Exam 102:

CERT

In 1988, a small Computer Emergency Response Team formed at the Software Engineering Institute (SEI), a research and development center operated by Carnegie Mellon University. The Defense Advanced Research Projects Agency (DARPA) originally funded its work. It is now known as the *CERT Coordination Center* (CERT/CC), and "CERT" no longer officially stands for anything. Funding comes from a mix of federal, civil, and private sources.

CERT/CC is made up of network security experts who provide 24-hour technical assistance for responding to computer security incidents. It also analyzes product vulnerabilities, publishes technical documents, and presents security-related training courses. CERT/CC may be found at: *http://www.cert.org*. Specifically, security advisories may be found at: *http://www.cert.org/advisories*.

A periodic visit to the CERT/CC site can keep you informed of developments in computer security and on problems found with various software packages.

BUGTRAQ

In 1993, a mailing list was created to publicly disclose demonstrated bugs in popular software, with the intent of forcing responsible parties to fix the problems quickly. The list has grown into a respected resource on security topics and has thousands of subscribers. To subscribe to the BUGTRAQ list, follow the instructions in the BUGTRAQ section of *http://www.securityfocus.com*. Archives of BUGTRAQ are also available there.

Attention to these and other resources can help you keep your system up-to-date. You'll be aware of problems found in software you're using, and since updates are almost always produced quickly in response to these notifications, you can upgrade, patch, or replace software as needed to keep your systems secure.

Objective 3: Set Up User-Level Security

Even after you've taken the precautions listed earlier, the potential for valid users of your system to cause problems by consuming resources still exists. Such a problem could be accidental, but if it happens intentionally, it is called a Denial of Service (DoS) attack. For example, a user could create processes that replicate themselves and never exit. Eventually your system would grind to a halt because of thousands of processes, each trying to create more clones. You could also have a user begin allocating memory until the system cannot cope with the requests. In either case, you'd probably need to restart the system, if it responds at all. Clearly, prevention is more desirable for everyone.

You can prevent these scenarios without undue restrictions on users by using **ulimit**. This is a **bash** built-in command* that sets maximums on various system resources for users. To enforce limits on users, include **ulimit** commands in */etc/profile*.

---

ulimit

Syntax

    ulimit [*options*] [*limit*]

Description

The **bash** built-in **ulimit** provides control over resources available to the shell and its child processes. For each resource, two limits may be set: a *hard* limit and a

---

* **tcsh** has the **limit** command with similar functionality.

soft limit. Hard limits can be changed only by the superuser; soft limits may be increased by users up to the value of the hard limit. Hard and soft limits are specified with the special **-H** and **-S** options, respectively. Other options specify specific limits. If an option is provided with a *limit* value, the corresponding limit is set. If *limit* is not provided, the current limit is displayed. *limit* is either the special word *unlimited* or a numeric value.

Options

-H

Specify the hard limit. Unless **-H** is specified, the soft limit is assumed.

-S

Explicitly specify the soft limit. This is the default.

-a

Display all current limits. This option does not accept a *limit* value.

-f

The maximum size of files created by the shell. This is the default resource if options are not specified.

-u

The maximum number of processes available to a single user.

-v

The maximum amount of virtual memory available to the shell.

Example 1

Display all limits for an account:

```
$ ulimit -a
core file size (blocks)    1000000
data seg size (kbytes)     unlimited
file size (blocks)         unlimited
max memory size (kbytes)   unlimited
stack size (kbytes)        8192
cpu time (seconds)         unlimited
max user processes         256
pipe size (512 bytes)      8
open files                 1024
virtual memory (kbytes)    2105343
```

Example 2

Set the maximum number of processes to 128:

```
$ ulimit -Hu 128
```

Example 3

Set the maximum working number of processes to 128 but allow the user to raise his limit as high as 150:

```
$ ulimit -Su 128
$ ulimit -Hu 150
```

Exam 102
Review Questions and Exercises

This section presents review questions to highlight important concepts and hands-on exercises that you can use to gain experience with the Topics covered on the LPI's Exam 102. The exercises can be particularly useful if you're not accustomed to routine Linux administration and should help you better prepare for the exam. To complete the exercises, you need a working Linux system that is not in production use.

Hardware and Architecture (Topic 1.1)

Review Questions

1. Describe the general functions of the PC BIOS and how its embedded routines are used by LILO.

2. Why is there a concern for Linux systems regarding disk cylinders beyond 1024?

3. Name three files in the */proc* filesystem that contain information on resource allocations.

4. What is the general procedure to configure a SCSI controller to boot from a device at SCSI ID 3?

5. Why are you unlikely to be able to use a WinModem on a Linux system?

Exercises

Exercise 1.1-1: PC BIOS

1. Boot your PC and enter the BIOS configuration utility using the method defined for your system. Locate the section that covers date and time. Is the programmed time correct?

2. Examine the enabled serial and parallel ports. Can you manually configure the interrupts and/or I/O ports assigned to them?

3. If you have an IDE hard disk, examine the BIOS reported cylinder count. Does the disk have more than 1024 cylinders? If so, what precautions are required when locating LILO and kernel images on the disk?

Exercise 1.1-2: NIC

1. Examine your network interface. Is it a standalone card or is the interface included on your system board? If it is a card, is it a PCI or ISA card? If it is an ISA card, determine what resources it is using by examining jumpers or running its configuration utility.

2. Examine the kernel's interrupt assignments by executing **cat /proc/interrupts**. Is your NIC correctly described? Are there any surprises in the list?

3. Repeat number 2 for */proc/dma* and */proc/ioports.*

Exercise 1.1-3: SCSI

1. If you have a SCSI controller, reboot your PC and enter the SCSI BIOS using the method defined for your system. What device number is selected, if any, for boot? How are the controller's onboard terminators configured? What data rate is the controller configured for?

Exercise 1.1-4: Modems

1. Using **minicom**, attach to your modem. For example:

```
# minicom /dev/modem
Welcome to minicom 1.82

OPTIONS: History Buffer, F-key Macros,
Search History Buffer, I18n
Compiled on Mar 21 1999, 21:10:56.

Press CTRL-A Z for help on special keys

AT S7=45 S0=0 L1 V1 X4 &c1 E1 Q0
OK
AT
OK
```

Does the modem respond to the AT command with OK? Try manually dialing your Internet Service Provider and watch the output of the modem.

Exercise 1.1-5: Sound

1. Examine */etc/conf.modules* or */etc/modules.conf.* Do you see sound configuration parameters? Try to determine what each parameter does and why it is in the file.

Linux Installation and Package Management (Topic 2.2)

Review Questions

1. Why is it beneficial to keep the root partition relatively small?

2. Why is the /var directory usually located in a partition of its own?

3. As a system administrator for a network with many workstations and a central NFS file server, how can you safely share /usr with your users while still maintaining control of its contents?

4. Describe how a tarball is made and how its contents are extracted.

5. In general terms, describe the procedure used to compile and install free or open source software from source code.

6. What is a shared library? How can you determine what library dependencies exist in a compiled executable?

7. Briefly describe the major functional modes of RPM.

8. Why might a Debian Linux administrator use **dpkg –iG** instead of simply **dpkg –i** to install a package?

Exercises

Exercise 2.2-1: Disk layout

1. In a shell, examine your disk layout using **cfdisk** or **fdisk**. For example:

```
# fdisk
Command (m for help): p

Disk /dev/sda: 255 heads, 63 sectors, 1109 cylinders
Units = cylinders of 16065 * 512 bytes

   Device Boot    Start      End    Blocks   Id  System
/dev/sda1             1       51    409626   83  Linux
/dev/sda2            52     1109   8498385    5  Extended
/dev/sda5            52       90    313236   83  Linux
/dev/sda6            91       97     56196   83  Linux
/dev/sda7            98      136    313236   83  Linux
/dev/sda8           137      264   1028128+  83  Linux
/dev/sda9           265      519   2048256   83  Linux
/dev/sda10          520      532    104391   83  Linux
/dev/sda11          533      545    104391   82  Linux swap
/dev/sda12          546     1109   4530298+  83  Linux
```

Is the entire disk consumed by the existing filesystems?

2. Examine how system directories are mapped to disk partitions on your system. Are /var and /tmp in their own partitions? Is /boot in its own partition within cylinder 1024? Is the root filesystem relatively small?

3. Where is LILO installed on your system? If it is installed in the boot sector, does your configuration allow for multiple boot scenarios? If it is installed in the root partition, is it within the first 1024 cylinders?

4. Locate a tarball (from *freshmeat.net*, for example), and install it on your system with the following steps:

    a. Unpack it using **tar xzvf** *file*.

    b. Configure with **./configure**.

    c. Build the software using **make** as directed in the documentation.

    d. Install the software using the instructions provided.

    Were there any difficulties with this procedure?

5. Use **ldd** to examine library dependencies of executable programs on your system. For example:

```
# ldd `which xterm`
    libXaw.so.7 => /usr/X11R6/lib/libXaw.so.7 (0x40019000)
    libXmu.so.6 => /usr/X11R6/lib/libXmu.so.6 (0x4006a000)
    libXt.so.6 => /usr/X11R6/lib/libXt.so.6 (0x4007e000)
    libSM.so.6 => /usr/X11R6/lib/libSM.so.6 (0x400c7000)
    libICE.so.6 => /usr/X11R6/lib/libICE.so.6 (0x400d0000)
    libXpm.so.4 => /usr/X11R6/lib/libXpm.so.4 (0x400e6000)
    libXext.so.6 => /usr/X11R6/lib/libXext.so.6 (0x400f4000)
    libX11.so.6 => /usr/X11R6/lib/libX11.so.6 (0x40101000)
    libncurses.so.4 => /usr/lib/libncurses.so.4 (0x401c4000)
    libc.so.6 => /lib/libc.so.6 (0x40201000)
    /lib/ld-linux.so.2 => /lib/ld-linux.so.2 (0x40000000)
```

6. Using a system that utilizes **dpkg**, obtain a list of all packages installed under **dpkg** management with **dpkg -l | less**. Find a package in the list that looks unfamiliar, and query information about the package using **dpkg -s** *pkg_name*.

7. Using a system that utilizes RPM, obtain a list of all packages installed under RPM management with **rpm -qa | less**. Find a package in the list that looks unfamiliar, and query information about the package using **rpm -qi** *pkg_name*.

Kernel (Topic 1.5)

Review Questions

1. What is the procedure for removing and installing modules in the running kernel? Why is this procedure necessary?

2. Describe the differences between the **insmod** and **modprobe** commands.

3. Which file stores optional parameters used by kernel modules?

4. Describe the nature of a monolithic kernel and the consequences and/or advantages of using one.

5. Name the major steps required to configure, build, and install a custom kernel and its modules.

Exercises

1. Using the procedures found in Part 2, *Kernel (Topic 1.5)*, as well as the kernel HOWTO, configure, build, and install a custom kernel and modules. Boot the new kernel. Does your system behave normally? Are you able to boot both your original kernel and the new one?

2. Using **lsmod**, examine the modules attached to your running kernel (presuming you're running a recent, modular kernel, that is).

   a. Try removing a noncritical module—for example, **rmmod sound**. Did the command fail because the module was in use?

   b. Try inserting a module—for example, **modprobe fat**, followed by **lsmod**. Did the module get inserted correctly? Remove it with **rmmod fat**. Was the removal successful?

   c. What is logged in */var/log/messages* during these changes?

Text Editing, Processing, and Printing (Topic 1.7)

Review Questions

1. What is the difference between the commands :q and :q! when running **vi**?

2. What does it mean to put **vi** into *command mode*?

3. What does **lpd** do to handle incoming print jobs destined for empty print queues?

4. Describe the kinds of information included in */etc/printcap*.

5. What is the function of a print filter?

6. What does the -P option specify to the print commands?

7. When is it useful to pipe into the standard input of **lpr** instead of simply using a filename as an argument?

8. How is the Ghostscript program used in printing to a non-PostScript printer?

9. What filter is used on a Linux system to print to remote printers on Windows clients?

Exercises

1. Use **vi** to create a text file. Enter insert mode with **i** and insert text. Quit insert mode with **Esc** and move around using **h**, **j**, **k**, and **l**, then reenter insert mode and add more text. End the session with **ZZ**. **cat** the file. Is it as expected?

2. On a system with an existing printer, examine */etc/printcap*. Which print filter is used for the printer? Which queue or queues are directed at the printer?

3. Check the printer status with **lpq -P***printer* and **lpc status**. Print to the queue using **lpr -P***printer file*.

4. Examine */var/spool/lp* for the spool directory of your print queue. Examine the files you find there.

5. If **APSfilter** is not installed, install it and allow it to add new print queues. How are these queues different from one another and from your default queue?

Shells, Scripting, Programming, and Compiling (Topic 1.9)

Review Questions

1. Name the two major shell variants found on Unix and Linux systems.

2. What characteristic of a **bash** variable changes when the variable is exported?

3. Describe the concept of shell aliases.

4. When is a shell function more suitable than a shell alias?

5. Describe the function of */etc/profile*.

6. What must the author of a new script file do to the file's mode?

7. How does the shell determine what interpreter to execute when starting a script?

8. How can a shell script use return values of the commands it executes?

Exercises

1. Using **bash**, enter the **export** command and the **set** command. Which set of variables is a subset of the other? What is the difference between the variables reported by **export** and those reported by **set**? Finally, enter **which export**. Where is the **export** command located?

2. Examine */etc/profile*. How is the default **umask** set? What customizations are done in the file for system users?

3. Create a simple **bash** script using the #!/bin/bash syntax, set the executable mode bits, and execute the shell. If it runs correctly, add errors to see the diagnostic messages. Have the script report both exported and nonexported variables. Verify that the nonexported variables do not survive the startup of the new shell.

X (Topic 2.10)

Review Questions

1. When using XFree86 v3.3.x, what software installation may be required when changing to a different video chipset, and why?

2. Describe how the location of fonts is conveyed to the XFree86 X server.

3. How is the use of a font server different from the use of a font path?

4. Which file controls access to **xdm** by remote X terminals?

5. Describe the function of **xinit**.

6. Compare and contrast a window manager, a desktop environment, and an X server.

7. Name the three components of the DISPLAY environment variable.

Exercises

1. From *www.xfree86.org*, obtain XFree86 in the precompiled binary form for your system using the instructions found in Part 2, *X (Topic 2.10)*. Start with the *Xinstall.sh* script and run it with *./***Xinstall.sh –check** to determine which package to get.

2. Back up your old installation (*/etc/X11* and */usr/X11R6*). Install the new version using *Xinstall.sh* as directed in the instructions accompanying the package.

3. Use **xf86config** to configure the new X server. Are you able to get an X display? Is the resolution correct?

4. Try generating the X configuration using **XF86Setup** or **xf86cfg** (depending on the X version). Is the program successful? Does it yield a working X configuration?

5. Obtain a new Type 1 font from the Internet (try a search at *http://www.google.com* or your favorite search engine). Add the font to */usr/X11R6/lib/X11/fonts/local* and use the **mkfontdir** utility on that directory. Verify that the *local* font directory is in the font path. Restart X and use **xfontsel** to view the new font. Was the font added correctly?

6. Configure **xfs** as describe in Part 2, *X (Topic 2.10)*, and remove the Font-Path statements from *XF86Config*, substituting **unix/:-1**. Start the font server and restart the X server. Using **xfontsel**, are you able to verify the availability of the same fonts as were available before?

7. Start **xdm** on your system, and note that the system starts the X server and presents a login prompt. If all works correctly, change the default runlevel to that which starts **xdm** and reboot. Does the system now present a graphical login screen?

8. Examine the scripts and programs used on your system for starting X, beginning with **startx**. Look for how the system uses files in the user's home directory to control GUI startup.

9. Examine your window manager configuration. Which window manager are you using? Is it part of a desktop environment, such as KDE or GNOME? Determine where its menus are configured and add an item or two to the menus.

Networking Fundamentals (Topic 1.12)

Review Questions

1. Describe how the subnet mask affects the maximum number of hosts that can be put on a TCP/IP network.

2. Name the three default address classes and the subnet masks associated with them.

3. The UDP protocol is said to be connectionless. Describe this concept and its consequences on applications that use UDP.

4. What user command is frequently used to send ICMP messages to remote hosts in order to verify those hosts' functionality?

5. Describe the contents and use of /etc/hosts.

6. In what configuration file are DNS servers listed? What is intended if the local loopback address is included there on a workstation?

7. Name two modes of the **netstat** command and the program's output in each case.

8. Describe why the **route** command is needed for a single interface on a nonrouting workstation.

9. How does **traceroute** determine the identities of intermediate gateways?

10. Describe the advantages and consequences of implementing DHCP.

11. What utility is used to configure and dial a modem prior to the creation of a PPP connection?

12. What are the four authentication modes commonly used during PPP negotiations?

Exercises

1. Examine your system's TCP/IP configuration using **ifconfig eth0** or a similar command for your network interface. Are you using DHCP? What type of subnet are you running with? Is it a Class A, B, or C address? Are you using a private address? Experiment with taking the interface offline using **ifconfig eth0 down** and **ifconfig eth0 up**.

2. Examine the contents of /etc/services.

3. Use the **dig** command to locate information from DNS servers about a domain name.

4. Examine your /etc/hosts file. How much name resolution is accomplished in this file manually?

5. Examine your /etc/resolv.conf file. How many DNS servers do you have available?

6. Execute **netstat –r**. How many routes are reported? What are the routes to the local network and interface for?

7. Use **traceroute** to examine the route to a favorite web site.

8. If you are using DHCP, use **pump –r** to release your IP address, followed by **pump –R** and **pump –s**. Does the system still function correctly on the network?

9. Using a standard modem (not a WinModem), use **minicom** to connect to the modem and verify that it responds to the **AT** command.

10. Execute a manual PPP connection as described in Part 2, *Networking Funda mentals (Topic 1.12)*. Does your modem successfully connect to your Internet Service Provider? Examine */var/log/messages* for information on the PPP session.

Networking Services (Topic 1.13)

Review Questions

1. Describe the function of **inetd** and how it is configured.

2. Describe the TCP Wrappers security tool and how it can enhance security on a networked system.

3. Describe the use of mail aliases and how to enable new aliases.

4. What files are used to configure the Apache web server?

5. How does the administrator share a directory using NFS?

6. How does the administrator mount a directory shared by a remote NFS server?

7. What is the function of **nmbd**?

8. Which file is used to configure **smbd**?

9. Describe the function and location of the *resolver*.

10. Name two programs that can be used to do queries against an NFS server.

11. Describe in general terms the main difference between BIND v4 and BIND v8 configuration files.

Exercises

1. Examine your *inetd.conf*. Are **telnetd** and **ftpd** enabled? If so, are TCP Wrappers (**tcpd**) configured for them?

2. Enable TCP Wrappers and place ALL:ALL in */etc/hosts.deny*, then attempt a Telnet session. Is the inbound request ignored as expected?

3. Familiarize yourself with */etc/sendmail.cf* and */etc/aliases*. Run **newaliases**.

4. Familiarize yourself with Apache configuration files in */etc/httpd/html/*.conf* (or your directory location).

5. Examine your */etc/exports* file, if it exists. Are you sharing NFS volumes?

---

6. Examine your */etc/smb.conf* file. Are you sharing Samba printers or volumes?

7. Examine your resolver configuration in */etc/resolv.conf, /etc/hosts.conf,* and */etc/nsswitch.conf.* Is the local */etc/hosts* file consulted prior to DNS servers?

8. By examining */etc/named.conf* and noting format details, determine what general release of BIND you are using.

Security (Topic 1.14)

Review Questions

1. What daemon is associated with the control files */etc/hosts.allow* and */etc/hosts.deny.*

2. In general terms, describe a method to locate SUID programs in the local filesystem. Why might an administrator do this routinely?

3. What is the function of the **md5sum** utility?

4. Why might a user run SSH instead of Telnet?

5. Describe shadow passwords and the file where the passwords are stored.

Exercises

1. Use **find** as described in Part 2, *Security (Topic 1.14)*, to locate SUID files. Is the list larger than you expected? Are the entries on your list justifiably SUID programs?

2. Use the **md5sum** utility on a binary program file and examine its output.

3. Using the instructions in Part 2, *Security (Topic 1.14)* (or a package from your distribution), install SSH. Start **sshd** and attempt to connect to your own system with **ssh localhost**. The connection should proceed in a manner similar to a Telnet session.

Exam 102 Practice Test

Exam 102 consists of approximately 72 questions. Most are multiple-choice single-answer, a few are multiple-choice multiple-answer, and the remainder are fill-in questions. No notes or other materials are permitted, and you have 90 minutes to complete the exam. The answers are provided on page 487.

Questions

1. How many hosts can exist on a subnet with mask 255.255.255.128? Select one.

   a. 512

   b. 256

   c. 128

   d. 127

   e. 126

2. When running a text-mode FTP client, which command retrieves multiple files? Select one.

   a. **get *.txt**

   b. **retrieve *.txt**

   c. **mget *.txt**

   d. **mretrieve *.txt**

   e. **get -m *.txt**

3. For an Internet workstation with a single network interface, what routes must be added to interface *eth0* after it is initialized? Select one.

   a. None

   b. Interface

   c. Interface and default gateway

   d. Interface, local network, and default gateway

4. Which of the following is true regarding the *XF86Config* file? Select all that apply.

   a. Can set the screen resolution setting

   b. Can set the bits-per-pixel (color depth) setting

   c. Includes keyboard and mouse selections

   d. Includes information on which window manager to run

   e. Contains information on where to find fonts

5. What is the correct syntax to remove *mypkg* entirely from a Debian GNU/ Linux system, including configuration files? Select one.

   a. **dpkg –r mypkg**

   b. **dpkg ––remove mypkg**

   c. **dpkg ––kill mypkg**

   d. **dpkg –R mypkg**

   e. **dpkg ––purge mypkg**

6. On a Linux server, what service is most likely "listening" on port 25? Select one.

   a. Apache

   b. News

   c. Sendmail

   d. Samba

   e. FTP

7. Your system's FontPath directives include only one entry:

   unix/:-1

   Which of the following is true? Select one.

   a. Error -1 has occurred during X startup

   b. Only the default font will be available to applications

   c. An X font server is to be used

   d. An X font server failed to initialize

   e. No fonts were found by XFree86 or by a font server

8. Which one of these protocols is used as a datagram delivery service by the remaining three? Select one.

   a. TCP

   b. IP

   c. UDP

   d. ICMP

9. How do you use **dpkg** to verify the status of an installed package *mypkg?* Select one.

a. dpkg -s mypkg

b. dpkg -S mypkg

c. dpkg -stat mypkg

d. dpkg --stat mypkg

e. dpkg --Status mypkg

10. Which of the following statements is true about an X server? Select one.

a. An X server is a high-performance system offering graphical programs over a network.

b. An X server sends its graphical output to a window manager.

c. An X server is under the control of a window manager.

d. A window manager is under the control of an X server.

e. A window manager is also known as an X server.

11. Which command will display information about Ethernet interface *eth0*? Select one.

a. cat /proc/eth/0

b. ifconfig eth0

c. ipconfig eth0

d. ipconfig /dev/eth0

e. cat /etc/eth0.conf

12. What are the two interrupts usually associated with a PC's onboard serial interface?

_____

13. Which of the following commands will cause a kernel module to be included in the running kernel? Select all that apply.

a. modinsert

b. modprobe

c. insmod

d. prbmod

e. rmmod

14. When is the PPP interface *ppp0* created? Select one.

a. At boot time by the kernel.

b. At installation time by mknod.

c. At dialup time by the chat script.

d. At dialup time by pppd.

e. When the modem powers up.

15. What program is run on a client machine to request an IP address from a DHCP server? Select one.

   a. **dhcpd**

   b. **inetd**

   c. **pump**

   d. **dhcp_client**

   e. **bootp**

16. What does the **printcap** entry **sd** indicate? Select one.

   a. The system default printer

   b. A printer's spool directory

   c. A device file for the printer

   d. A location where errors are stored

   e. The printer driver

17. How can you query the RPM database for a list of all installed RPM packages? Select one.

   a. **rpm -q**

   b. **rpm -qa**

   c. **rpm -a**

   d. **rpm -al**

   e. **rpm -qal**

18. Where are TCP Wrappers configured and where are they enabled?

   a. Configured in *tcpd.conf*, enabled in *tcpd.conf*

   b. Configured in *inetd.conf*, enabled in *inetd.conf*

   c. Configured in *hosts.deny* and *hosts.allow*, enabled in *inetd.conf*

   d. Configured in *inetd.conf*, enabled in *hosts.deny* and *hosts.allow*

19. Which pair of **dpkg** options are equivalent and what do they do? Select one.

   a. **-C** and **--configure**; they reconfigure an unpackaged package.

   b. **-C** and **--clear-avail**; they erase existing information about what packages are available.

   c. **-A** and **--audit**; they update information about what packages are available.

   d. **-C** and **--audit**; they provide resource consumption information on installed packages.

   e. **-C** and **--audit**; they search for partially installed packages.

20. Which of the following is a valid entry in */etc/fstab* for a remote NFS mount from server fs1? Select one.

   a. `fs1:/proc /mnt/fs1 nfs defaults 9 9`

   b. `/mnt/fs1 fs1:/proc nfs defaults 0 0`

```
c. fs1:/home /mnt/fs1 nfs defaults 0 0
d. /mnt/fs1 fs1:/home nfs defaults 0 0
e. /home:fs1 /mnt/fs1 nfs defaults 0 0
```

21. Which network protocol is used by Telnet and FTP? Select one.

    a. ICMP

    b. UDP

    c. TCP

    d. DHCP

    e. PPP

22. Which of the following programs will display DNS information for a host? Choose all that apply.

    a. **host**

    b. **nslookup**

    c. **nsstat**

    d. **dig**

    e. **ping**

23. Consider the following entry in /etc/exports:

    ```
    /home          pickle(rw,no_root_squash)
    ```

    How is this entry handled by the NFS daemon? Select one.

    a. Directory /home is shared to everyone, without requiring passwords.

    b. Directory /home is shared to everyone, requiring passwords.

    c. Directory pickle is mounted on /home.

    d. Root is not allowed access to the shared directory.

    e. The mount attempt will fail.

24. From the user's point of view, which answer describes the appearance of an NFS mounted directory? Select one.

    a. A new device in /dev.

    b. A new local volume accessed using a volume letter, such as D:.

    c. A new local volume accessed using the NFS server's name.

    d. Part of the local filesystem, accessed using ordinary pathnames.

    e. Part of the NFS server's filesystem, accessed using the NFS server's name.

25. Which of the following statements regarding the ICMP protocol is not true? Select one.

    a. ICMP is connectionless.

    b. ICMP provides network flow control.

    c. ICMP is also known as UDP.

    d. ICMP is used by ping.

26. What will happen when **rpm** is launched as follows? Select one.

   rpm -Uvh *file*

   a. The RPM file will be verified.

   b. An installed package may be upgraded with the version in file, with verbose output.

   c. An installed package may be upgraded with the version in file, with verbose output and hash marks indicating progress.

   d. An error will occur because a major mode is not specified.

   e. An error will occur because no file options were specified.

27. Consider the following C program:

```
#include <stdio.h>
main() {
  printf("Hello, world\n");
}
```

   and its compilation command:

   `# gcc -o hw hw.c -static`

   Assuming that the compilation is successful, what will result from the following command? Select one.

   `# ldd ./hw`

   a. An error message indicating that an option is required.

   b. An error message indicating that **hw** is the wrong file type.

   c. An error message indicating that **hw** is not dynamically linked.

   d. A list of source and header files from which **hw** was compiled.

   e. A list of shared libraries upon which **hw** is dependent.

28. How are changes to the system BIOS made? Select one.

   a. Using **linuxconf**.

   b. By manually editing text files.

   c. Using the **lilo** command.

   d. At boot time using system-specific menus.

   e. At boot time using LILO commands.

29. What is CHAP? Select one.

   a. The PPP chat script.

   b. An authentication protocol using clear text.

   c. An authentication protocol embedded in the PPP data stream.

   d. The **pppd** configuration utility.

   e. A modem communications protocol.

30. After a new kernel is compiled and copied correctly to the appropriate locations, what command must be run to ensure that the new kernel boots properly? Select one.

    a. **make install**

    b. **make config**

    c. **make lilo**

    d. LILO

    e. **lilo**

31. What server daemon resolves domain names to IP addresses for requesting hosts?

_____

32. During the two-way communication that takes place during a chat script used to start PPP, what is **chat** communicating with? Select one.

    a. The **pppd** daemon.

    b. The PPP server.

    c. The kernel.

    d. The modem.

    e. The **syslogd** daemon.

33. What function does a print filter serve? Select one.

    a. It collates output from multiple users.

    b. It translates various data formats into a page description language.

    c. It rejects print requests from unauthorized users.

    d. It rejects print requests from unauthorized hosts.

    e. It analyzes print data and directs print requests to the appropriate **lpd**.

34. Consider the following excerpt from file */etc/resolv.conf* of a Linux workstation:

```
nameserver 127.0.0.1
nameserver 192.168.1.5
nameserver 192.168.250.2
```

What can be said about this configuration? Select one.

    a. Two DNS servers on the public network are being used for resolution.

    b. One DNS server on the local network is being used for resolution.

    c. The configuration contains errors that will prevent the resolver from functioning.

    d. A caching-only name server is running.

    e. The resolver library will consult `nameserver 192.168.250.2` first.

35. Which of the following is true regarding BIND v4 and BIND v8 configuration files? Select one.

   a. The information is largely the same, but the syntax is different.

   b. The syntax is largely the same, but the information is different.

   c. The two BIND versions use the same configuration file.

   d. BIND v4 uses a binary configuration file instead of text.

   e. BIND v8 uses a binary configuration file instead of text.

36. What file is used to configure sendmail? Include the entire path.

   _____

37. Name the file that contains simple mappings between IP addresses and system names.

   _____

38. What is the meaning and location of the following kernel configuration file excerpt? Select one.

   options opl3 io=0x388

   a. Kernel option opl3 is set to use I/O port 0x388; */usr/src/linux/.config*.

   b. Kernel module option opl3 is set to use I/O port 0x388; */usr/src/linux/ .config*.

   c. Kernel module opl3 is set to use I/O port 0x388; */usr/src/linux/.config*.

   d. Kernel option opl3 is set to use I/O port 0x388; */usr/src/linux/.config*.

   e. Kernel module opl3 is set to use I/O port 0x388; */etc/conf.modules* or */etc/modules.conf*.

39. When using **xdm**, which of the following files can be used to start a window manager? Select one.

   a. **Xservers**

   b. **Xaccess**

   c. **xdm-config**

   d. **Xsession**

   e. **Xsetup_0**

40. What program can be used to interactively change the behavior of a print queue? Select one.

   a. **lpd**

   b. **lpr**

   c. **lpq**

   d. **lprm**

   e. **lpc**

41. What command displays queued outgoing mail? Select one.

    a. mailq

    b. mailqueue

    c. mqueue

    d. mq

    e. sendmail -mq

42. When partitioning a disk with more than 1024 cylinders, which of the following could affect the system's ability to boot? Select all that apply.

    a. Location of LILO on disk.

    b. Location of /boot on disk.

    c. Location of /var on disk.

    d. Disk transfer rate.

    e. Disk seek time.

43. Which of the following represents a valid sequence of commands to compile and install a new kernel? Select one.

    a. make modules_install; make modules; make bzImage; make clean; make dep

    b. make dep; make clean; make bzImage; make config; make modules; make modules_install

    c. make config; make dep; make clean; make bzImage; make modules; make modules_install

    d. make config; make bzImage; make dep; make clean; make modules; make modules_install

    e. make dep; make clean; make bzImage; make modules; make modules_install; make config

44. What program will display a list of each hop across the network to a specified destination? Select one.

    a. tracert

    b. rttrace

    c. traceroute

    d. routetrace

    e. init

45. Which of the following is a reasonable size for a swap partition for a Linux workstation with 128 MB RAM? Select one.

    a. 1 KB

    b. 0.5 MB

    c. 100 MB

    d. 5 GB

    e. 10 GB

46. What is XDMCP, and how is it used? Select one.

 a. An X utility, used to copy files between a host and an X terminal.

 b. An X utility, used to configure XDM.

 c. An X utility, used to configure IP addresses on X terminals on the network.

 d. An X protocol, used to discover/listen for X terminals on the network.

 e. An X protocol, used to exchange graphics information between X clients and X servers over the network.

47. What is the first step in compiling software obtained in a compressed **tar** archive *myapp.tgz*? Select one.

 a. **make install=myapp.tgz**

 b. **make myapp**

 c. **tar xzf myapp.tgz**

 d. **tar xvf myapp.tgz**

 e. **tar cvf myapp.tgz**

48. How many target devices can be added to an 8-bit SCSI-2 bus? Select one.

 a. 6

 b. 7

 c. 8

 d. 15

 e. 16

49. Which file holds configuration information used during the process of kernel compilation? Select one.

 a. */usr/src/linux/config*

 b. */usr/src/linux/.config*

 c. */usr/src/linux/kernel.conf*

 d. */etc/kernel.conf*

 e. */etc/sysconfig/kernel.conf*

50. After a PPP connection is established and authenticated, what needs to be done before the interface can be used? Select one.

 a. Add a route to **ppp0**.

 b. Enable **ppp0**.

 c. **ifup ppp0**.

 d. Run **pppd**.

 e. Turn on the modem.

51. Which of the following is not the name of an Apache configuration file? Select one.

    a. *httpd.conf*

    b. *html.conf*

    c. *srm.conf*

    d. *access.conf*

52. What is the **startx** command? Select one.

    a. A script included with XFree86 to make startup user friendly.

    b. A script used to start **xdm**.

    c. A compiled binary program that directly launches the X server.

    d. A configuration file created by X configuration tools such as *XF86Config*.

    e. A script originated by Linux distributors to tailor X startup to their particular X implementation.

53. Which statement is true regarding the configuration of a printer on a remote Windows machine? Select one.

    a. It can be configured like a TCP/IP network–attached printer.

    b. The input filter must be set to **smbprint**.

    c. The Windows printer must contain PostScript capability.

    d. The **rp** directive must be used in the *printcap* file.

    e. Linux can't print to Windows printers.

54. How can you obtain a list of files contained in an *.rpm* file? Select one.

    a. **rpm -q** *file*

    b. **rpm -i** *file*

    c. **rpm -ql** *file*

    d. **rpm -qlp** *file*

    e. **rpm -qal** *file*

55. What types of files are located in the directory tree specified by the Apache DocumentRoot configuration directive? Select one.

    a. Apache documentation files.

    b. Apache configuration files.

    c. Web site HTML files.

    d. Web site configuration files.

    e. Apache startup and shutdown commands.

56. How can root change the attributes of file *myfile* so that its owner is *user1* and its group is *group1*? Select one.

    a. **chgrp user1.group1 myfile**

    b. **chown user1.group1 myfile**

c. chmod user1.group1 myfile

d. chage user1.group1 myfile

e. chattr user1.group1 myfile

57. Which of the following commands will display a listing of files contained in a tar archive tape in */dev/st0*? Select one.

   a. tar cf /dev/st0

   b. tar xf /dev/st0

   c. tar tf /dev/st0

   d. tar –zf /dev/st0

   e. tar –zcvf /dev/st0

58. Which of the following accurately describes the contents of the *xdisp:1.0* DISPLAY environment variable? Select one.

   a. System *xdisp* is to send X programs to the first display of the local X server.

   b. System *xdisp* is to receive X programs on the first display of its X server.

   c. System *xdisp* is to receive X programs on the second display of its X server.

   d. Local program **xdisp** is to use the second display of the local X server.

   e. Local program **xdisp** is to use the second display of any available X terminal.

59. Which file contains information on the I/O port assignments in use? Select one.

   a. */dev/ioports*

   b. */etc/ioports*

   c. */etc/sysconfig/ioports*

   d. */etc/proc/ioports*

   e. */proc/ioports*

60. What is the system-wide **bash** configuration file called? Include the entire path.

   _____

61. What happens when **ldconfig** is executed? Select one.

   a. The binary index file of library locations is rebuilt.

   b. The text index file of library locations is rebuilt.

   c. **make** is run to rebuild libraries whose source code has changed.

   d. The disk is scanned for libraries to include in the index.

   e. Nothing, unless libraries have been recompiled since **ldconfig** was last run.

62. How can a nonprivileged user configure **sendmail** to forward mail to another account? Select one.

  a. He can add a new entry in */etc/aliases*.

  b. He can create a *.forward* file containing the new address.

  c. He can create an *.alias* file containing the new address.

  d. He can create a *sendmail.cf* file containing the new address.

  e. He cannot forward mail without assistance from the administrator.

63. How does a process indicate to the controlling shell that it has exited with an error condition? Select one.

  a. It prints an error message to *stderr*.

  b. It prints an error message to *stdout*.

  c. It sets an exit code with a zero value.

  d. It sets an exit code with a nonzero value.

  e. It causes a segmentation fault.

64. Consider the following trivial script called *myscript*:

```
#!/bin/bash
echo "Hello"
echo $myvar
```

Also consider this command sequence and result:

```
# set myvar='World'
# ./myscript
Hello
```

The script ran without error but didn't **echo** *World*. Why not? Select one.

  a. The syntax of the **set** command is incorrect.

  b. The script executes in a new shell, and *myvar* wasn't exported.

  c. The #!/bin/bash syntax is incorrect.

  d. The $myvar syntax is incorrect.

  e. The script is sourced by the current shell, and *myvar* is available only to new shells.

65. Why might an administrator use the **--force** option for **rpm**? Select one.

  a. To overwrite a previously installed package.

  b. To overwrite a Debian package.

  c. To prevent confirmation messages.

  d. To force the deletion of installed packages.

  e. To force the deletion of package dependencies.

66. Which of the following commands cannot be used to exit from **vi** when in command mode? Select one.

    a. **ZZ**

    b. **:x**

    c. **:q**

    d. **:q!**

    e. **:bye**

67. What does this short configuration file excerpt tell the Samba daemon? Select one.

```
[home]
  path = /home
  guest ok = yes
  writable = yes
```

    a. The location of the Samba software is rooted at */home*.

    b. A printer called home uses */home* as a spool directory.

    c. A share called home is located on */home* and is writable by authenticated users.

    d. A share called home is located on */home* and is writable by anyone.

    e. A share called home on remote system *guest* will be mounted at */home*.

68. Which is not a valid **dpkg** installation command? Select one.

    a. **dpkg -i** *package_file*

    b. **dpkg -iL** *package_file*

    c. **dpkg -iR** *package_dir*

    d. **dpkg -iG** *package_file*

    e. **dpkg -iE** *package_file*

69. How can the **finger** daemon be enabled? Select one.

    a. Uncomment the *in.fingerd* line in */etc/inetd.conf*.

    b. Use **cron** to run **fingerd** once per minute.

    c. Include **fingerd** in the TCP Wrappers configuration.

    d. Remove **fingerd** from *hosts.deny*.

    e. Add **fingerd** to *hosts.allow*.

70. Which of the following is not a major **rpm** mode option? Select one.

    a. **-U**

    b. **-V**

    c. **-e**

    d. **-q**

    e. **-v**

71. Which of the following is the text file that contains directories where the dynamic linker should look for libraries? Select one.

   a. *ld.so.conf*

   b. *conf.ld.so*

   c. *ld.so.cache*

   d. *so.config*

   e. *configld*

72. Where is quota information for users of volume */home* stored? Select one.

   a. */etc/sysconfig/quota/quota.home.user*

   b. */etc/quota/quota.home.user*

   c. */home/quota.home.user*

   d. */home/quota.user*

   e. */home/quota.home.user*

Answers

1. e. With the top bit of the last byte set in the subnet mask (.128), we have 7 bits left. 2^7 is 128, less the network address and broadcast address, leaving 126 addresses for hosts.

2. c. FTP clients use **mget** with wildcards.

3. d. Routes to the interface and the network are required to exchange information on the local LAN. To act as an Internet workstation (i.e., using Netscape), a default gateway is also necessary.

4. a, b, c, and e. *XF86Config* does not specify a window manager.

5. e. The **--purge** option is a variant of **-r**, remove.

6. c. As defined in */etc/services*, port 25 is the SMTP port, often monitored by **sendmail**.

7. c. The directive indicates that a font server should listen on its default port.

8. b. IP is the underlying datagram protocol.

9. a. The appropriate option is either **-s** or **--status**.

10. d. A window manager is a client, controlled by the X server. Answers a and b are incorrect because they imply that the X server originates the graphical output. Answers c and e are common misconceptions.

11. b. The **ifconfig** command is used to configure and display interface information. **ipconfig** is a Windows utility.

12. 3 and 4.

13. b and c.

14. d. PPP interfaces are not persistent. Instead, they are initialized when needed.

15. c. The DHCP client is called **pump**, after the lady's shoe of the same name. That's an extension from a "boot" because DHCP is a descendant from **bootp**.

16. b. The spool directory directive looks like this:

```
sd=/var/spool/lpd/lp
```

17. b. The query mode is required, which implies **-q**. The **-a** option in query mode yields all packages.

18. c. The *hosts.deny* and *hosts.allow* files contain configuration information for TCP Wrappers. The files won't be used, however, unless **tcpd** is included in *inetd.conf*.

19. e.

20. c. Answer a attempts to mount the */proc* filesystem. Answers b, d, and e have incorrect syntax.

21. c. Both Telnet and FTP are connection-oriented and use TCP for reliable connections.

22. a, b, and d.

23. b. Read/write access is available to everyone, including root.

24. d. NFS-mounted directories seamlessly blend into the local filesystem, requiring no special syntax for access.

25. c. While both ICMP and UDP are connectionless, they are different protocols.

26. c. Provided that *file* is an RPM file, the –U indicates that an upgrade should occur. **-h** turns on hash marks.

27. c. Because the program was statically linked using the **–static** option to **gcc**, there are no library dependencies, and **ldd** will yield an error.

28. d. Linux has no control over the BIOS settings.

29. c. CHAP is one of the PPP authentication techniques that embeds its information inside the PPP stream. It is an alternative to clear text passwords.

30. e. **lilo** must be run to rebuild the boot loader after a new kernel is installed.

31. The DNS daemon is **named**. It is included in a package called BIND.

32. d. The intent of the chat script is to prepare the modem with appropriate settings to establish a PPP connection.

33. b. A print server translates formats, such as PostScript to PCL.

34. d. The presence of the *localhost* address 127.0.0.1 indicates that **named** is running. Since the system is a workstation, it's safe to assume that it is not serving DNS to a wider community.

35. a. BIND v8 has a newer, more modular format, but the information is about the same.

36. */etc/sendmail.cf*.

37. */etc/hosts*.

38. e. **options** lines in */etc/modules.conf* or */etc/conf.modules* configure kernel modules.

39. d. **Xsession** is the system-wide default application startup file.

40. e. **lpc** is the line printer control program.

41. a.

42. a and b. Both the second stage of **lilo** and the kernel should be kept within the 1024-cylinder boundary.

43. c. Answer a is wrong because it installs modules before compiling them. Answers b and e are wrong because they build the kernel after configuring. Answer d is backward.

44. c. **tracert** is a Windows utility with the same function as **traceroute**.

45. c.

46. d. X terminals use XDMCP to attach to **xdm** daemons.

47. c. The *.tgz* extension indicates that the file is a compressed tar archive. This requires the use of the **z** option. **x** directs **tar** to extract. **f** directs **tar** to use the filename found next on the command line.

48. b. An 8-bit SCSI bus has three address lines. 2^8 is 8, less the address of the controller, which leaves 7 target addresses.

49. b.

50. a. Just as with any interface, routes must be added before communications can occur.

51. b. Apache uses *httpd.conf*, *srm.conf*, and *access.conf*. Some implementations may roll all of these files into a single *httpd.conf*.

52. a. **startx** is included with XFree86 as a suggestion, and customization is encouraged.

53. b. The **smbprint** filter is provided by the Samba package for printing to Windows printers.

54. d. Use **q** for query mode. Use the **l** query option to list, and use the **p** query option to specify a file rather than an installed RPM.

55. c.

56. b.

57. c. **t** is the option to list the contents of an archive.

58. c. The format is [*host*]:*display*[.*screen*]. The first display is :0; the second display is :1.

59. e.

60. The file is */etc/profile*.

61. a.

62. b. The *.forward* file is placed in the home directory containing a single line with the target email address.

63. d. Zero exit values usually indicate success.

64. b. Instead of using **set**, the command should have been:

```
# export myvar='World'
```

This gives the myvar variable to the new shell.

65. a. Without options, **rpm** won't overwrite an existing package installation.

66. e.

67. d.

68. b. Options **–i** (install) and **–L** (list installed files) are incompatible and don't make sense together.

69. a. For security purposes, **fingerd** is usually disabled using a comment in */etc/inetd.conf*.

70. e. The valid modes are Update (**–U**), Verify (**–V**), Erase (**–e**), and Query (**–q**).

71. a. *ld.so.conf* is the text file in which you add library directories. *ld.so.cache* is the binary index resulting from *ldconfig*.

72. d. Quota files are stored on the volume they control.

Exam 102
Highlighter's Index

Hardware and Architecture

Objective 1: Configure Fundamental System Hardware

PC BIOS

- The BIOS is the PC's firmware.
- The BIOS sets date and time for onboard clock, storage device configuration, and so on via menus.

Resource assignments

- Interrupts (IRQs) allow peripherals to interrupt the CPU.
- I/O addresses are locations in the microprocessor's memory map for hardware devices.
- DMA allows certain devices to work directly with memory, freeing the microprocessor (see Table 2-21).

Table 2-21: Some Common Device Settings

Device	I/O Address	IRQ	DMA
ttyS0 (COM1)	3f8	4	NA
ttyS1 (COM2)	2f8	3	NA
ttyS2 (COM3)	3e8	4	NA
ttyS3 (COM4)	2e8	3	NA
lp0 (LPT1)	378-37f	7	NA
lp1 (LPT2)	278-27f	5	NA

Table 2-21: Some Common Device Settings (continued)

Device	I/O Address	IRQ	DMA
fd0, fd1 (floppies 1 and 2)	3f0-3f7	6	2
fd2, fd3 (floppies 3 and 4)	370-377	10	3

1024-cylinder limit

- LILO and the kernel image should be kept within the first 1024 cylinders on hard disks.

Objective 2: Set Up SCSI and NIC Devices

NICs

- NICs have been configured using hardware jumpers, nonvolatile memory, and automated means.
- The *proc* filesystem includes information on interrupts, I/O ports, and DMA in */proc/interrupts*, */proc/ioports*, and */proc/dma*.

SCSI

- The Small Computer System Interface (SCSI) defines a bus for multiple storage devices.
- SCSI capabilities range from 5 MBps to 80 MBps and higher for the newest types.
- 8-bit SCSI offers up to seven devices plus the controller on a single bus.
- 16-bit SCSI offers up to 15 devices plus the controller on a single bus.
- Each device on the bus has a unique SCSI ID, 0–7 or 0–15. Controllers often default to address 7.
- Linux device files for SCSI disks are typically */dev/sda*, */dev/sdb*, and so forth.
- Linux device files for SCSI tape drives are typically */dev/st0*, */dev/st1*, and so on.
- SCSI buses must be terminated on both ends. Many SCSI devices include internal terminators to eliminate the need for external terminators.
- PC SCSI adapters have their own BIOS, where the default boot device, bus speed, and onboard termination settings can be made.

Objective 3: Configure Modems and Sound Cards

Modems

- Modems are serial devices. Some are external and are attached to a serial port. Others are installed in a computer and include serial port electronics onboard.
- Some modems are cost-reduced by implementing portions of their functionality in Windows software libraries. These so-called "WinModems" often aren't compatible with Linux without add-on drivers.

Sound devices

- Sound is well-supported under Linux.

- **pnpdump** output is stored for use at boot time by **isapnp**, which does plug-n-play configuration.

Linux Installation and Package Management

Objective 1: Design a Hard Disk Layout

Guidelines

- Keep / small by distributing larger parts of the directory tree to other filesystems.

- Separate a small */boot* partition below cylinder 1024 for kernels.

- Separate */var* into its own partition to prevent runaway logs from filling /.

- Separate */tmp*.

- Separate */usr* if it is to be shared read-only among other systems via NFS.

- Set swap size to be about the size of main memory.

Objective 2: Install a Boot Manager

- LILO is a popular Linux boot loader.

- LILO consists of the **lilo** command, which installs the boot loader, and the boot loader itself.

- LILO is configured using */etc/lilo.conf*.

Objective 3: Make and Install Programs from Source

- Software often comes in a tarball, a compressed **tar** archive file.

- Larger source code packages include a *configure* script to verify that every-thing is in order to compile the software.

- **make** is then used to build the software.

- **make** is also often used to install the software into directories such as */usr/local/bin*.

Objective 4: Manage Shared Libraries

- System libraries provide many of the functions required by a program.

- A program that contains executable code from libraries is *statically linked*, because it stands alone and contains all necessary code to execute.

- Since static linking leads to larger executable files and more resource consumption, system libraries can be shared among many executing programs at the same time.

- A program that contains references to external, shared libraries is *dynamically linked* at runtime by the dynamic linker, *ld.so*.

- New locations for shared libraries can be added to the `LD_LIBRARY_PATH` variable. As an alternative, the locations can be added to */etc/ld.so.conf*, which lists library file directories. This file is translated into the binary index */etc/ld.so.cache* using *ldconfig*.

Objective 5: Use Debian Package Management

- **dpkg** automates the installation and maintenance of software packages.

- **dpkg** has a number of options.

Objective 6: Use Red Hat Package Manager (RPM)

- RPM automates the installation and maintenance of software packages.

- Package dependencies are handled automatically.

Kernel

Objective 1: Manage Kernel Modules at Runtime

- The Linux kernel is modular, and device driver software is inserted into the running kernel as needed.

- Module files are *objects*, stored under */lib/modules*.

- Kernel modules can be managed using:

  lsmod
  > List modules.

  insmod
  > Insert a module into the kernel.

  rmmod
  > Remove a module from the kernel.

  modinfo
  > Get information about a module.

  modprobe
  > Insert modules along with their prerequisites.

- Modules are configured in */etc/conf.modules* or */etc/modules.conf*.

- **modprobe** determines module dependencies using a file called *modules.dep*. This file is usually created at boot time using **depmod**.

Objective 2: Reconfigure, Build, and Install a Custom Kernel and Modules

- To build a kernel, you need the compiler, assembler, linker, **make**, kernel source, and kernel headers.

- These are typical kernel compilation steps, done in */usr/src/linux*:

  1. Make a configuration using **make oldconfig** (existing setup), **make config** (basic interactive text program), **make menuconfig** (interactive text menu program), or **make xconfig** (graphical program). Each method creates the *.config* file containing kernel options.

  2. Modify EXTRAVERSION in *Makefile*, if desired.

  3. Build dependencies using **make dep**.

  4. Clean old results with **make clean**.

  5. Create the kernel with **make bzImage**.

  6. Create modules with **make modules**.

  7. Install the modules with **make modules_install**.

  8. Copy the new image to */boot*.

  9. Update */etc/lilo.conf* for the new image.

  10. Update the boot loader by running the **lilo** command.

Text-Editing, Processing, and Printing

Objective 1: Perform Basic File-Editing Operations Using vi

- Start **vi** with **vi** *file1 file2*. See Table 2-22.

Table 2-22: Basic vi Editing Commands

Command	Description
ZZ	Write the file contents (if changed) and quit.
:x	Write the file contents (if changed) and quit (the **ex** equivalent of **ZZ**).
:q	Quit without saving changes.
:q!	Quit without saving changes and without confirmation.
:n	Next file. When multiple files are specified for editing, this command loads the next file.
Esc (the Escape key)	Exit insert mode and put the editor back into command mode.
h	Left one character.
j	Down one line.
k	Up one line.
l (ell)	Right one character.

Table 2-22: Basic vi Editing Commands (continued)

Command	Description
0 (zero)	Beginning of the current line.
^	First non-whitespace character on the current line.
$	End of the current line.
H	Top of the screen.
L	Bottom of the screen.
G	End-of-file.
Ctrl-F	Down one screen.
Ctrl-B	Up one screen.
i	Enter insert mode to place text before the cursor.
a	Enter insert mode to place text after the cursor (append). This is necessary at the ends of lines.
C	Delete to end-of-line and enter insert mode.
R	Enter replace mode (a variant of insert mode) and overwrite existing characters.
dm	Delete a text block defined by a movement command **m** relative to the location where the command started.
dd	Delete the entire current line.
D	Delete to end-of-line (same as *d$*)
ym	Yank (copy) a text block defined by a movement command **m** relative to the location where the command started.
yy	Yank the entire current line.
P	Paste text on a line before the cursor.
p	Paste text on a line after the cursor.
/pattern	Search forward for *pattern*.
?pattern	Search backward for *pattern*.
n	Repeat the last search.
N	Repeat the last search in the opposite direction.

Objective 2: Manage Printers and Print Queues

- Printers are assigned to queues, which are managed by **lpd**, the print daemon. **lpd** listens for inbound print requests, forking a copy of itself for each active print queue.

- **lpr** submits jobs to print queues.

- **lpq** queries and displays queue status.

- **lprm** allows jobs to be removed from print queues.

- **lpc** allows root to administer queues; it has both interactive and command-line forms.

- **filters** translate data formats into a printer definition language.

- Spool directories hold spooled job data.

Objective 3: Print Files

- Files are printed with the **lpr** command:

```
# lpr /etc/lilo.conf
# man -t 5 myfile.txt | lpr -Pqueue2
```

Objective 4: Install and Configure Local and Remote Printers

/etc/printcap

- New printer definitions are added to */etc/printcap*:

```
lp|ljet:\
        :sd=/var/spool/lpd/lp:\
        :mx#0:\
        :sh:\
        :lp=/dev/lp0:\
        :if=/var/spool/lpd/lp/filter:\
        :lf=/var/spool/lpd/lp/log:
```

The lines in this example are defined as follows:

`lp|ljet:\`
> This parameter defines two alternate names for the printer, *lp* or *ljet*.

`sd=spool_directory`
> This parameter specifies the spool directory, under */var/spool/lpd*.

`mx=max_size`
> The maximum size of a print job in blocks. Setting this to `#0` indicates no limit.

`sh`
> Suppress header pages. Placing this attribute in *printcap* sets it, eliminating the headers.

`lp=printer_device`
> The local printer device, such as a parallel port.

`if=input_filter`
> The input filter to be used. See the following section, "Filters," for additional information.

`lf=log_file`
> The file where error messages are logged.

Filters

- **APSfilter** is implemented as executable scripts. Installation configures */etc/printcap* automatically. Multiple queues may be defined to give the user access to specific printer capabilities.

- **Magicfilter** is a binary program; installation does not automatically create print queues.

Remote queues and Samba printers

- Printing on a remote system or network printer is done through a local queue. */etc/printcap* for the local queue looks something like this:

```
rlp:\
        :sd=/var/spool/lpd/rlp:\
        :rm=lphost:\
        :rp=rlp:\
        :mx#0:\
        :sh:\
        :if=/usr/local/bin/magicfilter:
```

- Printing to Windows printers is similar and uses the *smbprint* filter:

```
winpr:\
        :sd=/var/spool/lpd/winpr:\
        :mx#0:\
        :sh:\
        :if=/usr/bin/smbprint:
```

Shells, Scripting, Programming, and Compiling

Objective 1: Customize and Use the Shell Environment

- A shell presents an interactive Textual User Interface, an operating environment, a facility for launching programs, and a programming language.
- Shells can generally be divided into those derived from the Bourne shell, **sh** (including **bash**), and the C-shells, such as **tcsh**.
- Shells are distinct from the kernel and run as user programs.
- Shells can be customized by manipulating variables.
- Shells use configuration files at startup.
- Shells pass environment variables to child processes, including other shells.

bash

- **bash** is a descendant of **sh**.
- Shell variables are known only to the local shell and are not passed on to other processes.
- Environment variables are passed on to other processes.
- A shell variable is made an environment variable when it is *exported*.
- This sets a shell variable:

  ```
  # PI=3.14
  ```

- This turns it into an environment variable:

  ```
  # export PI
  ```

- This definition does both at the same time:

  ```
  # export PI=3.14
  ```

- Shell aliases conveniently create new commands or modify existing commands:

  ```
  # alias more='less'
  ```

- Functions are defined for and called in scripts. This line creates a function named lsps:

  ```
  # lsps () { ls -l; ps; }
  ```

- **bash** configuration files control the shell's behavior. Table 2-23 contains a list of these files.

Table 2-23: Bash Configuration Files

File	Description
/etc/profile	The system-wide initialization file; executed when you log in.
/etc/bashrc	Another system-wide initialization file; may be executed by a user's *.bashrc* for each **bash** shell launched.
~/.bash_profile	If this file exists, it is executed automatically after */etc/profile* when you log in.
~/.bash_login	If *.bash_profile* doesn't exist, this file is executed automatically when you log in.
~/.profile	If neither *.bash_profile* nor *.bash_login* exists, this file is executed automatically when you log in.
~/.bashrc	This file is executed automatically when **bash** starts.
~/.bash_logout	This file is executed automatically when you log out.
~/.inputrc	This file contains optional key bindings and variables that affect how **bash** responds to your keystrokes.

Objective 2: Customize or Write Simple Scripts

- Scripts are executable text files containing commands.
- Scripts must have appropriate execution bits set in the mode.
- Some scripts define the interpreter using the #!/bin/bash syntax on the first line.

Environment

- A script that starts using #!/bin/bash operates in a new invocation of the shell. This shell first executes standard system and user startup scripts. It also inherits exported variables from the parent shell.
- Like binary programs, scripts can offer a return value after execution.
- Scripts use file tests to examine and check for specific information on files.
- Scripts can use *command substitution* to utilize the result of an external command.
- Scripts often send email to notify administrators of errors or status.
- Refer to *Part 2, Shells, Scripting, Programming, and Compiling (Topic 1.9)*, for details on **bash** commands.

X

- X is a client-server GUI system. XFree86 is the X implementation used for Linux.

- An X server is software or hardware that renders graphical output on a display device.

- An X client is software whose output is displayed by an X server and is usually managed by a window manager.

- An X window manager is a client that applies frames and controls to other client windows.

Objective 1: Install and Configure XFree86

Selecting and configuring an X server

- XFree86 configuration depends on the software version, the video chipset in use, and the monitor's capabilities.

- XFree86 can be installed from Linux distribution packages (*.rpm*, *.deb*), precompiled binaries, or compiled from source.

- Configuration of XFree86 is done in the *XF86Config* file.

- *XF86Config* contains sections that define input devices, monitors, graphics modes, and so on.

- *XF86Config* files differ between XFree86 Versions 3.x and 4.x.

X fonts

- The X server uses X fonts to satisfy font requests from X clients.

- Fonts are enumerated either through a static list presented in */etc/X11/XF86Config* or through a *font server* such as **xfs**.

- **xfs** is configured using its configuration file, */etc/X11/fs/config*.

.Xresources

- X resource settings in the *.Xresources* file control client program parameters. For example, this line defines a black background for an **xterm**:

  ```
  xterm*background: Black
  ```

Objective 2: Set Up xdm

- **xdm**, the X Display Manager, handles X sessions on physical displays both locally and across the network.

- **xdm** handles authentication.

- **xdm** is configured by a series of files in */etc/X11/xdm*.

- **xdm** is typically started automatically in runlevel 5 by making the appropriate settings in */etc/inittab*.

- **xdm** may be personalized by changing the resources in */etc/X11/xdm/Xresources*.

- Command-line options for the X server can be added to the */etc/X11/xdm/Xservers* file.

X stations

- X stations, also known as X terminals, are low-cost hardware systems that implement an X server and display.

- **xdm** can listen for inbound connection requests from X terminals using the *xdmcp* protocol.

- Specific access rules for X terminals to the **xdm** daemon can be configured in */etc/X11/xdm/Xaccess*.

Objective 3: Identify and Terminate Runaway X Applications

- X applications can occasionally become unresponsive or remain running after the X server is terminated.

- Use the top utility to identify processes.

- Use **kill** or **killall** to terminate processes.

- If the X server is unresponsive, use **Ctrl–Alt–F2** to switch to another console, and kill offending processes.

Objective 4: Install and Customize a Window Manager

- An X server doesn't supply a working user environment.

- Starting X usually involves launching not only the X server but also a window manager and other clients.

- A default window manager, such as the basic **twm**, is started by a combination of the **startx** script and **xinit**.

- **xinit** also calls scripts that include a window manager and default clients.

- Default system X configuration can be overridden by files in the user's home directory.

Window managers

- Each window manager and desktop environment has its own style of configuration.

- **twm** uses *.twmrc* in the user's home directory. If that file doesn't exist, it uses the systemwide */etc/X11/twm/system.twmrc*.

- Window manager configuration files can contain font and color selections, bindings between actions (such as mouse clicks) and responses, and menu definitions.

xterm

- A *terminal emulator* is a program that offers a command-line interface in a GUI window.

- **xterm** is the standard terminal emulator; there are many others.

- **xterm** can be configured in */usr/lib/X11/app-defaults/XTerm*.

X libraries

- X applications are dependent upon shared X libraries.

- Various graphical toolkits such as GTK or Qt can be used to develop X client applications.

- Software that depends on a particular library will not run unless that library is installed.

- You can determine which libraries an executable requires *with* **ldd**.

Remote X clients

- X clients can be displayed on remote X servers.

- The DISPLAY environment variable is used to indicate the destination for X client displays.

- DISPLAY has the format [*host*] : *display*[*.screen*] where *host* is a remote host-name or IP address, display is the display target (starting with 0), and *screen* is the screen to use on multiheaded displays.

- DISPLAY must be exported.

Networking Fundamentals

Objective 1: Fundamentals of TCP/IP

Addressing and masks

- An address mask separates the network portion from the host portion of the 32-bit IP address.

- Class A addresses have 8 bits of network address and 24 bits of host address.

- Class B addresses have 16 bits of network address and 16 bits of host address.

- Class C addresses have 24 bits of network address and 8 bits of host address.

- Subnets can be defined using the defined "class" schemes or using a locally defined split of network/host bits.

- The all-zero and all-ones addresses are reserved on all subnets for the network and broadcast addresses, respectively. This implies that the maximum number of hosts on a network with n bits in the host portion of the address is 2^n-2. For example, a Class C network has 8 bits in the host portion. Therefore, it can have a maximum of $2^8-2=254$ hosts.

Protocols

TCP/IP is a name representing a larger suite of network protocols. Some network protocols maintain a constant connection while others do not.

IP

> The Internet Protocol is the fundamental building block of the Internet. It is used by other protocols.

ICMP

> This connectionless messaging protocol uses IP. It is used for flow control, detection of unreachable destinations, redirecting routes, and checking remote hosts (the **ping** utility).

UDP

> The User Datagram Protocol is a connectionless transport agent. It is used by applications such as DNS and NFS.

TCP

> The Tranmission Control Protocol is a connection-oriented transport agent. It is used by applications such as FTP and Telnet.

PPP

> The Point-to-Point Protocol is used over serial lines, including modems.

TCP/IP services

- Inbound network requests to a host include a *port number*. Common port numbers are listed in Table 2-24.

Table 2-24: Common Port Assignments

Port Number	Assigned Use	Description
20	FTP data	When an FTP session is opened, the binary or ASCII data flow to the server is conducted using port 20, while control information flows on port 21. During use, both ports are managed by an *ftp daemon*, such as **wu-ftpd** or **PROftpd**.
21	FTP control	
23	Telnet server	Inbound Telnet requests are sent to server port 23 and processed by **telnetd**.
25	SMTP server	This port is used by mail transfer agents (MTAs), such as **sendmail**.
53	DNS server	This port is used by the Domain Name System server, **named**.
67	BOOTP/DHCP server	This port is used by BOOTP or the more commonly used DHCP server.
68	BOOTP/DHCP client	This port is used by the client side for BOOTP/DHCP.
80	HTTP server	Web servers, such as Apache (**httpd**), usually listen in on this port.

Table 2-24: Common Port Assignments (continued)

Port Number	Assigned Use	Description
110	POP3	The Post Office Protocol (POP) is used by mail client programs to transfer mail from a server.
119	NNTP server	This port is used by news servers for USENET news.
139	NetBIOS	This port is reserved for Microsoft's LAN network manager.
143	IMAP	An alternate to POP3, IMAP is another type of mail server.
161	SNMP	Agents running on monitored systems use this port for access to the Simple Network Management Protocol.

- Ports are assigned to specific programs. Definitions are stored in */etc/services*.
- Ports 1–1023 are privileged ports, owned by superuser processes.

TCP/IP utilities

- **ftp** implements the File Transfer Protocol client for the exchange of files to and from remote hosts.
- The **telnet** client program implements a Telnet session to a remote host.
- **ping** sends ICMP echo requests to a remote host to verify functionality.
- **dig** obtains information from DNS servers.
- **traccroute** attempts to display the route over which packets must travel to a remote host.
- **fwhois** queries a **whois** database to determine the owner of a domain or IP address.

Objective 3: TCP/IP Troubleshooting and Configuration

Network interfaces

- Interfaces are configured through a number of configuration files.
- */etc/hostname* contains the assigned hostname for the system.
- */etc/hosts* contains static mappings between IP addresses and names.
- */etc/nsswitch.conf* directs system library functions to specific name server methods such as local files, DNS, and NIS.
- */etc/host.conf* controls name resolution for older libraries.
- */etc/host.conf* is only rarely used and is replaced by */etc/nsswitch.conf*.
- */etc/resolv.conf* contains information to direct the resolver to DNS servers.

- */etc/networks* sets up equivalence between addresses and names for entire networks.

- The **host** command returns DNS information.

- The **hostname, domainname**, and **dnsdomainname** commands set or display the current host, domain, or node name.

- The **ifconfig** command configures network interfaces. It is used to create and configure interface parameters, usually at boot time. Parameters include the IP address and subnet mask.

- The **netstat** command displays network connections, routing tables, interface statistics, masquerade connections, and multicast memberships.

- The **route** command displays the routing table and can add or delete routes from the table.

DHCP

- DHCP is the Dynamic Host Configuration Protocol. It is used to assign an IP address and other information to a client system.

- The DHCP server is **dhcpd**.

- A DHCP server offers an address for a finite amount of time known as a *lease*.

Objective 4: Configure and Use PPP

- PPP is used to make a network connection over a serial interface. This could be a direct cable or modem connection.

- PPP is a peer protocol; there are no clients or servers.

- **pppd** is the PPP daemon, called when a PPP interface is needed. It uses a chat script to send configuration commands to a modem prior to dialing.

- Basic authentication for PPP can be done in clear text via the *chat* script. However, the PAP, CHAP, and MSCHAP methods encode their authentication information into the PPP data stream.

Networking Services

Objective 1: Configure and Manage inetd and Related Services

- **inetd** is the Internet super daemon; it listens on multiple inbound ports and launches the appropriate child daemon to service the requests.

- **inetd** uses TCP Wrappers (**tcpd**) to add access security to services.

- **inetd** is configured in */etc/inetd.conf.*

- You can eliminate an inbound service managed by **inetd** simply by commenting out its declaration in */etc/inetd.conf* and restarting or signaling **inetd**.

- TCP Wrappers allow the administrator to define access rules for hosts. The configuration files are */etc/hosts.allow* and */etc/hosts.deny*.

Objective 2: Operate and Perform Basic Configuration of sendmail

- **sendmail** is a Mail Transfer Agent (MTA).

- **sendmail** is configured in */etc/sendmail.cf*. This file is generally regarded as difficult to configure.

- The "smart host" parameter is used to configure a local **sendmail** daemon to transfer mail to a site's official mail system.

- */etc/aliases* is a file that stores aliases for inbound mail addresses; it can redirect mail to one or more users.

- Whenever */etc/aliases* is modified, **newaliases** must be executed.

- Each user can forward her own mail using a *.forward* file, containing the forwarding email address, in her home directory.

- Outbound mail that is trapped due to a network or other problem will remain queued; it can be examined using the **mailq** command.

Objective 3: Operate and Perform Basic Configuration of Apache

- Apache is configured using *httpd.conf, srm.conf,* and *access.conf.* On some installations, these may all be combined into *httpd.conf.*

- The configuration files contain configuration directives, one per line, consisting of a keyword and an argument list. For example:

```
DocumentRoot /home/httpd/html
```

sets the root directory for HTML files on the system.

- Apache is typically started at boot time using the system's startup methods.

Objective 4: Properly Manage the NFS, smb, and nmb Daemons

NFS

- Traditional Unix file sharing is done with NFS, originally developed by Sun Microsystems.

- NFS is a client-server package, and any system can hold both roles simultaneously.

- Exporting (sharing) a local filesystem with NFS is done by including a line in the */etc/exports* file, consisting of a directory and list of allowed systems, along with NFS options. For example:

```
/usr    (ro) orion.mydomain.com(rw)
/home   *.mydomain.com(rw)
```

- Remote NFS filesystems are mounted using the **mount** command:

```
# mount -t nfs server1:/home /mnt/server1
```

- NFS is typically started at boot time using the system's startup methods.

Samba

- The Samba suite implements Server Message Block (SMB) protocols used on Microsoft and IBM LANs.

- **smbd** handles file and printer sharing and authentication.

- **nmbd** implements the WINS service.

- Samba is configured in */etc/smb.conf.* The file consists of sections, each with a series of *keyword = value* pairs.

- Samba 2.0 and later comes with a web-based configuration tool called SWAT; it is usually configured to be monitored by **inetd**.

Objective 5: Set Up and Configure Basic DNS Services

- DNS is the distributed database of name-to-IP-address translations.

The resolver

- The resolver is a library used by networked applications when a domain name needs to be translated into an IP address.

- The resolver uses local files, NIS, and DNS to resolve hostnames as directed by */etc/resolv.conf.*

Domain registration

- Domain names are assigned through a registration process with one of the *domain name registrars* on the Internet.

- The DNS server daemon is **named**, part of the BIND package.

- **named** can be configured to speed up a local system by acting as a non-authoritative caching-only name server.

- **named** is configured using */etc/named.conf.*

- The **nslookup, host,** and **dig** utilities can be used to retrieve information from DNS servers.

- BIND Version 4 and Version 8 have significantly different configuration file formats, although the information contained in the files is similar.

Security

Objective 1: Perform Security Administration Tasks

TCP Wrappers

- Configuring TCP wrappers (**tcpd**) using */etc/hosts.allow* and */etc/hosts.deny* can enhance security for daemons controlled by **inetd**.

- **tcpd** is often configured to deny access to all systems for all services (a blanket deny), then specific systems are specified for legitimate access to services (limited allow).

- **tcpd** logs using **syslog**, commonly to */var/log/secure.*

Finding executable SUID files

- **find** can perform searches for file attributes such as SUID using the **–perm** option.

Verifying packages

- RPM packages are verified using the Verify mode, enabled using the **–V** (capital) option.

- The output for each package contains a string of eight characters that are set to dots when the attribute has not changed. The columns represent each of eight different attributes: MD5 checksum, file size, *symlink* attributes, the file's *mtime*, device file change, user/owner change, group change, and mode change.

SGID workgroups

- The SGID bit can be applied to directories to enforce a policy whereby new files created within the directory are assigned the same group ownership as the directory itself.

The Secure Shell

- The Secure Shell, or SSH, can be used as an alternative to Telnet for secure communications.

- SSH can also protect FTP and other data streams, including X sessions.

- The Secure Shell daemon is **sshd**.

Objective 2: Set Up Host Security

Shadow passwords

- Enabling the use of *shadow passwords* can enhance local security by making encrypted passwords harder to steal.

- The use of shadow passwords causes the removal of password information from the publicly readable *passwd* file and places it in *shadow*, readable only by root.

- A similar system is implemented for shadow groups, using the *gshadow* file.

Objective 3: Set Up User-Level Security

- Limits can be placed on users by using the **ulimit** command in the **bash** shell. This command allows enforcement of limitations on soft and hard limits on processes and memory usage.

Glossary

This Glossary contains a complete list of terms that you should be familiar with before taking the LPI exams. Knowledge of these terms will be important in preparing for LPI exams, but no exam question should depend on knowledge gleaned solely from this list.

This Glossary is copyrighted by the Linux Professional Institute (*http://www.lpi.org*) and is provided under the terms of the LPI Open Content License (*http://www.lpi.org/license.html#OCL*). This list was compiled by (in alphabetical order): Les Bell, David DeLano, Alan Mead, Tom Peters, Richard Rager, with additions by Jeff Dean and editing by O'Reilly & Associates, Inc.

*nix
> A term for any operating system resembling Unix, including Linux and a large number of free and commercial systems; also Un*x.

100BaseT
> Ethernet over UTP cables, using hubs to produce a star topology; supports a maximum (theoretical) transmission of 100 MBps.

10Base2
> So-called Thin Ethernet, using RG-58 coax cables and BNC connectors to construct a chain of cables; supports a maximum (theoretical) transmission of 10 Mbps.

10Base5
> The older Thick Ethernet, which used vampire taps into a single cable; supports a maximum (theoretical) transmission of 10 Mbps.

10BaseT
> Ethernet over UTP cables, using hubs to produce a star topology; supports a maximum (theoretical) transmission of 10 Mbps.

access
> To connect to and utilize a device (computer, printer) or file.

account
> The symbol or number that refers to a user for accounting purposes.

address
> 1. A location in memory; specifically, the I/O port used by a device to communicate with the processor.
>
> 2. A unique identifier assigned to an interface on a network-attached device such as a network interface card. Notice: a host can have multiple interfaces, hence multiple addresses.
>
> 3. The name or number given to a computer, device, or resource so it can be identified, found, and accessed on a network.

administer
> To control the operation and use of a computer or other device; the task of a system administrator.

algorithm
> A formal description of a procedure that, when suitable input is entered, will generate output as a result that satisfies specific requirements.

alias
> 1. Within a shell, a substitute word for a command string (e.g., **alias dir = "ls -- color"**).
>
> 2. An additional IP address on an interface.
>
> 3. Refers to another name given to an email account, in order to accept mail for one email address and forward it to another.

Alt
> The Alternative key on a keyboard.

analog
> Refers to a physical measure that can take any value within a continuous range (e.g., the voltage used to encode loudness when transmitting a signal over a conventional copper telephone line). See also *digital.*

ANSI
> Short for American National Standards Institute (*http://www.ansi.org*). A standards body responsible for many protocols.

API
> Short for Application Programming Interface. A specification that allows simple access to functionality of a library or other system resources when writing a program; operating system functionality is made available through an API.

application
> A program that runs on top of an operating system.

application layer
> The top layer of the four-layer TCP/IP protocol model. Includes protocols such as Telnet, FTP, HTTP, SMTP, and so on.

archive
> 1. A backup of data to be preserved.
>
> 2. A file that contains one or more components and an index (e.g., in *tar, cpio, rpm,* or *deb* format).

argument

A piece of information passed to a command or function (usually typed in behind it) that modifies its behavior or that is operated upon by the command or function (i.e., in **cat motd**, **motd** is the argument). See also *parameter*.

ARP

Short for Address Resolution Protocol. A protocol that, given an IP address on the local network, returns the Ethernet address of the corresponding interface.

ASCII

Short for American Standard Code for Information Interchange. A specification of characters widely used in the Unix world and beyond.

aspect ratio

The ratio between the width and the height of a pixel on a computer display.

assembler

A program that compiles programs written in assembly language into object code.

assembly language

A low-level computer language that can be translated directly to the object code of the computer processor.

background

A state of process execution that does not produce output to the terminal (execution may stop if the process tries to write to the terminal); it is common to run system processes and long-running user applications in the background. See also *foreground*.

backup

1. A copy of essential data stored on- or off-site as insurance against failures of system hardware, software, or user.

2. To make a backup.

binary

1. Taking two discrete values (e.g., bits), as opposed to decimal (taking ten discrete values).

2. A file that is not intended to be read by applications or the operating system instead of by humans; especially in plural ("binaries") for compiled sources. See also *text*.

BIOS

Short for Basic Input/Output System. A simple, low-level operating system that supplies a uniform API to higher-level operating systems; BIOS is generally implemented in ROM of some sort.

bit

The smallest entity of information; can have one of two states (0/1, on/off, open/closed, etc.).

bitplanes

The number of bits available for each display pixel to code for visual appearance (color, proximity, etc.).

block device

A device that exchanges data with the operating system in sizable blocks (e.g., 512 bytes) at a time.

boot

To cause the operating system to begin to function. Takes its name from "pulling oneself up by the bootstraps," a whimsical analogy applied to the BIOS loading itself and then running the boot loader. "Reboot" is the term for a repeat of the process.

boot loader

Software, usually installed on the MBR of Intel machines, which exists to load the operating system kernel and begin its functioning.

BOOTP

Short for Boot Protocol. A protocol used to provide information to diskless workstations or devices over a network. See also *DHCP*.

broadcast

A frame or datagram addressed to all interfaces on a network.

BSD

Short for Berkeley Software Design. A variant of Unix originally developed at the University of California, Berkeley. The BSD TCP/IP stack is the model for most subsequent TCP/IP implementations.

buffer

Temporary storage. See also *cache*.

BUGTRAQ

A mailing list for discussions regarding network security (daemons, programs, operating systems, routers, etc.).

build

To run a sequence of compile and link steps to produce a new version of an executable program.

bus

A cable for transmitting signals between various components within one computer system.

byte

A datatype of 8 bits.

C

A compiled computer language closely associated with Unix.

C++

An object-oriented computer language derived from C that needs a compiler.

cache

Any readily accessible storage area used to keep handy data that is (somehow) indicated to be needed again shortly; the purpose being to speed up the access of that data and improve system performance. Specifically, the fast computer memory that is used as a buffer for data and program instructions between the CPU and the slower main memory. See also *RAM*.

caching-only DNS

A domain name server that does not have any domains files.

Caldera OpenLinux

A commercial Linux distribution.

call

Execute a subprogram or library procedure in an executable program.

card

Any device that can be plugged into a computer expansion slot.

CD-ROM

A removable medium of considerable popularity that comes in several variations, the most popular being ISO9660.

CERT/CC

A team of people that studies Internet security and provides incident response services; see *http://www.cert.org*.

CGI

Short for Common Gateway Interface. A standard for allowing server applications to be executed as part of an HTTP request.

CHAP

Challenge Handshake Protocol, an authentication scheme used in PPP.

char

C datatype (usually 1 byte) used to store letters. See also *character*.

character

A letter or sign usually represented by 1 byte in ASCII code.

character device

A device that exchanges data with the operating system in one character (or byte or even word) at a time.

child process

Any process created by another so-called parent process; usually used in reference to a particular parent process.

CIDR

See *variable length subnet mask*.

CIFS

Short for Common Internet File System. Microsoft's successor to SMB, a suite of protocols for sharing file and print services (among Windows machines or Un*x machines running CIFS servers like Samba).

clean

In reference to a drive being mounted, "clean" means that the drive was unmounted properly and thus (theoretically) does not need to be checked; otherwise, a drive is "dirty."

client

A computer or process that connects to and receives a service from a server computer or process.

coax

Short for "coaxial." A type of cable with inner and outer conductors used for TV cables and for Ethernet LANs, where the computers usually have T-joints to attach to a single chain of cables that needs to be terminated by resistors.

colormap

A table used to encode a palette of colors for images.

command-line interface

An interactive user interface that allows commands to be given to a computer program or shell through a text-based terminal (or terminal emulator in a window within a graphical user interface).

compiler

A program that examines program source code and translates it into an equivalent object code file. See also *interpreter*.

compression

Removal of redundant information from a file or data stream to reduce its size, the storage space it needs, or the time needed for transmission. Lossy compression actually discards information that is considered nonessential and is appropriate only for data such as images or sound.

computer

A digital, electronic, general-purpose, programmable, information-processing automate.

console

The primary, directly attached, user interface of a computer. Some system administration functions may be performed only at a console.

control panel

A collection of buttons, switches, lights, or displays used to configure and control a router, printer, computer, or other device.

core dump

The content of memory written to a file on disk when a program crashes (usually called a "core").

corrupted

Damaged (said of a file or disk contents).

CPU

Short for Central Processing Unit. The main component that makes a computer work; these days, usually a "microprocessor" on a single silicon chip. See also *processor*.

crack

To gain access to a computer system without proper authorization (e.g., by guessing a legitimate user's password) and possibly interfere with its normal operation or integrity.

cracker

a. Someone who tries to crack into another computer system. See also *hacker*.

b. A software program used to crack, for instance, by guessing passwords.

crash

A sudden stop of normal operation. Supposedly, the original hard drives would sometimes experience a catastrophic failure in which the read/write heads would crash into the media, possibly sending the media flying; hence, a crash is an unintentional termination of software or hardware due to some failure or error—especially a termination in a final, catastrophic, or unpleasant way.

CSLIP

Short for Compressed SLIP. SLIP with added VJ compression of IP headers.

Ctrl

The Control key on a keyboard.

current working directory

The location within a filesystem where a program works. This is the default location for many commands unless another directory is explicitly defined.

cylinder

A number of tracks located at the same radius on the several surfaces of a hard disk. A hard disk with four platters has eight surfaces, so that at each position of the read/write heads, eight tracks can be read without head movement; these eight tracks form a cylinder.

daemon

A program that runs in the background to offer system services.

data

"That which is given," for instance, as input to a computer. See also *information*.

data link layer

Layer two of the ISO/OSI seven-layer model. Responsible for establishing an error-free communications path between network nodes over the physical link layer, frames messages for transmission, checks the integrity of received messages, manages access to and use of the media, and ensures proper sequencing of transmitted data. These functions are generally provided by a network card driver.

database

1. A usually large collection of ordered and readily accessible data.

2. A program to manage a database and extract information from it.

datagram packet

Especially as used in UDP. Not IP-specific; other protocols use the term "datagram" in their documentation.

Debian

A GNU/Linux distribution built by a volunteer organization.

default

The value of a parameter that a program uses if it is not explicitly given a value.

Del

The Delete key on a keyboard.

delete
Remove or erase a file, character, directory, and so on.

dependency
A state in which other libraries, programs, or packages are required to make a program work.

DES
Short for Data Encryption Standard. A U.S. government-sanctioned standard for the encryption of data now considered insecure to high-end brute force attacks.

desktop
The screen from which all programs are started and run on X.

device
1. A "peripheral" piece of hardware that is an optional part of or can be attached to a computer (even one that is actually housed within the computer's casing): interface cards, drives, printers, and so on.

2. The software interface used within Unix (Linux) to represent a computer peripheral: interface cards, drives, printers, and so on; see */dev* directory.

DHCP
Short for Dynamic Host Configuration Protocol. Provides for automatic downloading of IP address and other configuration data from a server to a client. Allows for reuse of IP addresses so that the number of hosts can exceed the number of available IP addresses. DHCP is an upgrade to the BOOTP protocol.

dial-in, dial-up, or dial-out
Refers to a connection made over the Public Switched Telephone Network (PSTN), as opposed to a permanent, or leased-line, connection.

die
To cease execution, especially in a final or complete manner.

digital
Refers to an entity that can assume only a limited number of discrete states and not any value (e.g., binary). See also *analog*.

directory
A special type of file that contains information about other files, such as filename, location, permissions, size, and so on.

dirty
A filesystem that was not cleanly unmounted. See also *clean*.

disk
Rotating magnetic media that support direct or random access. See also *floppy disk, hard disk*.

display
A human-readable device to display text, graphics, or other data.

distribution
A (usually) complete collection of software needed to operate a computer including the Linux kernel and various utilities and applications.

DMA

Short for Direct Memory Access. A hardware protocol that allows a special controller circuit (DMA controller) to transfer a block of data from a peripheral device's buffer memory directly to main memory without CPU involvement. See also *PIO*.

DNS

Short for Domain Name System. A hierarchically structured distributed directory service that translates human-intelligible names like *http://www.lpi.org* into the corresponding IP addresses.

domain

1. One or more computer networks that serve an organizational group.

2. The name assigned to a network domain.

domain name server

A system running BIND serving DNS-name-to-IP-address translations.

drive

Any device that can store and retrieve data in a relatively permanent fashion on media (which may be removable or built into the device).

EIDE

Short for Enhanced Integrated Device Electronics. An improved version of the IDE interface, used to connect hard drives and CD-ROMS to a PC.

email

Electronic mail.

emulate

To simulate the actions of a device or program so that the simulation can actually perform the same functions as the original.

emulator

A program that emulates the functions of some device or other program.

environment

A collection of variables associated with a process so that it knows about the user preferences and configuration of the system; they are inherited by a child process.

environment variables

The variables that define an environment.

ergonomic

Easy to use by humans.

Esc

The Escape key on a keyboard.

Ethernet

A type of LAN computer interface using coax (10Base2 or 10Base5) or UTP cables (10BaseT or 100BaseT).

execute

To set to work (a program). See also *run*.

Glossary

execute permission
> Permission set on a file on a Unix filesystem so that it may be run as a program by the "operating system."

executable
> A file that is a binary or a script that can be run as a program (may assume execute permission).

export
> To share, as in a filesystem or volume.

FAT
> Short for File Allocation Table. A simple filesystem that uses a table to index files on a block device (floppy or hard disk). It comes in the varieties of FAT-12 (MS-DOS), FAT-16 (MS-DOS, Microsoft Windows 3.x) and FAT-32 (Microsoft Windows 9x).

FHS
> Short for Filesystem Hierarchy Standard. A proposed standard for the location of files on a Unix system. See *http://www.pathname.com/fhs/*.

file
> A named sequence or stream of bytes at a known location in storage.

filesystem
> The data structures placed on a logical disk or partition (by **mkfs**) that allow the operating system to record information about files stored there.

filter
> To remove unwanted data.

floating-point
> Used with numbers that may represent a fraction. See also *integer*.

floppy disk
> A magnetic storage medium with a flexible disk inside. See also *hard disk*.

floppy drive
> A device that can read and write floppy disks.

font
> The shape of each of the letters in a character set.

foreground
> 1. The context in which a process is having access to a terminal for output (i.e., is not running in the background).
> 2. The color of text on a computer display (as opposed to the text's background).
> 3. Refers to the window "in front of" all others and with which the user is interacting.

fork
> When an executing process creates an exact executing duplicate (except for the different PID) of itself. See also *child process, spawn*.

format

1. Specification regarding how data is stored.

2. To apply the requisite format to storage media in preparation to making a filesystem.

forwarding

The act of receiving an email and then resending it to another destination.

frame

A packet as assembled and transmitted over the physical layer of a network (e.g., Ethernet, Token Ring, etc.).

free

1. Not costing anything.

2. Not inhibited. As applied to source code, it allows modification, study, and adaptation, not inhibited by excessively restrictive commercial license terms. See also *FSF, GPL*.

FSF

Short for Free Software Foundation. The FSF is a tax-exempt charity that raises funds for work on the GNU Project; see *http://www.fsf.org*.

FSSTND

Short for Filesystem Standard. A standard for the location of files on a Linux system; replaced by the FHS.

FTP

Short for File Transfer Protocol. A protocol for transferring files over the Internet and the software to accomplish the transfer.

gateway

A device that routes IP datagrams between networks in an Internet; a router. (In common usage today, a gateway is a general-purpose computer with a general-purpose operating system—e.g., Linux—that *may* be performing other functions, although security considerations may render this inadvisable. A router is a special-purpose computer with a special-purpose operating system—e.g., IOS—generally from a specialist supplier—e.g., Cisco.) Gateways do *not* perform protocol translation.

GB

An abbreviation for *gigabyte*, or 1000 MB.

GID

Group ID. See also *UID*.

global

A variable, configuration section, procedure, and so forth having a scope that is unlimited (i.e., applies everywhere unless contradicted locally).

GNU

Short for "GNU's Not Unix." An FSF Project to build Unix-compatible utilities and programs exclusively based on free program source code.

GPL

Short for GNU Public License. The GPL is a license that permits the copying, modification, and redistribution of free software. It was created by the FSF for software developed by the GNU Project and has been applied to Linux as well. See *http://www.gnu.org/copyleft/gpl.html*.

graphical user interface (GUI)

An interactive interface using a graphics display. Refer to a "graphical user interface" only if there actually is a graphical interface (like X); do not use the term for interactive programs on text terminals (based on *ncurses* or *slang*). Use "interactive interface" as a catchall. See also *command-line interface*.

graphics

Images, pictures; in contrast to text.

group

Refers to a list of one or more users having the same access rights. See also */etc/groups*.

hack

To accomplish a result in an unorthodox way.

hacker

Someone who hacks; a title assigned to people with remarkable computing skills. See also *cracker*.

hang

See *crash*.

hard disk

A computer device that uses solid disks as magnetic media to store data. See also *floppy disk*.

hard link

In Unix filesystems, an entry in a directory that points to a file in another directory on the same disk or partition and shares the *inode* of that file. See also *symlink*.

hardware

All physical parts making up the computer.

high-level

Refers to a computer language with a higher level of abstraction from the computer architecture than a low-level language.

host

Any computer attached to an IP-based Internet, especially computers that can act as a server to a client program or computer.

HOWTO

A series of documents, each on a particular topic, that form a significant portion of the documentation for Linux. HOWTOs originated with, and are generally published by, the Linux Documentation Project (LDP).

HTML

An abbreviation for HyperText Markup Language, a term coined by Tim Berners Lee. A standard for specifying the structure of a document indicated by tags in the document text; used on the World Wide Web with HTTP. HTML has been replaced with XHTML, an XML-like version of HTML.

HTTP

Short for HyperText Transfer Protocol. The succession of application layer protocols used for communication between a WWW browser and a WWW server.

I/O

Input/output.

ICMP

Short for Internet Control Message Protocol. A required protocol for the notification of errors between gateways and hosts on IP-based Internets.

ID

Short for "identifier" or "identity."

IDE

Short for Integrated Device Electronics. A popular interface on PCs to attach hard drives, constructed in such a way that much of the interface circuitry is integrated into the disk drive. See also *EIDE*.

idle

Inactive; waiting for a task or a wake-up call.

IMAP

Short for Internet Message Access Protocol. Protocol permitting access to electronic mail or bulletin board messages that are kept on a mail server.

implement

To create an actual object (program, device) that conforms to abstract specifications.

include file

A file that contains constants and parameters, possibly shared between two or more programs and included into the source code when these programs are compiled.

information

Something worth knowing, in contrast to just plain data.

inode

In Unix filesystems, a single block of administrative data defining a file on a disk partition.

input

Any data entered into a running program or into a file.

install

Transferring a new program to a computer's permanent storage (e.g., hard disk) and performing any necessary configuration or administration.

integer

> A data type used to represent a whole (integer, nonfraction) number within a limited range.

integrity

> In filesystems, a stable and noncorrupt state.

interactive

> Adjective meaning having the property to be able to interact (i.e., respond to stimulation from the outside). Used in the context of programs or interfaces.

interactive interface

> An interface between a computer and a user that allows them to interact and exchange input and output (commands and data).

interface

> A connection (through a hardware device or through a software program) between different components of a computer system (usually performing some kind of translation between protocols internal to the components); used especially in the contexts of network communication or communication between computer systems and their users.

Internet

> The worldwide distributed network of computers linked by the Internet Protocol.

interpreter

> A program that examines a script or program source code and executes it, line by line. See also *compiler.*

interrupt

> An electronic or software signal sent to a CPU to initiate a high-priority service, interrupting that which was in process.

intranet

> A network (usually a LAN) based on IP, but unlike the Internet, allowing only restricted access.

invoke

> Induce execution of. See also *call.*

IO port

> The memory address peripheral devices use to communicate with the CPU.

IP

> Short for Internet Protocol. The network layer protocol used on IP-based networks, including the Internet.

IRQ

> Interrupt request. See also *interrupt.*

ISA

> Short for Industry Standard Architecture. An increasingly obsolete PC bus standard for peripheral devices.

ISDN

Short for Integrated Services Digital Network. A technology for sending voice, video, and data over digital telephone lines or normal telephone wires. ISDN supports data transfer rates of 64 Kbps (64,000 bits per second). Most ISDN lines offered by telephone companies give you two lines, called B channels, at once. You can use one line for voice and the other for data, or you can use both lines for data to give you data rates of 128 Kbps.

ISO

Short for International Standards Organization. One of several bodies that exist to promote standards, including computer standards.

ISP

Short for Internet Service Provider. A company that provides connections to the Internet.

job

A task that has been sent to the background or has been submitted for later execution.

k or K

A factor of 1000, but with computers usually 1024 (2^{10}).

KB

Kilobyte; 1024 bytes.

Kbps

Data transfer rate in units of 1000 bits per second.

KBps

Data transfer rate in units of 1024 bytes per second.

kernel

The core of an operating system, which provides multitasking (process creation, interprocess protection, interprocess communication), memory management, and basic I/O management.

key

1. A token that is used to encrypt plain text or decrypt cipher text in an encryption system.

2. A database field that may be used as the basis of a query.

3. A marked switch on a keyboard that used to be a common computer input device.

keyboard

An input device having many keys marked with letters and other symbols.

LAN

Short for Local Area Network. A small network, usually with one or a few segments, which supports broadcasting and direct connections between hosts (e.g., Ethernet, Token Ring, AppleTalk, and ARCNet). See also *WAN*.

LDP

Short for Linux Documentation Project. A project intended to create free, high-quality documentation for GNU/Linux. See *http://www.linuxdoc.org*.

library

A collection of (often-related) subroutines to be linked to a program.

LILO

The Linux boot loader; a program that loads the kernel so Linux can boot. LILO can also be used to boot other operating systems.

link

To bind a program to the subroutines it references (calls). These are typically located in object modules or libraries.

Linux

A Unix-like operating system first developed, still maintained by, and named after Linus Torvalds. It is freely available under the General Public License.

load

To transfer from disk into memory.

local

Within easy reach, on the local area network, not remote.

log file

Record of activities.

low-level

Refers to a computer language in which statements are similar to instructions for the processor (or in which statements are more like object code than in a high-level language).

Mail User Agent

An end-user program used to access, process, read, archive, compose, and send email messages. Such email programs often include some MTA functionality, in particular the ability to use SMTP to send email to an outgoing mail server, and POP3 or IMAP to download mail from an inbound mail server. See also *MTA*.

manpage

Standard Unix manual page (usually available on the computer system in *nroff* format, called with the **man** command).

manual

1. A document, often of book length, discussing the design or operation of a software package or device.

2. By hand (as opposed to some more automated means).

masquerade

To pretend to be another host for the purposes of sharing one IP address among several local hosts hidden to the outside world for reasons of resource shortages or security. See also *NAT*.

MB

An abbreviation for Megabyte; 1000 KB (or sometimes 1024).

Mbps

Data transfer rate in units of 1 million bits per second.

MBR

Short for Master Boot Record. An area of the outermost cylinder of a hard disk that contains the partition table. The MBR contains four entries identifying the types, starting cylinder, and sizes of up to four partitions on the hard disk. One of the entries is flagged as *active*; this entry marks the partition from which the machine will boot. Floppy disks don't have an MBR, since they don't have a partition table. Instead, they just have a boot sector (same as a logical disk), which contains a Media Descriptor Table (MDT) and bootstrap loader. The MDT describes the format of a floppy disk or logical disk.

media

The physical device by which data is transmitted or (more commonly) stored.

memory

The place where a computer stores data and/or programs for direct access by the CPU. RAM or ROM (and also cache memory), not disks.

mini-HOWTO

A slimmer, more focused document; otherwise like a HOWTO.

modem

A device that converts between digital signals from the computer and analog signals for communication over a telephone line.

mouse

An input device that allows pointing to, selecting, and activating objects displayed in a graphical user interface.

MTA

Short for Message Transfer Agent. A program that routes email based on the header and invokes the correct delivery agent, especially SMTP, in order to route the mail toward its ultimate destination. For example: **exim, qmail, sendmail**, and **smail** are all MTAs. The term "Mail Transport Agent" is used in the online "Network Administrator's Guide" to refer to rmail, which is used to process incoming mail from UUCP before passing it on to sendmail. This usage is at least confusing, if not incorrect.

MTU

Short for Maximum Transfer Unit. Maximum size of an IP packet that will be accepted for transmission without fragmenting it into smaller datagrams. An optimal size is usually determined automatically; typical sizes are 296 bytes (40 header + 256 data for phone lines) and 1500 bytes (the maximum for an Ethernet connection).

NAT

Short for Network Address Translation. A generic description of the process whereby the IP address of a host on a private Internet is translated into an IANA-assigned unique address on the wider public Internet. This can be accomplished by several techniques: masquerading, circuit-level gateways such as SOCKS, transparent proxying, or application-level gateways.

NetBEUI

The current implementation of the NetBIOS protocol used in MS-DOS, MS-Windows, and OS/2.

NetBIOS

A lightweight transport protocol developed by Sytek, IBM, and Microsoft for use on personal computers. NetBIOS defines the protocol on the wire (datagram formats), the code that implements the protocol, and the API used to employ the protocol. An example of an application that uses the NetBIOS API is Microsoft Networks, the workstation and server code implemented in MS-DOS 3.0 and later, OS/2, and various Windows incarnations, though other applications do exist. NetBIOS employs name registration and broadcast discovery rather than addressing and is consequently a nonroutable protocol. See also *NetBIOS over TCP/IP, SMB.*

NetBIOS over TCP/IP

A layer of code that implements the NetBIOS API, but utilizing TCP and UDP datagrams, which are encapsulated in IP datagrams. Since IP is routable, this overcomes the most significant limitation of NetBIOS.

netmask

Short for *network mask;* the network part of an IP address. See also *variable length subnet mask.*

network

An interconnected set of hosts and other network devices that share a common physical layer such as Ethernet, X.25 and so on. See also *LAN, WAN.*

network interface card

An expansion board allowing a computer to access a network.

network layer

The layer of a network protocol stack that is concerned with addressing and delivery of datagrams across a network or Internet. In the TCP/IP protocol stack, the main network layer protocol is IP.

NFS

Short for Network File System. A protocol (developed by Sun Microsystems) enabling a *nix machine to mount a remote disk area as part of its local filesystem; widely considered of questionable security.

NIS

Short for Network Information Service (formerly "yellow pages"). Protocols to provide network services (such as authentication) for NFS.

object code

Instructions that can be executed by the computer processor.

offline

Not connected to a computer system or network. See also *online.*

online

1. Connected to a computer system or network. See also *offline.*

2. Stored on and accessible through a computer system or network.

operating system

Central set of programs that manages the various components and devices of the computer and its interaction with application programs and users (e.g., MS-DOS, Windows 95/98/NT/2000, Mac OS, Unix, Linux, etc.).

OSI

Short for Open System Interconnection. A layered suite of protocols for network communications. The concept of a "stack" of protocols (hence "TCP/IP stack") is due to the OSI seven-layer model, even though TCP/IP has only four distinct layers (certain OSI layer concepts are combined in TCP/IP).

output

Any data generated by a process.

owner

The account that has its user ID (UID) number associated with a file.

package

A set of related files and programs, especially a single-archive file (*tar*, *rpm*) that contains them.

packet

A quantum of data transmitted over a network. Specifically, a unit of TCP traffic carrying the information necessary to deliver itself, especially using the *UDP* protocol (datagram).

parallel

Several bits at the same time, over time (over multiple wires).

parameter

A variable with a specific value that has a meaning or function, which belongs to a program function or command. See also *argument*.

parent process

A process that started one or more other, so-called child processes.

partition

An arbitrary region of a storage device (almost always a hard drive) created by partitioning software before data was stored. Specifically on IBM PC compatibles: one of up to four distinct areas on a hard drive that can be dedi cated to different operating systems. One of the partition types, *extended*, supports further partitioning into a maximum of four logical disks.

password

A token that authenticates a user at login time.

PC

Short for Personal Computer. A computer designed to be used by one individual at a time. Often associated with computers compatible with the architecture of the original IBM microcomputer.

PCI

Short for Peripheral Component Interface. A PC bus to connect peripheral devices to the processor, PCI is thought of as a replacement for the original ISA bus.

peripheral

A device that is an optional attachment to the core components of a computer (CPU and memory).

physical layer

The lowest layer of both the ISO/OSI and TCP/IP protocol stacks. Consists of the cables, connectors, and associated hardware such as driver chips to implement a network such as Ethernet or Token Ring.

PID

Short for Process ID. A numerical identifier used to track processes by the kernel.

PIO

Short for Programmed Input/Output. A technique whereby the CPU executes a tightly coded loop in which it copies data from a peripheral device's buffer memory and writes it back out to main memory. See also *DMA*.

pipe

A data structure that connects a file handle in one process to a file handle in another; by convention, *stdout* of one process to *stdin* of the next. Established on the shell command line with the | symbol.

pixel

A "picture element"; the smallest addressable portion of a computer display. Screen resolution is usually cited in pixels.

PLIP

Short for Parallel Line Internet Protocol. IP protocol over a parallel cable (between two machines physically connected and not too distant).

PnP

Short for Plug 'n' Play. A specification intended to automate configuration of ISA peripherals in PCs.

POP

Short for Post Office Protocol. Protocol to retrieve mail from a mail server. Various software servers typically have names derived from "pop" such as ipop3d, ipop2d, and popper.

port

1. The name given to an individual, numbered "slot" that is available to Internet-working software. For example, HTTP servers generally listen to port 80. See also */etc/services, IO port.*

2. To adapt a computer program to operate in a new computing environment and/or in a new programming language.

PostScript

A page description language developed and marketed by Adobe Systems, Inc., widely implemented in laser printers, especially where high-quality output is required (e.g., phototypesetters), and under Linux, widely emulated in software for non-PostScript printers.

PPID

Short for Parent PID. The PID of a process' parent process. See also *child process, parent process, PID.*

PPP

Short for Point-to-Point Protocol. A physical layer protocol that can be used to encapsulate IP and other network protocols, making it an excellent way of extending LAN protocols to dialup users. PPP comprises an HDLC-like framing protocol, a link control protocol, and a family of network control protocols, each of which corresponds to a network protocol that PPP can encapsulate. PPP can also use PAP or CHAP for authentication.

presentation layer

The top layer of the ISO/OSI seven-layer model, which specifies character representation (e.g., ASCII) and graphics formats, such as NAPLPS (North American Presentation Layer Protocols). In TCP/IP, the presentation layer is subsumed into the application layer, but perhaps the closest equivalent standards are ASN.1, ANSI, and HTML/XML.

process

A running program; an instance of program execution.

processor

The main component that makes a computer work; these days, usually a "microprocessor" on a single silicon chip. See also *CPU.*

program

A sequence of instructions for the computer that implements an algorithm, especially when stored in a file in the form of either directly executable object code or source code for an interpreter or compiler. When loaded into memory and executed, the object-code program typically becomes a process.

prompt

An indication produced by a shell or application program that it is ready for further user commands or input.

protocol

A definition of data structures and formats to be exchanged by two programs over a network.

queue

A data structure that implements a first-in, first-out list (e.g., a print queue, which contains a list of jobs to be printed in order).

RAM

Short for Random Access Memory. Volatile, writable memory that a computer uses as its main memory. Comes in flavors such as EDO, ECC, SDRAM, and so on, which are not equivalent but from the perspective of a system administrator are very similar under normal use. See also *ROM.*

read permission

Authorization within a filesystem to display the contents of files and directories.

README

An important document that usually comes with a software package to call attention to important issues. README files usually have their name in uppercase letters, so that it appears at the top of a directory listing.

reboot
> See *boot.*

Red Hat
> A commercial Linux distribution offered by Red Hat Software, Inc.

redundant
> Superfluous; said of information in the contexts of compression or the preservation of data integrity.

regular expression
> A formal expression of a string pattern that can be searched for and processed by a pattern-matching program such as vi, grep, awk, or Perl.

RFC
> Short for Request For Comments. Despite the name, a *de facto* specification of Internet protocols and standards. See *http://www.cis.ohio-state.edu/hypertext/ information/rfc.html.*

ROM
> Short for Read-Only Memory. Computer memory, usually involving some enduring medium, such as a silicon chip or a burnt laser disc, which can be read but not altered. This is inconvenient when the data can change, and just to be confusing, some special ROMs can be modified under certain circumstances. See also *RAM.*

root
> 1. The administrative account (UID 0) on a *nix system that has all privileges. See also *superuser.*
> 2. The topmost, first, or originating node or object (e.g., root directory, /).

route
> 1. The path across one or more networks from one host to another.
> 2. To examine the destination network IP address in a datagram, and by consulting a table, direct the datagram to the next router along the path to the destination or to the destination itself.

router
> A device that routes IP datagrams between networks in an Internet; a gateway.

RPM
> Short for Red Hat Package Manager. A system that eases installation, verification, upgrading, and uninstalling of Linux packages. See the RPM HOWTO for more information.

run
> To let it work (a program). See also *execute.*

runlevel
> Mode of operation of a Unix system, offering different services on each level.

Samba
> An open source project to implement the SMB protocol and its network functions, including file and printer sharing.

script
A computer program that is written in an interpreted programming language and therefore stays in human-readable text format. See also *binary, executable.*

SCSI
Short for Small Computer System Interface. A multidrop bus cable architecture particularly suitable for both internal and external attachment of mass storage devices such as hard drives, tape drives, and CD-ROMs.

segment
A (limited) length of cable. Segments can be joined by repeaters (rare), bridges (common), routers, or switches (which are hardware logic bridges and routers).

serial
One bit after another, over time (over a single wire).

server
A process, or a host computer, that provides a particular service to client processes (e.g., web server, print server).

service
A process that accepts requests and returns responses in an almost endless loop; a *daemon.*

session layer
The ISO/OSI session control layer establishes and controls system-dependent aspects of communications sessions between specific nodes in the network. It bridges the gap between the services provided by the transport layer and the logical functions running on the operating system in a participating node. In the TCP/IP network stack, there is no session control layer; its functions are implemented partially in the transport layer and partially in the application layer.

shell
A program that mediates between the user and the operating system, typically accepting commands and invoking the corresponding programs.

signal
A logical interrupt to a process, which the process must generally deal with synchronously. A form of interprocess communications.

single mode
Single-user mode, runlevel 1.

SLIP
Short for Serial Line Internet Protocol. A way of encapsulating IP datagrams for transmission over asynchronous modem connections. See also *PPP.*

SMB
Short for Server Message Block. A Microsoft protocol developed originally to transport MS-DOS, and later OS/2 and Microsoft Windows, API calls, and their arguments across a NetBIOS LAN. Primarily used under Linux as a protocol for file and print sharing with Windows machines. See also *Samba.*

SMTP

Short for Simple Mail Transport Protocol. A conversational protocol used by mail servers for delivery of email via the Internet.

SNR

Short for Signal-to-Noise Ratio. The relative amount of useful information in a signal, as compared to the noise it carries.

socket

A TCP application layer connection.

software

A computer program.

source code

The plain text code written in a programming language that specifies the detailed operation of a program. Source code needs to be processed by a compiler to produce a program that can be run (i.e., be executed) by the computer.

sources

The files containing the source code for a program or program system, from which the executable program or library can be built or ported to another computer platform.

spawn

To create a child process by means of a *fork()* and an *exec()*.

stderr

The standard Unix error output device (by default to the terminal display).

stdin

The standard Unix input device (by default, the terminal keyboard).

stdout

The standard Unix output device (by default, the terminal display).

sticky bit

A permission bit on an executable file that causes the kernel to keep the memory image of the process after it has terminated, in order to avoid the overhead of reloading it when it is re-invoked.

stream

A sequence of data bytes with sequencing and flow control, such as that implemented by the TCP protocol within TCP/IP.

subnet mask

A value used in configuring the TCP/IP stack that specifies which part of a 32-bit IP address is the network address and which part is the host address.

SUID

Short for Set User ID. A permission bit for files in Unix-compatible filesystems based on the UID of the user who owns the file, rather than the user who created the process.

superuser

The user of the root account.

SuSE
>A commercial Linux distribution.

swap space
>Virtual memory; called swap space because processes swap location between fast RAM and slow virtual memory if their priority changes.

symlink
>Symbolic link. In Unix filesystems, a symlink is an entry in a directory that points to another filename in the filesystem. See also *hard link*.

synchronize
>1. To make the events in two separate sequences happen at the same time (used in communications).
>
>2. To make the content and state of data stored in two separate locations identical (e.g., cache, FTP sites).

syntax
>The formal rules that determine how keywords or commands and their components need to be combined when writing the source code of a computer program or forming shell commands.

sysadmin
>System administrator. A person who administers a computer system and keeps it working.

system
>A computer system; a term loosely used to refer to hardware and/or software. See also *operating system*.

TCP
>Short for Transmission Control Protocol. A session-oriented streaming transport protocol that provides sequencing, error detection and correction, flow control, congestion control, and multiplexing. See also *UDP*.

TCP/IP
>A suite of protocols basic to Internet transmissions, which includes TCP and IP.

terminal
>The outlet of a computer, usually consisting of a display for output of text (or possibly graphics) and a keyboard (and possibly a mouse) for input, used as a device for interaction between the computer and a user. See also *workstation*.

terminate
>To disconnect, end, finish, quit, stop, and so on.

terminator
>A resistive load to indicate the end a chain of devices, usually a SCSI chain or a coax network chain.

text
>A series of characters that can be displayed on a terminal display or printed on paper for human reading.

TFTP
>Short for *Tiny FTP*. A protocol similar to FTP, but much simpler and even less secure. Used mainly for cracking computers and booting diskless network clients.

third-party

A company or organization not directly involved in developing an original product. For example, a software company (such as Red Hat Software) that offers new products to an existing piece of software (such as Linux).

tools

Programs or utilities that provide administrative functionality, such as a compiler or language interpreter.

transport layer

The ISO/OSI seven layer model transport layer provides end-to-end control of a communication session once the path has been established, allowing processes to exchange data reliably and sequentially, independent of which systems are communicating and their locations in the network. The transport layer in TCP/IP is not defined in the same way, although TCP provides sequencing and error correction. UDP, which is also a transport layer protocol, does not have a session concept and is unreliable. The TCP/IP transport layer primarily provides multiplexing through the use of ports.

troubleshoot

The process of finding the reason(s) or problem(s) with networking, programming or hardware.

tune

To make small changes to configuration in order to produce more efficient operation.

TurboLinux

A commercial Linux distribution.

UDP

Short for User Datagram Protocol. A connectionless, unreliable transport protocol that provides multiplexing and error detection for applications that require a low-cost protocol for one-shot transactions. See also *datagram packet, TCP.*

UID

Short for User ID, the numeric identifier used on Linux and Unix systems to specify users.

uninstall

Remove hardware or software from a computer system.

unload

Remove services or software from a server so that more resources (CPU time, disk space, etc.) become available.

unreliable

In the TCP/IP sense of the term, a protocol that does not perform error correction (relying on "upper" layers to detect and correct errors, usually through retransmission).

upgrade

To update hardware or software to a better state.

URL

Short for Uniform Resource Locator. An identifier for an address on the Internet, preceded by the name of the protocol that must be used to reach that address (e.g., *ftp://ftp.kernel.org* or *http://www.oreilly.com*).

USB

Short for Universal Serial Bus. A recently developed bus standard for connecting peripheral devices in a chain.

user

1. The person that is using the resources of a computer.

2. A person's account or process; identification listed in */etc/passwd*.

user interface

See *interactive interface*.

UTC

Short for Coordinated Universal Time. Official world time, formerly Greenwich Mean Time.

utility

A program to help you do a task easier.

UTP

Short for Untwisted Pair. Network cables with several parallel wires used for Ethernet. The network usually has a star topology with hubs and does not need terminators.

variable length subnet mask

See *CIDR*.

vendor

A company that provides a service or a product.

virtual

Functionality provided without additional hardware or software, often without the user needing to realize this economy (e.g., virtual memory, virtual console, or virtual web server).

virtual memory

Extra memory made available on a system by using space on a hard disk. Usually referred to as *swap space*.

WAN

Short for Wide Area Network. A network that links geographically widespread facilities (and often LANs at those locations) using point-to-point (leased-line, SLIP, or PPP) or packet-switched network (X.25, frame relay) links that does not support the broadcast and direct connection capabilities of LANs.

wildcard

A placeholder used to represent any character or group of characters.

window

A region on a graphical desktop; the user interface for I/O with a child process of the desktop.

Windows NT

A 32-bit operating system available from Microsoft.

WinModem

A modem that has only a Digital Signal Processor and uses MS Windows–specific software to encode and decode data.

WINS

Short for Windows Internet Naming Service. An automatic NetBIOS name database to resolve NetBIOS names to IP addresses.

word

A datatype consisting of 2 or 4 bytes; on i386 architectures, a word is 4 bytes (32 bits) in size.

workspace

Computer resources that are assigned to a computer user.

workstation

A computer, usually with a graphical display, for interactive use by an individual. See also *server*.

write permission

Authorization within a filesystem to modify the contents of files and directories.

WWW

Short for World Wide Web. Global distributed archive of HTML documents linked via HTTP.

X Window System

Also known as "X," the X Window System is a graphical windowing environment, originally created at MIT.

yellow pages

See *NIS*.

Index

Symbols

& (ampersand), 54
{ and } (curly braces), 344, 452
> (right-angle bracket), 42, 43, 345
>> (append redirection operator), 43
* (asterisk), 233
\ (backslash), 62, 233, 234
\; (backslash semicolon), 452
! (bang-on), 16
$? (bash status variable), 356
^ (caret), 233
: (colon)
    and less command, 147
> (default PS2 prompt), 15
$ (dollar sign), 18, 233, 343, 345
# (hash character), 308, 346, 347
- (hyphen), 294
< (left-angle bracket), 43
. (period), 233
+ (plus), 234
? (question mark), 233
; (semicolon), 15
' (single quotes), 62, 343
| (vertical bar), 42, 234
 ! (she-bang), 353
/ (root filesystem), 74, 492
#!/bin/bash, 498
~/ (home directory), 346

Numbers

1024-cylinder limit, 79, 491

A

a2ps software package, 332
abort command, lpc, 328
access control, 104–116, 237
    executable files, 355
    tcpd, 448
        rules, 449
    via IP address or domain name, 427
access modes, 104, 110, 237
    binary representation, 107
    modifying, 112
    octal notation, 107
    setting, 238
    string, 108
access.conf, 432
active partitions, 73
address masks, 501
addresses, 390
    Classes, 390–392
    masks, 390
aliases, 340, 343, 430
    conf.modules, 308
    database, 431
alien command, 293
.allow files, 428

We'd like to hear your suggestions for improving our indexes. Send email to *index@oreilly.com*.

About the Author

Jeffrey Dean is a freelance author, editor, and consultant in Philadelphia, Pennsylvania. Jeffrey has professional experience in IT management, training delivery, and system administration of Linux, Solaris, VMS, AS/400, and Windows NT/2000. Jeffrey holds an undergraduate degree in electrical engineering from the University of Pittsburgh and a master's degree in engineering with emphasis in computer design from Penn State. He holds the Linux Professional Institute Level 1 (LPIC-1) and Red Hat Certified Engineer (RHCE) certifications.

Colophon

Our look is the result of reader comments, our own experimentation, and feedback from distribution channels. Distinctive covers complement our distinctive approach to technical topics, breathing personality and life into potentially dry subjects.

The animal on the cover of *LPI Linux Certification in a Nutshell* is a Bull. Christopher Columbus originally brought cattle to the New World from Spain. Descendants of these animals mated with English cows, and the offspring gradually evolved into the breed we know today.

Mary Brady was the production editor and proofreader, and Norma Emory was the copyeditor for *LPI Linux Certification in a Nutshell*. Nicole Arigo and Claire Cloutier provided quality control. Edith Shapiro and Sada Preisch provided production assistance. John Bickelhaupt wrote the index.

Ellie Volckhausen designed the cover of this book, based on a series design by Edie Freedman. The cover image is an original illustration created by Lorrie LeJeune. Emma Colby produced the cover layout with QuarkXPress 4.1 using Adobe's ITC Garamond font.

David Futato designed the interior layout based on a series design by Nancy Priest. Anne-Marie Vaduva converted the files from Microsoft Word to FrameMaker 5.5.6 using tools created by Mike Sierra. The text and heading fonts are ITC Garamond Light and Garamond Book; the code font is Constant Willison. The illustrations that appear in the book were produced by Robert Romano and Jessamyn Read using Macromedia FreeHand 9 and Adobe Photoshop 6. This colophon was written by Mary Brady.

Need in-depth answers fast?

Related Titles Available from O'Reilly

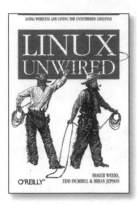

Linux

Building Embedded Linux Systems

Building Secure Servers with Linux

The Complete FreeBSD, *4th Edition*

CVS Pocket Reference, *2nd Edition*

Essential CVS

Even Grues Get Full

Extreme Programming Pocket Guide

Learning Red Hat Enterprise Linux and Fedora, *4th Edition*

Linux Desktop Hacks

Linux Device Drivers, *2nd Edition*

Linux in a Nutshell, *4th Edition*

Linux iptables Pocket Reference

Linux Network Administrator's Guide, *2nd Edition*

Linux Security Cookbook

Linux Server Hacks

Linux Unwired

Linux Web Server CD Bookshelf, *Version 2.0*

Managing & Using MySQL, *2nd Edition*

Managing RAID on Linux

MySQL Cookbook

MySQL Pocket Reference

Practical PostgreSQL

Programming with Qt, *2nd Edition*

Root of all Evil

Running Linux, *4th Edition*

Samba Pocket Reference, *2nd Edition*

Understanding the Linux Kernel, *2nd Edition*

User Friendly

Using Samba, *2nd Edition*

Keep in touch with O'Reilly

1. Download examples from our books

To find example files for a book, go to:

www.oreilly.com/catalog

select the book, and follow the "Examples" link.

2. Register your O'Reilly books

Register your book at *register.oreilly.com*

Why register your books? Once you've registered your O'Reilly books you can:

- Win O'Reilly books, T-shirts or discount coupons in our monthly drawing.
- Get special offers available only to registered O'Reilly customers.
- Get catalogs announcing new books (US and UK only).
- Get email notification of new editions of the O'Reilly books you own.

3. Join our email lists

Sign up to get topic-specific email announcements of new books and conferences, special offers, and O'Reilly Network technology newsletters at:

elists.oreilly.com

It's easy to customize your free elists subscription so you'll get exactly the O'Reilly news you want.

4. Get the latest news, tips, and tools

http://www.oreilly.com

- "Top 100 Sites on the Web"—PC Magazine
- CIO Magazine's Web Business 50 Awards

Our web site contains a library of comprehensive product information (including book excerpts and tables of contents), downloadable software, background articles, interviews with technology leaders, links to relevant sites, book cover art, and more.

5. Work for O'Reilly

Check out our web site for current employment opportunities:

jobs.oreilly.com

6. Contact us

O'Reilly & Associates
1005 Gravenstein Hwy North
Sebastopol, CA 95472 USA

TEL: 707-827-7000 or 800-998-9938
(6am to 5pm PST)

FAX: 707-829-0104

order@oreilly.com
For answers to problems regarding your order or our products.
To place a book order online, visit:

www.oreilly.com/order_new

catalog@oreilly.com
To request a copy of our latest catalog.

booktech@oreilly.com
For book content technical questions or corrections.

corporate@oreilly.com
For educational, library, government, and corporate sales.

proposals@oreilly.com
To submit new book proposals to our editors and product managers.

international@oreilly.com
For information about our international distributors or translation queries. For a list of our distributors outside of North America check out:

international.oreilly.com/distributors.html

adoption@oreilly.com
For information about academic use of O'Reilly books, visit:

academic.oreilly.com

O'REILLY®